AGENT ORANGE ON TRIAL

AGENT ORANGE
ON TRIAL

Mass Toxic Disasters in the Courts

PETER H. SCHUCK

THE BELKNAP PRESS OF
HARVARD UNIVERSITY PRESS
Cambridge, Massachusetts
and London, England 1986

Copyright © 1986 by Marcy Schuck, Trustee
Printed in the United States of America
10   9   8   7   6   5   4   3   2   1

This book is printed on acid-free paper, and its binding
materials have been chosen for strength and durability.

Library of Congress Cataloging-in-Publication Data
Schuck, Peter H.
Agent Orange on trial.
Bibliography: p.
Includes index.
1. Products liability—Agent Orange—United States.
2. Class actions (Civil procedure)—United States.
I. Title.
KF1297.C4S38   1986   346.7303'82   86-7360
347.306382
ISBN 0-674-01025-6 (alk. paper)

Book designed by Gwen Frankfeldt

To the Vietnam veterans and their families,
whose heroic sacrifices we must redeem
through a more just legal and social order

Preface

GREAT lawsuits involve the clash of fundamental legal principles and important social interests. That is why parties bring them, lawyers and judges cite them, law professors analyze them, and law students pore over them. But beneath and behind the abstract doctrines, obscured by the momentous stakes, are the unique individuals whose particular purposes and intelligences organize and drive the litigation. Of them, the lawbooks say little. My ambition in writing this book has been to repair this omission. I have sought to expose the human forces that have shaped the Agent Orange case, while exploring the larger meaning of the case for American law and public policy.

The book is divided into three major parts. Part I, "The Context" (Chapters 1 and 2), traces the historical roots and the social, political, and legal environments in which the Agent Orange case arose. Part II, "The Case" (Chapters 3 through 11), consists of a detailed, essentially chronological narrative of the Agent Orange litigation. It begins with the stories of the veterans and lawyers who organized and launched the lawsuit in 1978 and concludes with Judge Weinstein's series of controversial decisions concluding the litigation at the trial court level in May 1985. The narrative is interspersed with analyses of the many novel legal issues that the case presented, and is written to be accessible to readers with no sophisticated understanding of legal doctrines, procedures, or institutions. Part III, "The Future" (Chapters 12 and 13), offers several different perspectives on the broader social and legal significance of the Agent Orange case and explores its implications for future legal policy concerning the control of mass exposures to toxic substances. Although this part, especially Chapter 13, which analyzes a variety of alternative public policies and legal structures, is somewhat more technical, I trust that the dauntless general reader will persist, buoyed by the encouraging array of re- form options presented there.

The Agent Orange litigation has now entered a new phase in the appellate courts. The book, although based primarily on research conducted through the summer of 1985, carries the story through early February 1986, just before the filing of final briefs in the United States Court of Appeals for the Second Circuit. Oral argument in that court is scheduled to occur in April 1986, and a decision is expected some time thereafter. Review may then be sought in the Supreme Court of the United States.

This book could never have been written without the help of the many participants in the case who were willing to share their percep- tions with me. Some of them also reviewed the entire manuscript. Most will find their contributions acknowledged in the notes at the end of the book; a few, who felt constrained to insist upon confiden- tiality, must take my gratitude on faith. Other people, far removed from the action, assisted me by reading and commenting upon por- tions of the manuscript. These good souls include David Brittenham, Arthur Galston, Daniel Givelber, Jeffrey O'Connell, Fred Rowe, Jan Stolwijk, and the participants in the Yale Law School and University of Toronto Law School faculty workshops, to whom I presented a draft of Chapters 11, 12, and 13. Portions of Chapter 8 were included in an article published in volume 53 of the *University of Chicago Law Review* (1986).

My debts do not stop here. I received outstanding research assis- tance from Yale Law School students James Wooten, class of 1988; Wendy Wagner, class of 1987; and Andrew Tomback and Eric Mogilnicki, class of 1986. Pat DeLucca and Sherrill Kolakowski typed countless drafts with infinite patience and unerring accuracy. Aida Donald of Harvard University Press shepherded the manuscript through to publication with enthusiasm and dispatch; her colleague, Peg Anderson, deftly copy edited it. My family—Marcy, Chris, and Julie—never allowed me to forget that there is life beyond the type- writer. Generous institutions also played an invaluable supporting role. The book was researched and largely written while I held a John

Simon Guggenheim Memorial Fellowship. As ever, the Yale Law School facilitated my work in ways too numerous to mention but too precious to ignore.

Peter H. Schuck
March 1986
New Haven, Connecticut

Contents

I

THE CONTEXT

1

A New Kind of Case

THIS book is about two urgent social problems and about the extraordinary lawsuit they have spawned.

The first problem arose from the smoldering ashes of Vietnam. For many of the millions of American soldiers who returned home from that charnel house, the future was filled with bitterness, dread, controversy, and debilitating illness. In 1978 the veterans sued a number of chemical manufacturers, blaming them for various diseases and traumas that they and their families had allegedly suffered because of exposure to Agent Orange, a herbicide the United States Army had used to defoliate Vietnam's luxuriant jungle cover. The law, the veterans hoped, would assuage their pain and vindicate their sacrifices. Today, almost a decade later, they are still waiting. For many of them, the law has become a mockery of justice, an object of derision.

The second problem arose from a very different set of social facts. We live in the midst of a burgeoning technological revolution. For several decades a torrent of new synthetic chemicals has cascaded out of our laboratories.[1] Complex industrial processes have been developed, and intricate patterns of distribution, consumption, and disposal have evolved. These innovations have benefited American society enormously, but they have also created new kinds of risks. Agent Orange, originally hailed by some environmentalists and even by one of the veterans' lawyers as a model herbicide,[2] was later found to harbor insidious dangers as well; in this respect it was a characteristic product of the great scientific advance.

It might seem surprising that these two disparate social problems—the one produced by unspeakable human suffering, the other by unparalleled human ingenuity—came together in a courtroom. On the surface, each of these problems seems quite unsuited to resolution at the instance of private parties wrangling before a judge. War, after all, leaves many bitter legacies; distributing its burdens is ordinarily the stuff of national politics, not of private litigation. By the same token, environmental risk management is an immensely complex technical task; controlling such risks is usually the responsibility of legislatures and regulatory agencies, not of courts.

Students of the contemporary legal system, however, know better. Times have changed. Traditionally, tort (personal injury) cases were generally regarded as essentially isolated disputes in which the law's role was simply to allocate losses between putative injurers and victims according to a moral conception that Aristotle called corrective justice;[3] the law required that a wrongdoer return to a victim, typically in the form of money damages, what the former had "taken" from the latter. Such disputes were readily managed by the parties and the court system. Typically, the parties would adduce a relatively simple, comprehensible body of evidence before a detached arbiter, usually a jury. Applying general and familiar norms of conduct to the facts of the case, the jury would reach a decision, one that bound the parties but, because it was so fact-specific and was not explained by the jury, had little precedential effect on other cases.

Today, the law books abound with tort cases, especially in the product liability area, that involve not a few individuals but large aggregations of people and vast economic and social interests.[4] These cases are not preoccupied with corrective justice between individuals concerned solely with past events. Instead, they concern the public control of large-scale activities and the distribution of social power and values for the future. The court and jury in these cases do not simply prescribe and apply familiar norms to discrete actions; they function as policy-oriented risk regulators, as self-conscious allocators of hard-to-measure benefits and risks, and as social problem solvers.

The Agent Orange case carries this trend to its logical (or, as we shall see, perhaps illogical) extreme. Apart from its locus in a courtroom, it bears little resemblance to traditional tort adjudication. Its magnitude and complexity beggar the imagination, as a few crude numerical indicators will suggest.[5] The case is actually a consolidation into one class action of more than 600 separate actions originally filed by more than 15,000 named individuals throughout the United States, and almost 400 individual cases not included in the class action ("opt-out" cases). The parties in these consolidated actions consist of some 2.4 million Vietnam veterans, their wives, children born and unborn, and soldiers from Australia and New Zealand; a small number of civilian plaintiffs; seven (originally twenty-four) corporate defendants; and the United States government.

In a typical case litigated in the federal district court in which the Agent Orange case was heard, the docket sheet is one or two pages long and contains perhaps sixty individual entries, each representing a filed document. The Agent Orange docket sheet in the district court alone is approximately 425 single-spaced pages long. It contains over 7,300 individual entries, many representing documents that are hundreds of pages long. The files of briefs, hearing transcripts, court orders, affidavits, and other court documents in the case were so voluminous that the already cramped clerk's office had to take the unprecedented step of devoting an entire room, staffed by two special clerks, to house them.

The financial and personnel demands of the case are even more staggering. The plaintiffs are represented by a network of law firms that numbered almost 1,500 by May 1984, located in every region of the country; the documented cost of their activities to date certainly exceeds $10 million and increases daily. It has been estimated that the defendants spent roughly $100 million merely to prepare for the trial, utilizing hundreds of lawyers and corporate staff in their Herculean effort.

The court has also borne an enormous administrative burden. The current district court judge—the second to preside over the Agent Orange case—had to create a considerable bureaucracy within his chambers simply to enable him to run it, employing additional law clerks and paralegals. And although it is highly unusual for a judge to appoint even one special master to handle particular aspects of a litigation for him, this judge used no fewer than *six* special masters (four or five of them simultaneously) plus a federal magistrate, and they in turn sometimes hired consultants to assist them.

Finally, the case resulted in the largest tort settlement in history. That settlement, reached in May 1984 after almost six years of litigation, created a fund of $180 million; with accrued interest, it now totals more than $200 million, increasing at the rate of more than $40,000 each day. The case is now on appeal; since the settlement has been challenged, the court will not be in a position to begin distributing that fund for years, even if the plan is ultimately upheld. Nevertheless, simply to maintain the fund, the court has already been obliged to disburse more than two million dollars. For example, it has had to create an Agent Orange computer center to process the almost 250,000 claims that class members have filed against the fund.

But the significance of the Agent Orange case is not confined to the features that have been mentioned—its symbolic reenactment of the war, its heralding of a new role for courts and juries, or its gigantic dimensions. Even more important is what the case reveals about a new and far-reaching legal and social phenomenon—the "mass toxic tort"—and society's response to it.[6] The Agent Orange case is not the first mass toxic tort litigation (the diethylstilbestrol, or DES, and asbestos litigations began earlier), but it is probably the most revealing and perplexing example of that legal genre.[7] In the Agent Orange case, we confront an unprecedented challenge to our legal system: a future in which the law must grapple with the chemical revolution and help us live comfortably with it.

The mass toxic tort has only become possible in recent years, as a vibrant chemical technology converged with mass distribution techniques and mass markets. We have not yet grasped its full meaning and implications. To begin to understand what is truly distinctive about it, we must isolate the three constitutive elements—mass, toxic, and tort. In the course of discussing these elements, I shall highlight some of the themes of the book.

The Mass Tort

In the traditional tort case, A intentionally or negligently injures B. A and B are usually, but not always, individuals. The classic examples are assault and battery or a "fender bender" traffic accident. Sometimes, A's conduct injures more than one victim, as when his negligent driving causes a multivehicle collision. Even in those cases, however, the number of claimants is seldom large enough significantly to alter either the nature or the manageability of the litigation.

The mass tort differs from the conventional tort both in degree and in kind. In the mass tort, the number of victims is large; there may even be millions of claimants, as in the Agent Orange case. Its scale inevitably creates qualitative, not just quantitative, changes in the character of the case and in the ways in which it must be litigated and judged.

This point may become clearer if we consider the enormous "transaction costs" generated by a mass tort litigation. These costs are of many different kinds. A large number of potential claimants must be identified and perhaps organized into groups for litigation purposes. Mechanisms must be established to coordinate the activities and communications of the numerous lawyers and clients. The court system must administer the cases. Lawyers must conduct pretrial "discovery," through which they seek to obtain documents, testimony, and other information that may be relevant to the effective presentation of the parties' claims and defenses. Each case, unless settled, must then be tried for weeks or months, almost certainly before a jury. The parties must be permitted to pursue time-consuming appeals through one or more levels of appellate court review. If the appellate court finds that the trial court erred and sends the case back for further proceedings, many of these steps may have to be repeated. In the event of a recovery, the award must be distributed to the plaintiffs according to certain procedures and criteria.

As the number and diversity of plaintiffs increase, the cost of undertaking these activities in any individual case rises geometrically. To minimize these costs, lawyers may seek to aggregate numerous plaintiffs' claims into clusters of issues thought to be common to some or all of the plaintiffs; these claims may be suitably handled on a group or "class" basis. By spreading the costs among a large number of people, it may become economically and administratively more feasible to prosecute the multitude of claims.

Such class actions are common in certain areas of the law, such as antitrust and securities cases. There, numerous individuals may be affected in similar ways by similar courses of conduct by the same defendant(s). Although the cost-reducing potential of class actions in these areas is well established, this device has seldom been used in mass toxic tort cases, where important aspects of the plaintiffs' proof—especially on the issues of exposure, causation, and damages—may differ significantly for each individual plaintiff. And as we shall see, a class action indeed creates many difficulties in a mass toxic tort case. In that context a class action transforms the relationships among litigants, their lawyers, and the judicial system in ways that are poorly understood and that raise some serious concerns. These problems explain why no appellate court had ever allowed a mass toxic tort case before Agent Orange to proceed as a class action.[8]

The "mass" character of a tort case engenders other special difficulties as well. For the defendants, the stakes in such a case are so high, the potential liability so great, that their financial exposure may well exceed their insurance coverage, perhaps even threatening them with bankruptcy (as Johns-Manville alleged in the asbestos cases).[9] If punitive damages are possible (they were awarded in some asbestos cases), the risks become essentially uninsurable, and the specter of bankruptcy looms.[10] Defendants' desperate efforts to avoid these threats often trigger bitter, protracted disputes with other potential defendants and with insurers and stockholders. An already complex litigation becomes even more labyrinthine and impenetrable.

The enormous risks of litigation to defendants—and the huge court-awarded fees that may be awarded to plaintiffs' lawyers—mean that the incentives to settle mass tort cases informally are quite powerful. However, the process of negotiating and coordinating a settlement is infinitely more complex than in even a large conventional case, especially one not brought as a class action. The tortuous effort to settle the individual asbestos personal injury cases testify eloquently to these difficulties. The obstacles to settlements and class actions in mass tort cases also complicate the ethical issues concerning the relationship between plaintiffs' lawyers and their clients, as the bitter challenges to the Agent Orange settlement and the lawyers' role in securing its approval demonstrate.[11]

The Toxic Tort

A second distinctive feature of such cases is that the alleged injury is caused by a toxic substance. In the traditional tort case, the nature of the injury is typically rather straightforward: an actual assault, physical collision, trespass on land, defamatory statement, act of professional malpractice, or other relatively determinate, well-defined, traumatic interaction between the injurer and victim. Of course, difficult issues often arise even in conventional tort cases concerning who did what to whom, when, and with what effect. But these difficulties can usually be addressed more or less routinely. And when they cannot be, the putative victim is unlikely to pursue the claim, if only because most personal injury lawyers—who typically prosecute such claims only on a contingency fee basis (under which they are paid a percentage of any recovery) rather than an hourly rate basis—will not accept the case.

In the toxic tort dispute, the nature of the injury is very different and the processes of establishing, defining, and measuring that injury are far more complex. A chemical agent (or, less commonly, ionizing radiation) is suspected of having harmed one or more individuals. Often the pathways of causation are difficult to detect, the time periods extend over decades, and the effects are not readily isolated or scientifically understood. In some cases the victims may not even know that they have been harmed or that their harm is associated with a particular agent. Indeed, the victims may even be impossible to identify! In other cases the identity of the particular injurers may be unknown, and even if known, it may be impossible, either in principle or in practice, to accurately allocate responsibility for the harm among them.

These extraordinary difficulties in some toxic tort cases—the problems of so-called indeterminate plaintiffs and indeterminate defendants—usually reflect not only the high cost of establishing certain facts, but also the limited ability of existing scientific theory and methodology to establish those facts at *any* price.[12] This problem in turn may actually reflect a more elementary epistemological uncertainty concerning what we mean by a "fact" in the peculiar social-scientific context from which toxic torts arise.

The distinctive character of a toxic tort fundamentally affects the nature and course of the litigation. Entirely different forms of proof, demanding new kinds of evidence and witnesses, are usually necessary. Different rules of procedures, evidence, and substantive law may be required. And if implemented, these new legal arrangements inevitably alter the roles and relationships of litigants, lawyers, trial judges, juries, appellate judges, research institutions, regulatory agencies, and other governmental organs in profound ways. As we shall see, the Agent Orange case illustrates each of these problems.

The Tort Case

The third characteristic feature of these cases is that they remain at bottom *tort* disputes. This observation is not meant to be either tautological or paradoxical. We saw earlier that a tort case traditionally entailed a very distinctive model of adjudication, one that possessed a unique moral and legal structure and a characteristic array of advantages and disadvantages.[13] Increasingly, I suggested, this model has been joined by another, quite different one, of which the mass

toxic tort case is perhaps the clearest example. This newer model calls
into serious question many of the premises that underlie the first.

It would be a great mistake, however, to assume that the newer
model has fully obliterated the "tort" aspect of the mass toxic tort
case, leaving no trace of its traditional moral claims and legal forms.
Quite the contrary is true. As we shall see, the older model of tort
litigation survives, continuing to exert powerful gravitational forces
on the mass toxic tort case, confusing and constraining the ways in
which the dispute may be defined, litigated, and resolved.

The Agent Orange case dramatically illustrates each of these distinctive characteristics of mass toxic tort litigation. Its *mass* aspect, as we
have already seen, is especially striking, creating the prospect of ru-
inous liability for defendants, stupefying organizational complexity
for plaintiffs, and unprecedented problems of procedural, evidentiary,
and substantive law for the court.

Even more than the mass character of the claims, however, the *toxic*
nature of the injury in Agent Orange defines the case as extraordinary. This is especially evident when Agent Orange is compared with
the two most important and difficult toxic tort litigations that had
been brought previously, those involving asbestos and DES. Although
each of these litigations presented its own unique array of complications, the issue that would prove most perplexing in Agent Orange—
the question of whether the chemical *caused* plaintiffs' injuries—was
far more straightforward in the asbestos and DES cases.[14] First, the
objective symptoms of asbestosis and mesothelioma, the two most
common asbestos-related diseases, and of the vaginal adenocarcinoma
caused by DES, are relatively exposure- and disease-specific, distinctive, and easily observed. Second, the long latency periods for those
diseases (often twenty years or more) had already run their courses
by the time many of the cases reached trial. Third, the exposure levels
of asbestos workers and of women who had ingested DES during
pregnancy were relatively high and sustained.

None of these conditions obtained in the case of Agent Orange: the
cancers and birth defects that it allegedly caused were not distinctive;
the exposures had occurred less than fifteen years earlier and thus
may not yet have fully revealed their toxic effects; and the levels of
dioxin (the highly toxic contaminant of Agent Orange) to which the
veterans were exposed were generally quite low. For these and other
reasons, the obstacles to establishing general causation and damage,

easily overcome in the earlier toxic tort cases, would prove decisive in shaping the Agent Orange litigation and settlement and the public reaction to them.

By the same token, the task of establishing the liability of particular defendants was far more daunting in the Agent Orange case. The DES cases presented the indeterminate defendant problem; the pills, although manufactured by many different drug companies, were fungible and had been consumed long ago. Some asbestos cases presented the problem of indeterminate plaintiffs; certain injuries, especially cancer, were not asbestos-specific.[15]

The Agent Orange case, however, presented *both* the indeterminate defendant and indeterminate plaintiff problems and in extreme forms. The Agent Orange was produced by different companies, but their formulations were mixed together in nonidentifiable steel drums before being sent to Vietnam. The most serious injuries of which the veterans complained apparently are not dioxin-specific. And although in the asbestos cases the issue of which particular firms were liable was sometimes complicated by a number of variables (type of asbestos, condition of packaging and handling, use of respirators) that were not usually relevant to Agent Orange, the issues of which individuals were exposed and at what levels were even more difficult in Agent Orange.

But this case also reveals in an unusually clear and arresting form the distinctive moral dilemma that characterizes *tort* disputes. From the perspective of the veterans who sued, the case's significance lay less in large questions of public policy, such as the conduct of the Vietnam War and the social control of toxic substances, than in their claim to what tort law has traditionally promised—corrective justice. The veterans viewed the case as their opportunity to settle accounts, to recover from the government and the chemical manufacturers some portion of what the Vietnam War had taken from them in the name of duty: their youth, their vigor, and their future. The case came to symbolize their most human commitments and passions: their insistence upon respect and recognition, their hope for redemption and renewal, and their hunger for vindication and vengeance. For them, it was a searing morality play projected onto a national stage. These deeply personal aspirations pervaded the case, influencing the strategies of plaintiffs' counsel, shaping certain issues, and casting a shadow over the negotiated settlement that would obscure its legal status for years to come.[16]

Agent Orange, however, is more than a paradigm of a particularly difficult kind of mass toxic tort case. It also exemplifies a long historical development in the structure and underlying assumptions of tort law generally. This development consists of three interwoven themes whose character and implications will become clearer in the chapters that follow. First, tort law has moved from an individualistic grounding toward a more collective one. In defining the parties' legal rights and duties, tort law has come to be concerned with them less as discrete, idiosyncratic actors than as relatively interchangeable units of large, impersonal aggregations—broadly defined classes, epidemiological populations, or stochastic events. Second, the criteria for evaluating the parties' behavior have moved from moral categories to more functional ones. Evaluations of conduct based on fault, specific causation, and corrective justice norms have increasingly given way to considerations of compensation, deterrence, and administrative efficiency. Third, tort law has come to legitimate a judicial role that is less arbitral and more managerial in nature. Today's judge does not simply decide between the competing proofs and legal theories offered by the parties; he or she is also widely expected to administer large-scale litigation with an eye to achieving broad social purposes. The judge is supposed to allocate scarce resources wisely, develop legal rules that advance sound public policy, ensure that lawyers adequately represent their clients, and consider the social and political implications of settlements.

This steady evolution toward a more collectivist, functional, and managerial tort law seems certain to continue, for it reflects deep, probably irreversible social forces. The Agent Orange case represents their high-water mark to date. Indeed, the case promises to reinforce and accelerate those changes because of its high public profile and the remarkable reputation for wisdom and innovation of the judge who rendered its most important decisions. It is natural, therefore, to inquire whether the Agent Orange litigation is "typical" or "representative" of the kinds of mass toxic tort cases likely to arise in the future, or whether the case should instead be viewed as a fascinating but ultimately aberrational episode in our law.

This book attempts to answer this question through a kind of descriptive-analytical process of triangulation, one that seeks to locate the Agent Orange case on the map of American legal development. Certainly, no earlier case has been quite like it, at least in terms of the scale of the litigation, the novelty and difficulty of the questions presented, the widespread public interest in its subject matter, and the inventiveness of the court that managed and ultimately settled it. And it is equally certain that no future case will be similar in all crucial respects. This is most obviously true of the case's linkage with the Vietnam War and its consequent political coloration, but it may also be true of other aspects as well, such as its class action character and the immunities from liability of a key participant, the United States government.

But for all its unique features, it would be profoundly mistaken to regard the case as only an interesting oddity, a sort of legal sideshow of interest to veterans, to be sure, but without larger significance for American society generally. Had it been only that, I should never have undertaken this study. In reality, the Agent Orange litigation prefigures a grim dimension of our future; it is a harbinger of mass toxic tort cases yet to come.[17] Future disputes will surely possess their own idiosyncratic elements; for example, they may involve pharmaceuticals, food additives, industrial compounds, pollutants, toxic wastes deposited in landfills, radiation, or some other effusion of modern technology. The causal linkages between toxic agents, exposure levels, and pathological symptoms may be more or less elusive than was true of Agent Orange. The injurers' identity and responsibility may be more or less determinate than in this case. The judges who adjudicate future cases may have very different conceptions of the court's role and of the nature of mass toxic tort litigation than did Judges Pratt and Weinstein. Other differences will surely exist. The contours of new cases are no more predictable today than the Agent Orange case was twenty-five years ago.

What cannot be doubted, however, is that more mass toxic tort cases will come to court, that many will bear some strong resemblance to the Agent Orange case, and that all of the cases will be obliged to reckon with this one. The technological revolution that gave birth to Agent Orange continues to accelerate, pressing against the frontiers of existing chemical, toxicological, and epidemiological knowledge. Yet the system of regulatory controls that we have devised for dealing with many of these new risks is still very much in its infancy. Indeed, most of these controls are less than a decade old, and some, such as those involving the cleanup of hazardous waste dump sites through the Superfund, were adopted only after 1980.[18] Still, it is already clear that the system is pitifully inadequate in important respects. In May 1985, for example, the Congressional Budget Office reported that there were roughly 19,000 hazardous waste sites, of which the Environmental Protection Agency (EPA) had completed preliminary assessments of 10,700. By September 1985, EPA had designated about 850 as "national priority" sites. The list will grow to approximately 2,000 during the next few years; Congress's Office of Technology Assessment puts the eventual number at over 10,000, requiring cleanup costs of up to $100 billion. Any one of these sites (or others not yet identified) could turn out to be another Love Canal disaster. In September 1985, EPA began cleanup operations on about 450 of them.[19]

The problem seems certain to increase, not recede. Like the Three Mile Island incident in 1980, the disaster in Bhopal, India, in December 1984, involving an American chemical manufacturer, and the Sequoyah Fuels leak of a uranium compound in January 1986 are stark reminders of what can go wrong even—or perhaps especially—in technically intricate systems in which an extensive array of controls is already in place.[20] A case like Bhopal, it is true, will probably be like child's play compared to Agent Orange, at least in terms of the ease of establishing causation, calculating damages, and apportioning responsibility. And the outcome of the Agent Orange case itself may discourage some of the more complicated mass tort claims from being brought at all. But many of the mass toxic tort disputes that will be litigated in the future will involve some of the problems that make Agent Orange so difficult. And when litigants and courts struggle to resolve them, Agent Orange will surely be the prominent landmark, the starting point for analysis.

But emphasizing the case's significance as a lodestar for future litigants and judges is to miss what in the end may be an even more profound lesson. The Agent Orange case is not simply a response to the veterans' anguish and to the social risks from toxic chemicals. It is, most pointedly, an attempt to solve these problems in a particular way. Tort litigation is an exceedingly valuable mechanism of social integration and control, a mechanism of which Americans appear to be unusually fond.[21] But it is by no means our only, or necessarily our most promising, remedy for mass toxic harms. It is only one in a repertoire of policy instruments, including regulation, administrative compensation schemes, collective bargaining, and insurance, by which society can attempt to control risks and compensate harms.[22] And by revealing what mass toxic tort litigation entails—not simply in the abstract but as actually implemented by flesh-and-blood lawyers, clients, and judges in a here-and-now case—a study of Agent Orange should place us in a far better position to evaluate the proper role of this particular legal tool.

It may seem odd to close this introduction by emphasizing the particularized, idiosyncratic, human dimension of the Agent Orange case. After all, I have stressed that its causes, character, and consequences are firmly rooted in technological developments, fundamental legal structures, and large historical and political forces. These are social phenomena in which the role of individuals might seem to be insignificant or at most merely epiphenomenal. Yet the truth is that almost every aspect of the Agent Orange litigation has been influenced by contingent human choices. Dedicated but deeply divided veterans; flamboyant trial lawyers; class-action financial entrepreneurs; skillful, Machiavellian special masters; a Naderesque litigation organizer; a brilliant, crafty judge—these forceful personalities continually collided in a kind of Brownian motion of strategic choice, high idealism, seat-of-the-pants innovation, and human folly. Seldom has the contradiction between the popular, intuitive aspiration for law and its technical, formal reality been more vividly revealed. The Agent Orange case reminds us that great historic developments not only play upon, but may also be the playthings of, ordinary men and women who are sometimes capable of doing extraordinary things.

2

The Chemical and the Courts

A POIGNANT paradox, one of many that pervade this bitter conflict, is that Agent Orange began in a moment of great promise,
an exciting technological breakthrough. As early as the 1930s, agri-
cultural chemical research had revealed a number of synthetic compounds capable of regulating and suppressing plant growth. These
herbicides promised to be of great value to farmers in eradicating
weeds, but their potential military applications were also widely appreciated. The most effective herbicide was a formulation known as
2,4-D. During World War II the U.S. Army undertook defoliant research at Fort Detrick, Maryland, where previously known compounds, including a potent herbicide, 2,4,5-T, were successfully
formulated. These compounds were regarded as more effective, easier to apply, and safer than existing weed killers. After the war ended,
they were marketed commercially; as production increased rapidly,
unit costs plummeted. Australia also conducted research on these
herbicides at this time, and the British, embroiled in a colonial war in
Malaya, successfully used 2,4,5-T to destroy enemy crops and cover.[1]

By 1960 the U.S. Army had already tested a large number of herbicides in the laboratory and in the field. The results, buttressed by a
successful field test in Vietnam, led President Kennedy to accept the
joint recommendation of the State and Defense Departments to approve Operation Hades (later Ranch Hand), in which various mix-
tures of 2,4-D, 2,4,5-T, and other chemicals—known as Agent Blue,
White, Purple, Green, or Pink, according to the colored stripe on
their container drums—were sprayed on the Vietnamese jungle from
low-flying C-123 aircraft. The operation evolved into an offensive
strategy designed to destroy enemy crops as well as to clear roads and
communication lines. Applications of the chemicals increased to an

average of three gallons per acre; frequently even heavier concentrations were used.

When United States involvement in Vietnam escalated in late 1964 after the Gulf of Tonkin resolution, aerial spraying activities increased as well. Agent Orange, made up of equal parts of 2,4-D and 2,4,5-T, was introduced in early 1965. It proved especially effective in defoliating woody and broad-leaved vegetation and largely displaced Agents Pink and Green; White and Blue, however, continued to be sprayed as well. Agent Orange use intensified, peaking in 1969 when 3.25 million gallons were sprayed (compared to only a third of a million gallons in 1965). For a number of reasons, however, Operation Ranch Hand began to wind down in 1967, and in April 1970 the use of Agent Orange ended. During the five years of the program, some 11.2 million gallons of it had been sprayed over as much as 10 percent of South Vietnam's land area, including forests, transportation routes, and cultivated areas; this amount was 60 percent of all herbicides used there.[2]

Well before this time, concerns about the toxicity of herbicides in general, and of Agent Orange in particular, had been raised both publicly and privately.[3] As early as 1952, army officials had been informed by Monsanto Chemical Company, later a major manufacturer of Agent Orange, that 2,4,5-T was contaminated by a toxic substance. In 1963 the army's review of toxicity studies on 2,4,5-T found some increased risk of chloracne (a severe but usually reversible skin condition) and respiratory irritations; this risk was heightened when the chemical was applied at high concentrations by inexperienced personnel. That year the President's Science Advisory Committee reported to the Joint Chiefs of Staff on the possible health dangers of herbicide use.

Fifteen years later, after the Agent Orange case had commenced, the questions of precisely when and how the chemical companies and the government learned of the herbicide's toxicity and what they knew would become central issues in the litigation and in the debates that surrounded it. Even in the late 1960s, however, the source of the danger was clear. It came not from the compound itself but from a by-product of an intermediate stage of the 2,4,5-T manufacturing process, a contaminant that remained in the final product, usually in tiny amounts. This contaminant carries the chemical name 2,3,7,8 tetrachlorodibenzo-p-dioxin; it is one member of a family of compounds known as dioxins, distinguished from its relatives only by the position of its chlorine atoms on the molecule. This particular dioxin, known as TCDD, has been described as "perhaps the most toxic molecule ever synthesized by man."[4]

One cannot fully appreciate the significance of the Agent Orange case without understanding just how toxic TCDD is. Writing in early 1979, shortly after the case was filed, Arthur Galston, a biologist at Yale who specializes in herbicide research, summarized what was then known about the substance. Most striking was the fact that even "vanishingly small" quantities of dioxin in the diet produced adverse health effects in test animals. Galston reported that dioxin concentrations as low as 5 parts per trillion (ppt)—an amount roughly equivalent to one drop in 4 million gallons of water—"can, when supplied on a daily basis, induce a cancerous condition in rats. Concentrations about 1 ppb [part per billion] result in premature death from more acute causes, and concentrations above 50 ppb produce rapid signs of acute toxicity and early death . . . [Researchers] have found that lower concentrations of TCDD produce the same effects as higher concentrations, but merely take longer to do so . . . Even the purest 2,4,5-T currently available commercially contains about 0.05 ppm (mg/kg) of TCDD."[5]

Despite these findings, Agent Orange's actual toll on human health remained a controversial matter. First, the herbicide's potential toxicity was a function of, among other things, the quantity of dioxin it contained, but in any particular field application that quantity could not be known with certainty. The most reliable estimate, based on an assumed average TCDD contamination of 2 ppm (the average quantity found in the 2.2 million gallons of Agent Orange remaining in government storage after the war), was that the Agent Orange used between 1965 and 1971 contained 240 pounds of TCDD. Individual samples, however, contained levels as high as 140 ppm.[6] Second, information on the dioxin levels in the Agent Orange to which American soldiers were exposed was even less reliable. The areas in which aerial spraying missions had been conducted were known, but it was impossible to know how much of the herbicide reached the ground where people could ingest or inhale it; the levels to which specific individuals had been exposed was impossible to learn. Third, although dioxin at certain levels was clearly capable of causing serious diseases, those same diseases could also result from other causes. It followed, then, that inferences concerning Agent Orange's causation of particular diseases in particular individuals would remain weak and speculative; this fact more than any other would determine the future course of the Agent Orange litigation. Nevertheless, practical judgments had to be made in the presence of uncertain dangers. Extrapolating from the concentrations of TCDD found in the Agent Orange used in Vietnam, Galston concluded that "American servicemen who worked with Agent Orange or who saw duty in the heavily defoliated zones of Vietnam have a legitimate basis for asking the government to look into the state of their health."

Even in the late 1960s, more than a decade earlier, most scientists would have agreed with this conclusion. By that time the defoliation program had become a very visible and controversial element in the growing opposition to the Vietnam War.[7] Many scientists in the United States and abroad denounced the program, warning about its possible long-term effects on the people and ecology of Vietnam. These protests, which began in 1964 with a few scientists strongly critical of the war effort, spread to more prestigious and politically neutral technical bodies, including the mainstream American Association for the Advancement of Science (AAAS) and influential scientific journals. In 1966 and 1967, petitions calling for an end to chemical and biological warfare and signed by thousands of scientists, including many Nobel laureates, were sent to President Johnson and received wide publicity. These protests intensified when the Nixon administration, publicly committed to ending the war, assumed office in 1969.

International protests against the program also increased. In the United Nations, resolutions were introduced as early as 1966 charging the United States with violations of the 1925 Geneva Protocol limiting the use of chemical and biological weapons. Although the United States was able to defeat most of these resolutions, the General Assembly, over strong American opposition and the abstention of many allies, adopted a resolution in December 1969 that clearly defined the United States' defoliation program as a violation of the protocol. Even some American officials in Vietnam urged that the defoliation program be terminated, maintaining that its destructive scale and intensity were undermining efforts to "pacify" the countryside, feed the population, and win the support of the Vietnamese.

But it was a scientific event that galvanized opposition to the program most strongly and provided an occasion for ending it. In 1965 the National Cancer Institute had contracted with the Bionetics Research Laboratories to study the possible toxicity of a number of herbicides and pesticides, including 2,4-D and 2,4,5-T. Somewhat unexpectedly, a preliminary report on the research in 1966 had indicated that 2,4,5-T caused many birth defects in mice and rats whose mothers had been exposed to relatively high levels (up to 30 ppm) of dioxin and that 2,4-D was also potentially teratogenic. But these findings were not publicly released until 1969, when Matthew Meselson, a Harvard scientist and opponent of the defoliation program, obtained a copy of the report that had been leaked to "Nader's Raiders" and persuaded Lee DuBridge, President Nixon's science adviser and Meselson's former colleague at California Institute of Technology, to convene a meeting of scientists to discuss its implications. Although some leaders in the Pentagon insisted that the exposure levels used in the research were much higher than those experienced in Vietnam, they could no longer deny that a serious danger existed. On April 15, 1970, three Cabinet secretaries announced the suspension of most domestic uses of herbicides containing 2,4,5-T, and the Pentagon temporarily suspended all military use of 2,4,5-T, including Agent Orange. Although Agents White and Blue continued to be used in Vietnam through 1970, the military never reauthorized the use of Agent Orange.[8]

Between 1970, when the spraying of Agent Orange ended, and the summer of 1978, when the first Agent Orange lawsuit was filed, a number of important developments occurred that would culminate in, and profoundly shape, the Agent Orange case. Those developments included the tortuous process of assimilating Vietnam veterans into postwar American society, the accumulating evidence of dioxin's toxicity, the growing, increasingly visible health problems of the returned veterans, the response of the Veterans Administration, political organization by the veterans, and the evolution of the legal system, especially product liability law.

The Veterans' Assimilation

The Vietnam combat soldiers came home to a remarkably chilly reception. Compared with earlier postwar periods, the reabsorption and integration of these men into American society was painfully slow, incomplete, and grudging. In part, of course, this simply reflected the war's unpopularity. In the spasm of recrimination and national self-doubt that followed the strategic withdrawal from Vietnam, the veterans became unwanted reminders to many Americans of our perceived defeat and humiliation.

The returning veterans also presented more difficult adjustment problems than their predecessors. In part because of improved evacuation techniques and emergency medical care, the Vietnam War produced more disabled veterans than any earlier war. The wounded-to-killed ratios in World War II and Korea were about 3 to 1 and 4 to 1; in Vietnam, the ratio was 5.6 to 1. Of those discharged for disabilities during World War II, 18 percent were amputees and 3.1 percent were paralyzed; the comparable figures for Vietnam were 28.3 percent and 25.2 percent. Many Vietnam veterans were drug-dependent, and many more required psychiatric treatment.[9]

Emotional isolation at home flowed naturally from the lack of troop solidarity in Vietnam, another striking departure from past wars. The military's humane policy of short (one-year) tours of duty and frequent rotations in Vietnam weakened the attachments among soldiers that were common in earlier wars, increasing their feelings of separateness and alienation. Upon their return, this isolation discouraged the reunions and reminiscences that had eased the shock of reentry into civilian life for veterans of earlier eras. As Frank McCarthy, a combat veteran who would figure prominently in the Agent Orange story, said: "The thing with us—we came back one at a time. We were snatched out of society, put into a war situation alone, snatched out alone, and brought back into a society alone that was apathetic to our needs, that wanted to forget the Vietnam War."[10]

Finally, their return coincided with a prolonged period of economic crisis, the worst since the Great Depression. The veterans were greeted with double-digit inflation, rising unemployment, and spiraling interest rates, and many simply could not compete in this turbulent economic setting. These veterans possessed substantially less labor market experience than their predecessors; their average age was only twenty-three, compared with twenty-five and twenty-seven for Korea and World War II veterans. Many had been eligible for military service only because of lowered standards on Selective Service tests (the so-called Project 100,000). Although the economic disadvantage of Vietnam veterans apparently largely disappeared by the early 1980s, it was keenly felt during the first years after their return.[11]

Knowledge about Dioxin

With the release of the Bionetics Laboratories studies in 1969, concern about the effects on human health of dioxin-contaminated 2,4,5-T intensified. Reports from public health authorities throughout the world described a number of alarming incidents that appeared to implicate the herbicide. In 1969, for example, the Saigon press reported new and unexplained birth abnormalities that began in 1967 when the Agent Orange spraying program accelerated. Following an explosion in a 2,4,5-T plant in England, seventy-nine workers developed chloracne, as did some members of their families. Several workers died, apparently from severe liver damage. The next year, after the federal government responded to political pressure and the Bionetics studies by canceling all 2,4,5-T uses on food crops intended for human consumption, a technical advisory committee was formed (at the request of the chemical companies) to prepare recommendations to the EPA. The committee's report, submitted in 1971, urged restrictions on allowable dioxin levels in 2,4,5-T for still-permitted uses; even so, many scientists criticized the report as inadequate. That same year, it was learned that the spraying on roads of waste oil containing high concentrations of dioxin-contaminated 2,4,5-T had killed animals in a town in eastern Missouri. (Eventually, the entire town had to be evacuated and abandoned.)[12]

During the early 1970s, Matthew Meselson reported having found high dioxin concentrations in various locations in Vietnam and in fish, suggesting that dioxin might be building up in the food chain. The EPA, however, followed an erratic regulatory path, withdrawing its cancellation order on the use of 2,4,5-T on rice crops in 1974 and vacillating for several years thereafter over whether dioxin was entering the food chain. In 1976 another explosion in a 2,4,5-T plant, this time in Seveso, Italy, littered the surrounding area with dioxin, leading to serious illnesses and evacuation of the community. These events prompted publication the following year of several books directed at lay audiences and highly critical of the government's laxity in dealing with 2,4,5-T. And in 1978, researchers at the University of Wisconsin reported that more than 65 percent of the monkeys fed a diet containing dioxin-contaminated food at concentrations of 500 ppt had died; according to the scientists, this demonstrated "the ability of dioxin to persist and accumulate in the living tissues of primates." In a second study, the Wisconsin group found that more than half of the rats fed dioxin levels as low as 5 ppt a day had developed tumors, indicating the possibility of carcinogenicity.

By mid-1978, then, the available scientific evidence on dioxin strongly suggested that even at "low" levels it could be a virulent toxicant, that it inevitably accompanied commercially manufactured 2,4,5-T, and that it accumulated in the food chain and in the fatty tissues and secretions of animals. Yet the many remaining questions about dioxin's effects divided scientists and engendered continuing uncertainty. Some of these ongoing disputes were methodological; the most important concerned appropriate test dosages and concentration levels, the animal species used for testing, control variables, and extrapolation from animal data to health effects on people. Some disputes reflected the different training and emphases of traditional toxicologists, primarily concerned with short-term effects, and specialists such as cancer researchers and geneticists, more concerned with long-term abnormalities. Finally, some disputes revolved around what scientists call "trans-scientific" questions—for example, how "safe" is safe enough—that science can pose and perhaps narrow but can never answer authoritatively.

The Veterans' Health Problems

With the passage of time, a steadily growing number of Vietnam veterans died prematurely or reported debilitating illnesses or claimed that their children were born with serious congenital defects. Few veterans linked their conditions to exposure in Vietnam to Agent Orange; indeed, it was not until the spring of 1978 that they had any reason to make that connection, and most did not do so until much later. Some months earlier, Maude deVictor, a benefits counselor in the Chicago regional office of the VA, learned about a veteran with terminal cancer who claimed that Agent Orange was responsible for his illness; the VA had rejected his claim. When deVictor questioned other veterans and their widows about Agent Orange exposures and physical symptoms, she thought she discerned a pattern. When she gathered and publicized statistics that explicitly linked Agent Orange and veterans' symptoms, however, she ran into a bureaucratic stone wall. A sympathetic Chicago television station aired a special report on her findings, entitled "Agent Orange: The Deadly Fog," which attracted considerable attention from veterans who now thought they saw an explanation for conditions that had previously seemed inexplicable. Soon, Agent Orange–related inquiries, and even some disability claims, began to reach the VA.[13]

The VA's Response

The VA, established more than fifty years earlier, was the successor to a long line of programs and agencies stretching back to colonial times, created to provide care and support for veterans of American wars. Expanded after each new military conflict, the VA by 1978 was one of the largest federal agencies (second in number of employees, third in budget), operating hundreds of hospitals, outpatient clinics, and nursing homes and serving almost 20 million patients.

If the VA had one principle firmly embedded in its bureaucratic mind, it was that any problems suffered by veterans exposed to Agent Orange (which the VA eventually presumed to include *all* Vietnam veterans) were not, with the exception of chloracne, caused by the herbicide. In the absence of some other proof that their problems were in fact service-connected, the VA denied their disability claims. (The VA, it should be noted, was supported in this by the Veterans of Foreign Wars.)

When Maude deVictor's suspicions were televised in March 1978, the VA responded with a press release stating that only 27 of the 2.5 million claims it had decided during the past year had been herbicide-related. In May it issued a disability rating memorandum stating that chloracne was the only service-related disability recognized as having been caused by exposure to herbicides. Several weeks later the agency circulated another memorandum, again insisting that chloracne was the only chronic condition associated with herbicides; any other neurological symptoms were "fully reversible." It also instructed VA personnel not to make any file entries suggesting "a relationship between a veteran's illness and defoliant exposure" unless that diagnosis was confirmed unequivocally after the case was referred to VA headquarters. VA employees, the memorandum continued, must not initiate examinations for dioxin "poisoning" or make statements regarding Agent Orange without prior review by headquarters. VA officials also downplayed concerns about dioxin in other ways; one even claimed that Agent Orange was no more toxic than aspirin!

Persistent veterans' criticisms coupled with congressional pressure for a more liberal policy on benefits, however, began to soften the VA position slightly. By late 1978 the VA had established a protocol for physical examinations of veterans claiming Agent Orange–related illness, the findings from which were entered into a computerized Agent Orange Registry. Even so, no claims other than chloracne were recognized.[14]

Veterans' Organizations

In view of the VA's adamant position on Agent Orange, one might have expected Vietnam veterans to organize politically to seek to reverse it. But the established veterans' groups, although a formidable political force, were not organizations a new veteran was likely to turn to for help. The American Legion and the Veterans of Foreign Wars, which enjoyed very close relations with the VA (the Legion is given free space in VA headquarters and represents many veterans before the agency), were made up largely of aging men with markedly conservative, promilitary political views. Vietnam veterans, in contrast, were very young and not as reflexively traditional. Finding their wartime service a stigma even to some members of the old-line veterans' organizations, the younger soldiers refrained from joining them, retreating instead into further isolation. One combat soldier's hostile reception by older veterans was probably experienced by many: "Walking across the Boston Common his first day home, his service uniform and gear fully apparent, he was greeted by peace demonstrators with shouts of 'Killer! How many babies did you burn over there?' Returning home, his brother offered, 'You asshole! Why did you go to Vietnam anyway?' Seeking solace and companionship that night in the American Legion Hall, he was confronted with 'Hey buddy! How come you guys lost the war over there?' "[15]

Uncomfortable with existing organizations but craving solidarity, understanding, and political strength, many Vietnam veterans organized new groups. Unlike the established ones, most of these groups were either antiwar or politically neutral. All were primarily concerned with the problems of Vietnam veterans. Vietnam Veterans Against the War (VVAW), for example, combined traditional lobbying for VA benefit changes with "new politics" advocacy of immediate United States withdrawal from southeast Asia. After being infiltrated by the FBI and CIA, however, VVAW was effectively destroyed. Citizen Soldier, a New York–based group with roots in the antiwar movement, sought an amnesty for Vietnam-era draft evaders. The National Association of Concerned Veterans, in contrast, avoided ideological politics, concentrating almost exclusively upon assisting veterans to adjust and obtain governmental benefits. None of the newer veterans' groups was large. "They fought not at the big unit level, as in World War II," one of their lawyers observed, "but at the squad level. They came home and organized in the same way.

They were very effective in small groups but not really capable of large-scale organization."[16]

The publicity surrounding the TV documentary on Maude deVictor's findings galvanized a number of the newer veterans' organizations into action. Like other new groups, Citizen Soldier used the Agent Orange issue to bolster its organizing efforts and criticisms of government policies. The group established a "Search and Save" campaign to identify victims of Agent Orange, and two of its staffers began work on a book, GI Guinea Pigs, denouncing the government's policies. Later, when several other new veterans' groups formed a task force to press the Agent Orange issue, Citizen Soldier was excluded; the group then turned to a litigation strategy. Other groups, notably the confrontational Vietnam Veterans of America (VVA) and the more moderate, single-issue Agent Orange Victims International (AOVI), also began to search for lawyers to represent the veterans who had been exposed to Agent Orange. This organizational fragmentation, with its overlay of ideological division, was to plague the Agent Orange litigation.

Changes in the Legal System

In the decade preceding the Agent Orange litigation, the legal system experienced unprecedented changes that were highly favorable to the kinds of claims the veterans were to assert in that case. Procedurally, the law was more receptive to common group claims through the device of the class action and encouraged litigants to use new types of expert evidence, often of a statistical or epidemiological nature. These innovations, although developed primarily in other legal contexts such as antitrust, employment discrimination, and environmental litigation, could be applied to tort claims as well.[17]

Changes during the 1970s affecting the ethical rules of the legal profession also facilitated cases like Agent Orange. State bar associations, under pressure from the Supreme Court, virtually eliminated long-established restrictions on lawyers' freedom to advertise for, solicit, and finance clients, especially in personal injury, civil rights, and "public interest" cases. As a result, lawyers were left virtually free to conceive, initiate, sustain, and terminate litigation themselves, less constrained than ever before by individual, identifiable clients.[18]

The most dramatic and significant changes, however, occurred around substantive tort law—the legal doctrines and institutional practices that determine what kinds of personal injury claims the courts will recognize. By the late 1970s, a series of judicial decisions by a few innovative state and federal courts and echoed in a large number of other jurisdictions had radically transformed the doctrinal foundations of tort law. Many of these innovations applied to the field of tort law generally, but their greatest impact by far was in the area of manufacturers' liability for defective products.[19] Not coincidentally, product liability law became the substantive basis for the veterans' claims in the Agent Orange litigation.

The swiftness and scope of this transformation may more easily be grasped if we briefly consider how product liability law had evolved during the two decades prior to the Agent Orange litigation. I shall organize this discussion around the discrete elements of a plaintiff's prima facie burden in a tort dispute—that is, what he must prove in order to avoid having his claim dismissed before it can reach a jury.

To reach a jury, the tort plaintiff is required to establish four elements on the basis of evidence that a reasonable juror might accept and in the light of previously developed legal standards. He must establish that the defendant owed him a duty of care, that the defendant breached that duty, that defendant's breach of duty caused plaintiff's harm, and that the plaintiff sustained damages of the kind the law regards as compensable. (In some jurisdictions the plaintiff must also establish that his own behavior did not contribute to causing the injury; most, however, impose upon the defendant the burden of proving the plaintiff's "contributory fault"). Generally speaking, the judicial innovations of the 1960s and 1970s made it much easier for a plaintiff to establish each of these four elements with sufficient probability that his claim would be submitted to a jury. At that point, the jury's natural sympathy for innocent individuals victimized by corporate or governmental misbehavior or neglect could be expected to favor a plaintiff's claims.

The Defendant's Duty of Care

Until quite recently, the manufacturer of most products, other than food, owed a duty of care—a duty to produce and market nondefective products. That duty was owed not to the world in general but only to those purchasing the product from the manufacturer. Beginning with the landmark case of *MacPherson* v. *Buick Motor Co.*, decided in New York in 1916, that duty was gradually extended to those who purchased from other sellers in the chain of distribution, such as retailers. Led by a 1960 decision by the Supreme Court of New Jersey, *Henningsen* v. *Bloomfield Motors, Inc.*, courts began to rule that a manufacturer's potential liability extended beyond the purchasers themselves to include members of their families and others who were likely to use or otherwise be exposed to the manufacturer's product. In the years that followed, courts took the further step of enlarging that duty to protect anyone who was injured by the product, including a victim who had no contractual relationship to the manufacturer, the purchaser, or the consumer, so long as the victim's exposure to the product could be said to be reasonably foreseeable. When one considers the vast contemporary expansion in the number of products, such as toxic chemicals, that pose a potential risk to large numbers of people—few or none of whom purchased them—the significance of this greatly enlarged scope of manufacturers' legal duties becomes apparent.[20]

The Defendant's Violation of the Duty

Traditionally, a manufacturer's liability for a defective product could be premised solely on a showing that the manufacturer had produced the product negligently. This "negligence" or "fault" standard required that the plaintiff prove that the manufacturer had failed to use reasonable care in producing it—for example, by violating industry-wide standards, by violating the firm's own standards, or by failing to warn of latent hazards. This requirement was often difficult for a plaintiff to satisfy. Beginning with the Supreme Court of California's *Greenman* decision in 1963, however, most state courts repudiated the negligence standard for manufactuers' product liability in favor of a standard of "strict liability" (or "liability without fault").[21] Under a strict liability rule, a manufacturer became liable for all injuries caused by "defective" products, defined as products that were "unreasonably dangerous," regardless of whether or not it had been negligent in the manufacturing process. Under such a rule, then, a manufacturer cannot defeat liability by showing that it took all reasonable precautions against defects.

Moreover, by the late 1970s, the notion of defective product had itself been expanded to include not only the familiar concept of a manufacturing defect (that is, a departure from the manufacturer's own production standards), but a so-called design defect as well. Within broad limits, this latter concept leaves open to a jury a decision that a product, although manufactured according to design specifications and in accordance with statutory and regulatory requirements, was nevertheless defective. Under the concept of design defect, this conclusion would follow if the jury believes that the product should have been designed differently (more safely) or perhaps should not have been produced at all.[22]

The precise effect of these moves from a negligence to a strict liability standard for defective products, and from a manufacturing to a design defect standard, is much debated among legal scholars. The question is complicated by the fact that vestiges of the negligence standard remain in the legal definition of defect. What seems clear, however, is that strict liability, coupled with a design defect rule, enables plaintiffs to get their cases to a jury more easily, thereby enhancing their prospects for a jury verdict or for a favorable settlement with the manufacturer.

Causation

Until quite recently a plaintiff was obliged to demonstrate causation by establishing two analytically distinct links between the defendant's conduct or product and the plaintiff's injury. First, plaintiff had to show that a particular course of conduct or a particular product had caused his injury. This may be called the "determinate plaintiff" requirement. Second, he had to show that a particular defendant was responsible for that injurious conduct or product. This may be called the "determinate defendant" requirement. Although neither of these requirements ordinarily creates significant obstacles for plaintiffs in traditional tort cases, both created extremely difficult problems for plaintiffs in the Agent Orange litigation. In certain categories of traditional cases in which causation was likely but might be especially difficult for a plaintiff to prove, such as medical malpractice claims or airplane crashes, the courts long ago made proof of causation easier by adopting special rules that shift from plaintiff to defendant the burden of producing evidence or of persuading the jury.[23]

Since the 1960s, some courts have gone considerably further in relaxing both causation requirements, especially the need for a "determinate defendant." For example, they now permit a plaintiff to get to a jury on the causation issue merely by showing that the defendant's conduct or product might be a "substantial factor in bringing about the harm." According to the *Restatement (Second) of Torts*, a

compilation of tort doctrine that significantly influences judicial decisions, this standard is satisfied if "the defendant's conduct has such
an effect in producing the harm as to lead reasonable men to regard
it as a cause, using that word in the popular sense." Moreover, courts
increasingly permit plaintiffs to seek to establish causation by adducing evidence of a statistical, epidemiological, or experimental nature,
in lieu of more particularistic evidence. Although the admissibility
and probity of such evidence remains controversial, and courts continue to be uncomfortable with it, its routine use in employment
discrimination and regulatory cases has led to its growing acceptance
by courts hearing complex pharmaceutical and other toxic tort
cases.[24]

In situations in which general causation can be readily established
but plaintiffs cannot identify precisely who was responsible for the
harm, courts in the late 1970s also began to adopt techniques for
facilitating plaintiffs' proof of firms' liability. The most important of
these techniques has been the so-called "alternative liability" rule.
Generally speaking, a plaintiff faced with indeterminate defendants
can fix firms' responsibility under this rule by showing that a fungible
product was the cause of his harm, so long as a rational method exists
for allocating damages among the manufacturers of that product. This
approach, prefigured in a case in 1948 concerning a two-defendant
hunting accident, was first extended to the mass toxic tort context in
the important *Sindell* case, which wound its way through the California courts during the late 1970s just as the Agent Orange litigation
was getting under way. In that case, a DES victim, unable to identify
the particular manufacturer whose pills her mother had purchased
and consumed during pregnancy a generation before the lawsuit, was
permitted to proceed with her claim. She simply had to show that
DES caused her injury, that manufacturers representing a substantial
share of the DES market were before the court as defendants, and that
their individual shares of the DES market could be established.[25]

Damages

In the decade or two preceding the Agent Orange litigation, the courts
steadily enlarged the kinds of personal injuries for which the law
would provide compensation, and juries continually increased their
awards of both compensatory and punitive damages in tort cases.
Until quite recently, damages in tort cases, especially in product lia-

bility actions, were legally confined to the traditional categories of compensable harm—medical and other out-of-pocket expenses, lost earnings, and "pain and suffering." Jury awards of compensatory damages, designed to compensate victims for injuries sustained, were modest in size, seldom exceeding $1 million. Awards of punitive damages, designed to punish the defendant for malicious or extremely reckless behavior and to deter others from such conduct, were quite rare and were generally confined to particularly egregious cases of malicious and outrageous wrongdoing.[26]

All of that changed during the 1960s and 1970s. First, following a 1968 California decision, *Dillon* v. *Legg*, courts began to permit plaintiffs to recover not merely for the traditional categories of compensable damages, but also for emotional distress. In the past, damages for emotional distress had generally been limited to a few categories: intentional torts, torts in which the defendant's negligence would almost certainly cause emotional trauma (the classic examples were the mishandling of a corpse by an undertaker and delivery of a telegram erroneously announcing the death of a close relative), and torts in which the defendant had caused a physical impact upon the plaintiff's body. After *Dillon*, however, courts increasingly allowed recovery for emotional suffering in situations in which the plaintiff, although not physically touched, was traumatized by having observed injury to a child or other close relative while plaintiff was within the so-called zone of danger. By the late 1970s, even these constraints had been relaxed somewhat; plaintiffs, for example, began to recover for emotional trauma associated with the birth of a defective, stillborn, or unwanted child whose condition had been caused by a physician's negligence, or for trauma brought on by fear of cancer after exposure to toxic chemicals.

Second, juries began to award compensatory damages at, or even well above, the million-dollar level with some regularity. Many of these large awards occurred in product liability cases. Third, punitive damage awards became far more common and larger in amounts, especially in cases involving business defendants. Moreover, punitive damages were sometimes granted in product liability cases in which no real evidence of malice on the part of the manufacturer had been presented. This occurred during the late 1960s in the MER/29 litigation in which a series of large punitive damage awards was rendered against a single manufacturer for a single defective drug. Surely the most dramatic and well-publicized example of changed attitudes con-

cerning punitive damages among juries and courts was the Ford Pinto
case, decided in 1978. In that lawsuit, a jury rendered a verdict for a
teenage boy that included not only $2.8 million in compensatory dam-
ages but punitive damages of $125 million (which the trial judge
reduced to a mere $3.8 million)! Here, as in other such cases, nothing
more malicious or reckless on the manufacturer's part was shown
than a calculated, conventional decision to design a product in a way
that traded safety off against cost and other marketing and engineering considerations.[27]

By the late 1970s, these judicial innovations expanding the scope of
a manufacturer's duty to design and produce safe products, multi-
plying the categories of persons entitled to sue to enforce that duty,
easing the causation requirements, and upholding unprecedented
damage awards were well-established elements in the legal systems
of California, New York, and many other populous and influential
states. These innovations reflected a growing consensus, already rip-
ening into what can only be called a conventional wisdom, that the
traditional moral foundations of tort law, as symbolized in the negligence standard and its individualized case-by-case determination of
fault, should be replaced by a more functional system. According to
the functional approach, a tort system should be evaluated according
to how well it achieves a variety of social policy goals. The most
prominent of these goals are: to deter harmful conduct, to compensate victims, to internalize social costs to the activities that generate
them, to spread losses widely throughout society—preferably through
insurance and the price system—to minimize system costs, and—
somewhat more controversially—to improve (or at least not worsen)
the distribution of wealth. The transformation of product liability law
during the 1960s and 1970s was perhaps the most dramatic, unequivocal expression of the functional approach and represented its most
complete triumph.[28]

To be sure, these developments did not lack for critics, and they
raised many difficult questions of principle and practice. Nevertheless, they usually commanded the enthusiastic support of most pol-
iticians, legal scholars, and commentators. (This was also true,
although to a lesser extent, of certain other important expansions of
product liability law during this period, such as the steady erosion of
"product misuse" and some other manufacturer defenses to product
liability claims.) Clearly, then, the expansion of product liability res-
onated to more fundamental economic changes and intellectual cur-

rents shaping society's attitudes toward this area of the law. The displacement of face-to-face local transactions by a mass production economy based on anonymous national markets, the spread of liability insurance, the growing insistence upon the social responsibilities of business, the rising ethos of consumer protection, a more activist judiciary, and the increasing prominence of the "law and economics" critique of traditional legal institutions all played a part.[29]

Another legal trend, more embryonic and less visible than the changes in product liability law, enlarged the scope of the government's tort liability. The rapidly rising scale of governmental activity during the 1960s and 1970s led to a number of federal court decisions that significantly expanded the potential tort liability both of individual executive officials at all levels of government and of state and municipal government entities. In 1974 Congress amended the Federal Tort Claims Act, the federal government's statutory waiver of its sovereign immunity, to broaden somewhat the categories of governmental wrongs for which it could be sued for damages. Moreover, commentators increasingly criticized some of the remaining enclaves of federal governmental immunity, including the so-called *Feres* doctrine, which precluded all liability for the federal government's tort against its own military personnel. The ancient structure of sovereign immunity, largely impregnable until recent decades, had begun to crumble under the pressures generated by a ubiquitous, activist government.[30]

The 1970s also saw the emergence of mass tort litigation as an important legal phenomenon. Airplane crashes, dangerous drugs, hotel fires, building collapses, passenger train derailments—and the lawsuits that almost inevitably followed—became familiar front-page stories. Many of these mass tort disputes involved toxic substances. Cases involving the Dalkon Shield, toxic shock syndrome, Love Canal, DES, and a host of environmental pollutants often dominated the evening news. Of these, the most important and notorious were the asbestos cases. In August 1982, approximately 16,500 of these were pending against Johns-Manville; plaintiffs sought compensatory and punitive damages for personal injuries totaling many billions of dollars.

The incontrovertible toxicity of asbestos, the unprecedented magnitude of this litigation, and the almost unimaginable potential liability it entailed received a great deal of public attention during the 1970s. After several rulings favorable to plaintiffs, most notably the seminal *Borel* decision in 1973 in which the "conservative" Fifth Circuit Court of Appeals rejected an array of manufacturer defenses and applied expansive product liability principles to occupational asbestos-related diseases, the extraordinary possibilities of mass tort litigation became unmistakably clear. (As this is being written, the courts are experiencing a blizzard of new actions involving claims by school districts and others of property damage caused by asbestos.)[31]

For present purposes, the important point that these changes suggest is this: many legal obstacles to tort litigation generally, and mass toxic tort litigation in particular, were being systematically dismantled by the court, with the apparent approval of political and legal commentators, at precisely the time that the Vietnam veterans were beginning to consider what court remedies might be available to compensate them for the devastating injuries that they believed Agent Orange had inflicted on them. However ignorant most veterans may have been about this larger legal transformation, its implications—its promises of financial recompense and symbolic justice—were not lost upon either their leaders or their lawyers.

II

THE CASE

3

The Agent Orange War

EARLY in 1978, Edward Gorman, a personal injury lawyer on Long Island, received a telephone call from a stranger, Paul Reutershan, who told Gorman a harrowing story. Reutershan was a Vietnam veteran, having enlisted as a seventeen-year-old in the army, where he served as crew chief on a resupply helicopter for an engineer unit. Upon his return from Vietnam, Reutershan, who neither smoked nor drank and who considered himself something of a "health nut," contracted virulent abdominal cancer, for which he was hospitalized in 1977. Although his doctors declared his condition terminal, Reutershan returned to his civilian work as a conductor on a commuter train in Connecticut.

One day he read a *Daily News* account about Maude deVictor's data correlating health problems and exposure to Agent Orange in Vietnam. Reutershan immediately recalled his own experiences with the chemical some ten years earlier, when he had served on a helicopter crew and had flown through clouds of the chemical during spraying. Convinced that he had identified the cause of his mysterious illness, he wrote to President Carter asking him to intercede to gain admission to a VA hospital. Reutershan's desperate call to Gorman followed, and in late July Gorman filed suit in a state court in New York, naming Dow and two other chemical manufacturers as defendants. On December 14, 1978, Reutershan died of cancer, deeply in debt for medical expenses and for his efforts to inform other veterans about Agent Orange.[1]

Reutershan, however, left two far-reaching legacies. The first was his lawsuit which, although still embryonic, would soon grow into a full-scale assault on the chemical manufacturers, the United States government, and the conscience of the American people. The second legacy, essential to the first, was his creation of the combat unit that would actually conduct the assault. In his last months, knowing that the end was near, Reutershan drew together his mother and sister, some family friends, and a small group of veterans whom he had come to know through his efforts to publicize the Agent Orange issue. Agreeing on the need to perpetuate his work, they formed a nonprofit organization, Agent Orange Victims International (AOVI). AOVI would carry on the struggle under the leadership of Reutershan's designated successor, Frank McCarthy.

McCarthy was a natural for the job. His personal history is worth recounting, for although he did not claim to be an Agent Orange victim, he was otherwise rather typical, at least in broad outline, of the Vietnam veterans he was to recruit and lead in the Agent Orange war.[2] As a high school dropout from Philadelphia, inspired by the new young president who had been a war hero, McCarthy joined the army in 1961. He was an eager enlistee, determined to make a glorious career of soldiering. He wanted to emulate the uncle for whom he was named, a thirty-year army veteran who had been the father figure in Frank's broken home and whose stories of the Iwo Jima, Guadalcanal, and Korea campaigns had stimulated the boy's dreams. The seventeen-year-old recruit trained with the 101st Airborne Division in Kentucky and then served in Korea.

Early in 1964, McCarthy's life took a momentous turn. The First Infantry Division, celebrated in American military history as the Big Red One, was being formed up for service in South Vietnam. McCarthy underwent a year of exceptionally rigorous training at Fort Riley, Kansas ("As difficult as 'Nam," he recalls, "except that nobody was shooting at us"), where he became deeply imbued with the glorious tradition of the Big Red One, which had led the assaults on Omaha Beach and in North Africa and the South Pacific during World War II. McCarthy then shipped out to Vietnam, landing at Vung-Tau on the southeastern coast in September 1965. He remembers the moment vividly:

> After twenty days on the boat, wrestling with the soldier's eternal questions—will I be a coward, can I look the enemy in the eye and blow him away, will my family be proud of me—I had concluded that I would do my duty and was prepared to die for my country and my buddies if necessary. We were there to defend freedom and decency against the Communists, whose agent, Oswald, had killed my president. I was fiercely proud to be part of the Big Red One, and I also thought of a

Churchill quote that I had read somewhere: "The reason men go to war is because the women are watching." These motivations were all intertwined in me.

McCarthy's battalion was sent to the western edge of the Iron Triangle, a dense jungle on the Cambodian border. His "year of disillusionment," as he now recalls it, began immediately. McCarthy, as the "point man" in a reconnaissance platoon, was usually the first man in the lead column that would advance through the almost impenetrable, Vietcong-infested jungle looking for the enemy, booby traps, mines, and "panji pits" (camouflaged holes studded with pointed stakes). A short, wiry man, McCarthy was also a "tunnel rat," whose job it was to crawl through the network of tunnels that the enemy dug beneath the jungle floor.

> If was a booby trap for us. I had to watch my closest buddies suddenly get blown to smithereens without being able to do anything about it. Except in free-fire zones, we were under strictest orders, punishable by court-martial, not to fire at the VC, even if they were running away in clear view, without first radioing to headquarters for permission. All our training went out the window. After our guys got killed the first time, we fired back, shot up our radios, and returned to camp, explaining that we hadn't been able to radio for permission. After a few weeks, nobody mentioned the order again. Maybe they ran out of radios.

By late 1966, the esprit that had sustained McCarthy had turned sour. Of the thirty-two men originally in his platoon, only six were left; the others had been replaced by green soldiers ("newbies"), mostly draftees who had been inadequately trained, who shared little of the career soldier's reverence for the legacy of the Big Red One, and on whom (or so the hardened veterans assumed) one could not rely in tough situations. McCarthy and the others also felt betrayed by the political controls on the day-to-day conduct of the war. "We all knew that we could defeat the enemy and drive them back to the North if they would only let us bomb Hanoi and cut off the Ho Chi Minh Trail . . . Because we did not use the military capability we knew we had, we lost the honor we went there with; there was no honor in just killing. It began to seem endless."

At about this time McCarthy and the others in his platoon began to receive hate mail from the United States. "I would read a letter from home and feel a glow and then read one from a stranger that said, 'While you are there killing babies, we're home fucking your sister.'

(McCarthy feels great bitterness toward many antiwar activists who he says later refused to help Agent Orange victims. "A sixth grade class scraped together six hundred dollars, a little old lady sends us twenty-five dollars a month from her Social Security check, but Jane Fonda, who traveled to Hanoi and made millions off of her war movies, wouldn't give the war's American victims a dime." Abbie Hoffman, he claims, refused a plea for help with fund-raising by saying only, "You shouldn't have been in Vietnam anyway.")

McCarthy left Vietnam in March 1967 as a staff sergeant, decorated with the Bronze Star for heroism with valor and a Purple Heart. He also carried deeply embedded shrapnel from which he continues to suffer great pain today. His spiritual wounds were equally debilitating. "In addition to my pain and partly because of it, I was a very troubled guy," he recalls. "I remained patriotic and proud, but I was thoroughly disillusioned. My early ideals mocked me, making me bitter and hard." After a year as a drill instructor at Fort Dix, where he trained brand-new soldiers destined for Vietnam ("I could hardly bear telling them what lay in store for them"), he was honorably discharged in March 1968. He moved to New York City, where he lived on odd jobs and enrolled in the Art Students' League to study sculpture under the GI Bill.

For the next ten years Frank McCarthy the civilian spent much of his time in a new war—this one with the Veterans Administration. Until 1975 he battled for himself; thereafter, he waged the war on behalf of his fellow Vietnam veterans. McCarthy's litany of endless wrangling with the VA bureaucracy apparently differed only in detail from those of thousands of other veterans. Immediately after his discharge, when he went to the VA to obtain relief from the shrapnel lodged in his body, he was told that he could not see a VA doctor for three months. "I threw my papers at them and walked out feeling hopeless," McCarthy says, "until I looked at the rows of guys sitting there in wheelchairs who would never walk again." In 1973 the VA's long delays in sending his disability and educational assistance checks caused him to be evicted from his apartment; his belongings were strewn on the sidewalk and stolen by thieves. Enraged, he stormed into the VA office in New York and "threw quite a scene" until two New York City police officers intervened and the VA admitted its error. Even then, the check arrived only after two months and some pointed inquiries from Senator Javits's office. For several weeks, McCarthy had no place to sleep and lived on the streets. "That was the worst time of my life," he recalls, "worse even than Vietnam. I felt that my country had forsaken me."

At some point, McCarthy managed to pull himself together, and in 1975 he received a retroactive compensation check from the VA for $5,000. With that to live on, he organized the Vietnam Veterans Unifying Group to fight the decision of the New York City Board of Education to disaccredit the Art Students' League from the GI Bill program. After McCarthy obtained 10,000 signatures on a petition, held a show of veterans' art work at Lincoln Center, and generated some grassroots opposition to the board's action, Governor Rockefeller reversed the earlier decision. This victory had a profound effect on McCarthy, convincing him that he could change the system through legal means. The Unifying Group, which eventually grew to 350 members organized in different chapters, began to work directly with veterans, counseling them about how to obtain their benefits and deal with the VA. McCarthy's knowledge of the Vietnam veteran community and its problems grew rapidly.

But what he regards as the transforming event in his life was still to come. In June 1978, a friend gave McCarthy a newspaper article describing Paul Reutershan's battle with cancer. McCarthy telephoned Reutershan in the hospital and told him about the Unifying Group. "To me," McCarthy says, "Paul seemed like just another veteran with a problem. But when he asked me to come immediately to Norwalk Hospital and I went, he changed my entire life." Although they spent the entire day discussing Reutershan's plan to alert the veterans to the Agent Orange danger, McCarthy did not take Reutershan's claims altogether seriously at first. "I thought Agent Orange, if that's what the chemical was, was great stuff. We were fighting in a triple-canopy jungle in the Iron Triangle, and I wanted those planes to melt the whole thing away so we could see the enemy that was all around us. And why would our government poison us?" But he knew Reutershan was not crazy. He had, after all, convinced a hard-nosed lawyer to file a $10 million lawsuit against Dow Chemical.

When Reutershan was discharged from the hospital, McCarthy began to visit him at his mother's home, where he worked. "The phone rang all day," McCarthy recalls, "vets, vets, vets—all with problems that broke our hearts." McCarthy began to see Agent Orange as a metaphor for Vietnam veterans' helplessness and suffering, a symbol that could exert a far more powerful galvanizing effect than the elusive bureaucratic enemy at the VA. Just as he had done back in the early 1960s, McCarthy decided to join an army and a war, enlisting his remaining ideals and energy in the struggle against Agent Orange.

In late 1978, Reutershan's army was still only a tiny contingent, confined largely to his VFW post in Stamford, Connecticut. That post, however, was not typical. McCarthy remembers it as one of the "toughest" in the country, perhaps the first to be completely run by Vietnam veterans, most of whom were hardened combat soldiers harboring lots of painful and angry memories. Its commander, Jimmie Sparrow, also believed in Reutershan and made the post the core of the fledgling AOVI organization.

AOVI viewed Reutershan's lawsuit as an important part of its broad-gauged strategy to alert the nation to the Agent Orange menace. The lawsuit, however, was already experiencing some of the difficulties that have continued to plague it down to the present day. It seemed clear that Reutershan's attorney, Edward Gorman, was not the man to be the solitary field marshal in the Agent Orange war. Even before the suit was filed, Gorman had discerned some of the minefields through which the case would have to pass, and he reached out for help. In August 1978, Gorman invited another Long Island lawyer, Victor J. Yannacone, Jr., to lunch, where he sought Yannacone's advice on how to proceed in the case.[3]

In some ways Yannacone seemed a logical choice. Since beginning practice with his father in 1959, Yannacone's specialty had been workmen's compensation claims. This work, combined with his technical aptitude (he had begun college as a premed student), led him to learn a great deal about the broader problem of toxic chemicals. "Workmen's compensation practice involves minimal fees," Yannacone points out, "but can generate an extraordinarily large volume of cases. Before long, I had handled cases involving asbestos, beryllium, ketone, arsenic, industrial oils, and many other toxicants. That's how I saw my first chloracne victim."

By Yannacone's account, workmen's compensation law is not a demanding kind of practice. "It is relatively common to earn sixty to a hundred thousand a year without filling all your time. The Compensation Board is frequently in recess, and I can handle my 3,000 open cases easily from a table in the state office building cafeteria." That left the squat, burly, energetic lawyer with time for other things. More than a decade earlier, Yannacone had compelled a public health agency in Suffolk County, New York, where he lived and worked, to discontinue the spraying of DDT. Yannacone recalls that when the local judge who heard the DDT dispute asked what legal principles could possibly justify a ban, Yannacone quickly coined a new phrase, "environmental law." Although he claims never to have seen or heard the term before, environmental law blossomed into a major legal specialty within only a few years. Yannacone went on to help form the Environmental Defense Fund, today a leading environmental advocacy group, with which he launched a David and Goliath legal campaign—eventually successful—against DDT and certain other chlorinated hydrocarbons.

Yannacone, then, was more than a lawyer who could make legal arguments and muster scientific data to advance a client's interests. He was also a passionate partisan, a crusader who was personally and ideologically committed to subduing toxic chemicals in the interest of preserving ecological balance and human health. The incandescent intensity of his commitment, resonating through his flamboyant oratory, charismatic persona, and eccentric operating style, was to shape the course of the Agent Orange litigation in profound, bizarre, and (for us) instructive ways.

Gorman exhorted Yannacone to become personally involved in the Reutershan case, especially in its technical scientific aspects. Yannacone, however, doubted that Reutershan's symptoms alone could establish the necessary causal linkage with Agent Orange. He later recalled his pessimistic evaluation: "A toxic tort is like being hit by a chemical bullet. The difference is that, unlike being hit by a car, you have to negate other possible causes. Here, there was the added problem that the victims of Agent Orange were indeterminate. I had already paid my dues to society in the DDT litigation, and I recognized that to take on another case of that magnitude without any resources, with a much more difficult scientific problem, and with much more well-entrenched chemical companies than in the DDT cases was basically a hopeless task." After looking into the technical reports on dioxin and even attending a congressional hearing on the subject in October, Yannacone declined Gorman's request.

When Reutershan died in December, relations between Gorman and AOVI rapidly deteriorated. On his deathbed, Reutershan had repeated his earlier desire that the case be expanded into a class action. Gorman, however, resisted doing so. Shortly after Reutershan died, McCarthy, as AOVI's new leader, began to search for a new lawyer who would fulfill Reutershan's dying wish. It was an exercise in frustration. "I went from lawyer to lawyer and from law office to law office," McCarthy remembers with fresh bitterness. "Some of them treated me like a kid, some like a psychopath, and some laughed at me. One guy on Park Avenue kept me cooling my heels in his reception area for six hours, and when I caught him on his way out, he expressed amazement that I would wait so long."

Just when McCarthy had almost given up hope, Gorman's associate telephoned to say that Yannacone might be persuaded to take the case. McCarthy immediately drove his battered van out to Yannacone's home in Patchogue, Long Island, and demanded that the lawyer help. According to McCarthy, Yannacone again declined, explaining why the effort would be too costly to sustain and could not succeed, except perhaps on behalf of a class he could not then identify. But Yannacone could not get the case out of his mind. Several days later, after he had heard about some new cancer cases among Vietnam combat veterans, a class action began to seem more viable. He telephoned McCarthy and said, "You must realize what we would be up against." McCarthy, sensing Yannacone's change of heart, replied, "I don't care. We have to do it." They immediately met and began to map out a comprehensive campaign. The centerpiece was a national class action lawsuit, but their plan also incorporated other elements: a legislative strategy at the federal and state levels, outreach to veterans and their families, mobilization of the scientific community, and pervasive use of the mass media.

From the very first day, the veterans viewed Yannacone, in the military metaphors that McCarthy and others almost always use in discussing the case, as their "legal field commander." Yannacone asked McCarthy what the veterans hoped the lawsuit would accomplish. In Yannacone's version, McCarthy said the veterans wanted four things: "We want to turn the American people around so that the Vietnam combat soldier will no longer be abused and dishonored. We want to get the benefits that we are entitled to. We want to find out what is killing us. And we want the American taxpayer not to have to pay for injuries the chemical companies caused." McCarthy claims to have had somewhat more limited goals: "Yannacone has always seen the [Agent Orange case] as a public interest litigation," he recalls. "To us it was and still is a remedial measure" designed to compel the chemical companies to pay for medical testing and treatment and compensation for the veterans and their families.[4]

Yannacone assured McCarthy that the veterans' goals would guide his conduct of the case. Gradually, he devised a litigation strategy consisting of several related elements. He would first file a class action suit, then mobilize lawyers throughout the country to file similar suits on behalf of veterans in their jurisdictions. He would seek to have all of the local suits consolidated into one national class action in federal court in New York, which he would personally orchestrate. Finally, he would have to obtain adequate financing to support the litigation. Working with McCarthy and other veterans, Yannacone quickly initiated, and eventually accomplished, all but the last objective. That goal consistently eluded him.

The first step was the easiest. Yannacone rewrote the Reutershan complaint, using his technical flair to summarize the scientific studies on dioxin and phenoxy herbicides in a lawyer's tendentious fashion. On January 8, 1979, he filed the amended Reutershan complaint as a class action in the United States District Court for the Southern District of New York, in Manhattan.[5] From the instant the suit was filed, the media loved it. Yannacone, who proudly proclaims he has never written a press release or called a press conference, recalls the moment with obvious relish. "The phones rang off the hooks all day— 150 calls, with the last coming at 3 A.M. from soldiers in Australia." Yannacone had assured McCarthy that this would be no ordinary personal injury suit, and he was right.

The complaint, which named Dow, Monsanto, and three other chemical manufacturers as defendants (others were added later), defined the class as "all those so unfortunate as to have been and now to be situated at risk, not only during this generation but during generations to come." Less than a month later, after receiving a call from a Marine whose child exhibited the same deformities that dioxin was thought to cause, Yannacone amended the definition to include children born with birth defects. It eventually included 2.4 million Vietnam veterans, as well as their spouses and afflicted children, born and unborn.

The legal theories that Yannacone advanced to establish the liability of the chemical companies were fairly standard for a product liability case. These theories eventually included negligence, strict product liability and failure to warn, breach of warranty (nonperformance of a promise), intentional harm, and others.

The veterans' demand for relief, however, was highly unconventional. They sought damages "in the range of $4 billion to $40 billion." Alleging that the defendants' liquid assets would be insufficient to cover this liability and fully compensate the plaintiffs, Yannacone asked the court to establish a trust fund out of defendants' current earnings, a reserve from which the claims of present and future victims of Agent Orange could be satisfied. He also hoped that once Agent Orange's toxicity to the veterans had been established, the federal government would begin paying them and their families benefits for death, disability, and medical costs under the VA and Social Security programs. (The VA cash and medical benefits, he estimated, would be worth almost $50,000 per year for life.)

The trust fund idea embodied a number of Yannacone's theories about mass toxic tort litigation. The creation of such a fund could avert the specter of bankruptcy that Yannacone predicted (correctly, as it turned out) would soon confront the asbestos industry. And it would symbolize—and in the long run, enforce—what he regarded as a nondelegable fiduciary duty on the part of the chemical manufacturers to be the trustees of the public health and welfare in the use of their products. "The business press was much taken with the idea of 'corporate stewardship' during this period," Yannacone recalls, "and this was a way to realize that ideal." (He later described the original Agent Orange case as having been "patterned after the early days of environmental litigation. It followed for the first two or three years almost step by step the DDT litigation of the 1960s.")

The idea of a class action in a mass toxic tort case of national scope was unprecedented. As a matter of procedural law, its validity was seriously in doubt; indeed, the draftsmen of Rule 23 of the Federal Rules of Civil Procedure, which authorizes the class action device, explicitly advised against its use in such situations.[6] Although the class action entailed some grave risks to defendants, who faced the possibility of massive liability to the class, it also would create some obstacles for plaintiffs and their lawyers, who would have to prepare and try a much more costly, cumbersome kind of case than in an individual dispute. Indeed, the mere costs of providing individual notice to all class members, if required, could bankrupt the lawyers. Moreover, they would also cede to the court some control of the litigation, including their fee arrangements. These risks, however, were far down the road and probably seemed hypothetical to Yannacone and McCarthy in January 1979. But they were very real, and they haunted the case in later years.

The second step relied very heavily upon McCarthy's energies and organizing skills. He, Yannacone, and some of the other Long Island lawyers whom Yannacone started to recruit to help finance the case began to barnstorm throughout the country. Arriving in a new city, AOVI would activate the extensive Vietnam veterans' grapevine and convene public meetings at which McCarthy, a quiet but intense and eloquent man, would educate the veterans about Agent Orange and the lawsuit. McCarthy would then refer the veterans to "Yannacone and Associates" (as the Agent Orange litigation finance team styled itself), which encouraged them to sign notices of intention to join the class. In addition, Yannacone would meet with local lawyers and convince them to sign associate counsel agreements, thereby bringing themselves and their clients into the case. Armed with class action complaint forms that required only filling in the blanks, Yannacone and the local lawyers would then proceed to the nearest federal courthouse and file a class action complaint. Somehow the press always managed to be there to record Yannacone announcing the latest chapter in what he billed as the largest class action in history. His speeches to the local veterans were always inspirational. "The veterans loved him," McCarthy later said of Yannacone. "He's got the balls of a racehorse. He's a champion. He would stand up there and tell them the truth. He told them, 'We can't win, but I'll at least get you your day in court.' " Yannacone's hold over the veterans, his ability to evoke their fierce loyalty, would become a crucial factor in the evolution of the Agent Orange case.[7]

One such veteran was Michael Ryan. Now a police sergeant on Long Island, Ryan had become mysteriously ill in Vietnam while helping to build an advance camp for a cavalry regiment. In 1971, four years after his return to civilian life, Ryan's wife, Maureen, gave birth to a daughter, Kerry, with multiple birth defects. Maureen's mother-in-law, an experienced obstetrics nurse, attended Kerry's birth and was aghast at the child's condition. "If anyone tells you that it was your fault," she told Maureen, "tell that S.O.B. to see me. I've delivered thousands and thousands of babies and this is one of the worst cases I have ever seen. There had to have been a massive insult to the embryo." For the next seven years, the Ryans journeyed from specialist to specialist, hospital center to hospital center, seeking an explanation, hope, and treatment for Kerry.

On one of those visits, while sitting in the waiting room at Johns Hopkins, Maureen happened to glance at a magazine that carried an article describing unusual physical symptoms associated with herbicide use. Maureen did not know what herbicide meant, but the symptoms reminded her of those Michael had suffered in Vietnam. She began to piece together a theory and a course of action, slim shards of coincidence and circumstance—information about Michael and exposure to Agent Orange ten years earlier, a newspaper account of Reutershan's death and, early in 1979, news of a class action suit against the chemical companies brought by a lawyer named Yannacone who happened to live nearby.

The Ryans decided to call Yannacone and tell him their story. The lawyer arranged to meet immediately with Michael at the police station where Ryan was working the night shift. At eight o'clock the next morning, having spent hours going over Yannacone's evidence and strategy for victory, the two men left the station house. In the Ryan family, Yannacone had the articulate, photogenic, all-American parents and the lovable but tragically damaged child that he needed as the lead named plaintiffs in the case. In Yannacone, the Ryans had a champion, a lawyer whose unflagging fidelity to their cause continues to inspire their devotion today, more than seven years later.

Later, tensions developed between the Ryans and McCarthy, Yannacone's "clients." (McCarthy's group, AOVI, included many veterans who believed that they were Agent Orange victims.) Their Vietnam experiences had obviously molded Ryan and McCarthy in radically different ways, much as it had divided the nation. "Frank," Ryan says, "was the kind of veteran who refers to Vietnam as 'Nam, who cannot stop living the war. He wanted desperately to build a veterans' organization around that nightmare. He was always looking back to Vietnam, saying 'We got fucked over in 'Nam and now it's happening again here.' " Ryan, in contrast, thinks of himself as a "loner in a three-piece suit," as a crusader not so much on behalf of veterans as against what he sees as the growing chemical contamination of the world. "It is too late for the veterans and their children," he says. "It is their—our—grandchildren I want to save. If you write about me, don't put me in the veterans' camp. Put me out there by myself."[8] The conflict between these two strong figures and their separate visions of justice would not flare up for some time; meanwhile there was a lawsuit to be shaped.

Yannacone's third step was to have all of the Agent Orange actions consolidated into one gigantic case in New York. This procedural move was perhaps the easiest and least controversial of all. Dow, joined by the other defendants, actually took the lead in requesting it. Leonard Rivkin, a pugnacious, fast-talking lawyer who built a solo practice in plaintiffs' personal injury claims into the largest suburban law firm in the country, had handled Dow product liability litigation for almost a decade and was representing the company in the Reutershan case.[9] Rivkin had already had the case removed from state to federal court and then transferred to the Eastern District of New York, which covered all of Long Island, where Rivkin lived and worked. "At that point," Rivkin says, "this looked like a run-of-the-mill product liability case."[10]

When Yannacone took over the Reutershan case, the lawyers agreed for their own convenience to move it even farther east, from the district's Brooklyn headquarters to its "Long Island annex" in Uniondale. By then, several new Agent Orange cases had been filed against Dow in other parts of the country. Rivkin was also concerned that an adverse finding in even one isolated Agent Orange case might be used against Dow in the others through the legal doctrine known as "offensive collateral estoppel."[11] He therefore decided to ask Yannacone if he would join in seeking to consolidate and transfer all Agent Orange cases to the Uniondale division of the Eastern District. (Reflecting on this decision six years later, Rivkin noted that when Johns-Manville filed for bankruptcy in 1982, it was spending $2 million a month to litigate the asbestos cases, involving a roughly comparable number of named plaintiffs as in Agent Orange, in different courts all over the country.) Yannacone, who needed to minimize litigation costs and wanted to assure personal control of the cases, readily agreed.

The two lawyers therefore petitioned the Judicial Multidistrict Litigation Panel, a group of federal judges who decide whether to consolidate a series of closely related cases (and if so, in what judicial district) originally brought in disparate jurisdictions for discovery purposes and perhaps for trial as well. There had been some previous multidistrict litigation (MDL) in product liability cases, but nothing of this magnitude. In May 1979 the panel granted the petition; the case, now consolidated into an MDL proceeding and designated as *In re Agent Orange Product Liability Litigation*, was removed to Uniondale, where it was assigned to Judge George C. Pratt. Victor Yannacone was designated as lead counsel for plaintiffs.

These preliminary developments exemplify the proposition, so familiar to lawyers, that procedure and substance are often intimately intertwined. The location of the case in the Eastern District of New York, its assignment in the first instance to Judge Pratt, and Yannacone's designation as lead counsel seemed like essentially mechanical decisions, exciting no controversy and little attention or comment at the time. Nevertheless, as we shall see, each of these factors profoundly influenced the development, outcome, and significance of the litigation.

McCarthy, like Reutershan before him, had never viewed the lawsuit as anything more than one part of the veterans' overall political and educational strategy—important, to be sure, but only one of the several theaters in which the Agent Orange conflict must be waged. He now believes, however, that the lawyers always saw the matter differently. "To them," McCarthy says, "the lawsuit was all there was." Ryan disagrees, at least as far as Yannacone was concerned. "Victor and the veterans," Ryan insists, "were always on the same wavelength."[12]

But the case would change and grow, transcending Yannacone's early vision of it. The lawyers' preoccupation with the litigation came to reflect more than idealism and professional tunnel vision, more than the natural human tendency to magnify the importance of whatever one spends one's time doing. To the veterans' lawyers, the Agent Orange case would also represent an enormous investment of time, money, and reputation, perhaps the largest investment of their professional lives—and one of the riskiest. The nature and magnitude of this investment cast a shadow over all aspects of their handling of the case—their decision to initiate it, the litigation strategies they adopted, the financing and management of the case, their approach to settlement, and their posture toward the court.[13]

Although Victor Yannacone, like everybody else, underestimated what it would eventually cost to mount a credible, effective legal challenge to the chemical industry and the federal government, he recognized that the effort would be very expensive. For all his unusual talents, Yannacone was only a workmen's compensation lawyer operating a local practice; he was not equipped to sustain this kind of case. The costs of legal research, expert witnesses, stenographic transcripts, depositions, travel, computer services, photocopying, secretarial help, postage, and administrative overhead, not to mention the costs associated with conducting a lengthy trial, would quickly consume his personal resources and those of AOVI. (One idea, of trying to finance the litigation through one-dollar donations from individual veterans, was rejected.)[14]

Yannacone's entire litigation strategy, indeed his own ability to maintain control over the case, was soon threatened by the efforts of two enterprising Houston attorneys, Benton Musslewhite and Newton Schwartz. They were filing more than a hundred individual Agent Orange lawsuits on behalf of individual veterans in Texas, and they also represented Citizen Soldier, a veterans' group in New York City. The Texans, Yannacone quickly learned, were not at all interested in signing associate counsel agreements with Yannacone. Holding retainers from a large number of individual clients, they felt no inclination to surrender control over their cases to Yannacone.[15]

In several respects, then, Yannacone needed help with the burgeoning Agent Orange litigation, and he needed it fast. He began by enlisting the assistance of a group of lawyers—at McCarthy's insistence, they were mostly veterans of World War II and Korea—whom Hy Herman, a revered trial lawyer in the area, had recruited for him from small Long Island personal injury law firms. Meeting with them in the spring of 1979, super-salesman Yannacone made a strong pitch to their imaginations, patriotism, idealism, and profit motives. He emphasized that he would manage the case with the aid of state-of-the-art computer technology and could bring it to trial for $1 million. Although some in his audience thought Yannacone's plan grandiose and naive, others were tantalized and agreed to put up their money.[16]

On September 20, 1979, the consortium of Yannacone & Associates began business. It consisted of twelve partners—Yannacone, Hy Herman, Al Fiorella, Eugene O'Brien, Billy Levine, David Dean, Ed Hayes, Ed Gorman, Milton Mokotoff, Jim Kelly, Irving Like, and Donald Russo. Under the consortium agreement, Yannacone, as unsalaried executive director, would receive an equal share in any fee that the court might eventually award to the consortium out of a settlement or plaintiffs' recovery; he would work on the case full time but need not contribute any money to its support. The individual clients that McCarthy had helped him to secure (according to Yannacone, the other consortium members had no clients of their own) by now numbered more than 1,000 and eventually totaled more than 3,000; they became the clients of Yannacone & Associates, augmented by the clients covered by the associate counsel agreements entered into between the firm and other lawyers throughout the country. According to Yannacone, the consortium eventually represented 8,300 clients, and the number of associated counsel agreements eventually rose to almost 1,300.

Yannacone later testified that the consortium was established solely to establish defendants' liability, not to litigate the questions of causation and damage to individual veterans.[17] That would be the work of the local counsel. Any counsel fees awarded by the court would be divided between the consortium and the local counsel in a ratio that would depend upon the local counsel's experience.

Each of the law firms in the consortium assigned an individual lawyer to the case on a limited basis, so as not to interfere unduly with their existing practices. Most were "trauma" litigators; none except Like and Yannacone had had much experience with complex, class action litigation or with occupational disease or epidemiology problems. Five of these men (Gorman, O'Brien, Fiorella, Russo, and Kelly) had worked as defense lawyers, typically for insurance companies; they would give Yannacone "a window into the minds of defense counsel." Like was chairman of the law committee; he and Hayes were assigned responsibility for legal research. Keith Kavenagh, a historian by training and a partner in Yannacone's own firm, had overall responsibility for the final preparation of documents. A trial committee led by Dean coordinated discovery and would try the case in court. Fiorella was chairman of the group.

Instead of adopting a formal budget for the conduct of the litigation, the member firms agreed to advance an initial $2,000 each; any additional amounts would be forthcoming only to reimburse expenses that the firms deemed necessary. The initial allotment was quickly spent, no budgets were ever approved, and a series of increasingly bitter quarrels ensued over the appropriateness of reimbursing additional expenses that Yannacone either planned or had already incurred.[18]

From the outset, Yannacone emphasized his intention to buttress the veterans' causation argument, which would clearly be the weakest link in their case, by conducting his own epidemiological study.[19] With the assistance of his wife, Carol, he planned to take computer-coded case histories on the individual veterans—including their prewar medical condition, their exposure to Agent Orange in Vietnam, their postwar symptoms—and those of their families, and store these on computer tapes. Starting with this information base, he would then refine the data in an effort to develop patterns of exposure, symptomatology, etiology, and legal responsibility that could stand up in court. Although he had been warned that a creditable study would cost tens of millions of dollars, Yannacone insisted that a three-year study could be completed for less than a million.

His skeptical partners, led by Like and Fiorella, refused to put up the money; they insisted that the consortium should not expend its resources on the causation issue, which would probably not be litigated for some time.[20] Yannacone remains convinced that the consortium rejected the study for a more sinister reason than cost. "It might impede settlement of Agent Orange litigation," he testified in February 1985, "since it might establish clearly that there were substantial numbers of Vietnam combat veterans who had significant disability and damages associated with their service in Vietnam . . . the one thing no one wanted was a large number of sick plaintiffs, since the case would not be amenable to a settlement before trial."[21] The audacious Yannacone, however, decided to proceed with the study anyway. He claims that his wife began to develop the medical histories, eventually compiling over 3,000 of them, a claim that his partners ridicule. (When they later reviewed Yannacone's files, Like recalls, "We found very few medical profiles of any value to the litigation, let alone an epidemiological study.")

Yannacone's demand for this study, which was never completed, bracketed the entire litigation. His bitterness about its demise and about the consortium's refusal to reimburse him and his wife for the costs of developing the study, never abated. A central part of his evidentiary strategy from the very beginning, the study also became the subject of Yannacone's dramatic swan song at the conclusion of the case, when he demanded that the court use part of the settlement fund to finance its completion.[22]

The consortium members were also embroiled in constant disputes over who would review documents obtained through discovery, about the need for computerizing the document base, and about who would perform which tasks. These and other squabbles were grim auguries of difficulties yet to come, and their cumulative corrosive effects on the plaintiffs' case later became important. For the time being, Judge Pratt knew nothing of them. Indeed, Pratt's continuing ignorance concerning the internecine strife within the plaintiffs' camp was an important lever in Yannacone's struggle with his legal associates. On many occasions, when pressed by them over finances, media relations, or litigation strategy, Yannacone would threaten to go to Judge Pratt and reveal the lawyers' disarray.[23] He thus played skillfully on their fears that Pratt might conclude that Yannacone & Associates was no longer capable of adequately representing the class, as required by Rule 23, and might decide to designate others, such as Musslewhite and Schwartz, as plaintiffs lead counsel. Not only would the Long Island consortium have to relinquish control of the case, the fees that the court might eventually award to them would also be significantly reduced. If that happened, Yannacone might suffer the same fate, but that possibility was no guarantee that he would not go to Pratt. "Victor," one of his associates emphasized, "was totally unpredictable, an unguided missile. To destroy the enemy he would willingly risk blowing his own side up."

By most accounts, Pratt approached the Agent Orange dispute as a more or less conventional product liability case, albeit one with some obvious peculiarities. This attitude was not altogether surprising to those who were familiar with Pratt's background and judicial philosophy.[24] After graduating from Yale Law School near the top of his class in 1953 and clerking on the high court of New York state, he had settled down to a law firm practice on Long Island. In 1976, President Ford appointed him to the federal bench.[25] Nothing in his practice, court experience, bar association work, or Republican Party activities had prepared him for a case like this.

At first, Judge Pratt tried to move the case forward quickly. On August 14, 1979, only four months after receiving it from the multidistrict litigation (MDL) panel, he addressed some crucial issues in the Agent Orange case.[26] The defendants had moved to dismiss the complaint on several legal grounds. Some of their arguments, if upheld by the court, would have ended the lawsuit then and there. The most important of these related to the applicability of federal law, an issue that later proved crucial in the litigation and that will almost surely shape many mass toxic tort cases in the future. For a variety of legal, strategic, and other reasons, one party or another in a case may want their claims heard by a federal court applying federal law rather than by a state court applying state law. A federal forum may be especially attractive to plaintiffs in a class action in which the plaintiffs reside in many different states, complex questions of federal law may arise, and more permissive class action procedures may be desirable. Some or all of these elements commonly occur in mass toxic tort situations, especially those, like Agent Orange, in which the federal government's role may be significant.

Even when a federal court hears the case, however, two crucial questions remain. First, shall the court apply federal law or state law to each procedural or substantive issue? Second, if state law applies and (as was true in the Agent Orange case) a number of different jurisdictions can plausibly claim a connection with the dispute (for example, the forum state, New York; the states in which the defendants had manufactured the herbicide; perhaps even Vietnam itself), *which* jurisdiction's law shall apply to which issues? This last is known as the choice-of-law question. These are immensely difficult and tangled questions, particularly in a case like Agent Orange; indeed, the three courts that eventually considered them during the course of the litigation—Judge Pratt, the Court of Appeals, and Judge Weinstein— took quite different approaches to them. (The notorious uncertainty and plasticity of choice-of-law principles is suggested by Judge Weinstein's quip: "Whenever I have a case that is difficult to settle, I say to the lawyers, 'Have you considered the choice-of-law problems in this case? Go out into the hallway and discuss them.' "[27]

The consortium had argued that plaintiffs' claims were based on, among other things, federal common law—that is, federal principles derived not from the Constitution or federal statutes, but from the decisional law of federal judges. Defendants had maintained that the case must be governed by the product liability laws and statutes of limitations (which prescribe the period within which a suit must be brought) of each state rather than by a uniform federal common law. It was not so much that state law favored them and federal common law was against them; defendants' preference for state law was more complicated, more of a gamble, than that. In fact, until they knew *which* state law would apply, they could not know for certain whether state law would on balance help or hurt their cause. While some state statutes of limitations would bar the veterans' claims, for example, others would not; similarly, the substantive product liability law of the states was a mixed bag, with California law particularly unsympathetic to the manufacturers' interests. Defendants' real reason was that no federal common law of limitations or of product liability existed, and they feared what a judge—even one as sensible as Judge Pratt—might decide to write on this *tabula rasa*.

A great deal turned on this seemingly technical dispute. If federal common law did not apply, the court's jurisdiction, its power to hear the case, would be based entirely on the so-called diversity jurisdiction (jurisdiction based on the fact that plaintiffs and defendants reside in different states). And if the Agent Orange case were treated as a diversity case, then state law, not federal, would control the content of the substantive law and the question of *which* state's law should apply. That single factor—the applicable law—could easily determine the outcome of the case. Indeed, many veterans' claims might already be barred by certain states' statutes of limitations. Because of the posture in which the federal common law question came before him, however, Pratt could avoid squarely ruling on it for now, deferring a decision until plaintiffs had an opportunity to develop a more complete factual record.

But Pratt's decision did reach the merits on one important question. Yannacone, as we have seen, regarded the mass media as an indispensable ally in his crusade to activate the public conscience against Agent Orange; he had actively used every court filing, every development in the case as an occasion to denounce the chemical companies and their product. Defendants, alarmed by the effect these attacks might have on the public and on prospective jurors, sought a gag order from Judge Pratt to restrict communications between Yannacone and the media. They also complained that Yannacone was using the media to solicit clients in violation of the legal profession's ethical canons.

Although gag orders had occasionally been granted in other cases, the consortium pointed out that such an order raised serious constitutional problems in that it would inhibit litigants' ability, protected by the First Amendment, to seek to influence government officials and public opinion, as well as to inform veterans of their legal rights. Yannacone was personally indignant. "I have been involved in public interest litigation for years," he told Judge Pratt. "I have never once in twenty years called a newspaper reporter, held a press conference, or issued a press release," an assertion some of his consortium colleagues regarded as disingenuous.[28] Alluding to the veterans' efforts to affect VA and environmental policy and to obtain legislative relief, Pratt refused to enter the order. "The unique nature and public importance of this litigation" demanded that public debate on the issues raised by the Agent Orange litigation proceed unimpeded.[29]

Within only three months, the issue of whether federal or state law would apply to the case was back before Judge Pratt for decision. In October, Yannacone, who regards frequently amended pleadings as a valuable technique of "public-interest" litigation, had filed yet another version of the complaint—his third. (Judge Pratt later criticized his "disregard for the filing requirements.") The defendants had moved to dismiss it, contending once again that the court lacked jurisdiction because plaintiffs' claims did not involve any "federal question."[30]

This time Pratt faced the issue squarely. On November 20, he ruled that federal common law applied to the litigation. He began by noting that federal common law was not ordinarily applied in a case like Agent Orange in which private parties were suing other private parties; it was reserved for only those private cases in which substantial federal interests were involved that would be adversely affected if state law were applied and in which important state interests would not be impaired if federal common law displaced state law. Here, Pratt reasoned, those tests were clearly satisfied. The Agent Orange case concerned the rights not only of large numbers of American soldiers and their families but of war contractors as well. Moreover, applying state law would create great uncertainty and perhaps injustice; "essentially similar claims, involving veterans and war contractors identically situated in all relevant respects, would be treated differently under different state laws." Thus federal common law was clearly appropriate here even if no prior mass tort case had ever before applied to it: "The reason may be that no tort claim has heretofore implicated such significant federal interests involving so many persons in any area so little regulated by state law."[31]

Plaintiffs had won the first skirmish, one they could not afford to lose. Recognizing what was at stake, the chemical companies immediately appealed. The Agent Orange case—perhaps the last battle of the Vietnam War—was now truly under way.

4

Judge Pratt Rules

AS a legal battle, the Agent Orange case was surely an oddity; a central combatant was missing from the field. The United States government, which had tested herbicides since before World War II, had sent the soldiers to Vietnam, had contracted for the production of Agent Orange, had directed its application in Vietnam, and had taken responsibility for the physical well-being of its troops, *was not a party to the lawsuit*. Litigating the Agent Orange case without the federal government, Judge Weinstein said later, was like playing *Hamlet* without the Prince of Denmark.[1] What, then, could possibly account for the veterans' failure to sue the government?

The most obvious answer—but, as it turns out, not the decisive one—was "sovereign immunity," a hoary legal doctrine that in general the government cannot be sued without its consent. This immunity has been severely criticized for many years and on many grounds. Some legal scholars have argued that the doctrine, which was established in English law as early as the thirteenth century, simply reflects its medieval origins; the divinely invested king, as the source of all law, could not be limited by it. Others have contended that the traditional idea "the king can do no wrong" has been seriously misunderstood; far from suggesting the king's immunity from justice, they maintain, the phrase meant that the king would not suffer injustice to be done to a subject without remedying it. Both critiques have emphasized that in a democratic society, one in which the rule of law binds government as well as citizens, sovereign immunity should play a very different and much reduced role.[2]

These scholarly criticisms, however, have had only a modest effect on the immunity doctrine, at least at the federal level. Congress, in enacting the Federal Tort Claims Act of 1946, did establish a general waiver of the United States' sovereign immunity, but then riddled the waiver with numerous exceptions.[3] Some of these exceptions, such as the one for governmental torts committed while engaged in "discretionary functions," are quite broad. More pertinent to the Agent Orange litigation, the courts have interpreted the Act to preserve sovereign immunity with respect to so-called "intramilitary torts." In a 1950 decision, *Feres* v. *United States,* the Supreme Court held that the federal government continued to be immune from liability for torts committed against soldiers "where the injuries arise out of or are in the course of activity incident to service."[4] The Court based this rule, which came to be known as the *Feres* doctrine, on three factors: the distinctively federal character of the relationship between the government and its armed forces, which would be threatened if state tort law (upon which all tort suits authorized by the Tort Claims Act are based) governed that relationship; the statutory "no fault" scheme for compensating governmentally inflicted harms to soldiers that Congress had established under the Veterans Benefits Act; and the corrosive effects that intramilitary tort claims would have on military discipline.

The *Feres* doctrine would almost certainly bar any damage claims against the United States by veterans exposed to Agent Orange during the Vietnam War; their Agent Orange–caused injuries, if any, were clearly service-related. This might have been a reason for the veterans not to sue the government. But the plaintiff class also included the veterans' wives and children, and it was far less certain that *Feres* barred *their* claims. They claimed independent injuries not simply derivative from those of the veterans; their miscarriages, the wives asserted, had been caused by Agent Orange–related damage to their husbands' sperm; the children's claim was that their birth defects were caused by genetic damage to the fathers.

The scope of the *Feres* immunity principle subsequently played a central role in the Agent Orange case. But the consortium's decision not to sue the government actually rested on two rather different considerations having little to do with legal doctrine. First, suing the government would greatly protract the litigation. "The government's cooperation was essential to building our case, especially on our low budget," Irving Like observed. "The feds helped us with discovery and witnesses, which they would not have done if we had made them active antagonists."

A second consideration, which some of the veterans' own lawyers still find difficult to accept, was emotional. Frank McCarthy and the

AOVI, the original instigators of the case, felt quite strongly that they did not *want* to sue the government, whether or not *Feres* applied. Even today, long after the government's knowledge about dioxin was revealed through discovery, McCarthy firmly maintains that position. "For the veterans, it has always been a moral point. We think that it is wrong to charge the government—our government—with what amounts to criminal responsibility without far stronger evidence of culpability than we have seen. The chemical companies are the responsible parties. The government did no more than use stuff that my mother used to kill weeds in her garden."

Yannacone shares McCarthy's view. "Look, when I was developing the DDT case back in the 1960s, I and my colleagues knew all there was to know about herbicides. Until 1969, when we and the government learned about dioxin, every scientist I spoke to regarded 2,4,5-T as a model herbicide—unlike DDT, it was specific, nontoxic to animals, and biodegradable. Under the circumstances, I felt morally obligated not to sue the government, and Frank and the other veterans whom I spoke to felt even more strongly about it. Even after all they had been through, these guys felt, and still feel, an extraordinarily high level of patriotism. You know, 'My country right or wrong.' " Benton Musslewhite, who along with Yannacone and Robert A. Taylor, Jr., a young associate in the Washington, D.C. law firm of Ashcraft & Gerel, was one of the few plaintiffs' lawyers in the case with a significant number of veteran clients, also emphasized the veterans' patriotic ardor.[5]

But the chemical companies had no such concerns. Seeing an opportunity to reap strategic advantage by bringing the government into the case, they decided to seize it.[6] The manufacturers accomplished this in two different ways. First, they sought to join the United States as a "third-party defendant" in the case. Their theory was that the government, for a variety of reasons, including its negligent use of and failure to warn about Agent Orange, was obligated to indemnify the manufacturers for any liability to the plaintiffs that the court might ultimately impose on them. These indemnity claims, however, faced a major obstacle—indeed, the same one the veterans would have faced had they sued the government themselves. Although *Feres*, strictly speaking, applied only to claims asserted by soldiers and thus did not bar the manufacturers' third-party claims, an extension of *Feres*, known as the *Stencel* doctrine, precluded third-party claims for indemnity against the United States where those claims derived from claims that would themselves be barred by *Feres*.[7] By combining *Feres* and *Stencel*, the government argued that its immunity should stand not only against service-related claims by soldiers asserted directly against the government, but also against those claims asserted indirectly under an indemnity theory. As Judge Pratt observed to the lawyer for Dow, the chemical companies' argument placed them "in a schizoid position because you are saying, well, we don't agree with the government unless we get the same protection."[8]

The manufacturers had a second, fallback strategy. Even if they could not bring the government into the case directly, they could nevertheless try to spotlight its responsibility for Agent Orange and escape their own. This theory, known as the "government contract" or "shared immunity" defense, was both straightforward and powerful.[9] The idea was that the circumstances surrounding the manufacture and use of the herbicide were so clearly controlled and dictated by the government through its approximately seventy procurement contracts that the manufacturers should be protected from liability. From the manufacturers' point of view, the genius of this theory, which had previously been used in only a few cases, was that instead of being a claim against the government (barred, as we have seen, by *Feres/Stencel*), it was a defense against the claims of the *plaintiffs*. If successful, this tactic would not merely deflect attention from the veterans' injuries and the manufacturers' conduct and put the onus on the government, it would defeat the veterans' claims altogether. In any event, it would surely bog the case down in years of discovery.

In an era in which government has increasingly acted through private contractors, the government contract defense seemed justified by the same considerations that favored governmental immunity. Just as *Stencel* was designed to prevent end runs around the government's immunity by third parties seeking indemnity for *Feres*-barred claims, so a government contract defense would prevent the government, which could not be held liable directly, from having to absorb liability indirectly. Without such a defense, contractors would insist that the government indemnify them contractually for liability costs arising out of their work for the government. And that would defeat the whole purpose of the defense—or so the argument ran.

But whether the government contract defense should be upheld in a particular case depends ultimately upon the precise way in which the defense is defined by the court and the factual evidence adduced to support its applicability in the specific instance. In the Agent Orange case the manufacturers were claiming that the government had long experimented with herbicides, had invented Agent Orange, knew that dioxin was a by-product of 2,4,5-T, and knew about dioxin's toxicity as early as 1962. They were claiming that the government had compelled the manufacturers, using various forms of legal and extralegal coercion, to produce Agent Orange; had refused to allow them to manufacture such herbicides for the civilian market; had unilaterally prescribed the terms and specifications of the contracts under which the defendants manufactured the herbicide; had monitored defendants' compliance with those contract terms and specifications; had assured the availability of the raw materials needed to produce it on a high-priority basis; and had unilaterally determined and controlled the nature and extent of Agent Orange's use in Vietnam. If these allegations could be proved, the defense might well be established.

The government contract defense posed another tactical problem for the plaintiffs' lawyers, especially those, like Musslewhite and Taylor, who hoped eventually to sue the federal government directly.[10] In order to defeat the government contract defense and thereby hold the manufacturers liable, the lawyers would probably have to prove that the manufacturers had written the product specifications and had failed to warn the government about dioxin's dangers and its presence in the herbicide. But to hold the government directly liable (assuming they could overcome the *Feres* obstacle and their clients' objections), the lawyers would probably have to show that the government had known enough and had exercised sufficient control that it should be deemed negligent. These two positions were not necessarily logically inconsistent; plaintiffs might be able to show that the government's knowledge was sufficient to vitiate the government contract defense yet was great enough to establish negligence. But they were certain to complicate plaintiffs' evidentiary presentations and confuse the jury. This difficulty was an important tactical reason for the veterans not to sue the government.

The plaintiffs' predicament, of course, spelled opportunity for the manufacturers. Invoking the government contract defense, they moved in March 1980 for summary judgment—a technique for quickly resolving a case in which only issues of law, which the court can decide itself on the basis of agreed-upon facts, are in dispute, thus obviating the need for a trial. At the same time, the government moved to dismiss the companies' claims on the basis of sovereign immunity, as elaborated in the *Feres/Stencel* doctrine.

The plaintiffs' lawyers worried about the prospects for survival of their lawsuit. David Dean, who would eventually be designated as plaintiffs' chief trial attorney, recalls their concern about the government contract defense:

> We went to the law books and concluded that it was a good legal defense. I was also very troubled about how it might affect the jury. As it turns out, I had reason to be scared. Years later, as the trial approached, we ran a jury simulation to get its reaction to my opening and to our case. When we listened to the mock jury deliberate, it became clear to us that although the jurors were prepared to believe that the chemical companies were capable of almost any wrongdoing, they also believed that the government was also capable of it. We realized that the defendants could be let off the hook completely."[11]

The consortium had two other causes for serious concern. One was the critical question of whether federal common law or state product liability law should apply to the various issues in the case, and, if state law applied, *which* state's law. Although they had already persuaded Judge Pratt to apply federal common law, the issue was far from settled. The chemical companies had requested permission to take an interlocutory appeal of Pratt's decision to the Second Circuit Court of Appeals; this would allow them to appeal *immediately* rather than having to wait until after the entire case was tried and decided, as is ordinarily required. Yannacone, who claims that his colleagues saw this as an opportunity to save money by precipitating an early settlement or dismissal, had acquiesced in the companies' request. (Like, however, maintains that Yannacone, in agreeing to the appeal, overrode the consortium's contrary instructions.) If the appeals court, which agreed to hear the appeal, reversed on this issue and ordered that the litigation proceed under state law, the veterans' case could be mortally wounded.[12]

The consortium's other concern involved two equally important procedural questions: whether they could get the court to certify the case as a class action and, if so, what the contours of the class (and perhaps subclasses, of which plaintiffs had requested fifteen) would be. If the case could not be sustained as a class action, the veterans and their families would have to litigate their claims individually; in that event, of course, few would be able to proceed at all. Even if the court agreed to certify a class, the costs of providing adequate notice to the individual class members, which the Supreme Court had held to be constitutionally required by the due process clause, might be

prohibitive (depending upon the type and size of the class and the notice required).[13] Finally, the issue of which jurisdiction's law applied
was intimately linked to class certification. If the Second Circuit ruled
that the tort law of many different states must be applied, then the case
might not qualify as a class action because the many variations among
the laws of different states would violate what might be a key prereq-
uisite for class certification: that common factual and legal questions
underlie the veterans' claims. (Alternatively, numerous subclasses
might be necessary.) In order to have a viable lawsuit at all, therefore,
the veterans probably would have to prevail on both issues: federal
common law and the class action.

Their prospects for success did not seem bright. Although Judge
Pratt had strongly endorsed their federal common law theory, it remained a novel one in a product liability case, an area governed by
state tort law, and the appellate court might well reject it. The class
certification issue was even more problematic. Intuitively, one would
think the Agent Orange case especially appropriate for class action
treatment. Certainly, two legal requirements for class certification—
that the members of the class be numerous and that many of the
issues be common—were easily met. The veterans, after all, had
fought in the same war and had been exposed to the same product,
and many of the factual and legal claims (for example, the government contract defense and the issue of Agent Orange's defectiveness)
had to be resolved in the same way for all. A third requirement—that
the claims of the individual veterans representing the class be "typical"—could probably be satisfied, perhaps by breaking the class into
subclasses, each with representative parties and common claims.
Yannacone had suggested just this approach to the court.

But other preconditions for class certification might be more difficult. One, the requirement that the representative plaintiffs "fairly
and adequately protect the interests of the class," involved a judicial
evaluation of the qualifications of counsel for the veterans who would
be representing the class, and the absence of antagonism or conflicting interests among class members. Yet the relationships between
lawyers within Yannacone & Associates had already deteriorated
alarmingly; by late 1980, the internecine quarrels threatened to erupt
into open warfare. Was Judge Pratt aware of this problem? If so, what
would he do about it? The consortium could not be sure.

Even if plaintiffs could satisfy all of these preconditions to class
certification, they must also somehow fit the Agent Orange case into

one of four categories of class action prescribed by Rule 23(b) of the Federal Rules of Civil Procedure. One of these categories—for suits seeking injunctive or declaratory relief—seemed inapplicable to an action for damages, even one that sought a court-ordered trust fund; another, designed to keep defendants from having to meet incompatible legal standards, also seemed irrelevant. A third, intended to avoid premature depletion of a limited damages pool, did not seem to apply to financially well-heeled chemical companies like Dow, Monsanto, and Diamond Shamrock.

Although the consortium argued otherwise, the veterans' best hope probably lay with the so-called (b)(3) class action. This was for cases in which "the questions of law or fact common to the members of the class predominate over any questions affecting only individual members, and . . . a class action is superior to all other available methods for the fair and efficient adjudication of the controversy." The Agent Orange case did implicate some common issues. But many other issues—for example, the exposure levels of individual veterans and the herbicide's effects on individual veterans in light of their particular medical histories, life circumstances, and other unique conditions—would be plaintiff-specific. Most daunting for the veterans were the comments on (b)(3) class actions made by the advisory committee that drafted the provision: "A 'mass accident' resulting in injuries to numerous persons is ordinarily not appropriate for a class action because of the likelihood that significant questions, not only of damages but of liability and defenses to liability, would be present, affecting the individuals in different ways. In these circumstances an action conducted nominally as a class action would degenerate in practice into multiple lawsuits separately tried."[14]

Dow's lawyers would forcefully point out to Judge Pratt that at least ten district courts had explicitly refused to certify (b)(3) class actions in mass tort cases involving DES, asbestos, airline and bus crashes, and air pollution. Of the three mass tort cases in which courts had certified a class, two were single-accident cases; in the third, the court certified a class only for certain specified legal issues and later rescinded even that certification. Most important, no court had certified a class where the crucial issue of causation was fiercely contested, as it would be here. Finally, no appellate court had approved a class certification in a mass tort case.[15]

On November 24, 1980—just as Judge Pratt was preparing to rule on these issues, and only a few weeks after a presidential election in which the government's treatment of Vietnam veterans was a prominent issue—a panel of the Second Circuit, by a vote of two to one, delivered a devastating blow to the plaintiffs. In a very brief opinion by Judge Amalya Kearse, the majority reversed Judge Pratt's earlier decision to apply federal law to the case; it held that there was no "identifiable federal policy at stake in this litigation that warrants the creation of federal common law rules." This ruling meant that the Agent Orange case could be heard by the federal court only on the basis of its diversity jurisdiction. This in turn meant that state law—and indeed, a different state law for each state—would govern most of the crucial issues in the case, an extremely far-reaching result.[16]

This result was irrational on its face, as Chief Judge Wilfred Feinberg maintained in his strong dissent. "To the nonlegal mind," Feinberg wrote, "it would be an odd proposition indeed that this litigation, so patently of national scope and concern, should not be tried in federal court." He reviewed a recent Second Circuit decision emphasizing the important federal interest in assuring the uniform treatment of federal prisoners, a precedent that Judge Kearse had brushed aside in a most unpersuasive fashion. Feinberg noted how anomalous it was for the law to treat federal soldiers differently, depending solely upon the statutes of limitations and product liability rules of the state in which they happened to reside, rules that were still very much in flux. Drawing upon Judge Pratt's earlier reasoning, Feinberg pointed out that "if the laws of thirty or forty state jurisdictions are separately applied, veterans' recoveries for Agent Orange injuries will vary widely—despite the fact that these soldiers fought shoulder to shoulder, without regard to state citizenship, in a national endeavor abroad."[17]

Feinberg's careful analysis of the federal interest in uniform legal treatment of the veterans was clearly correct. One need not go as far as Professor Aaron Twerski, a lawyer for the plaintiffs, who argued that applying disparate state laws to the veterans' claims in this case would violate the equal protection clause, in order to see that Kearse's approach was indefensible. It would work great individual injustices, would create extraordinary burdens on the federal courts (which would now have to discover and apply unfamiliar and often unsettled state law to a multitude of complex legal questions), and would symbolically repudiate the special relationship between the government and its soldiers, one that the Supreme Court had described as distinctly federal in character."[18]

Judge Kearse's decision was a classic example of the perils of treating Agent Orange as a larger version of a conventional tort dispute. Her approach, perfectly defensible in the ordinary case in which one or a few soldiers sue concerning a discrete incident, made no sense at all in a mass action going to the heart of a broad federal policy. Nevertheless, her ruling stood. Plaintiffs appealed the decision to the Supreme Court, filing a brief with which some members of the consortium were very dissatisfied. But the Court, acceding to the urging of the solicitor general (the United States' advocate before the Supreme Court), declined, as it does in most appeals, to hear the case. Kearse's decision would stand. Judge Weinstein later lamented that it had "injected great legal complexity and doubt into the litigation, making further appeals after trial a near certainty." This observation, carefully couched in the respectful language of a district judge bound by a higher court's decision, was characteristically understated.[19]

Five weeks later, in late December 1980, Judge Pratt ruled on the principal outstanding motions by the chemical companies, the government, and the veterans. His decision was momentous, profoundly shaping the subsequent course of the litigation. First, relying on *Feres/Stencel,* he dismissed all pending claims against the government, both those by veterans and those by family members. The United States was out of the case. Second, he held that the government contract defense was legally viable but that the chemical companies must still prove that it applied factually to the Agent Orange dispute. Meanwhile, the parties must submit briefs containing their views of what the precise elements of the defense ought to be.

Judge Pratt then promulgated a "case management plan" to govern the next phase of what he recognized as an extraordinary case. A large number of Agent Orange cases had already been consolidated in his court, he noted, and many more cases would be brought. Because the plaintiffs came from most of the fifty states, New Zealand, and Australia, many different legal standards would have to be applied, since the Second Circuit had rejected federal common law. Each of the numerous defendants had potentially different involvements and legal responsibilities. The causation issues were especially complex, quite unlike those presented in single-incident tort cases. The case presented "numerous questions of law that lie at the frontier of modern tort jurisprudence." Much Agent Orange–related damage to the veterans might still be only latent. On numerous technical issues, the available data were probably inadequate to support scientifically sound conclusions. Important and conflicting public policy issues were at stake. Compounding these difficulties, he noted, was the striking disparity between the plaintiffs, "who have limited resources with which to press their claims and whose plight becomes more desperate and depressing as time goes on," and the defendants, "who have ample resources for counsel and expert witnesses to defend them, and who probably gain significantly . . . , from every delay that they can produce."[20]

Pratt's list is interesting for several reasons. It undermines the notion, widely shared by the Agent Orange lawyers, that Pratt viewed the case as a conventional tort dispute. It also identifies factors, including data limitations, that are crucial to understanding what subsequently transpired in the case. And it includes several realities, such as the suffering and financial straits of plaintiffs, that judges seldom acknowledge publicly but that may strongly influence how they respond to a case like Agent Orange.

Pratt's case management plan consisted of four main parts. First, he anounced his intention to certify the case as a (b)(3) class action, a decision he had deferred while awaiting the Second Circuit's ruling on the federal common law question. Although enormous management problems were inevitable in a class action of this magnitude and complexity, "the truly overwhelming problems that would attend any other management device" made class certification necessary. Pratt's decision to certify the class, it seemed, was made out of sheer practical necessity. To separately try the individual Agent Orange cases "would take far too long a time; probably neither the litigants nor this court would live long enough to see the last case tried."

Although Pratt's class action decision was defensible, his reasoning was poorly supported. For example, he failed to discuss the advisory committee's carefully considered stricture against the use of the class action device in mass tort litigation. He also failed to mention any of the precedents bearing on this question or to cite any authority whatsoever that might support his action. He did not analyze the relevance to the class action issue of the Second Circuit's rejection of his federal common law theory, nor did he explore the possibility that Yannacone & Associates was too divided and poorly financed to represent the class adequately. Finally, he failed to issue a formal certification order and did not specify how the millions of veterans and their families would be notified of the pendency of the class action. As we shall see, his decision to defer these matters to another day had

profound legal, financial, strategic, and ultimately political consequences.

In the second element of his plan, Pratt indicated that he would
immediately take up the difficult question of whether statutes of
limitations automatically barred some or all of the veterans' claims.
Statutes of limitations were not designed to apply to toxic torts involving low-visibility, continuous exposures, long latency periods,
and difficult-to-diagnose diseases. To make matters worse, the Second Circuit had now rejected federal common law, and the New York
legislature would soon liberalize its statute of limitations but leave
unclear which veterans it covered.[21] Judge Weinstein later described
the difficulties of trying to unravel the statute of limitations knot:

> The primary statutes of limitations issue is whether a single bar period
> should apply to all members of the class or whether each of the groups—
> servicepersons, wives and children—need to be treated separately and,
> in turn, subdivided among the various jurisdictions where they reside
> and where critical events occurred. More than one hundred and fifty
> subclasses, covering each of the states and foreign countries, might be
> involved. Each jurisdiction has separate statutory limitations periods,
> points in time from which the statute is measured (such as time of
> exposure to the toxic substance or time of manifestation of the disease)
> and tolling provisions and case-law glosses applicable to the
> servicepeople, spouses and minor children. Complex subsidiary prob-
> lems of "when" and "where" the serviceperson's injury took place,
> "when" and "where" manifestations "were" or "should have been"
> noted by the individual claimant, and what actions by defendants may
> have operated to toll the statute because of alleged "coverup" of infor-
> mation or other reasons would all need to be considered.[22]

The third element of Pratt's plan was to order a series of trials, if
necessary, with respect to issues common to the class. Because the
government contract defense was potentially dispositive of the entire
Agent Orange case—that is, if defendants could prove its applicability, plaintiffs would be out of court and the case would be over—the
judge wanted to move first to an early trial of the factual issues relevant to that defense. If plaintiffs overcame that defense, the court
would then proceed to try additional common, potentially dispositive
issues, such as negligence, defectiveness, and so-called general causation (that is, the issue of whether and under what circumstances
Agent Orange could have caused certain types of injuries). If plaintiffs lost on any of these issues, the case would be over. If they

prevailed, however, the jury would make findings on these issues in the form of special verdicts (in which the jury answers particular questions that the court has put to it). Those verdicts would then be used, either in individual trials before Judge Pratt or in trials held by the courts in which the cases were originally filed, to help resolve two issues—individual causation (whether a particular veteran was exposed to Agent Orange and with what results) and individual damages.[23]

The consortium had proposed this serial trials approach to the court. In their brief, the lawyers, with rhetorical flourish, likened it to the unfolding of a classic Greek tragedy:

> Plaintiffs' fate, unbeknownst to them, lay in the hand of the corporate defendant chemical companies, not the obvious enemy . . . The initial trial of the liability issues can be likened to the chorus in a Greek tragedy reciting the collective and common experiences of the principals; the second generic causation phase depicts the several catastrophes visited upon the battalions of the participants, while the final phase of the litigation unveils the life histories of the individual soldiers whose trials are its catharses.[24]

The defendants immediately saw the danger in the serial trials approach. Serial trials beginning with the government contract defense meshed perfectly with the consortium's litigation strategy. To establish that defense, the manufacturers would have to show that the government knew as much as they did about Agent Orange's dangers. This, the consortium believed, might make it awkward later on for the manufacturers to deny that there *were* dangers. The consortium hoped to win a quick victory on this important threshold issue, build up the pressure on defendants, minimize their own litigation costs, and demonstrate the strength of their case. If they could accomplish all this without precipitating a marathon, all-or-nothing, comprehensive struggle, they would either induce a swift and favorable settlement or, if their case were ultimately destined to fail, cut their losses and get out early.[25]

The chemical companies, for whom delay, attrition, and litigation costs were powerful weapons, vigorously opposed the serial trials approach as unworkable, premature, and based on the false premise that the issues in the case could be neatly separated. On the other hand, if this approach had to be used, they were delighted that the first trial would be on the government contract defense. That issue, unlike causation or product defect, involved proof of the government's knowledge, not of emotionally charged facts. That proof could be offered through documents rather than through testimony by cancer-ridden veterans about their babies with birth defects.[26]

The final element of the judge's plan modified his original order, which had barred virtually all discovery in the case until further notice. That further notice had never been given; hence, during the almost two years of the Agent Orange litigation, little progress had been made in developing what would surely be a massive factual record. The litigation had stalled. Indeed, according to Pratt, the parties could not "even agree on the form in which the large quantities of discovery documents should be prepared" or on "even the most basic aspects" of how the documents would be computerized and shared. And although the lawyers had pressed for more discovery, Pratt feared that if his decision were reversed on appeal, any proceedings based upon federal common law would have to be retried, causing "a colossal waste of time."[27]

But now that the federal common law issue was resolved, Pratt reasoned, discovery could properly proceed. He thus ordered "Phase I discovery" to commence in January 1981; it would be limited, however, to written interrogatories directed at the government contract defense. This discovery order was a small beginning, but a beginning nonetheless.

5

Discovery Begins

As 1981 began—the third year of the Agent Orange case—the veterans had some cause to celebrate. Judge Pratt's case management plan, with its emphasis on class action, serial trials, and expedited discovery, fulfilled the consortium's fondest hopes. By recognizing the government contract defense, it is true, Pratt had dealt the veterans a setback that could prove fatal to their lawsuit. But the chemical companies still had to prove that the defense applied to Agent Orange; even if they were able to prove this, the consortium would be better off knowing that at an early stage than having to undergo a costly and protracted litigation, only to lose in the end. Pratt's serial trials plan would minimize that dire possibility. But no one was thinking of defeat. "We had survived powerful defendants' best efforts to defeat us," Yannacone recalled, "and that was achievement enough."[1]

The veterans were advancing on another front as well. Led by the colorful, headline-grabbing Yannacone, they waged their war against Agent Orange outside the courtroom as well as within it. As Dean recalls:

> In many news articles Agent Orange was described as a "killer" or as a "poison," without even an "alleged." We always referred to the veterans as "innocent victims." From our pollster, we knew that 80 percent of the prospective jurors had heard of Agent Orange and believed it was harmful. While we took every opportunity to cultivate reporters and denounce the callous chemical companies, our opponents for some reason were very unsophisticated about this. They were not accessible to the press, and I think they saw it as a legal problem to be dealt with by lawyers rather than a PR problem. Only as trial approached did some of them begin to send out press packets explaining their testing results, the tiny dioxin levels, etc., but by then it was too late.

The defendants' reticence, Dean and some others believed, reflected the conservative, buttoned-up style of the Wall Street lawyers who mainly represented them. "The contrast to us," Dean laughs, "could hardly have been greater. Their paper work was superb; we sometimes filed our briefs without staples, cutting and pasting on our way to the courthouse. The Wall Street boys would file errata sheets correcting an incorrect page cite; we made so many errors we didn't bother. We were almost all trial lawyers; except for Rivkin, their most experienced trial lawyers, like Henry Miller [a former president of the New York Trial Lawyers Association who represented T.H. Agriculture and Nutrition], didn't really get involved until late in the game."[2]

But despite their tactical gains, there was little rejoicing in the veterans' camp; the lawyers were too busy wrangling over money, strategy, and status. Some consortium members, concerned about how Yannacone was running the case, retained a management consultant to review the financing and administration of the case. The report was highly critical. The consortium, the consultant found, was "an accident waiting to happen," and it was wasting what little money it had: "It was impossible to estimate costs," he concluded. "No one knew where the litigation was going. There was no money in the bank. They didn't even know who was going to keep the books. It was ludicrous. We asked them, 'Where is the money going to come from to fund this thing along the way?' Their answer was 'We don't know.' " The consultant was especially critical of Yannacone, whose grandiose and high-handed manner seemed to be "their biggest problem." Given the defendants' massive resources, he concluded, only a large infusion of new money would enable the plaintiffs to remain in the game.[3]

Money was not the only source of friction within Yannacone & Associates, but it affected all the others. Yannacone insisted on traveling around the country to recruit ever more veterans for the lawsuit; he hoped to enlarge the class as much as possible. His partners, however, viewed these ventures as little more than ego-tripping and resented having to pay the bills. Their dispute was in part over tactics and ideology. To Yannacone, the case was as much a vehicle for political organization, veteran consciousness-raising, and public education as it was a self-contained judicial proceeding; in contrast, many of the others saw the case as a professional and financial venture, a calculated investment in the prospect of a large settlement and award of counsel fees.[4]

But the conflict was also over personality and operating style. Dean, who had originally been brought into the consortium by Fiorella, and who ended up being Yannacone's sole defender within the group, recalls that Fiorella and Yannacone were constantly at each other's throats: "When Al wanted a document that Victor had, he would call me and say, 'Get me that paper from that prick bastard,' and when I asked Victor for it, he would rant and rave about Al. They reminded me of two Sicilian street fighters. I was sure," Dean added jokingly, "that assassination crossed each of their minds."[5] Frank McCarthy increasingly shared Yannacone's hostility toward the consortium, which McCarthy claims ruined him financially by reneging for years on assurances that he would be reimbursed for his travel expenses in connection with his efforts to mobilize veterans and lawyers throughout the country. Many of the consortium partners reciprocated Yannacone's animosity; to them, his grandiosity, condescension, and manipulativeness were becoming intolerable.[6]

As the consortium plunged deeper into dissension and turmoil, it was buffeted by external pressures as well. Early in 1981, Rob Taylor, of Ashcraft & Gerel, joined with Benton Musslewhite, Newton Schwartz, and several other attorneys to request that Judge Pratt create a new lawyers' group to coordinate Phase I discovery for plaintiffs; they did not want to leave that responsibility to Yannacone & Associates, which Pratt had designated as lead counsel in the case.[7] Ashcraft & Gerel represented a large number of veterans who had filed Agent Orange claims. Many were associated with Vietnam Veterans of America, which was active on the Agent Orange issue and linked politically with the Kennedy wing of the Democratic Party. VVA had achieved some notoriety when some of its leaders made a well-publicized trip to Hanoi in December 1981 to meet with North Vietnamese leaders.[8] Musslewhite, who had been a top aide to Ralph Yarbrough, a liberal senator from Texas, claimed to have obtained retainers from more than 1,100 veterans; most of these were members of Citizen Soldier, which had lobbied for amnesty for Vietnam-era draft evaders. Between Ashcraft & Gerel, Musslewhite, and their allies, these lawyers claimed to represent almost half of the 3,400 named plaintiffs in the Agent Orange cases and anticipated adding almost 600 more. These clients did not intend to join in Yannacone's class action but would instead "opt out" of the class, as they had a clear right to do under Rule 23. Their own lawyers would proceed to litigate their cases individually, and they would technically not be bound by the outcome of the class action case, although that outcome might well influence the courts and juries that would hear their claims.

Speaking for this group, Taylor and Musslewhite complained to Judge Pratt about Yannacone & Associates' handling of the case and its lack of cooperation in supplying them with documents and information as the court had required. They also implied that the consortium was not providing competent representation to the veterans; they claimed it had not even read the 10,000 documents that the government, although no longer a party, had already produced for inspection and that Yannacone & Associates had no intention of reading them.[9]

The group therefore demanded a more prominent role in the management of discovery. Specifically, they asked that the court designate a steering committee for discovery purposes consisting of three lawyers representing VVA clients (from Ashcraft & Gerel), three representing AOVI clients (from Yannacone & Associates), and three representing Citizen Soldier (from the Musslewhite-Schwartz group). The court, they said, should also authorize Ashcraft & Gerel to act as spokesman for plaintiffs at pretrial conferences, to convene meetings of plaintiffs' counsel, and to serve as the official liaison or conduit for any notices and documents to which the non–class action counsel were entitled.

Yannacone & Associates vigorously denounced this "power play." While conceding an occasional "inadvertent slippage" in document mailings, the consortium contended that the other nonclass lawyers had participated only "minimally" in the case. If their clients joined the class, the consortium argued, they would be represented by Yannacone & Associates; if they opted out, their lawyers had no legitimate claim to participate in the management of the class action. Yannacone & Associates defended its efforts, including its disbursement of about $480,000 of the lawyers' money up to that point, and emphasized the "profound differences" between the two groups concerning how the case should be litigated. In particular, the consortium argued that the lawyers who wished to litigate individual cases and who had opposed Pratt's serial trials approach were actually playing the defendants' game. Their motion, the consortium implied, was a thinly veiled attempt to have the class bear the cost of their cases.[10]

Clearly, much more was at stake in this quarrel than the question of who would send documents to whom: it was a struggle over who would control the Agent Orange litigation. This struggle had at least three aspects, relating to the clients, the lawyers, and the court. The first was organizational and ideological in nature. Yannacone & Associates, Ashcraft & Gerel, and the Musslewhite-Schwartz group primarily represented three veterans' organizations—AOVI, VVA, and Citizen Soldier, respectively—that differed from one another in terms of their leadership, competition for the veterans' allegiance, geographical bases, political strategies, and views on the war.[11]

The struggle for control also involved the financial, reputational, and tactical interests of the various lawyers. All, by agreement with their clients, were working on a contingency fee basis. But the lawyers knew that if the case were litigated as a class action, any fee they would receive must, under Rule 23, ultimately be approved by the *court* and that the court would probably give the lion's share of the fee award to the lead counsel in the case; other lawyers, who simply supplied their clients as members of the class, would receive little or nothing. The economic value of the case to the lawyers therefore depended largely upon how central their role was in running the litigation.

The lawyers also knew that the case might well be the most visible, important tort case in history, and they wanted to be (and to be *seen*) in the middle of the action, not on the sidelines. They wanted to execute professional *tours de force* before the jury, not merely watch their competitors do so. Great professional reputations would probably be made in the Agent Orange case. As Dean later put it, "To be the chief trial lawyer in the largest personal injury case in history, that's what you pay your dues for." Only the lawyers who controlled the management of the case could make the crucial decisions that would shape the litigation; only they could play general on the legal battlefield and serve the interests of their clients as they thought best.[12]

To the consortium, which already occupied the position of lead counsel, these considerations made it imperative to retain control. To the insurgent lawyers, the same considerations suggested a strategy of trying to take over the class action. Failing that, they should stay out of the class, litigate in their own way, benefit as much as possible from the discovery conducted by the class action lawyers, and hope for a large settlement or recovery. In that happy event, as nonclass lawyers, their fees would not be regulated by the court. Until Pratt signed a formal class certification order, however, the insurgents' position would inevitably remain ambiguous.

The third aspect of the struggle for control concerned the court's role. In an ordinary lawsuit, the litigation is largely controlled and shaped by the lawyers for the individual parties; and the judge tends to be detached, reactive, and umpirelike. In a class action, however, the court inevitably plays a much more intrusive, dominant part in the design and management of the litigation. By defining the class (and subclasses), prescribing how notice will be provided, deciding who shall be lead counsel, monitoring the adequacy of the class's representation, approving any settlement, awarding counsel fees, and generally ensuring that the class's interests are well protected, the judge in a class action becomes the focal point, the orchestrator of the case.[13] In the Agent Orange case, this was true of Judge Pratt and even more true of his successor, Chief Judge Weinstein.

Although Judge Pratt could not know precisely how these factors affected each of the disputants, he certainly recognized that the insurgents' demand for a larger role was part of a bitter power struggle that would persist for the duration of the Agent Orange case. Pratt reserved judgment on their motion, indicating with thinly veiled sarcasm that he remained committed to the "perhaps . . . fictional view of litigation these days," that "the lawsuit belongs to the parties and not to the lawyers."[14] Meanwhile, Yannacone & Associates continued as lead counsel. Once again the increasingly fragile consortium had managed to repel a dangerous threat to its position. The insurgents, however, would be back.

Another problem for the plaintiffs came from an all-too-familiar quarter—the Veterans Administration. Although the filing of the Agent Orange case had not altered the VA's official position that illnesses other than chloracne had nothing to do with the herbicide, pressures against the agency began to build. In April 1979 the General Accounting Office, the congressional auditing agency, called for better record keeping and medical follow-up by the VA in cases involving exposure to herbicides. A month later, Citizen Soldier publicized a survey of veterans' experiences with the VA on Agent Orange–related claims, harshly criticizing the attitudes of VA doctors toward such claims.[15]

Even the president of the United States began to feel the heat. Just before Reutershan's death, Frank McCarthy had promised to "get to Jimmy Carter" with the Agent Orange story. When Max Cleland, the widely admired head of the VA, scheduled a special reception at the White House for 500 Vietnam veterans on Memorial Day, 1979,

McCarthy managed to get in. As Carter entered the reception room, McCarthy worked his way to the front of the crowd. McCarthy recalls the scene: "When Carter spoke, my memories of Reutershan complaining about Carter's failure to answer Paul's letter asking for help flooded over me. Suddenly, Max, who was good for the veterans except on the Agent Orange issue, caught my eye, and I shouted, 'What about Agent Orange victims, Mr. President? Thousands of our men are dying because of it! We need a study!' " According to the United Press account of the incident, "Carter, looking grim, heard McCarthy out and replied, 'Max and I agree.' " The assembled veterans and journalists applauded. After McCarthy's "ambush" (as he calls it) of Carter, AOVI members all over the country kept hounding Cleland to fulfill the president's commitment. (At a Senate hearing in California in 1980, for example, Cleland, a Vietnam veteran and a triple amputee, was taunted by veterans about the VA's inaction. "Did you lose your balls in Vietnam, too?" one of them shouted.)[16]

The publicity surrounding these and other dramatic incidents—including the visit by VVA leaders to Hanoi in December 1981 to discuss the impact of Agent Orange on the people and ecology of Vietnam—had several important effects. First, Agent Orange research began to receive a higher priority in the VA. Immediately after McCarthy's ambush, President Carter announced a study of the Operation Ranch Hand pilots to evaluate the health effects of their exposure to defoliants. In December 1979, preliminary results of a VA study revealed that dioxin could indeed remain in body fat for a long period, weakening the VA's official position that Agent Orange was not toxic. Most important, the VA, responding to a congressional mandate, finally announced in May 1981 that it would conduct a "definitive," multimillion-dollar study of Agent Orange health effects on Vietnam veterans. (In the event, however, the VA's credibility with Congress, scientists, and the Vietnam veterans on the Agent Orange issue had plunged so low that the much-criticized VA study, plagued by persistent allegations of bias, was transferred away from the agency's control—first to the Food and Drug Administration, then to the Air Force, and finally, in October 1982, to the Center for Disease Control.)[17]

Another result of the publicity was that Congress unanimously enacted a statute giving veterans who claimed herbicide-related illness a higher priority in obtaining access to free care in VA hospitals and nursing homes. These veterans, however, would remain in the non–service connected (nonentitlement) category; the new law neatly sidestepped the dispute over the health effects of Agent Orange by allowing care for exposed veterans "notwithstanding that there is insufficient medical evidence to conclude that such disability may be associated with exposure."[18]

Congress had made it clear that the new law applied only to medical care and should not affect claims for service-connected disability benefits. Still, the number of herbicide-related benefit claims steadily increased. From 100 in 1978, the number had grown to 6,146 in early 1981. After newly discovered military records revealed in September 1981 that numerous soldiers had been exposed to Agent Orange when C-123 planes on defoliation missions had jettisoned their chemical cargoes near U.S. bases, a further spurt of claims was made; the total reached 14,236 by the fall of 1982. Of these claims, however, the VA approved very few, involving serious chloracne.[19]

Yannacone, advancing a variety of imaginative legal arguments, went to court to challenge the VA's denial of benefits on these claims, demanding that the agency take detailed exposure histories, warn veterans about genetic risks from Agent Orange, and inform them of their legal rights against the VA. His position, however, was doomed. Congress had specifically provided that VA benefit determinations were "final and conclusive" and that no court possessed jurisdiction to review them. Since the Supreme Court in 1974 had interpreted this provision to permit judicial review only of *constitutional* challenges to VA benefit decisions, Yannacone framed his challenge in constitutional terms, but Judge Pratt refused to take the bait. He would not interject himself "into what appears to be a political struggle between veterans and the VA."[20]

In truth, the veterans' suit against the VA seemed a sideshow, more likely to attract attention than to obtain relief. The main event continued to be the class action against the chemical manufacturers, yet that seemed to have ground to a halt by early 1982, more than a year after Judge Pratt's December 1980 order initiating Phase 1 discovery. (The December 1980 order had itself been delayed for more than a year by Pratt's decision to await the Second Circuit's ruling on appeal of his federal common law holding.) Indeed, the case had come to resemble the "phony war" during World War II, when the initial invasion led to a hiatus of drift and lassitude, giving no hint of the furious firestorm that would follow. The most remarkable thing about the Agent Orange case during this period was not what had happened but what had *not* happened.

There were several reasons for the lack of movement. First, although Pratt had agreed to a class action, he had never formally certified the class. This meant that no class notice of the action's pendency could be approved or disseminated. Without notice, it was impossible to find out how many veterans would decide to opt out of the class, and thus the size of the class was unknowable. No serious discussion of settlement could occur under these conditions. Then, too, Pratt had never acted on the defendants' January 1981 request that he ask the Second Circuit to grant interlocutory review of the class action question.[21] Hence, defendants could not appeal his class certification decision. Nor had he ruled on the statute of limitations issue, despite his December 1980 decision to take that issue up "immediately." Furthermore, he had not ruled on the request by Ashcraft & Gerel and the Musslewhite group for designation of a steering committee to manage the litigation, and he had not ruled on the defendants' request that he allow an interlocutory appeal to the Second Circuit of his order dismissing their third-party claims against the United States.

Finally, although the parties had quickly responded to his December 1980 order to submit briefs on the elements constituting the government contract defense, which was to be the central focus both of Phase I discovery and of the first trial, Pratt had not yet decided this fundamental question. Without such a ruling, Pratt later conceded, "intensive discovery was not appropriate."[22] Not surprisingly, little had been conducted.

The reasons for Pratt's long delays are unclear. In August 1980, he had been assigned responsibility for the complex Abscam cases, and these demanded much time. As to class certification and notice, he may have hoped to spare plaintiffs the high costs of providing notice if the case should be ended because of the government contract defense or some other dispositive motion. The delay also gave the consortium more time to build the veterans' case. Some of the lawyers, however, have a different explanation. While expressing a high regard for Pratt's ability and conscientiousness, they believe he was simply paralyzed by the magnitude and complexity of the case and could not manage it. "He handled the case badly," remarks a very sympathetic and respectful lawyer for one of the defendants. "He didn't know what to do with it, failed to give it the full attention it demanded, and let a lot of time go by."[23]

On February 24, 1982, Pratt finally did address several of these outstanding questions. He denied the motion to designate a steering committee; his views concerning the adequacy of Yannacone & Associates' representation "remain[ed] unchanged," a position that seemed quite oblivious to the serious, deepening problems within the consortium. He also rejected the chemical companies' efforts to take an interlocutory appeal of his *Feres/Stencel* decision. On the class action question, however, Pratt did not issue a formal certification order (although he did state—falsely, as it turned out—that one "will soon be entered"), and he did not even mention defendants' long-pending request for interlocutory review. He decided to defer indefinitely ruling on the statute of limitations issue, noting only that that issue would be affected by the fact that the case was a class action, a fact he had known since December 1980, when he had decided to certify the class. By not ruling, however, he effectively preserved many veterans' claims, which probably would have been barred by the applicable statutes, some of which were in the process of being liberalized.

Pratt *did* rule on the fundamental substantive question of how the government contract defense should be defined. He enumerated three elements that each chemical company must prove in order to establish the defense and obtain immunity: that the government established the specifications for Agent Orange (regardless of the role the company played in developing them); that the Agent Orange supplied to the government by the company met those specifications in all material respects; and that the government knew as much as or more than the company about the hazards to people of using Agent Orange. The last of these requirements, which had been developed by Twerski, was the most important and controversial.[24]

Unfortunately, Pratt's delineation of the government contract defense glossed over a number of ambiguities concerning parity of knowledge, ambiguities that should have been evident to him even then. These included the questions of what it meant to "know" something as elusive, subjective, and indeterminate as whether a chemical agent was "safe"; what level of official must have that knowledge in order for it to be imputed to the government; at what level of generality a fact must be known in order to constitute knowledge under the legal standard (for example, was it enough to know that dioxin could be toxic at *some* level, if it was not known whether it was toxic at a *particular* level?); and whether the knowledge test would be satisfied if an official merely had "reason to know" or "reason to inquire," as distinguished from actual knowledge. Moreover, because knowledge *in vacuo* is not legally relevant, it is not apparent how Pratt could have believed that the knowledge questions could even be answered, much less used as the basis for terminating the lawsuit, without first resolving the questions of "generic causation" (whether and under what conditions Agent Orange was capable of causing harm) and of enterprise liability (whether one company's knowledge could be imputed to another). These unresolved ambiguities would come back to haunt Judge Pratt and the parties.

With the elements of the government contract defense laid out, Pratt went on to order that "intensive discovery is not only appropriate but required." He scheduled an off-the-record conference on discovery issues for March 18, but he did not issue his decision structuring the resolution of those issues until April 29. He then announced his appointment of Sol Schreiber as special master to act as the court's agent in supervising all discovery, assisting in any settlement negotiations, and preparing the pretrial order that would govern the Phase I trial. (The defendants, seeking better access to government documents needed to establish the government contract defense, had requested that Pratt appoint a special master for discovery, even offering to pay the costs, including the special master's $180 per hour fee.)[25]

Schreiber was an ideal choice. A former federal magistrate (a court official who performs many judicial functions, including holding hearings and making legal rulings on the court's behalf), Schreiber was an expert on the management of civil litigation and knowledgeable about insurance law. He had been a court-appointed master in several complex cases. During the early 1950s, Pratt and Schreiber had been Yale Law School classmates. Although they were not close friends, Schreiber was well known to Pratt and enjoyed the court's confidence.[26] Pratt scheduled an initial discovery meeting between the parties and Schreiber for May 13—almost seventeen months after he had ruled on the government contract defense and supposedly initiated Phase I discovery. Pratt also announced that the Phase I trial on the government contract defense would begin one year later, on June 13, 1983.

The advantages of having a special master were evident. For the parties, he offered a means to obtain swift decisions on discovery and related issues from someone with detailed knowledge of the case that was unavailable to a busy, generalist judge. Although the parties could always appeal the special master's decisions to the judge, they knew that frequent appeals would arouse resentment and probably be fruitless. (In fact, Pratt confirmed all of Schreiber's decisions except one, which was modified.) The special master could insulate the court from messy, time-consuming details, distancing it from the lawyers' incessant posturings and wrangling. The master also constituted a new tactical resource with which the court could hope to manipulate the parties toward agreement.[27] (For the special master himself, the appointment was the best of both worlds. "You are paid like a lawyer," Schreiber quipped, "and called Judge.")[28]

To David Shapiro, who would serve as a special settlement master in the case two years later, the master's role was a delicate balancing act requiring considerable sophistication and judgment. "He must know when he can speak in the judge's name, when he can't, and when he can say, 'I don't know what the judge would say but I would predict that . . .' " A special master, Shapiro observes, wears three hats: "He is the judge's man, the judge's buffer, and the judge's mediator. And he is a mediator at three levels—within each party grouping, as between plaintiffs and defendants, and as between the parties and the court. Finally, the special master must sometimes also negotiate with the judge."[29] As we shall see, these multiple, conflicting roles create tactical opportunities for the court, but they also pose serious ethical dilemmas and potential legal pitfalls.

With Schreiber's appointment and the setting of a trial date one year hence, the Agent Orange case entered a new phase. The "phony war" was over; the true stakes in the struggle had become more immediate and palpable, less distant and abstract. Imminent trial, as Dr. Johnson once said of the prospect of hanging, served to "concentrate the mind" on what lay ahead.

Some of the veterans' lawyers were distressed about having to litigate the government contract defense before reaching the merits, but they were confident they could defeat it, after which (or so they thought) they would be home free. Fiorella recalls their thinking: "The chemical companies had the burden of proof on the defense. We knew that the documents and depositions would show that they knew more than the government, which would defeat the defense. That would automatically trigger their failure to warn, which would leave us with the causation issue. By then, however, they would be rushing to settle."[30]

But as the pace of discovery quickened and the demands of trial preparation created new priorities, intensifying pressures within Yannacone & Associates produced problems that could no longer be ignored. Plaintiffs had managed to surmount defendants' earlier motions to dismiss with legal arguments culled from books in a law library and presented in briefs. To affirmatively prove every fact that plaintiffs *must establish to prevail*, however, was a far more difficult task, one for which the consortium's financial and human resources were clearly inadequate.

That task would require the lawyers to do what none of them had ever done before. Among other things, they must put together a highly specialized trial team, constantly litigate discovery motions, examine and digest millions of documents in the government's and defendants' files throughout the country, organize and computerize their document base, identify and interview expert witnesses, and prepare their own witnesses for pretrial depositions. They must conduct and digest hundreds of depositions of their own and their adversaries' witnesses, undertake large-scale legal research on many novel issues, keep hundreds of local counsel throughout the country (and in Australia and New Zealand) informed of litigation developments, prepare and file numerous pleadings, and devise and coordinate a trial strategy. These activities would demand enormous financial resources, management capability, specialized professional talent, secretarial and logistical support, and a deep reservoir of goodwill among the lawyers. All of these resources, however, were in desperately short supply, especially goodwill.

In March 1982, immediately after Pratt set a trial date, the consortium began a frantic search for new "investors," as they were unabashedly called. Bowing to the inevitable, it entered into negotiations with Ashcraft & Gerel and with the Musslewhite group, but these efforts bore no fruit.[31] Meanwhile, the consortium attempted once again to wrestle with the problem of Victor Yannacone. As always, the quarrels revolved around money and personality. Yannacone claimed he could not computerize the documents and conduct the litigation with the money he was being given; his detractors insisted that he was squandering even that money and should receive no more, and they said his imperious, belligerent manner was turning off potential investors. Many consortium lawyers were barely on speaking terms with him. Some favored firing Yannacone, but the same old considerations—his emotional hold on the veterans across the country, his close relationship with McCarthy and AOVI, his contacts with the press, and his threats to reveal the perilous state of the consortium's financing to Judge Pratt, who might name a new lead counsel—persuaded them to swallow their bitterness for the time being.[32]

As discovery proceeded, prodded by the special master, the dimensions of the problems of proof confronting plaintiffs' lawyers became increasingly apparent. Some of these problems were endemic to toxic tort litigation generally, and others were peculiar to the Agent Orange case. Dean described one endemic problem: "Our clients could not help us prove our case. After all, they had not been hit by a truck, victimized by a doctor, or injured by a drug or other consumer product. They didn't know what had happened to them or when. They only knew that something had gone wrong. Our causation case, therefore, had to be proved almost entirely from documents in the defendants' files."[33]

Another difficulty was identifying what company had made the product in order to establish who was liable. "Whose stuff was it?" Dean asked. "We didn't know and it was impossible to find out. In Vietnam, the barrels of Agent Orange manufactured by different companies had been mixed together before being sprayed and before our clients were even exposed to it. Again, our proof, such as it was, must come from the defendants' documents." These obstacles in turn created another problem in the trial lawyer's mind: "How could we make a case based largely on documents come alive to a jury? How could we get people, rather than just papers, before the jury?"[34]

But some documents can be more dramatic than a live witness. Through several intermediaries, the consortium had learned of a report in Dow's files concerning a meeting in March 1965 at which Dow, Diamond Shamrock, Hercules, and other chemical companies (but not Monsanto) had discussed the dioxin problem in some detail. Dean, who was assigned to find the document, vividly recalls the day early in 1982 when he came across it while rooting around in the Diamond Shamrock files at the plush offices of their prestigious New York counsel, Cadwalader, Wickersham & Taft.[35] "As soon as I read it," Dean recalls, "I shouted 'Holy Christ!' We had found the smoking gun."[36]

Dean's exultation was understandable, if premature. Dow had called the meeting to discuss health hazards involved in the production of 2,4,5-T and its precursor, trichlorophenol (TCP). (At the time of the meeting, Dow had not yet contracted to produce Agent Orange for the government, and the government was not present.) Dow had manufactured 2,4,5-T since 1948, had learned about the dioxin contamination problem in 1964, had developed a method of detecting it at concentration levels as low as 1 ppm, had concluded that dioxin at that level was "safe," and had succeeded in reducing dioxin levels in its 2,4,5-T to below 1 ppm. After mixture with equal parts of 2,4-D, this would result in a dioxin level of 0.5 ppm or less in its Agent Orange formulations. At the meeting, Dow explained that repeated exposure to 1 ppm of dioxin could be dangerous, that precautions were necessary, and that it had examined herbicides sold by some other companies and found some to contain "surprisingly high levels" of dioxin. (At that point the hazard being discussed was chloracne, not cancer, liver disease, or birth defects.)

The "smoking gun memorandum," especially in conjunction with other documents that came to light during this period, had extremely important implications for the culpability of different defendants, for the viability of the government contract defense, and for the prospects of settling the case. Dow's study and other data revealed that unlike DES, Agent Orange was not a generic product. The different manufacturing processes employed by the various chemical companies resulted in products containing different levels of dioxin. Some, like Dow's and Hercules', contained levels that were low relative to Monsanto's and Diamond Shamrock's products. Well into 1983, the plaintiffs' lawyers assumed that Dow's and Hercules' products contained less than 1 ppm of dioxin (although occasional higher levels came to light later). In contrast, the data suggested that some manufacturers' products contained dioxin levels as high as 47 ppm.[37]

Another file memorandum, dated July 12, 1965, was perhaps even more explosive. It concerned a telephone conversation in which a Dow official had indicated to Hercules that "Dow was extremely frightened that the situation might explode. They are aware that their competitors are marketing 2,4,5-T acid which contains alarming amounts of [a chloracne-causing substance] and if the government learns of this, the whole industry will suffer. They are particularly fearful of a Congressional investigation and excessive restrictive legislation on manufacture of pesticides which might result."[38]

Although Dow later insisted that there was nothing secret or conspiratorial about these incidents and that it had actually disseminated the information to many outsiders, a jury might be persuaded that the companies had avoided telling the government everything they knew about the hazards of dioxin in their products.[39] Two far-reaching consequences might follow, the lawyers thought. Plaintiffs might succeed in disproving parity of knowledge between the manufacturers and the government, thus defeating the government contract defense, and the jury might find the manufacturers' concealment sufficiently reprehensible to warrant punitive damages. It was not inconceivable that a punitive damage award could total billions of dollars.[40]

These documents also created an irresistible strategic opportunity for the plaintiffs' lawyers. By driving a wedge between the chemical companies, they could hope to pick the companies off one by one. Dow and Monsanto were the two largest producers of Agent Orange, with 28.6 percent and 29.5 percent of the market, respectively. Simply on a volume basis, therefore, they faced the greatest potential liability, and that risk would increase significantly if the government contract defense failed. But if Dow's product was much "cleaner" than Monsanto's and liability turned on dioxin content, the case against Dow was far weaker, especially if dioxin levels of less than 1 ppm were "safe." Plaintiffs therefore had little to lose in offering to settle with Dow; indeed, Dow's cooperation could strengthen their case against the remaining defendants.[41]

Other considerations pointed in the same direction. Dow, a very proud, sophisticated, self-confident company, had long set the industry standard in research on 2,4,5-T toxicology, detection methodology, risk control, and production techniques. It had taken some steps to alert its competitors to the danger, even telling them about the German firm from which Dow had obtained its dioxin testing process for only $35,000. It thus had an important stake in distancing itself from its laggard competitors.[42] And even a modest settlement payment by the well-heeled Dow would finance the consortium's litigation against the rest. The consortium would then use Dow employees' testimony to establish causation and culpability by the other defendants, either forcing them into settlement or producing a favorable jury verdict. The lawyers hoped to use Dow to win the veterans' case by skillfully exploiting the conflicting interests between Dow and the others and the haunting fear (even on Dow's part) of massive liability if the case reached a jury.

The consortium strongly suspected that Dow had other good reasons to be attracted to this settlement strategy. With the onset of intensive discovery, the company's litigation expenses were mounting rapidly. And even if Dow was correct in viewing itself as the least culpable of the manufacturers, it might still be tagged with a large liability. This was not simply because of its large market share and the possibility of punitive damages. If the defendants were held "jointly and severally liable," as the law permits when all defendants are shown to have acted in concert, *each defendant that remained in the case would be potentially liable for 100 percent of the judgment, regardless of its product's dioxin content.* The smoking gun memorandum and that of July 12, 1965, might provide the evidence that could persuade a jury of concerted action by the manufacturers.

In July 1982, Fiorella suggested to several defendants' lawyers that the parties discuss settlement possibilities. An initial meeting was scheduled at the New York offices of Hercules' lawyers, Kelley, Drye & Warren. The consortium designated Ed Gorman, who had a long, mutually respectful professional relationship with Len Rivkin, Dow's lawyer, as its chief negotiator; he would be assisted by Gene O'Brien and Al Fiorella. At the first meeting, the defendants' lawyers, who were very concerned about the enormous size of the class, demanded to know how many actual injuries in each of several categories of disease (birth defects, liver cancers, and so on) were alleged to be Agent Orange–related; Gorman agreed to supply the information. Fiorella immediately asked Yannacone, who with his wife was supposedly compiling and computerizing the individual veterans' medical histories, to provide it for the next meeting in September. This information was extremely difficult to come by; because Pratt had not yet actually certified the class, no notice had been sent to members. Nevertheless, Yannacone estimated that there were 20,000 "hard" injury cases (including birth defects) and another 30,000 lesser injuries; these were the figures reported to the defendants' lawyers.[43]

By the September meeting, a new development had affected the calculus. In late August, on the same day that Johns-Manville filed for bankruptcy to seek protection from massive potential liabilities from asbestos-related claims, an Illinois jury had awarded almost $58 million to forty-seven railroad workers. The workers had been exposed to only 22 ppb of dioxin during a chemical spill resulting from a train wreck. (Monsanto, which manufactured the chemical that contained the dioxin, had settled for $3.5 million on the day of trial, and two other defendants had settled for the same amount.) The Agent Orange defendants reacted with concern. "The jury's award scared the hell out of us," Rivkin recalls, "but there were extenuating circumstances. Monsanto had pulled out its expert witnesses when it settled at the last minute, and Paul Pratt, the very effective plaintiffs' lawyer in the case, practically owns the juries in that area."[44]

At the September meeting, the defendants' lawyers asked Gorman for thirty-six representative disease profiles. According to several consortium members (but not Yannacone), the following events transpired. Fiorella asked Yannacone to develop the profiles. The profiles were not ready for the October meeting, but Yannacone said he would come to the November meeting with a computer keyboard and hookup and would print out the data. Shortly before the November meeting, however, Yannacone told Fiorella that if he wanted profiles, he must come down to Yannacone's office and produce them himself. Consortium members recall that when they went to Yannacone's office, they discovered that many files had little medical information other than brief notes from the veterans or their wives. "We came away with no more than ten profiles after reviewing hundreds of files. Even Keith Kavenagh [Yannacone's partner] was exasperated with Victor." The desperate lawyers turned to Steve Schlegel and Dennis O'Malley, associated counsel in Chicago and Boston, who had many clients and could compile the profiles. In December, the Gorman group gave those profiles to the defendants' lawyers. At that point the negotiations petered out, and no further group meetings were held.

In December, however, Gorman and O'Brien had begun to meet secretly with Rivkin in an effort to split Dow off from the other companies. Rivkin told them he had no authority to negotiate a settlement by Dow but would listen to their proposals and transmit them to his client. In January 1983, they reported to the consortium that Rivkin had agreed to recommend to his client a "structured settlement," one that could be "sold" to the veterans as a $100 million settlement but would cost Dow only $40 million; Dow would pay $10 million up front and $30 million to an insurance company that would invest the money and pay out $90 million over the next twenty years. When Dean objected that Rivkin had previously mentioned to him a figure of $175 million, Gorman took up the discrepancy with Rivkin, who recalled no such discussion. Dean was then assigned to speak directly to Rivkin, who again denied having mentioned a higher figure, whereupon the consortium voted (over Dean's objection) to accept the Gorman-Rivkin agreement. At the same time, Fiorella was assigned to talk to Bill Krohley, Hercules' lawyer, about settlement. Krohley had learned of Rivkin's discussions and indicated that any Hercules settlement would have to dovetail with Dow's.

In February, Rivkin reported to Gorman that the Dow management had decided not to settle. Dow felt that it had not been at fault and did not want to be put into the position of financing the veterans' case. Since Dow had no idea how many claims were actually being asserted against it, it doubted the consortium's ability to procure releases of liability claims that would bind all potential plaintiffs. And Dow feared that even if it settled with the consortium, the government or one of the other defendants might bring it back in as a defendant under some third-party liability theory. Dow could not buy peace even if it wanted to.

Some consortium members believe that Dow rejected settlement for another reason. Yannacone's partners claim (and Yannacone denies) that he, unbeknownst to them, discussed settlement with Charlie Carey, Dow's in-house claims manager, and indicated that plaintiffs would not settle with Dow for less than $300 million; in addition, Dow would have to establish a special toxicological research facility and take other preventive steps. But if Dow settled, Yannacone allegedly told Carey, the lawsuit would focus on Monsanto, and when plaintiffs won, Dow could pick up the defeated Monsanto's business. Dean recalls that Yannacone planned to hold a press conference announcing such a settlement, at which the veterans would praise Dow for its corporate citizenship.[45] This discussion apparently left Dow considerably confused about who was speaking for the consortium and what could happen if Dow accepted Gorman's proposal and Yannacone then publicly denounced it. Although efforts were made to dispel the confusion, the damage had already been done, and the discussions with Dow ended.

Rivkin did not inform all of the other defendants' lawyers about the highly secret settlement discussions until after they had terminated. His colleagues were shocked to learn that Dow had met surreptitiously with the enemy; to them, it betrayed the spirit of leadership and cooperation that Dow had displayed up to that time.[46] But in heightening the tensions between Dow and the defendants whose product had contained relatively high levels of dioxin (especially Monsanto and Diamond Shamrock), this incident also underscored a fundamental reality: although the defendants shared common interests on many important issues (for example, the government contract defense and statutes of limitations), their positions on others remained highly conflicting, especially on knowledge about the dioxin problem, efforts to reduce dioxin levels, the levels at which dioxin might be dangerous, and, most significant of all, allocation of liability and damages. As Rivkin's separate settlement discussions suggested, these conflicts, which plaintiffs' counsel sought to aggravate and defendants' counsel sought to suppress, were beginning to force their way to the surface.

6

Three-Cornered Struggle

WITH the trial looming only months ahead, the lawyers wrestled with an increasingly demanding discovery schedule. Special master Schreiber pressed them hard to negotiate their countless disputes over documents and depositions rather than litigate them before Judge Pratt. Although Pratt had been elevated to the Court of Appeals in mid-1982, he had retained the Agent Orange case on his docket. Schreiber warned the lawyers that if the case were not ready for trial by June, the case would be assigned to another judge, who would have to begin from scratch.[1] Because the discovery concerned only the government contract defense, especially the government's knowledge about dioxin, government officials' files and memories were crucial; thus the government, although no longer a party to the case, remained the focus of it. The chemical companies initiated virtually all discovery; apart from a few depositions, the financially pressed consortium conducted almost none. Often it could not even afford to purchase copies of the documents that the defendants had discovered.[2]

Discovery, therefore, centered on what the government, not the chemical companies, knew. A three-cornered struggle ensued. The chemical companies, constantly complaining about the government's adversarial posture and obstructionism, demanded full access to information held by the Pentagon, the EPA, and the Department of Agriculture. The government insisted that it was cooperating with discovery but that it was entitled, and perhaps even obliged, to withhold information that, if disclosed, could compromise the deliberative processes of government or could reveal state secrets. The plaintiffs' lawyers, for their part, supported the government's position and sniped at the defendants whenever possible. (There were additional conflicts within the plaintiffs' camp; whenever Ashcraft & Gerel and the Musslewhite group sought a more influential role in shaping the discovery, they were met with the argument, usually sustained by Schreiber, that only the lead counsel group had that power and that if they wished to join the group, they must share the discovery costs.)[3]

The conflicting claims raised a number of difficult, often unprecedented issues. Because the chemical companies could not know precisely what the government knew and what information might help them prove their case, they needed to cast their discovery nets widely, yet Pratt would not permit them to go on a "fishing expedition" in government files. The government's state-secret privilege, moreover, was legally absolute; it could not be overcome even by a showing that a party needed the information to prove its case. Indeed, even inspection of the requested documents by a judge *in camera* (alone in chambers) to test the government's claim of this privilege—a routine practice in other kinds of document disputes—was ordinarily not permitted. To invoke this privilege, however, the government was required to submit an affidavit signed by the department head (in this case, officials of Cabinet rank) attesting that that official had personally reviewed each privileged document. In the Agent Orange case, this would require busy Cabinet officers to read thousands and thousands of documents personally.

Judge Pratt, on Schreiber's advice, resolved this dilemma in an innovative fashion.[4] The government was persuaded to provide Schreiber with a security clearance to admit him to a special guarded room in the Pentagon, where he spent several weeks examining the government documents at issue. Of these, he selected only 154 that he considered relevant—a limitation not previously applied to a state-secret privilege claim. He then gave the government lawyers an opportunity to submit the required affidavits claiming the state-secret privilege for these documents. This makeshift procedure worked; in the end the government suppressed only one document, a pattern of openness that the Justice Department considers "extraordinary."[5]

Additional problems were raised by the lawyers' desire to depose (interrogate on the record) a number of former Cabinet-rank officials, including Henry Kissinger, Robert McNamara, and General Maxwell Taylor, concerning their knowledge of the dioxin problem during the 1960s. Because the Supreme Court had severely limited the circumstances under which depositions of high-level officials might be taken, the government might have been able to bar these depositions. (The problem was complicated by the fact that many of these people were former officials and others, like Cyrus Vance, were again officials but now in different positions than they had been in during the Vietnam War.) Nevertheless, a schedule was worked out, and the depositions were taken.[6] All of these former officials testified that they had known nothing of the problem and that had they known of it, they would not have allowed the use of Agent Orange. A more difficult issue was never decided: whether, as a legal matter, the government could be said to have knowledge, for purposes of the government contract defense, if only lower-level officials possessed the information.[7]

Several other novel solutions to thorny discovery problems were devised. The first related to trade secrets and other information that the chemical companies had submitted to the Department of Agriculture and the EPA for regulatory purposes and that were legally entitled to confidential treatment. But because the parties had to have access to this information to litigate the government contract defense properly, Judge Pratt ordered that the lawyers on both sides be permitted, under special restrictions and protections, to examine and use the documents and that they destroy them afterward. Another innovation related to the design of a protective order governing the media's access to confidential information generated through discovery. By slightly shifting the burden of initial justification, the court successfully balanced the conflicting interests: sensitive First Amendment rights to have access to and disseminate information, versus the need for confidentiality, expeditious discovery, and fair trial. The order, however, left the media free to publish whatever information they managed to obtain in other ways. A third innovation related to defendants' desire to obtain the testimony of veterans who were *in extremis* because of imminent death or deteriorating health. (Deriding the extensive procedures proposed by the defendants, Keith Kavenagh, a hard-working, well-liked member of the consortium, mordantly observed that "if the veteran has not passed on by then, they will surely have questioned him to death.") Here the court permitted videotaped depositions under restrictions designed to minimize the risk of abuses.[8]

But litigating and resolving these and many other discovery issues took a great deal of time, and time was running out. On February 27, 1983, three months before trial was to begin, Kavenagh sent a memorandum to his colleagues expressing serious doubts that they could adequately prepare their case in time. He predicted that Ashcraft & Gerel and the Musslewhite group would soon make another move, this time seeking to oust Yannacone & Associates as lead counsel on the grounds of incompetence and insufficient resources to prosecute the case effectively. If the request was "properly phrased and argued," Kavenagh warned, the insurgents might succeed in obtaining access to internal consortium documents and take depositions of consortium members. "That would be embarrassing to say the least." Unless the consortium could show Judge Pratt that it had obtained additional financing to support trial preparation, Kavenagh feared, "not only do we stand a very good chance of being discharged, we also are in clear danger of being the recipients of some rather nasty malpractice actions."[9]

Kavenagh's concerns were widely shared within the consortium, and in March the group once again reached out in desperation for money and expertise. This time it was more successful. One lawyer who responded was Steven Schlegel, the Chicago litigator who had helped to develop the representative disease profiles during the abortive settlement negotiations. By his own account, Schlegel was not a "cause" lawyer; he handled tort cases for the money. He believed that if the Agent Orange case could be wrested away from the consortium's conventional personal injury lawyers (whom he derided as having a "rearender" or "bonebreaker" mentality) and tried by seasoned, sophisticated class action specialists, it might win them fame and fortune.[10] Ashcraft & Gerel and the Musslewhite group also responded, agreeing to join Schlegel and Yannacone & Associates in a newly constituted plaintiffs' management committee in which each member would retain control over its own clients and would contribute $3,000 per month to the litigation fund.

The plaintiffs were not alone in believing that the impending June 27 trial date was impossible to meet. In mid-March, most of the defendants requested a one-year extension, insisting that the government had "sabotaged" their efforts at discovery, much of which still remained to be conducted, and that the novelty and complexity of the case necessitated further preparation.[11] Some defendants also urged that Judge Pratt reject Schreiber's recommendation to defer class certification and notice to members until after trial. Although the defendants had vigorously resisted a class action, they believed that if the court insisted upon certifying it, it should require plaintiffs' lawyers to provide individual notice to the millions of class members *now;* this notice, they hoped, would prove so costly to the lawyers that the litigation would collapse of its own weight.

In April, all of the chemical companies except Monsanto and Diamond Shamrock (whose Agent Orange had contained relatively high levels of dioxin) moved for summary judgment, arguing that their government contract defense could be decided by the court purely as a matter of law because no genuine issues of material fact that would require a trial existed. If they could sustain this defense, plaintiffs' claims would have to be dismissed and the case would be over.

The defendants had originally resisted moving for summary judgment, thinking it hopeless. The government contract defense obviously raised issues of fact that required a trial. In addition, such a motion would foreclose a procedural compromise suggested by special master Schreiber that some believed could turn the Agent Orange case around and win an early dismissal. Schreiber proposed that the defendants consent to certification of a (b)(3) class (which would permit class members to opt out and pursue their claims individually) and pay for the costs of providing notice to the class; in return, the plaintiffs would agree to allow the government contract defense, which might end the case, to be tried to the court rather than to a jury. Schreiber's plan would relieve the plaintiffs' lawyers of the cost of notice, which could be enormous in a case like this, but would deprive them of a (presumably sympathetic) jury.

The proposal seemed especially attractive to the defendants; not only would they try the potentially dispositive issue to the court but, if they prevailed on it, a large class (whose members would be bound by the judgment) would be to their benefit. Rivkin was therefore extremely enthusiastic about Schreiber's proposal. He lobbied the other defendants' lawyers and even arranged for Dow's chief executive officer to lobby his counterparts at the other chemical companies.

Five of them agreed to go along, but Monsanto and Diamond Shamrock refused. As the manufacturers with the "dirtiest" products, they were almost certain to lose the government contract defense; what judge or jury, after all, would believe that the government had known that their dioxin levels were so high? Monsanto, represented by the law firm of Townley & Updike, which did not normally handle its work, was especially nervous. As the largest marketer of Agent Orange, it might have punitive as well as compensatory damages to an enormous class assessed against it. And if their "cleaner" codefendants prevailed on the defense or settled out of the case, the two companies might later have to confront the plaintiffs and an unsympathetic jury *alone*. Even bankruptcy could not be ruled out.

Their best hope was to put off trial, conduct more discovery, and hope that plaintiffs' lawyers would run out of money.

It was a close question whether *any* defendant should accede to a class action, a key element of Schreiber's proposal. Class litigation held certain undeniable advantages to the companies—lower litigation costs, a reduced risk of punitive damages (because the court has greater control of the case and wants to preserve defendants' assets for compensatory damages to the class), a far more tractable settlement process, and the opportunity to resolve the whole Agent Orange "ball of wax" in one proceeding. Some defendants' lawyers believed that the asbestos corporations, in successfully opposing MDL and class action treatment of the asbestos cases in the mid-1970s, had miscalculated badly; at enormous cost, they had had to litigate numerous cases to establish principles that could have been laid down in one.

On the other hand, some defendants felt that litigating all claims in a single, massive class action would foolishly risk everything on one roll of the dice. For some, the asbestos experience actually confirmed the wisdom of resisting consolidated litigation, especially in Agent Orange, where the lawyers in the field against them were so poorly financed. Finally, some urged that even those who favored a class action could have their cake and eat it too; by opposing class certification on the record, they would have one more issue to appeal should the veterans prevail at trial.

The rejection of Schreiber's proposal by Monsanto and Diamond Shamrock did not entirely doom the June 27 trial date. At a hearing on March 21, Dow and Hercules stated their willingness to accept Schreiber's proposal and go to trial alone or with any codefendant who wished to join them. Thompson Chemicals, it appeared, was also interested. At this point, the special master suggested that the government contract defense might be tried separately for those defendants willing to forgo further discovery in return for a nonjury trial before Judge Pratt. However, when Rivkin rose to address the issue at the hearing a week later, a plaintiffs' lawyer, Gene O'Brien, interrupted to tell him that if he believed he had an offer from the plaintiffs for a nonjury trial, he was mistaken. Rivkin and Krohley (Hercules' lawyer) both asserted that Yannacone, who was absent, had clearly made such an offer and accused the plaintiffs of "sandbagging." "The sandbagging," O'Brien replied, "was by the defendants . . . Our offer to them was then, as it is now . . . if all the defendants will say they are ready to go nonjury within twenty-four hours, we will have an answer for them." Monsanto's and Diamond Shamrock's unwillingness made this impossible, and Schreiber's new proposal died as well.[12] Pratt then insisted that the defendants move for summary judgment on the government contract issue, and seven of the companies did so. Again, however, Monsanto and Diamond Shamrock, knowing that the motion was futile and perhaps fearing that plaintiffs might cross-move for summary judgment against *them*, did not join. Here was the first open breach between defendants; it would not be the last.

When Yannacone received a "five-foot-tall stack of briefs" containing the defendants' arguments, he noted that they prominently featured testimony from Dr. Gordon MacDonald, a member of President Johnson's Science Advisory Committee (PSAC), whose deposition the defendants had recently conducted. MacDonald had testified that the issues of dioxin in 2,4,5-T and of dioxin's potential toxicity in humans had been informally discussed within PSAC between April and June 1965. Although Yannacone would argue that MacDonald's statement had been taken out of context, he immediately recognized the mortal danger to plaintiffs' case that this represented. "The first Panzer Division has just arrived," he told a colleague at the time.[13] If MacDonald's testimony were credited, if PSAC's knowledge of the danger were imputed to the government, and if that knowledge were enough to put the government on notice that there was a serious problem, then the chemical companies would have gone a long way toward establishing parity of knowledge, the crucial disputed element of the government contract defense. Even plaintiffs' most dramatic evidence—the smoking gun memorandum and Dow's (and other defendants') expressed fear that a knowledgeable government might take restrictive measures against 2,4,5-T—would be rendered legally irrelevant if, as MacDonald's testimony suggested, the government knew enough *anyway* to trigger the government contract defense.

On May 20, 1983, Judge Pratt decided the summary judgment motions. It would prove to be one of the most important decisions in the long, tortuous history of the Agent Orange case. He held that the chemical companies had proved the first two elements of the defense—that the government had prepared the specifications for Agent Orange and defendants had met them.[14] (Fifteen months later, these findings were seriously undermined when the government, newly restored to the case as a party, produced new evidence of the companies' role in specifying the product.)[15] Pratt then reviewed the evidence bearing upon the third element of the defense, the government's relative knowledge: notably, its knowledge of chloracne outbreaks during the 1950s among German workers exposed to TCP, a precursor chemical of 2,4,5-T; the 1959 Hoffman Report, containing "startling information" about dioxin's toxicity; testing at Edgewood Arsenal during the early 1960s; knowledge of the dioxin contamination problem among government scientists during the mid to late 1960s; discussions of the issue within PSAC; and the Bionetics studies. He concluded that "uncontradicted and uncontested evidence . . . reveals that the government and the military possessed rather extensive knowledge tending to show that its use of Agent Orange in Vietnam created significant, though undetermined, risks of harm to our military personnel."

As to the chemical companies' knowledge, however, the picture was far more complicated. The veterans' cases against three of them were quickly dismissed; Riverdale and Hoffman-Taff were ignorant of any hazards, and Thompson Chemicals knew less than the government. (Despite their ignorance, these companies would not automatically escape liability if the court accepted any of the plaintiffs' theories of enterprise liability, meaning, as Judge Weinstein later put it, that a chemical company had a duty to warn the government if it was or should have been aware of the dangers posed either by its own product *or* by a competitor's product that was to be mixed with its own.[16] But Pratt unaccountably failed to address the liability implications of these theories.)

Dow, however, presented a very different situation. It had begun producing 2,4,5-T in 1948, had long known of the potential hazards posed by chlorinated hydrocarbons, had developed the "rabbit-ear" test in 1945 to determine the presence of chloracnegens, had corresponded with German firms about this problem in the 1950s, and had known of chloracne outbreaks among its own and other companies' workers. Dow had developed the most sophisticated methods to monitor the presence of dioxin in TCP and 2,4,5-T; using gas chromatography, Dow could detect concentrations as low as 1 ppm, a level the company believed (or so its attorneys claimed) was "safe" as to chloracne and liver damage. No knowledge of cancer risks appears to have existed until years later, but plaintiffs argued that so long as Dow knew that dioxin probably caused *some* harm, even if minor, it was liable for dioxin-caused injuries that were more remote but also more serious.

Dow had sought to show the government's parity of knowledge in three ways. First, it argued, the only relevant knowledge was about hazards that accompanied use. Since the reported hazards related to workers exposed to dioxin in the production process at levels well above 1 ppm rather than to users of the finished product, Dow argued, it had no relevant hazards to report to the government. In response, the plaintiffs' lawyers cited the smoking gun memorandum of the March 1965 conference at which Dow informed Hercules and Diamond "that 1 ppm with repeat exposure can create a real problem" in the finished (2,4,5-T) product. Dow responded that this referred to a problem for test animals, not humans. Second, Dow insisted that even if high-level government officials lacked information, "crucial middle-level government experts . . . had extensive knowledge" about potential hazards to users as well as production workers. To this, the veterans responded that what the middle-level people knew was not specific enough. Finally, Dow insisted that even if it had told the government more, that would not have altered the defoliation program in Vietnam. The veterans countered that a more knowledgeable government would have terminated purchase of Agent Orange and restricted its domestic use.[17]

Pratt rejected Dow's arguments. Only a trial, he said, could resolve whether additional information might actually have affected the government's use of Agent Orange and whether Dow's product was in fact safe at the varying dioxin levels it contained, in which case there was no information about danger that must be reported to the government. (Similar fact issues, he ruled, also precluded summary judgment for defendants Uniroyal and T.H. Agriculture and Nutrition.)

Pratt's decision was correct as to Dow but seems curiously inconsistent with his treatment of Hercules, to which he granted summary judgment. Although Hercules' workers had not experienced chloracne outbreaks and the dioxin levels of its product were relatively low, it had attended Dow's March 1965 meeting. In Dow's case, this raised a question of fact concerning the difference that additional information on these matters might have made to the government. Why, then, should the same reasoning not apply to Hercules as well?

The most momentous feature of Pratt's decision concerned the relationship between the factual question of what level, if any, of dioxin could actually harm the plaintiffs, and the knowledge element of the government contract defense. "I have concluded," he wrote, "that a separate trial of the open issues on the government contract defense with respect to the remaining defendants is no longer appropriate." Pratt maintained that his original plan for serial trials had made sense at an earlier time but that "as we all have learned more about the development and use of Agent Orange in Vietnam, the issues in the action have become clearer. Plaintiffs undoubtedly will strongly emphasize a negligent failure to warn as a basis for liability. But when the "knowledge" factor of the government contract defense is placed alongside a liability theory of a negligent failure to warn, the issues, unfortunately, no longer remain discrete or separate. On the contrary, they tend to merge." Pratt concluded, therefore, that "justice would be served by combining what remains of the government contract defense issues with . . . a trial at the earliest reasonable date covering the issues of liability, general causation, and the government contract defense."[18]

Pratt's bland language scarcely concealed the thunderbolt he had hurled. Everyone's central assumption about the Agent Orange case—the structure that Judge Pratt had imposed upon it and that had guided its development for two and a half years—was suddenly out the window. A litigation organized around a focused, relatively well-defined set of issues to be tried only one month hence, possibly leading by stages to the trial of other defined issues, was instantly transformed into a completely open-ended free-for-all involving a diffuse, highly interrelated tangle of issues that would be subject to discovery, trial, and decision at some unspecified time in the (presumably distant) future.

The scales had finally fallen from Judge Pratt's eyes, and the wonder is that it had taken so long. His new vision of the case, especially the interconnectedness of the crucial factual issues, was correct. But his suggestion that only hindsight could have provided this view was wholly unconvincing. Had he thought through the nature of the government contract defense more systematically back in 1980, he would have had to conclude that the core issue of knowledge was actually a composite of questions. An inquiry into the distribution of *relevant* knowledge, for example, required information about the kinds of harms that dioxin could cause at different concentration levels, the responsibility of particular manufacturers under an alternative enterprise liability theory, and the nature of scientific bureaucracies in government. Moreover, if he had squarely confronted the plaintiffs' enterprise liability theories, he could not have granted summary judgment for Hercules (or for other firms that were dismissed), because under those theories even the "cleanness" of an individual company's product would not necessarily preclude its liability.

Despite the centrality of these questions, the judge had failed to

delineate them in order to guide the parties and had not even permitted discovery on them. Their interrelationships and salience should
have been evident to him from the start. Six months earlier, Yannacone
had argued that the issues could not really be separated and that a
single trial should be conducted, but Schreiber had predicted that
"the judge will not change his mind" and that he, Schreiber, probably
would not either.[19]

Both sides read Judge Pratt's decision with anguish. Dow was bitterly disappointed that it had not been dismissed from the case along
with Hercules; indeed, Pratt had unfavorably compared Dow's product to Hercules'. Dow knew now that the case against it would go
forward and that at the end of that road waited a jury that would be
receptive to the veterans' pleas for justice. At that moment, Dow
determined to adopt a new litigation strategy. Angered by Judge
Pratt's decision lumping it with what the company regarded as its less
scrupulous, free-riding competitors, Dow decided to break ranks
publicly. Hereafter it would seek to turn the court's attention more
directly to the issue of the relative dirtiness of its competitors' products, especially those of Monsanto and Diamond Shamrock, an issue
Dow had previously muted in the interests of maintaining a united
front. With that shift, the Agent Orange case was transformed.[20]

The consortium lawyers were even more despondent over Pratt's
decision. They had survived summary judgment motions, but otherwise their future seemed bleak. Pratt's new direction utterly con-
founded their earlier game plan. Instead of carefully phased litigation
in which they could gradually and at relatively low cost build up the
pressure on the chemical companies and induce settlement, the consortium now faced the prospect of having to conduct massive discovery on all issues for perhaps years to come. Pratt had failed to set a
new trial date; given the disparity of resources between the two sides,
the defendants would have little incentive to move toward settlement
until a trial was upon them. Meanwhile they could simply drag their
heels and wear the consortium down. As Irving Like put it, "We now
knew that it would be a long haul. We also knew that we lacked the
horses. Some changes would obviously have to be made, and made
fast."[21]

The first thing that would have to change, most of the lawyers felt,
was Yannacone's role in the litigation. It was not simply that there
were now new players—Ashcraft & Gerel, the Musslewhite group,
and Schlegel—who were watching and waiting for an opportunity to

take greater control of the case. It was also that the area of Yannacone's particular substantive responsibility—proof of generic causation—had now moved from the wings to center stage. There, many of his colleagues believed, his failures were glaringly evident.

These perceived failures took several different forms.[22] First, Yannacone's peremptory manner (Fiorella called him "a legend in his own mind") and his obvious disdain for his colleagues made teamwork almost impossible.[23] (This problem intensified when Keith Kavenagh, who had often been able to calm Yannacone down, died suddenly in late March 1983.) When the defendants had moved for summary judgment, for example, Yannacone had asked the consortium lawyers to gather at his office to prepare the massive filing in opposition to the motions. It was necessary to write and file a separate set of briefs and supporting affidavits and documentary exhibits directed at each of the chemical companies, a task that required them to review all of the depositions, documents, legal precedents, and other materials developed during almost five years of litigation, distilling them into carefully honed, skillfully woven legal and factual arguments. And all this had to be done within a matter of days!

On the night before their papers were due, with an enormous amount of synthesis, writing, editing, and typing still to be done, Like, Fiorella, Taylor, Schlegel, Hayes, Twerski, and a few others worked feverishly and without sleep. By many accounts (but not Yannacone's), Yannacone provided no help, went to bed, and blithely went off the next morning to a workmen's compensation hearing. Even more infuriating, his much-vaunted computerized data base turned out to have little useful information stored. Yannacone, however, maintains that these complaints are false and simply confirm his view that the consortium lawyers did not understand the case (they were merely "personal injury" lawyers, not environmental, "public interest" lawyers), were incompetent ("the data were all there, but they hadn't programmed it properly"), and were starving the lawsuit of funds.[24] "They'd heard me cry help for three years," he later told a journalist. "They'd pauperized my family. They'd laughed at my concerns."[25]

But the lawyers' grievance with Yannacone extended far beyond such incidents; it went to the very heart of their litigation strategy. According to the consortium's work plan, Yannacone's major responsibility in the lawsuit, besides dealing with the veterans and the media, was to develop the scientific case against dioxin, which required him not only to develop a scientific theory of causation but to mobilize the necessary technical experts. Some of these experts would testify at trial, but an even more important role was to help the lawyers develop the case and prepare for trial by advising them about whom to interview, which documents to seek on discovery, how to interpret them, what lines of inquiry to pursue in depositions, what defenses to anticipate and how to meet them. It was exceedingly exasperating, then, that Yannacone steadfastly refused to divulge to his colleagues the names of his experts.[26] Yannacone insisted that only he, not the personal injury lawyers on his team, was technically competent to understand the experts; moreover, he said, his colleagues would compromise the experts by revealing their news to the defendants.[27]

His partners became increasingly convinced that just as Yannacone's computerized data base was useless to them, he never really had the experts lined up either. Their conviction was fortified when Yannacone repeatedly demanded funds to support the epidemiological study based on the medical case records his wife was compiling, which he insisted was crucial to the case. The consortium members, pointing out that neither he nor his wife possessed the scientific credentials to withstand the predictable attacks by defendants' experts on the study's methodological adequacy, continually asked him to identify an epidemiologist who could help them develop a sound scientific protocol for it. Yannacone, however, demanded that they fund his study with no questions asked. And so it went on issue after bitter issue.[28]

In part (but only in part), these disagreements reflected fundamentally different conceptions of how the case should be litigated. His colleagues emphasized a purely practical consideration: their severely limited funds must first be allocated to overcoming the threshold obstacle, the government contract defense, which might then lead to a partial settlement that could finance the rest of the case. Yannacone, in contrast, was preoccupied by what he prophetically viewed as the essential problem of a mass toxic tort case: proof of causation. Yannacone believed that no single expert possessed the requisite knowledge to testify about dioxin in the traditional manner—that is, by stating that in their professional opinions, dioxin caused the plaintiffs' injuries—for the pathways of causation were complex and spanned numerous medical specialties. Instead, plaintiffs must prove the precise physiological mechanism of causation by constructing a series of building blocks, starting with effects at the cellular level and working up to the systemic level, demonstrating dioxin's toxicity through the testimony of a series of experts, each of whom understood one particular building block.[29]

Yannacone's conception of the quintessential problem of proving causation in a mass toxic tort case of this kind was insightful and, as events were to demonstrate, probably correct. His method, however, was also very daunting and maddeningly abstract. The difficulty was that he never troubled to persuade his colleagues that he had a coherent, realistic plan for accomplishing the task. "We could never sit down with him as attorneys and go over our case step by step," recalled Like, echoing the complaints of others. "We needed to meet the experts and prepare them for depositions, to test their credibility and their quality as witnesses. We also needed to sit down with them so that they could help prepare us for discovery. But Victor refused to work that way." Dean, Yannacone's most loyal supporter within the consortium and still an admirer, ruefully agrees with that criticism.[30]

Yannacone's response was to grumble about the hopeless scientific ignorance of his colleagues. He wrote to them in June 1983:

> To the best of my knowledge, none of the Consortium members have invested the time in reading the carefully culled scientific literature that I distributed at the beginning of this case . . . In order to establish causal relation, every member of the trial team must become intimately familiar with the rudiments of epidemiology as both a science and a "Black Art," the biochemical physiology of the liver and the metabolic processes associated with the liver, cancer biology, the principles and practices of animal studies in toxicology, and biochemical molecular biology or as some call it, biomolecular genetics. Lack of preparation in these areas of scientific concern and a lack of familiarity with the basic elements of their underlying academic disciplines can lead to critical embarrassment during the trial of the litigation and missed opportunities during pretrial discovery.[31]

His partners, for their part, waited in vain for Yannacone to indicate precisely how he planned to convert scientific articles into legal evidence through identifiable expert witnesses.[32]

By mid-June, the rancor between Yannacone and the consortium had erupted into all-out warfare. Special master Schreiber, who believed that the discord was beginning to jeopardize the veterans' case, told Fiorella that with the litigation entering a new phase, several changes were needed. In particular, the consortium needed a new spokesman in court and should remove Like as chairman of the law

committee. The consortium readily agreed with the first change and
voted, with Dean dissenting, to replace Yannacone with Dean. (In
court, Yannacone, not one to be pushed around, sometimes would
rise first and speak anyway.) But they supported Like and were puzzled by Schreiber's intrusion. At a consortium meeting, Fiorella accused Yannacone of having orchestrated a campaign to use Like, with
whom Yannacone had feuded for years, as a scapegoat for the
consortium's troubles. The consortium voted to reconfirm Like in his
position and reported this to Schreiber, who seemed upset by the
rebuff.[33]

But the retention of Like was only a minor eddy in the current of
change engulfing the consortium. Even Yannacone, whose role was
now confined to putting together the generic causation evidence,
recognized that that long-neglected part of the case must be developed quickly. He contacted Tom Henderson, a plaintiffs' lawyer from
Pittsburgh who specialized in proving causation in asbestos cases,
and invited him to join the consortium. They had met earlier at sem-
inars on occupational and environmental health, and Yannacone had
tried to interest Henderson in the case during the summer of 1981.
Henderson had demurred then and later, in February 1983, when
Yannacone had again approached him. He was too busy trying asbestos cases, and he believed that the serial trials structure that the
consortium had recommended and Pratt had endorsed was "crazy."
Serial trials, Henderson believed, played right into the chemical companies' hands by removing any pressure for settlement. "In cases like
this," he argued, "the only way to get defendants to settle is to drag
them before a jury as soon as possible on the human issues of causation and injury to the veterans, not on documentary, bloodless
issues like government contract defense." And Henderson had not
been impressed by the ability of the consortium lawyers—most of
whom, except Like and Twerski, he viewed as conventional "slip and
fall" personal injury practitioners—to build the kind of complex causation case that would be needed with Agent Orange.[34]

But when Henderson, fresh from some asbestos victories, learned
in June 1983 that Pratt's restructuring of the case had made causation
a central issue, his interest was kindled. Learning of Yannacone's
difficulties within the consortium, Henderson also saw an opportunity to take control of the scientific side of the case. "Victor had
misled the others into thinking he could prove cause," Henderson
said. "He had led them down the garden path." When Henderson

conferred with the consortium, "the hostility was so thick you could cut it with a knife. Fiorella and Yannacone were at each other's throats, and Yannacone and Dean were outvoted on everything."[35]

Henderson then met with Dr. Samuel Epstein, a professor of preventive medicine and a leading controversialist concerning the environmental and public health effects of pesticides and other toxic chemicals. Epstein, in a blizzard of technical and popular articles, congressional and court testimony, speeches, and books (most notably, *The Politics of Cancer*), had established himself as perhaps the most acerbic, passionate, and uncompromising scientific critic of the chemical industry.[36] With Epstein's urging, Henderson became convinced that a winning causation case could be constructed. In August he decided to take the plunge, arranging to spend all of his time on the case for the next year.

Henderson had no illusions about the difficulty of the task, which he defined somewhat differently than Yannacone did, but his experience in the asbestos cases, never far from his mind, fired his optimism. First, he hoped to get the causation issue to a jury not under the conventional "proximate cause" standard but under a less demanding "could cause" standard, and he believed that animal studies, biochemical testimony, and epidemiology could be used to satisfy this standard. Unlike Yannacone, he regarded animal studies as more important than epidemiological evidence in implicating dioxin. (Just the reverse had been true in the asbestos cases Henderson had litigated.) Second, he viewed the causal relationship between dioxin and chloracne as equivalent to that between asbestos and asbestosis, and he hoped to show that a combination of chloracne, systemic toxicity (such as liver dysfunction), and neurological damage could establish dioxin's capacity to cause more serious diseases.

Henderson, who had been warned about Yannacone's volcanic eruptions but had dismissed the reports as exaggerated, quickly found him impossible to work with. "Victor is brilliant and articulate," Henderson said, "but he is grandiose and cannot carry out what needs to be done to implement his ideas." As it turned out, he did not have to work with Yannacone for very long. The Long Island lawyers, who had brought in Schlegel, Musslewhite, and now Henderson in the desperate hope that new blood and outside financing would put their case on a sound footing, concluded that they simply could not carry the main burden any longer. The consortium had already spent more than $500,000—about $50,000 from each lawyer, not counting

their time and overhead—and yet the case was in a sense only beginning. (Yannacone claimed to have spent a great deal more, and he
faced financial ruin.) The new lawyers insisted that at least $1.2 mil-
lion more must be spent just to prepare the case for trial, and they
demanded that each member of the venture sign a $200,000 letter of
credit, a financial commitment that the Long Island contingent could
not undertake.[37] To add to their troubles, Schreiber, who was presumed to speak for Judge Pratt, was beginning to express dissatisfaction with the consortium's performance and prospects.[38]

The consortium lawyers decided to bail out. On September 19, they
requested that Judge Pratt remove Yannacone & Associates as lead
counsel, citing their inadequate financial resources.[39] Schreiber informed them that he intended to recommend to Pratt that Schlegel,
Musslewhite, and Henderson be designated as the new plaintiffs'
management committee, which they claim enraged Yannacone.[40]
Yannacone's agitation presented the lawyers with a dilemma. They
continued to fear that Yannacone, out of pique or calculated self-
interest, might advise the thousands of veterans who viewed him as
their champion (whether or not they were his clients or had become
clients of the consortium, a matter of some dispute among the lawyers) to opt out of the class action. And even his many detractors
acknowledged his talent and technical expertise. In any event,
Yannacone was asked (at Ashcraft & Gerel's urging) to assist
Henderson on the causation issue for a fee on a trial basis (a "short
leash," as Taylor called the arrangement).[41] In October, the lawyers
paid him $5,000.[42]

Having secured its flank, Ashcraft & Gerel now made its most
blatant power grab yet, threatening to withdraw its clients from the
class action unless it was given total control. According to Taylor, the
firm's hard-working associate on the case, "Speaking quite bluntly,
we wanted to be the dictator and just get the thing done." Schreiber,
however, would have none of this. Meeting with plaintiffs' lawyers,
the special master sharply rebuked the firm, emphasizing that it lacked
experience handling class actions of this kind and that no one firm
could run it. Criticizing the firm's threat to use its clients as a bargaining chip for control, Schreiber told the assembled lawyers that if
he were awarding fees, Ashcraft & Gerel would not receive a penny.
Schlegel, Musslewhite, and Henderson were designated as the lead
counsel who would begin to build a new plaintiffs' management committee (PMC).[43]

Yannacone, who hoped to be made executive director of this group, quickly managed to arouse Henderson's ire, and the relationship ended. His parting shot—"I don't work well as a slave"—could not conceal his virtually complete capitulation to the new regime.[44] But Yannacone's charismatic hold over many of the veterans made them willing to follow him wherever he might lead, including out of the class action altogether. Whether this threat would exact further concessions or would, like a nuclear bomb, prove too destructive to be used was the question that no one, not even Yannacone, could then answer.

By October, the furious struggles within the plaintiffs' camp for control over the case had subsided, and the dust had begun to settle. A new leadership group—fresh, confident, more experienced in complex litigation, and far better financed—was now in place. The nine remaining members of the old Long Island consortium, no longer subject to Yannacone's control and with the albatross of major financial commitment now removed, were optimistic about its prospects. With Fiorella negotiating the transition arrangements, they agreed to continue their participation under the direction of the PMC. The lines of responsibility were now clearer: Musslewhite would prepare their case on the government contract defense; Henderson would handle the generic causation issue; Dean would concentrate on proving Monsanto's liability; Schlegel and Fiorella, aided by Gorman, O'Brien, and Levine, would work on proving Dow's and Diamond Shamrock's liability; the law committee, consisting of Like, Fiorella, and several law professors who had been retained, would prepare the legal arguments and briefs; and all would conduct depositions and discovery in their areas. Prominent plaintiffs' lawyers from other parts of the country—Stanley Chesley, a mass torts specialist from Cincinnati, and Phil Brown, a San Francisco attorney—were being added, and the group now represented a cross-section of the legal profession. As Like put it, "We now had a national team to represent a national case."[45]

Although a staggering amount of work remained to be done, especially on causation issues, much had been accomplished. Plaintiffs, whose resources were dwarfed by those of the defendants, had succeeded in establishing conditional class certification, including much of the research needed to support final certification, such as identification of common issues and solution of the notice problem, and the federal court's jurisdiction over the case (although they had lost on the federal common law issue). Moreover, they had survived summary judgment motions and had built a strong basis for overcoming the government contract defense. Perhaps most important, they had (as Yannacone later said, with an ironic twist to the rhetoric of Vietnam) "begun to win the hearts and minds of the American people."[46] Although members of the new PMC later stated that the case had been poorly litigated by the old consortium, this assertion—made in part to magnify the new group's achievements and thus justify a larger fee award—seems rather harsh and unjust.[47] Given the severe financial and organizational disadvantages under which it had operated, and given Judge Pratt's original structuring of the case, it was notable that the consortium had managed to hang on so long and had placed the new PMC in a position from which they might now move the case forward to trial.

Yet in a case full of surprises, the most unexpected and momentous was about to occur. On October 14, Judge Pratt, who had been elevated to the Court of Appeals more than a year earlier but had retained the Agent Orange case on his docket, suddenly announced that in view of "the increasing pressure of work in the Circuit Court," he could no longer preside over the case.[48] (It was rumored that the chief judge of the Second Circuit had refused to release Pratt for the many months that the Agent Orange trial was expected to require.) Only days later it was revealed that Judge Jack B. Weinstein, widely hailed—and denounced—as perhaps the most unconventional jurist in the federal system, would take over. The Agent Orange litigation was not merely entering a new phase; it was about to be recreated. With Weinstein presiding, all bets were off.

7

Enter Judge Weinstein

A S all of the Agent Orange lawyers filed into Judge Weinstein's chambers on October 21, 1983, uncertainty and anticipation filled the air. After almost five years with Judge Pratt, the case had settled down into a rather placid, predictable pattern largely dominated by the minutiae of discovery, a routine undisturbed by any prospect of imminent trial. The lawyers knew Pratt as a fairly conservative, conventional, workmanlike judge who played by the established rules, one whose judicial philosophy, work habits, intellectual energies, and conception of the case were by now familiar and uncontroversial.[1]

Weinstein, in dramatic contrast, was a wild card. It was not that he was unknown to the lawyers. Quite the contrary. He had sat on the federal bench in one of the busiest districts in the country since 1967, had coauthored leading treatises on evidence and civil procedure, and enjoyed a towering reputation as a professor at Columbia Law School, one of the nation's most distinguished educational institutions. Some of his decisions were celebrated precedents, including several landmark school desegregation and civil rights cases and a tort case (*Hall* v. *E. I. DuPont*) in which he had devised a new theory for expanding defective product liability in indeterminate defendant cases to cover an entire industry. His political and ideological identity had been clearly etched in his term as attorney for Nassau County and, in the early 1970s, when he had narrowly lost a primary bid for a vacancy on the New York State Court of Appeals. A liberal Democrat who unabashedly believed in activist government and judging and who enjoyed being in the public eye, Weinstein proudly wore his liberalism and humanitarianism on his sleeve.[2] He often reached out to decide challenging issues at the frontier of the law. Many lawyers and law clerks assumed that he was not sorry to be assigned the Agent Orange case.

For all of these reasons (and because he was known to be a World War II veteran), the plaintiffs' lawyers entered the judge's chambers in an exuberant, feisty mood, while their adversaries from the chemical companies arrived with grim anticipation, fearing the worst. What they all failed to take into account was that Jack Weinstein was an extremely complex, unconventional man of vast imagination, Byzantine subtlety, and almost blinding brilliance, as uncomfortable with traditional formulations as any individual of genius in any field is. When Weinstein was on the bench, the lawyers often seemed superfluous. Instead of being the target of lawyer's wiles and manipulations, as most judges were, he was more often the master of those tactics, confounding lawyers and, when necessary, making up the rules as he went along. (The novel tort liability theory he had adopted in the *Hall* case, for example, had not even been briefed by the lawyers in that case.) As a judge, Weinstein was ultimately unknowable and predictably unpredictable.[3]

Upon entering the judge's chambers, the lawyers immediately experienced the Weinstein "treatment"—warm, disarming geniality dispensed by a tall, handsome man of about sixty with an open face and an easy flashing smile. Champagne and refreshments had been laid out (it was also the judge's wedding anniversary), and he invited the lawyers to introduce themselves one by one and indicate "what we ought to do with this case." Obviously surprised—they naturally assumed that an "in chambers" conference would simply be a get-acquainted session—the normally loquacious, aggressive lawyers seemed at a loss for words, and none really took advantage of this opportunity to tutor the new presiding judge.[4]

Weinstein immediately launched into a long, dazzling monologue.[5] Speaking very softly, displaying great courtesy, and being careful to provide no ground for legal challenge, he deftly and unmistakably turned the Agent Orange case around, inside out, and on its head. He began by indicating that he intended to move the case from suburban Uniondale, on Long Island, where Pratt sat, to Brooklyn, where Weinstein did; there he would establish a special Agent Orange document headquarters as an adjunct to the court, assuring the lawyers' convenience and even allowing conference call hearings to accommodate out-of-town counsel. The lawyers, as Weinstein well knew, were far less concerned with the question of facilities than with the effect of the new location on who would hear the case. A Uniondale jury would be drawn only from the suburban counties of Nassau and Suffolk, but a Brooklyn jury would be drawn from urban Kings County as well—a definite advantage to the plaintiffs.

With the preliminaries out of the way, Weinstein went directly to the heart of his message to the lawyers: "This case will be promptly disposed of." Taking out his calendar, he said that jury selection would begin on Monday, May 7, 1984, and the trial would begin immediately thereafter, running for a predicted four months to mid-September. While expressing "the greatest respect for Judge Pratt," whose views (so he said) were generally "converging if not identical" to his own, Weinstein left no doubt that he was repudiating Pratt's entire approach to the litigation.

Causation, he insisted, was the first and foremost issue, not the government contract defense. Indeed, he did not "think very much of [the latter] as a dispositive defense"; it should only be addressed "down the line" after causation was decided. With so many plaintiffs, an innovative trial structure was needed. It might be necessary, he proposed, for the plaintiffs' lawyers to select a small number "of their best cases as they see them, in their best categories as they see them, and then we will try those and see if there is anything to the case." The central problem of proof in a case like Agent Orange would be "one of showing causality through statistical analysis," a consideration Pratt had never mentioned.

He appreciated, Weinstein said, that "an early trial disadvantages the plaintiffs" because "some of the statistical material on carcinogens takes many years to develop." He pointed out, however, that the plaintiffs "brought the case . . . and if they can't prove it, and if in ten or fifteen years it turns out that the jury made a mistake, we can't help it. That is the way we have to proceed in a court of law." Furthermore, the defendants' liability would be "a very difficult thing to prove" in this case; indeed, "liability . . . is highly doubtful." The plaintiffs' lawyers, jubilant only moments before, were now aghast.

Turning to the class action issue, which Pratt had put aside for almost three years after conditionally certifying a class in 1980, Weinstein signaled his strong desire to certify one large class so that all parties would be bound by the verdict. He even hinted that he might certify the class so that its members could not opt out, thereby disposing of the litigation "in one fell swoop."

As for the government contract defense, Weinstein clearly indicated that Judge Pratt had gotten it all wrong. Not only was that defense not central or potentially dispositive in this case, as Pratt had maintained, but the crucial question was not the one Pratt had posed in defining the defense. As Weinstein put it, "It is not only a question of what you knew . . . in the case of a manufacturer but what you should have known." While acknowledging that liability rules should not impede the government's ability to use contractors to meet national defense requirements, he questioned "whether a manufacturer is free to produce a product under contract if the manufacturer knows that product will cause damage." The chemical company lawyers, who had only moments before gleefully watched Weinstein's words deflate their adversaries' soaring hopes, found it was now their turn to squirm.

But Weinstein was not content to discomfit only the plaintiffs and the defendants. He next turned to the parties Pratt had dismissed from the case, the United States government and several chemical companies, notably Hercules and Thompson Chemicals, whose lawyers had been invited to be present in chambers. Reminding them that Pratt had never formally signed a judgment of dismissal, Weinstein quickly came to the point: "It is clear that I have no intention of signing a judgment dismissing at this point any of these defendants . . . Everybody stays in until the litigation is over, unless there is a very good reason to let them out. At the moment, I am just not convinced anybody gets out, and that includes the United States."

The lawyers were stunned. (The Hercules lawyer, who had come to the hearing as a spectator and left as a defendant, only half jokingly asked the judge if he could have scotch instead of wine.) As general consternation swept through the room, Weinstein hammered away at a central theme—the responsibility of the government. The Agent Orange litigation, he suggested, presented not so much a case as a social problem, one "that is very difficult for the Courts to decide alone. It is a political as well as a Court problem. It involves the Executive, the Veterans Administration and the Legislature, which has to appropriate a lot of money for veterans and for their various problems, if they are attributable to their service." The government had a central role in the Agent Orange case, he maintained, and liability could not be fairly decided without the government's active participation.

Although he was uncertain "whether procedurally we can force the government to come in," he saw a possible solution. A number of civilians had filed claims that, unlike those of the veterans, might not be subject to the government's immunity under the Federal Tort Claims Act. (He neglected to add that Pratt had held to the contrary three years earlier.) These claims, he suggested, might be tried to a jury along with the claims against the chemical companies; since the Tort Claims Act precluded a jury trial of the government, the jury's findings on governmental liability would only be advisory to the court. Weinstein, who professed a high opinion of juries, immediately added: "I don't want anybody to waste too much time telling me [this case] can't be tried by a jury . . . This seems to me the kind of case where the community is going to have to be heard. They're going to tell the world what the answer is on all of these technical problems, whether they have a high school education or not."

But this case would be "better settled than tried. If it can be settled, let's. If I can help you, I will." Settlement would be difficult, he stressed, unless "the other two pieces"—the VA and Congress—could be brought into the case; unfortunately, he added, "we can't do that because of limited jurisdiction. The intelligent way to handle it would be if there is any liability . . . [for] the VA to take over the whole thing, then to just have the manufacturers make a lump sum donation to help defray some of the costs of the Veterans Administration paying the costs of the damages, if any, attributable to Agent Orange. I don't know how that is going to be handled. You'll have to think about it and I will, too."

Finally, Weinstein emphasized that he expected thorough pretrial preparation and the parties' full cooperation in quickly completing discovery. "I like very dull trials, everything laid out beforehand, everybody revealing everything, all the experts getting together so we don't have last-minute problems. As far as I'm concerned, it's going to be tried a little more complicated but much like an intersection case." When Uniroyal's lawyers asked if they could renew their motion, denied earlier by Pratt, to bring in other defendants, Weinstein shook his head. "After four years? I'm going to trial . . . It's just one old case that has to be disposed of. That's the way it will be treated."

As Weinstein concluded his remarkable disquisition, Yannacone spoke up, introducing himself, Henderson, Dean, and Musslewhite as "the plaintiffs' management committee." This was at best a half-truth insofar as Yannacone was concerned. Early that morning, before the conference in chambers, Yannacone had asked Henderson whether he, Yannacone, could help run the case, to which Henderson had replied, "No fucking way."[6] (Months later, Dean telephoned Henderson, who had just returned from church, to read him the *American Lawyer* account containing that quote. Henderson, who could not believe that his language had been presented verbatim, kept saying "Yeah, but what did the *article* say I said.")[7] The tenacious Yannacone had then visited special master Schreiber and persuaded him to press Henderson to give Yannacone at least a temporary status. Henderson, fearing as always that Yannacone, if spurned, might make waves and take his veterans out of the case, had reluctantly agreed.[8] Yannacone then told McCarthy, who awaited him outside, that he was now "acting executive director." When a puzzled McCarthy asked what that meant, Yannacone replied that it was an empty title, and he identified the new lawyers, including Henderson, who were being brought in to help run the case.[9]

Weinstein almost certainly knew none of this that afternoon in chambers. When Yannacone introduced the "committee," the judge responded that he preferred to have one spokesman for each side. To this, Yannacone replied, "I'm serving as executive director for the committee at the time being." Weinstein resisted the bait. "The word 'executive director for the time being' leaves me very unhappy. I want somebody who says 'I'm in charge of the case for the plaintiff' . . . Acting director for the time being is not the person I'm looking for at the moment." Yannacone, normally voluble and irrepressible, was stunned by Weinstein's unceremonious putdown. After the chambers conference, Yannacone immediately left the courthouse. His departure bespoke a larger estrangement that soon ripened into an irreconcilable schism. Yannacone became a bitter critic of the PMC, of Judge Weinstein, and of the new direction in which they were taking the Agent Orange litigation.[10]

McCarthy left the courthouse dejected:

> I was low as I could be. We had lost our attorney and were now being represented by people (except for Dean) who we didn't know, who did not see us as part of the litigation, who didn't understand our cause. Then and there, my respect for the legal system went down the tubes. I saw that as the final blow against Victor. I had seen him lose power steadily within the consortium, seen the lawyers lose respect for each other. Victor and his group were our commander, battalion leaders, down to the squad leaders in each state. We would do whatever they thought necessary. After that, I had little hope in the lawsuit. The new

lawyers called us occasionally and Dean tried to give us faith in them, but we had little confidence in them, and Victor's bitterness added fuel to the fire. After five years, it was like starting all over.[11]

Weinstein's first performance had been dazzling. However the veterans viewed the new turn of events, the lawyers on all sides were astonished and impressed.[12] Where Judge Pratt had run the case as an "absentee landlord" (as one defendant's counsel put it), confining himself to the lawyers' briefs and never meeting with them informally in his chambers, Weinstein's style was just the opposite. He had quickly mastered the essentials of the sprawling, five-year-old litigation. (In the weeks that followed, he displayed a remarkable grasp of the technical literature on chemical toxicity, acquired, so he jokingly said, in the course of a casual visit to the Library of Congress and in bedtime reading.) More than that, he had utterly reconceptualized the case, discerning (as Pratt apparently never had) the uniquely problematic feature of mass toxic tort litigation, especially the problem of indeterminate plaintiffs.

But Weinstein's genius was not simply synthetic and conceptual, for he had also immediately grasped what practical steps must be taken to get the case to trial. In addition, he had displayed unusual personal gifts—an adroitness in handling Yannacone, a charismatic ability to communicate a sense of urgency, a contagious can-do spirit, a courageous readiness to adopt unconventional, unpopular measures, extraordinary self-confidence, a keen political and strategic awareness, and an utter mastery of the process of complex litigation. As if to dramatize his engaging informality and palpable humanity, Weinstein—here as in other cases—almost invariably left his judicial robe in his chambers, appearing in open court clad in a business suit.

When the lawyers' wonderment finally subsided, they realized that Weinstein had transformed the nature of the Agent Orange case. For one thing, he had completely reversed its focus. To him, the pivotal issue should be plaintiffs' point of greatest vulnerability—in this case, the issue of causation. Weinstein recognized, as Pratt had not, that Agent Orange was not simply a tort case writ large; it was the focus of such intense public concern that resolving it on the basis of a technical "lawyer's issue," such as the statute of limitations or the government contract defense, would not end the dispute but would merely cause it to fester. For this reason, he felt, the case must either be resolved on the merits or be settled out of court. All of his subsequent actions were consistent with that conviction and with the direction of his judicial and scholarly careers, which had been concerned with the creative use of procedure to achieve substantive justice, not avoid it.[13]

Also, by seeking to bring the government and the other defendants back into the case, Weinstein might vastly increase the financial and political resources available for resolving the dispute and for addressing the veterans' larger problems. Convinced that the government had an important, indeed essential, contribution to make to each of these tasks, Weinstein intended in a sense to hold the government hostage in the hope that it would be forced to devise a more comprehensive, political solution.

Finally, he had turned up the pressure on the lawyers either to proceed directly to trial or to settle the case, pushing them simultaneously in both directions. By fixing a trial date only six months away and by making it crystal clear that he would not deviate from it by even a single day, Weinstein signaled his determination to manage the case aggressively. A dramatic example of his intransigence occurred only weeks before the May 7 trial date when Monsanto's law firm sought a delay, citing the sudden nervous collapse of its lead counsel. Weinstein, although sympathetic, quickly denied the request. "You have a large firm," he told Monsanto's lawyers. "Get someone else."[14] ("He would not have delayed that trial even if his mother died," observed a federal magistrate who was assigned to the case. "In fact, his mother was very ill during this period and died only months after the trial date.")[15]

From long experience, Weinstein knew that lawyers, if left to their own devices, would drag their feet.[16] This was particularly true of defendants' counsel; paid on an hourly basis, their optimal strategy was the classic "bury the plaintiffs' lawyers" technique, using procedural maneuvering and delay to increase the heavy financial burden on their adversaries, all of whom worked on a contingent fee basis. But delay was useful for the plaintiff's lawyers, too; they did want to get to trial (indeed, it was their desire to meet the May 7 trial date that dissuaded the new PMC from suing the government,[17] which the judge obviously wanted back in the case), but they also desperately needed more time to develop their causation case, which had been largely neglected.

Weinstein knew all of this, and he also knew that imposing an early, immovable trial date would help push the parties toward a settlement—an outcome that he fervently wished to bring about. Academics who theorize about the litigation process emphasize that the more certain the outcome is, the less likely disputants are to go to court and, if they do go to court, the more likely they are to settle once they are there.[18] But Weinstein viewed the matter very differently. In a case like Agent Orange, he saw, the consequences for both sides of losing could be so calamitous that uncertainty, if it made both sides more pessimistic, actually created a powerful inducement to settle. Imminent trial, as one participant put it, made Agent Orange "a giant crap shoot." The large chemical companies faced the chilling prospect of being hauled before a Brooklyn jury by extremely sympathetic plaintiffs—young men with cancers, children like Kerry Ryan with birth defects, families with shattered lives. But the prospect of a trial also underscored for plaintiffs the glaring weaknesses of their evidence on causation, weaknesses to which Weinstein had alluded in his initial meeting with the lawyers. The looming May 7 deadline, Weinstein sensed, would ultimately be his most effective goad to settlement. (He even placed a huge calendar, with the trial date circled, on a large blackboard that he kept in prominent view of the lawyers and to which he often pointed for emphasis. He also conspicuously ordered carpenters to expand the jury box to accommodate extra alternate jurors. In these and other ways, he constantly reminded the lawyers that he meant business.)[19]

The litigators were totally preoccupied by the demands of preparing for trial, demands that meant seven-day work weeks for many of them, month after month. Apart from the government contract defense, none of the many issues in the case had been developed through discovery. Most of the lawyers believed that years of additional preparation were necessary, yet Weinstein had given them only six months. Depositions had to be taken of friendly and hostile witnesses all over the country, often on short notice and over weekends. A blizzard of briefs and motions on dozens of complex, novel legal issues had to be researched, written, and argued before Judge Weinstein. Expedited appeals of unfavorable decisions had to be taken to the circuit court. Innumerable documents had to be requested, analyzed, and inventoried; if access was denied by defendants or government, the status of the documents had to be litigated before the special master and perhaps the judge. Expert witnesses had to be identified, retained, and prepared. The lawyers had to prepare for and attend frequent conferences with the judge and with the special master (later, two settlement masters and a discovery magistrate). A careful strategy of jury selection had to be devised. Associated counsel across the nation and in other countries had to be kept informed. And, perhaps most time-consuming of all, the complaining veterans' medical files and personal histories had to be analyzed in detail to select the handful of "representative plaintiffs" whose claims, according to Weinstein's plan, would be tried to the jury. The lawyers had to conduct these and numerous other pretrial activities without abandoning their busy and continuing litigation practices in their home cities, practices that must pay the bills during their protracted involvement in the Agent Orange case.[20]

Weinstein's renovation of the Agent Orange litigation created a mood of near-panic among the plaintiffs' lawyers. They knew, first of all, that even the recent infusions of new capital and manpower would be inadequate to meet the judge's extremely demanding schedule.[21] Their efforts to recruit additional financiers and lawyers, however, sometimes failed. In November, Fiorella reported to the group that Peter Johnson, a New York lawyer with big-case experience, was interested in joining the PMC. Musslewhite, Henderson, and several other PMC members visited Johnson and received his terms: in return for putting up $500,000 and five full-time lawyers, he wanted to be the PMC's lead in-court counsel. Musslewhite later testified that he and several others were enthusiastic about Johnson's offer but that Dean, whom Johnson would have displaced as spokesman, dug in his heels, saying, "I am going to be the court spokesman or I walk. And if I walk, it's going to hurt the case."[22] Dean's tactics engendered some bitterness, especially among the newer PMC members, some of whom doubted his physical ability to withstand the rigors of a long trial. Indeed, one of Dean's opponents on the PMC later accused him in a sworn public affidavit of having gone so far, to buttress his claim to chief trial counsel, as to insist that a "special relationship" existed between Dean's wife and Weinstein's wife and that Mrs. Weinstein had telephoned Mrs. Dean with words of personal support.[23] This bizarre allegation, never substantiated, suggests that the stakes in this decision were extremely high and not entirely professional. Nevertheless, when the PMC voted on the question, Dean prevailed. (Later, Dean won another showdown vote over whether he would handle the opening statement to the jury rather than share it with other trial lawyers.) Similar attempts by Musslewhite in late 1983 to effect a reconciliation with Ashcraft & Gerel, bringing that firm's money, manpower, and knowledge of the case onto the PMC, were also rebuffed within the group.[24]

Other recruitment efforts, however, succeeded, and by the year's end the PMC was much expanded. Henderson had recruited Gene Locks, a Philadelphia trial lawyer. Musslewhite recruited Newton Schwartz and John O'Quinn, Houston practitioners, but only after Musslewhite had agreed to sell them a share of his interest in a fee award.[25] (Dean, jokingly referring to the financially pressed character in Mel Brooks's film "The Producers," called Musslewhite "the Max Bialystok of the legal profession; he sold 10,000 percent of his case.")[26]

The new PMC, now consisting of nine members, set its internal finances on a new footing by negotiating a fresh arrangement for defraying expenses and sharing whatever fees the court might ultimately award. Under the agreement, as the court later interpreted it, five of them (Brown, Chesley, Locks, O'Quinn, and Schwartz) each contributed $250,000 for litigation expenses, Henderson contributed $200,000, and the three others (Dean, Musslewhite, and Schlegel) contributed their time but no cash for general expenses. In the event of an award, however, the cash contributors would receive "off the top" three times the amount they had advanced. Half of the remainder of the award would be allocated in equal shares among all PMC members, 30 percent in proportion to hours worked and 20 percent based on certain conventional "merit" factors (what Musslewhite calls "the golden spike").[27]

This new fee-sharing arrangement created yet another fissure within the PMC, dividing the financial interests of the litigators from those of the financiers (there was, of course, some overlap between the two categories). The financiers, who now stood to obtain their profit even if the fee award were relatively low and without regard to their time contributions, might find settlement at a relatively low figure more attractive than the litigators. If a settlement did take place, even the appearance of such conflicts might be used to impugn the integrity of the settlement. In the event, this is precisely what transpired; indeed, as we shall see in Chapter 10, the PMC fee-sharing agreement itself came under serious challenge.

Pressures mounted steadily after October 21. Schlegel, who was responsible for managing the development of plaintiffs' case, describes the "administrative nightmare." "By March 1984 I was coordinating the work of 120 lawyers, while having to spend hours each day just answering telephone calls from lawyers all over the U.S. and Australia who would ask 'What's going on?' Our expenses were enormous; the cost of transcribing depositions between March and May alone was almost $200,000."[28] (The transcription services were obliged to sue the PMC for some of this money.)[29] But the intensity of these pressures defied measurement. "This case," the twice-divorced Dean says, "ruined my health, my marriage, and my practice."[30] And other lawyers reported that the case either broke up or severely strained marriages. Constant anxiety and physical exhaustion were common conditions by the end. When a Monsanto attorney actually suffered a nervous collapse attributed to the stress of pretrial preparation, one plaintiffs' lawyer had a premonition of their own demise: "There we saw a breakdown by one of the great army's well-fed generals; here in the mountains, we guerillas were dying of malnutrition."[31]

After October, the PMC's preparation for trial proceeded simultaneously along three major fronts. They struggled to complete discovery. They litigated over several crucial legal issues. And they developed representative cases for trial.

Discovery

From the moment Weinstein took over the case, he expressed dissatisfaction with the pace of discovery and constantly pressed the lawyers to accelerate it. In December, the judge decided to appoint a new special master for discovery to replace Schreiber, Pratt's appointee. Although he was well disposed toward Schreiber, Weinstein wanted someone who would be stationed in the courthouse at all times, whose costs would be borne by the government instead of the defendants, and who would bring a fresh vigor to the case. He named Shira Scheindlin, a talented young federal magistrate, and she took over in late January 1984.[32] (Dean had objected to John Caden, Weinstein's first choice, on the ostensible ground that Caden was a veteran and thus might appear to be biased; Dean's real reason, however, was a trial lawyer's intuition that Caden would be less sympathetic to the plaintiffs than Schreiber had been.)[33]

Scheindlin, at Weinstein's urging, aggressively rode herd on all of the lawyers and quickly won their respect. The judge had instructed her (as he had Schreiber) not to discuss settlement with the lawyers as magistrates ordinarily do but to take them instead on a "forced march" to trial. She began by meeting with them weekly, but the

frequency increased as they approached trial. By May, she was holding three or four meetings each week as well as issuing many written
discovery opinions; many meetings convened at 10 A.M. and lasted
until 11 P.M. These meetings were supplemented by constant *ex parte*
conversations (in private, without all parties present) between
Scheindlin and the lawyers by telephone or in her chambers; this
innovation, which Schreiber had initiated, is ordinarily proscribed by
the canons of ethics. Here, it enabled the lawyers to let off steam and
to clear up questions without delay, as the pressured circumstances of
the case made essential, but such informalities carried risks as well.[34]

Through these meetings and conversations, Scheindlin could
closely monitor the case. Constant hand-holding was necessary, and
she found it difficult to inveigle the lawyers into preparing for trial.
("I couldn't credibly enforce deadlines," she confesses. "What was I
supposed to do if they failed to comply—delay the trial? dismiss the
case?") The problem was not with defendants' counsel, who were
prepared to throw legions of lawyers and paralegals into the fray.
Indeed, Dow and some other defendants were determined to meet
Weinstein's Draconian trial schedule, for they knew that the plaintiffs' lawyers were disorganized and hoped to catch them with their
pants down.[35]

Plaintiffs' lawyers posed the major obstacles to meeting the schedule, for organizational as well as substantive reasons. Despite
Schlegel's heroic efforts, they lacked an effective management structure capable of moving the case to trial by May. The PMC, after all,
was not a law firm in any meaningful sense. The PMC did not establish a litigation headquarters in Brooklyn until January; even then,
some lawyers continued to commute to their practices in other cities.
More important, the members of the PMC had never worked together
before. As personal injury specialists, their customary work style involved one senior partner on a case surrounded by a few young
associates. "The PMC consisted of egocentric, aggressive kingpins
who were essentially strangers to one another," one close observer
commented. "They had not developed a rapport through years of
partnership, and it was often hard for them to get along." Even
without Yannacone, the disparate personalities—the volatile, laconic
Henderson; the wisecracking, emotional Dean; the urbane, buttoned-
up Schlegel; and the blustery, smooth-talking Musslewhite—meshed
uneasily, especially under conditions of great stress.

Another internal division made it difficult to pinpoint responsibility. Ultimate authority—especially as to spending and settlement strategy—was in the hands of the financiers, such as Chesley and Brown; unlike the litigators, these men had not lived with the case and did not really know it. Although the financiers generally supplied Schlegel with the funds he requested to manage the case, the split was sometimes apparent, even within the Texas contingent; the financiers, Schwartz and O'Quinn, occasionally treated Musslewhite, who was in a financially precarious position, peremptorily. Yet of all the PMC lawyers, only Musslewhite and Schlegel actually represented a substantial number of veterans.[36]

These problems all took their toll on plaintiffs' ability to get ready for trial. They labored under severe constraints of time, money, and data, and even by April, only one month before trial, discovery was far from complete. Indeed, the plaintiffs' case remained so disorganized that Magistrate Scheindlin's pretrial order instructing the parties as to how they must specify their witnesses and evidence at trial, which should have been issued in October, could not be issued until March 26; through Schlegel's tireless efforts, the plaintiffs were able to comply by mid-April. And so unprepared were plaintiffs that Weinstein actually directed Scheindlin to *continue discovery throughout the trial*, scheduling discovery conferences every Friday until the trial ended.[37]

Legal Issues

In order to prepare a case for trial, the lawyers must know what legal standards and rules will govern the decision; only then can they determine what factual evidence must be adduced and what arguments will be relevant. As we have seen, Judge Pratt had addressed few nondiscovery issues other than the government contract defense before leaving the case. When Weinstein took over, he faced a dilemma. Clarifying the legal standards would facilitate preparation and trial; by resolving crucial issues, it might also stimulate settlement. On the other hand, to issue decisions specifying the law would consume a great deal of Weinstein's own time and would only encourage interlocutory appeals; if permitted, these could delay the onset of trial and might even result in reversal of his rulings.[38]

Characteristically, Weinstein charted a shrewd course through these shoals. Whenever possible, he avoided formal opinions and gave

many informal signals from the bench; these revealed his "preliminary" thinking to the lawyers without really committing him to a
position or inviting time-consuming appeals. (When a defendant's
lawyer complained shortly before trial that Weinstein had failed to
address a number of issues, he responded good-naturedly, "Ask me
anything you like and I'll tell you how I will probably rule.")[39] And he
refused to certify interlocutory appeals. On several issues, however,
he had to rule formally and decisively. These included the questions
of class certification, class notice, choice of law, and governmental
immunity.

Class Certification and Notice

In 1980 Judge Pratt had agreed to certify the case as a class action, but
he had never entered a formal order doing so. By late 1983, with
Weinstein anxious to expedite trial and facilitate settlement negotiations, certification had become essential. While acknowledging the
view of the drafters of Rule 23 that class actions should not be used in
mass tort cases, Weinstein maintained that the Agent Orange case
was different, emphasizing that many issues, especially causation
and the government contract and product misuse defenses, were
common to all plaintiffs. Here the judge was on shaky ground. No
previous class certification had ever been upheld in such broad terms
in a mass toxic tort case. Furthermore, Weinstein's opinion did not
adequately meet defendants' argument that the issues of generic causation (dioxin *could* cause the observed symptoms) and specific causation (dioxin *did* cause *this* individual's symptoms) were so closely
intertwined that the very idea of pure generic causation became essentially meaningless in a case like Agent Orange.

Up to this point, Weinstein was merely following Pratt's earlier
reasoning, but he immediately ventured far beyond Pratt (and
probably beyond any other judge). Defendants had argued that class
certification must be denied because so many disparate states' laws
(depending upon the individual plaintiff's residence) would control
important aspects of the veterans' claims. Weinstein responded:
"There is . . . a consensus among the states with respect to the rules
of conflicts and applicable substantive law that provides, in effect, a
national substantive rule governing the main issues in this case.
Since, in the main, one law applies to all the claims, certification of
one class is appropriate."[40] As I explain in the next section,

Weinstein's bland claim that a national consensus on a single substantive law existed and could be applied in this case was in fact highly controversial.

Weinstein nevertheless decided to rely on this claim to certify a (b)(3) class, one that permits class members to opt out and pursue their claims individually. He defined the class to include: (1) all American, Australian, and New Zealand veterans who served at any time between 1961 and 1972 and who claimed injuries while in or near Vietnam by exposure to Agent Orange or other phenoxy herbicides, including those containing 2,4,5-T or dioxin, and (2) all of the veterans' spouses, parents, and children born before January 1, 1984, who claimed direct or derivative injuries as a result of a veteran's exposure. He also certified a (b)(1)(B) class (a mandatory class from which members could not opt out); this included the same individuals in the (b)(3) class but was limited to their claims for punitive damages. (An earlier hearing convened by special master Schreiber had indicated that the defendants' combined net assets, including insurance, totaled approximately $9–$16 billion and that the number of individual claims might total 50,000. Although these assets were sufficient to pay any compensatory damage claims that might be upheld, Weinstein reasoned, punitive damage awards, which may be any amount a jury awards unless the judge deems it excessive, might break the bank. Although he expressed serious doubts about the appropriateness of punitive damages in the Agent Orange case, Weinstein ordered all class members to remain in the class for purposes of litigating any punitive damage claims; that way, if these claims were upheld, the limited fund could be divided among them.)[41]

Finally, Weinstein addressed the important question of how to notify the millions of class members about the pending action and their right either to participate or to opt out. Notice would enable the veterans and their families to protect their interests; it would affect the number of claims filed and hence the size of the settlement or recovery, should there be one; and it would affect plaintiffs' attorneys' fee award, should there be one. Certain forms of notice, however, could be prohibitively expensive for plaintiffs to provide. Looming over this question was the Supreme Court's 1974 *Eisen* decision, a securities class action case in which the Court had held that all class members must receive actual notice by mail or in person if they could be identified "through reasonable effort." If notice to the veterans proved to be legally inadequate under the *Eisen* standard, the judgment would not be binding on class members, thus vitiating the central purpose of a class action.[42]

Weinstein's solution, which the veterans' lawyers had proposed, was innovative but highly questionable as a matter of law. Barely mentioning *Eisen* and failing even to discuss defendants' argument that more individualized notice was reasonably feasible, Weinstein authorized mail notice to those individuals who had filed claims in court or were listed in the VA's Agent Orange Registry. For the rest, he permitted the use of radio and TV announcements with broad geographic coverage; newspaper announcements throughout the United States, Australia, and New Zealand; a toll-free telephone number that veterans could use to obtain information about the suit; and letters from the court requesting each state governor to use all efforts to notify veterans in their states. Weinstein also prescribed the contents and form of the notices and announcements.

Weinstein's class action decision, especially on notice, might have been vulnerable on a full appeal. Because his order could not be immediately appealed normally, defendants decided to file an interlocutory appeal of the order through a mandamus petition (an unusual remedy used only to challenge a trial court's "calculated and repeated disregard of governing rules"). In January, the Second Circuit denied the petition. Although the court expressed some "skepticism" about both Weinstein's separation of generic and specific causation and his belief in the existence of a national consensus among the states as to the principal legal issues, it emphasized the very narrow scope of review on mandamus petitions and the need to defer to the trial judge in so complex a case; it devoted only a single sentence to the notice issue. When the defendants sought review of the Second Circuit's decision, the Supreme Court predictably declined to hear their appeal. While their review petition was pending, however, the Second Circuit stayed Weinstein's class notification order; notice was not sent out until mid-March, rendering it ineffective for many veterans who may have wanted to opt out by the May 1 deadline.[43]

In certifying the class action, Weinstein created a special relationship between himself and the veterans and their families, for the judge in a class action is in a sense the trustee for the class, obligated to ensure that they receive adequate legal representation and to otherwise protect their interests. For Weinstein, this merely formalized a responsibility that he, like Judge Pratt, had felt keenly from the beginning. This special relationship provided a legal justification for his refusal to allow the lawyers to run their own case and let the chips fall where they may, a refusal that his activist judging style would in any event have assured.

Choice-of-Law

When the Second Circuit ruled in 1980 that federal common law did not govern the Agent Orange case, it necessarily decided that *state* substantive law did. The reason was that this ruling left the federal court (the forum court) with only so-called "diversity" jurisdiction; in such a situation, the forum court traditionally must behave as if it were a court of the state in which it sits and must apply the substantive law of that state. But this left two crucial questions: *which* state's law (including not only substantive law but choice-of-law rules) must the forum court look to? And once that state was identified, *which* particular choice-of-law rules would that state's courts actually apply? Pratt had never addressed these questions, and Weinstein had managed to skirt them in his class action decision by invoking "national consensus law" (a phrase coined by Twerski).[44] Yet the answers to these questions would determine more than whether the issues were common enough to justify certifying a class action (as Weinstein had already found). More important, because the laws of certain states were very unsympathetic to the veterans' claims, the answers would determine whether the veterans had any viable claims *at all*.

In February 1984, two months after his class action decision, Weinstein answered both questions, and did so in a manner that was strikingly bold and inventive, even for him. In essence, he defined the questions out of existence: it did not matter which state's law would apply, Weinstein held, because *any* state court "would look to a federal or a national consensus law of manufacturer's liability, government contract defense, and punitive damages."[45] By a wave of his magic wand, the judicial wizard had vaporized the choice-of-law problem.

Weinstein's journey to the safe harbor of "national consensus law" was a masterpiece of judicial navigation, a brilliant tour de force. Carefully marshaling his arguments, he led a fascinating excursion through five contending schools of choice-of-law theory in order to reach his desired conclusion: that each of the theories would encourage a state court judge (which the Second Circuit's earlier decision obliged Weinstein to emulate in this diversity case) to look to federal or national consensus law rather than to the law of any one of the numerous state and foreign jurisdictions that could claim some "contacts" with the case. Weinstein's approach was entirely justified as a matter of policy and equity; on those grounds, the Second Circuit's surprising rejection of federal common law in favor of state law was utterly perverse. Reliance upon state law would prevent the use of a class action and would probably defeat many veterans' claims on purely technical grounds, such as statutes of limitations. Furthermore, a just legal system, confronted by "legally identical claims involving servicemen who fought a difficult foreign war shoulder to shoulder and were exposed to virtually identical risks," as Weinstein put it, obviously should not treat those claims differently simply because the veterans happened to move to different states when they returned.

To avoid these deplorable results, however, Weinstein had to engage in some rather fancy footwork. First he had to circumvent Judge Kearse's troublesome 1980 opinion.[46] Kearse, after all, had stated quite explicitly that the federal interest in the outcome of the case was "as yet undetermined" and that "[t]he fact that application of state law may produce a variety of results is of no moment. It is in the nature of a federal system that different states will apply different rules of law." Her decision, moreover, was the "law of the case," inexorably binding on all lower court judges, especially Weinstein. ("I keep the court's opinion by my bedside," he assured the defendants' lawyers with his bright smile.)[47]

Weinstein maneuvered around this obstacle in several ways. Playing the Talmudic scholar, he first offered a fine distinction, arguing that the Second Circuit had decided only a jurisdictional question, the scope of "arising under [federal] law," the test for the court's so-called "federal question" (that is, nondiversity) jurisdiction, and had not ruled on the choice-of-law point. Although he was technically correct—indeed, it was the jurisdictional aspect of the issue that had made it open to interlocutory appeal in 1980—the two issues were really inextricably intertwined. More important, the appellate court had decided that the federal government possessed no "substantive interest in the content of the rules to be applied," a finding that seriously weakened Weinstein's position. Weinstein was unable to cite a single case to support his distinction.

Undaunted, he then argued that the earlier finding had been overtaken by events. But these supervening events—a statement by the

Second Circuit that it had not yet been decided whether the government contract defense was governed by federal law; VA studies and activities concerning Agent Orange; and the government's status as a third-party defendant—either were misstated or were mere makeweights, essentially irrelevant to the choice-of-law question. Weinstein's imaginative effort to neutralize the Second Circuit's decision and thus gain freedom to fashion a better rule, then, was ultimately unpersuasive.

Weinstein's second stratagem was even less convincing. The laws of different states were often inconsistent on crucial issues in the case, as Weinstein's own discussion of three areas of the law (product liability, government contract defense, and punitive damages) clearly demonstrated. Nevertheless, he sought to obscure that fact by asserting that there existed among the different states a "national consensus" on a single substantive rule on these issues. In truth, no such consensus existed, especially under the novel facts presented by the Agent Orange case. His tactic was to interweave two elements—a "national consensus" on these issues and a strong federal interest in their resolution—that he must have known were quite distinct. The first, as we have just seen, simply did not exist. The second, although it existed, had already been decided (albeit perversely) by a higher court and was thus out of his hands.

Weinstein's opinion, combining prestidigitation and rank insubordination, was redeemed only by the manifest wisdom and fairness of his position. Conjure as he might, no "national consensus law" existed on these issues. Significantly, he neither cited a case establishing that it did exist nor said what the content of that law was or even how one might go about divining it. That, he coyly observed, was "a subject for another memorandum"; his own opinion was merely "preliminary" and "provisional," "a first general guide to the parties of the court's present thinking," one that was always "subject to refinement and change." (Months later, in his opinion approving the fairness of the settlement, Weinstein shored up his earlier choice-of-law approach by finding that the government contract defense not only was governed by federal law itself but preempted state product liability law.)[48]

In a stroke, then, Weinstein had accomplished three extraordinary things. He had emasculated a higher court's ruling. He had created an entirely new choice-of-law doctrine, one of infinite plasticity that he could use to shape the substantive law—and thus the outcome—

of the case. And he had practically immunized his highly questionable ruling from appellate court review. Not a bad day's work for a
district judge.

Governmental Immunity

Weinstein could work both sides of the street equally well. Only five
days before his choice-of-law decision, Weinstein had called attention
to his lowly status as a trial judge in order to rationalize his decision
to respect precedent and refrain from making new law. That occasion
was the chemical companies' request that he reconsider Judge Pratt's
1980 decision dismissing their contribution/indemnity claims against
the United States on the basis of governmental immunity. Technically, Pratt's decision remained open because he had failed to implement the decision by formally signing a final judgment of dismissal.[49]
(He similarly failed to enter a class certification order.) In the case of
the government, Pratt probably had done this for two reasons: to
facilitate discovery against it on the government contract defense and
to prevent further delay because of piecemeal appeals by the companies. The companies now argued that recent Supreme Court decisions, as well as criticism by academic commentators, had undermined
the *Feres/Stencel* immunity doctrine; it should no longer bar governmental liability for whatever the companies might ultimately be found
to owe either to the veterans or to their wives and children. Upholding the government's *Feres/Stencel* immunity as to any third-party
claims based directly or indirectly on the veterans' own injuries,
Weinstein expressed a Uriah Heep–like humility: "Perhaps a pathbreaking appellate court" might limit *Feres/Stencel* as applied to the
veterans' claims, he wrote, but "this level of the hierarchy" should
not do so.

No sooner had Weinstein uttered that familiar piety than he proceeded to violate it flagrantly. Overriding all existing precedents, including the law of the Agent Orange case itself, he went on to make
new law by upholding the claims of family members in genetic injury
cases. Family member claims for "derivative" losses (for example, for
wrongful death or for loss of support or consortium) resulting from
the veteran's injury were clearly barred by *Feres/Stencel*, and Weinstein
so held. But "direct" or "independent" claims by family members
arguably were not barred.[50] In Agent Orange, wives were claiming
that their husbands' exposure to the herbicide damaged their sperm,

causing the wives to miscarry; children were claiming that genetic damage to their fathers had caused the children's birth defects. It was these claims, first brought by the family members against the chemical companies and now brought by the companies (via indemnity/contribution claims) against the government, that the government sought to bar under *Feres/Stencel*.

Judge Pratt, of course, had decided this same issue in the government's favor back in December 1980. This was the law of the case, treated as such by all parties ever since, and Judge Weinstein was obliged to adhere to it until an appellate court reversed it or unless he could demonstrate that Pratt had clearly erred. Weinstein nonetheless approached the matter as if the slate were entirely clean, as if Pratt had never decided the question, as if the only relevant consideration were Pratt's failure to sign his order of dismissal. (In stark contrast, Weinstein's later decision on the government contract defense deferred to Judge Pratt's law of the case even as he acknowledged that Pratt's position had been "criticized.")[51]

In Weinstein's creative hands, resolution of an "open" legal question is a marvelous thing to behold; his constructions come as close to true artistry as judicial craftsmanship can. Weinstein deployed this sublime skill with special strategic urgency in treating the family members' independent claims. What was at stake for him, after all, was the participation of the government, which he considered the key to resolving the Agent Orange dilemma. (As if to dramatize the government's centrality, Weinstein during hearings assigned government counsel to the front table, which is usually assigned to the principal defendants, even though the government was only a third-party defendant that had actually been dismissed from the case.)

He began by asserting that "it is clear that a civilian plaintiff may sue for his or her own independent injuries notwithstanding the fact that a serviceman family member whose suit would be barred by *Feres* was also injured in the same incident." For this proposition he cited only two supports. The first was *Orken v. United States*, a 1956 Sixth Circuit decision in which an air force plane had crashed into a dwelling occupied by a soldier and his wife and two children, killing all four.[52] *Orken* had held only that the claim by the soldier's estate was barred by *Feres*. Although *Orken* thus could not help the family members in Agent Orange, the resourceful Weinstein stressed that the government's brief in that case had "properly conceded" that *Feres* did not bar the suits for the death of the soldier's family members. His second support was a statement in the *dissenting* opinion in *Stencel*, which had sought to draw from the majority's reasoning a conclusion similar to Weinstein's.[53] Weinstein's precedents, then, were embarrassingly weak: a voluntary waiver of governmental immunity in one case (which the court there had not even bothered to mention) and a statement by a single, *losing* judge in another. These hardly seem premises from which "clear" principles are established. But as his invocation of national consensus law in the choice-of-law opinion demonstrated, Weinstein has occasionally made even more out of even less.

The next question for Weinstein was whether the family members' claims in Agent Orange were more like the derivative claims that were clearly barred by *Feres* or more like the independent claims the government had conceded (whether "properly" or not, of course, was now the issue) in *Orken*. He correctly observed that recent cases involving genetic injury to servicemen caused by radiation or toxic substances, claims in which wives and children had complained of sperm-mediated miscarriages and birth defects, fell somewhere in between: "The claims are like the [clearly *Feres*-barred claims] in that their injury would not have occurred if not for the fact that the husband or father was exposed to the harmful substance. In that sense, the claims are 'incident to service' and the claims of the family members are 'derivative' of those of the serviceman. Like the [claims in *Orken*], however, the family members are not suing for the serviceperson's injury but for their direct injury."[54] He also acknowledged that *every appellate court* that had faced the question had held ("albeit reluctantly and with some dissent") that even these independent claims of family members for their own direct injuries were barred by *Feres/Stencel*. Nevertheless, he brushed these appellate decisions aside, asserting that none of them had "analyzed in any depth the applicability" of the three reasons underlying the *Feres* doctrine. The higher courts, in other words, had been too sloppy, a defect he would not repeat. He then proceeded to analyze the *Feres* factors as applied to the Agent Orange case.

Two of those factors—the existence of a congressionally established no-fault compensation scheme for veterans and the inappropriateness of having state law govern the relationship between soldier and government (as it must in suits under the Federal Tort Claims Act)—were irrelevant to family members' claims, as Weinstein pointed out. But even Weinstein could not dispose of the third factor, the possible harmful effects on military discipline and effectiveness (broadly understood) of so easily allowing suits on such claims. The Supreme Court had only months earlier reaffirmed *Feres*, emphasizing that this "military discipline" rationale was the most important justification for the immunity.[55] More important, the family members' claims would raise the identical issues—including the military's wisdom in using Agent Orange and the risks and benefits of alternative military strategies—that the veterans' claims would raise. These were precisely the kinds of issues that *Feres* was designed to remove from the courts.

Faced with this formidable obstacle, Weinstein resorted to a rhetorical technique he had often used to brilliant effect as a law school professor: a sequence of hypothetical questions designed to draw one ineluctably toward a particular conclusion. The problem, he began, was "one where a civilian suffers an independent physical injury whose etiology is entwined with that of a serviceman's." Again citing only *Orken* and the dissent in *Stencel*, Weinstein asserted that in that situation "the serviceman is barred by *Feres* from suing but, as the government concedes, the civilian is not. The claims of the wives and children in this litigation," he concluded, "are analytically identical to [this] group of cases."

The government, however, had conceded no such thing. The only concession (other than that in the *Orken* case, which involved only a few claims and had been decided almost thirty years before) had occurred at a hearing before Judge Weinstein two months earlier, in December, at which the judge had posed a series of questions based on hypothetical situations to the Justice Department attorney, Gretchen Witt. In the first, a serviceman on duty is driving a military vehicle whose wheel flies off, injuring both the driver and his family members, who happen to be bystanders; in the next, a serviceman's militarily implanted pacemaker explodes, injuring both him and members of his family standing nearby; and in the last, a military chemical spray causes dermatological harm to the serviceman and to his wife through sexual contact with him.

In presenting each situation to Witt, the judge stated as a *fact* that the family members could sue the government. He then asked her to articulate a principled difference between the last case (involving the spray-induced dermatological harm) and a situation in which the chemical spray causes not dermatological harm but genetic damage to his sperm, inducing the wife's miscarriage and the child's birth defect. Witt, ordinarily articulate and unflappable, obviously felt flustered and under great pressure. (The parties had not been advised that the immunity issue would even be discussed that day; Weinstein, who had entered the courtroom with several textbooks in hand, simply launched into the subject.) She first said she could not think of a difference and then said, "The difference is, in this we are dealing with a combat situation." When further pressed by Weinstein, she said, "I can't articulate a difference in principle."[56]

In his decision two months later, Weinstein tried to limit the scope of *Feres* as applied to civilian plaintiffs. Repeating the hypothetical examples, he noted that the last was identical to the Agent Orange situation, and he referred again and again to the government's "concession" that in each case, the civilian (including a family member) could sue even though the serviceman could not. "It is indisputable," he concluded, "that *Feres* would not bar the claim of a civilian who was exposed in the same manner as the serviceman" even if the two trials would otherwise be identical.

Weinstein did not bother to explain how this conclusion could be "indisputable" when each of the seven courts (six circuit court opinions and Judge Pratt) that had confronted a family member's genetic injury claim in a concrete case had rejected that claim, and when *Orken* was so dubious a precedent.[57] (Indeed, when the decision went up to the appeals court on mandamus shortly after Weinstein's decision, even the chemical companies stated in their brief that "other circuit courts have concededly arrived at a conclusion contrary" to Weinstein's, and the brief made only a perfunctory attempt to distinguish those cases, emphasizing instead that Weinstein's decision was "well-reasoned.")[58] In addition, the Supreme Court had on five occasions declined to review those decisions. Even Weinstein's own Second Circuit (which had not yet had occasion to decide a family member's genetic injury claim) had held in a nongenetic injury case involving family members that *Feres* would bar any claim "involv[ing] the same issues as if a serviceman himself sued."[59] And it was precisely this *identity of issues*, which certainly characterized the family member claims in Agent Orange, that should have been Weinstein's analytical focus and would have led him to a contrary result.

Weinstein did not bother to explain why the government, with all those strong precedents available to it, would have conceded such a point in a landmark case involving thousands of family member claims, nor did he explain why Witt's inability to conjure an immediate, articulate response to an unexpected, difficult hypothetical question (whose crucial premise Weinstein had pressed upon her as if it were a fact) should be taken as a far-reaching concession by the United States government. Certainly, the government did not so regard it.[60]

Weinstein had successfully accomplished his mission: he had dragged the government back into the case. Noting once again that his opinion was only "preliminary" and "tentative," designed merely to "assist the parties in preparing for trial," he closed by inviting the government to "renew its motion to dismiss at any time." This invitation, however, could not have been seriously intended. Indeed, when the government shortly thereafter and on several occasions asked Weinstein to reconsider or certify an immediate appeal on the issue, he summarily rejected the request; the government, he insisted, must stand trial on May 7, only two months hence, unless a higher court intervened.[61] And when Arvin Maskin, the government's lead attorney on the case, indicated that the government expected its position to be vindicated on appeal and was not preparing for trial, Weinstein shot back: "I suggest that you inform your superiors that I consider that attitude very unusual in a case where the government has a potential liability of some billions, b-i-l-l-i-o-n-s, of dollars . . . you will be part of the trial."[62] So much for tentativeness.

Weinstein's action, although welcomed by the other parties in the case, also created significant problems for them. Judge Pratt, in his summary judgment opinion nine months earlier (with almost no discussion of the issue), had found for the defendants on the first two elements of the government contract defense—that the government had established the specifications for Agent Orange and that the chemical companies had met those specifications. Bound by that decision, the parties were feverishly preparing for trial on the third element, relative knowledge. But by bringing the government back into the case, Weinstein was reopening the first two elements as well. "I myself have not been able to see how Judge Pratt was so certain about it," Weinstein suddenly interjected at a hearing on February 15. "I am going to set aside his findings with respect to that aspect of the motion for summary judgment." When the chemical companies' lawyers protested that the earlier decision was binding, Weinstein pointed out that when Pratt ruled, "the Government was going to be out of the case. The Government is now in the case. You want the Government in the case, don't you?" The chagrined lawyers, recognizing that Weinstein had checkmated them once again, responded, "Absolutely." In this way the wily judge used Pratt's dismissal of the government three years earlier in two completely inconsistent ways. The dismissal would be effective for purposes of justifying Weinstein's decision to set aside Pratt's ruling on the first two elements; it did not, however, prevent him from restoring the government as a party.[63]

On March 22 the government filed a mandamus petition with the Second Circuit. Its brief, a far cry from the typical bland government paper, contained a stinging attack on Weinstein's behavior. Beginning with the October 21 hearing, the petition argued, Weinstein had made up his mind to bring the government into the case regardless of the law; thereafter he had "gerrymander[ed] the three branches of government" to bring about a settlement and apportion damages. This, the brief said, was grossly unfair and prejudicial to the government; in reliance upon its earlier dismissal, it had conducted no discovery or trial preparation and had maintained strict neutrality as a nonparty, furnishing the parties (now to be its adversaries) with documents and witnesses that it would have withheld as a litigant. As recently as mid-December, the brief pointed out, Weinstein had conceded that he did not see how the government could legally be made a party. Yet now he had suddenly ordered it to go to trial within a matter of weeks in a complex, billion-dollar class action that had been going on for six years. Weinstein's conduct, the government asserted, set "a new standard for judicial usurpation."

The Second Circuit, however, merely slapped Weinstein on the wrist. In an opinion written by a fellow district judge from across the river in Manhattan, who was sitting by designation on the appellate panel, the court noted that Weinstein's statements that the *Feres/Stencel* rule was "unfair" in this case and that the government should be made a party to "facilitate settlement . . . would better have been left unsaid." Had Weinstein based his decision on these views, the court added, that would constitute "an abuse of judicial power." Nevertheless, it found no abuse because he had made a "reasoned analysis" of the issues in his opinion.[64] (Months later, the Second Circuit dismissed the government's full appeal, fastening on Weinstein's description of his ruling as only "tentative," which rendered it therefore nonappealable.)[65] The glitter of Weinstein's hypothetical cases and other pyrotechnics carried the day with the appellate court, blinding it to the serious analytical weaknesses and arbitrariness of his opinion and the inadmissible purpose of his decision. In a striking, lamentable reversal of the pattern of decision that had made Weinstein justly famous, he had enabled procedural form to triumph over substantive fairness.

The "Representative" Plaintiffs

At the October 21 hearing, Weinstein had mentioned that plaintiffs might have to "select a limited number" of representative cases to try "and see if there is anything to the case." (This novel approach had been proposed by another judge in an article that Weinstein had recently read.)[66] Henderson, who was responsible for preparing plaintiffs' causation case, was ecstatic: "Getting to a Brooklyn jury with three cancers and four birth defects against seven chemical companies," he recalls thinking at the time, "would have rung the bell."

Henderson grouped the veterans' claims into five categories of pathology: (1) dermatological (chloracne); (2) systemic (for example, liver dysfunction); (3) neurological (for example, peripheral neuropathies); (4) cancers (for example, soft-tissue sarcoma); and (5) birth defects. He understood representative cases to mean individuals who exhibited as many of these pathologies as possible: "Michael Ryan [the lead plaintiff], for example, had (1) and (3), and little Kerry Ryan had serious birth defects that were consistent with male-mediated genetic injury to Mike's sperm. The more 'representative' the case was in this sense, the more winnable the case became. The very low probabilities of having any one pathology in the absence of a specific causal agent, when multiplied, became a truly microscopic probability of having several of them, as our representative plaintiffs did." Henderson also believed that epidemiological evidence on soft-tissue sarcomas and lymphomas (cancers of the lymphatic system) would suffice to get them to a jury, for unlike many other pathologies linked to Agent Orange, these produced distinctive, causally traceable tumors. Finally, he intended his representative group to include several veterans who had died from soft-tissue sarcomas and other unusual cancers.[67]

Selecting the representative plaintiffs, however, was a grueling process. The lawyers (at this point, the PMC consisted only of Henderson, Schlegel, and Musslewhite) had to assemble a large number of medical records from doctors, hospitals, death certificates, and personal questionnaires. Since relatively few of the veterans were direct clients of PMC members, they had to contact each veteran's local lawyer so that the veteran could be located and examined. By December, with the help of their remaining medical experts (Dr. Epstein and the PMC had already parted ways rancorously),[68] the PMC had chosen fifty candidate plaintiffs. They had not had time, however, to refine their criteria further or to interview the individuals in depth. This last step was especially important because the representative plaintiffs must be prepared for the extraordinary rigors to which they would inevitably be subjected. They must expect hostile depositions, physical examinations by batteries of defendants' physicians, brutal cross-examination, and the constant intrusions of the media anxious to dramatize their ghastly circumstances. "This was no ordinary lawsuit," Henderson noted, "and ordinary plaintiffs might not be able to take the pressure."[69]

Weinstein's specifications made the case selection process even more difficult. He strongly resisted Henderson's position that multiple-symptom veterans were representative, fearing that they would "fuzz over the issue of specific symptomology" and confuse the jury. Then, when Henderson had pared the group down, Weinstein forced him to eliminate the death cases, an unexpected blow to plaintiffs' presentation. It would be unfair to defendants, he reasoned, to allow plaintiffs to use individuals who could no longer by physically examined or cross-examined in depositions and at trial; death cases, moreover, would exacerbate the emotionalism that would inevitably surround the trial. (Dean recalls that Weinstein barred him from using the word "poison" to describe Agent Orange in his planned opening statement to the jury.)[70] Weinstein's legitimate concerns, however, ignored the facts that many of the veterans' diseases were fatal and that tort actions, known as "wrongful death" cases, are often brought on behalf of dead individuals. To Henderson, Weinstein's elimination of the death cases was more sinister; it was an integral part of what Henderson viewed as the judge's "grand design of settlement," which demanded that Weinstein keep the PMC's expectations of recovery low.[71]

In any event, the representative group was eventually reduced to six and then, when one veteran seemed unable to endure the physical demands of depositions and trial, to five: Dan Ford (soft-tissue sarcoma), David Lambiotte (lymphoma), Dan Jordan (liver damage, chloracne, and two children with birth defects), George Ewalt (liver damage, dermatological problems, peripheral neuropathy, skin cancer, and a disabled child), and Kerry Ryan. (Henderson thought it better strategically to have plaintiffs with provable cancers than with lung cancers that might be attributable to non–Agent Orange factors.) He visited each of the representative cases and prepared them for what was coming.[72]

These five cases, of course, had to be supported by an array of expert witnesses who could testify effectively on the crucial issue of causation. Henderson wanted to use no more than a dozen witnesses, but they must be capable of speaking authoritatively about such complex scientific specialties as biochemistry, toxicology, epidemiology, internal medicine, statistics, oncology, occupational medicine, genetics, immunology, neurology, and plant physiology. They must also be able to withstand a blistering cross-examination by defendants' well-funded trial team. And Henderson needed to link generic causation to specific causation. He hoped to accomplish this through the expert testimony of Dr. Ronald Codario, an internist who had personally examined more than five hundred Agent Orange plaintiffs, and through other experts who were not treating physicians but could nevertheless testify about specific causation based on their clinical experience and on their examination of individual veterans' medical records.

Depositions of these experts, whom Henderson had interviewed throughout the country and in Stockholm and had brought together in Washington for a two-day preparatory session, did not begin until March 6 but then continued at a frenetic pace into May. During the first four months of 1984, more than a hundred depositions—usually complex and lasting several days—were taken; more than sixty related to causation. Henderson recalled this as "the most grueling period of my life; I was away from home probably 85 percent of the time. Weinstein forced us to telescope three years of normal discovery into three months." The process was especially taxing because of Magistrate Scheindlin's innovative requirement that the lawyers prepare unusually detailed "Rule 26(b)(4) summaries" of the experts' qualifications and testimony before depositions could go forward. She used this requirement to force the plaintiffs' lawyers to organize their causation evidence quickly.[73]

While Henderson, with the help of Locks and Neil Peterson, Locks's partner, was struggling with causation, Dean and Schlegel were wrestling with the question of how to prove particular defendants' liability, and Musslewhite was developing arguments to overcome the government contract defense. Each of these questions presented formidable difficulties for plaintiffs. Because of the way in which the herbicides produced by the different manufacturers had been mixed before spraying, it was impossible to know which manufacturer's product had injured which particular veteran. Several recent decisions had adopted innovative theories holding manufacturers liable in analogous situations, theories that plaintiffs hoped the court would apply to the Agent Orange situation. The enterprise liability theory, based on Weinstein's own *Hall* decision, would require plaintiffs to prove either that the manufacturers had engaged in a conspiracy of silence or that they had a duty to warn the government of dioxin's dangers and to inform it about their latest detection methodologies and had failed as individual firms to discharge that duty. Under the "alternative liability" or "market share" theory, based on the *Sindell* decision, the court might hold all manufacturers of a fungible product liable for a portion of plaintiffs' damages according to their market shares of the product or some other allocation method.[74]

Faced with an imaginative judge, the author of the *Hall* decision, Dow was especially concerned. Like Monsanto, it had produced almost 30 percent of the Agent Orange and thus stood to lose the most from any market share allocation.[75] On November 30, Dow filed a brief opposing enterprise liability and alternative liability but arguing that if Weinstein adopted the latter, he should adopt an allocation that fully took account of the "staggering" difference in dioxin content—1.3 percent of the total as against 75 percent—between Dow's product and Monsanto's. This brief triggered an angry response from Monsanto, which disputed Dow's calculations and emphasized that the manufacturers' products had been mixed together.[76] The PMC, needless to say, watched this discord with delight.

Each of these legal theories of recovery depended on evidence concerning what the dangers of Agent Orange actually were, what each manufacturer knew and when, what information it revealed to the government and when, what the government's response to their disclosures was, what the government knew on its own, and how it would have responded had the manufacturers revealed more information sooner. These liability theories were closely linked, therefore, both to the causation issue, which affected what information should have been communicated and acted upon, and to the government contract defense, which Weinstein had informally redefined to require that the government know as much as the chemical companies knew "or reasonably should have known" about the dangers.[77] Weinstein had issued no written opinions on the liability and government contract defense questions and had provided only sketchy guidance as to how he would interpret the law. The discovery process, however, had raised factual issues on these questions that seemed sufficient to take the case to a jury. And plaintiffs' lawyers felt confident that if the jury heard the case, they would win—and win big.

They were far less certain, however, whether Weinstein would allow the causation issue to go to the jury; if he did not, the case was over, at least in his court. The defendants had developed evidence that purported to show that the representative plaintiffs' diseases and deformities could have been related not to Agent Orange but to unusual family medical histories and other factors.[78] And despite the lawyers' strenuous efforts to build their causation case in the months after October 1983, Weinstein's skepticism concerning their ability to make a prima facie case on that issue, an attitude he had revealed at their very first meeting, had continued to increase.[79]

As the exhausted plaintiffs' lawyers staggered toward the May 7 trial date, they had much reason for concern. Only weeks before the trial, Frank McCarthy, appalled at the weakness of the evidentiary presentation that the PMC had put together and at the judge's low opinion of it, launched a nationwide letter-writing campaign by veterans to persuade Weinstein to postpone the trial.[80] In addition to having a number of skittish clients and a consistently skeptical judge, their case appeared, even to Magistrate Scheindlin—a close, acute, and very sympathetic observer—to be tattered and perilously incomplete. Despite the interrelationship of issues in the case, the hundreds of depositions and the defendants' countless documents had not been computerized or cross-indexed; many had still not been analyzed. Much of the critical pretrial work was done only during the last week of April and the first days of May. And much was never done; as we have seen, it was necessary to take the extraordinary step of scheduling discovery throughout the trial itself.[81]

To Yannacone, now kibitzing from the sidelines, the culprits were obvious and the remedy was simple. "The computer programs were written, the system debugged and ready for more than two years," he later recalled. "The PMC and the former Yannacone Associates before them just refused to load the data!"[82] To most other PMC-watchers, however, the problems with the plaintiffs' case ran far deeper than inadequate computerization of information. By almost any standard, their case was in serious disarray.

8

Fashioning a Settlement

FROM the moment Weinstein entered the Agent Orange case, the goal of settlement was uppermost in his mind. He had said as much to the lawyers on October 21, and those who best knew his thinking—the special masters and his law clerks—believe that purpose guided his every action in the months that followed. For Weinstein, the attractiveness of settlement had much to do with his belief that a mass toxic tort with the special problematic features of a case like Agent Orange should not be litigated, at least under traditional rules. To try such a case, he felt, would consume an almost unthinkable amount of time (he predicted a very long trial), money, talent, and social energy, and with the inevitable appeals and possible retrials, the outcome might well be uncertain for many years to come. In the end, the only people who would surely benefit from such an endless litigation would be the defendants' lawyers, who were paid by the hour. And for all his courage and independence of mind, the liberal Weinstein must have dreaded the prospect that his genuine doubts about the veterans' causation evidence might oblige him to withhold their case from the jury or, if he submitted it to the jury and the jury found for plaintiffs, he might enter judgment for the chemical companies, notwithstanding that verdict. Finally, a negotiated settlement offered the prospect of everybody obtaining something rather than one side losing everything.[1]

He was aware, of course, that earlier settlement discussions had failed. These had taken place, however, without the spur of a formally certified, notified plaintiff class and an imminent trial date. In addition, as Feinberg saw it, the new PMC did not have Yannacone's fierce commitment, born both of ideology and of more than five years' experience with the case, to go to trial in order to vindicate principle and justify past sacrifices.[2] The new PMC's lack of intimate connection to the class, as well as its more rational, detached approach to the case, would make it far more open to settlement than Yannacone had been. Punitive damages, the prospect of which (Weinstein later wrote) "makes it impossible to settle and decide these cases on any rational basis," had now been excluded from the case by Weinstein.[3] Perhaps most important, neither the government nor the court had played any role whatsoever in the earlier discussions. By February 1984, then, the time seemed ripe for a risk-taking judge to begin a new, bold effort to settle the case.

Weinstein knew he could not settle a case as large, complex, and symbolically explosive as Agent Orange without employing agents to act as eyes, ears, tongues, and buffers. He also knew that with the highly competitive, aggressive lawyers gearing up for trial, he could only brake the emotional momentum toward conflict by diverting their attention to shared goals. Convinced that unusual political skills and contacts would be essential, Weinstein turned to several Washington insiders for help.[4] As the court's use of Schreiber and Scheindlin indicated, the appointment of adjuncts to assist in managing complex litigation was not uncommon. They were frequently used (as in Agent Orange) to expedite discovery, and Weinstein had also used them occasionally in other cases to help him fashion and implement a decree.[5] The idea of appointing special masters for settlement, however, was highly unusual if not unprecedented.[6] Under the Federal Rules of Civil Procedure, only "exceptional circumstances" could justify the appointment of one special master (much less three), and the Supreme Court had interpreted this narrowly, warning against their proliferation.[7]

Weinstein nevertheless decided to proceed. In February, he told the Agent Orange lawyers that he wanted their permission to retain, at the defendants' expense, an unnamed consultant to develop a settlement strategy and plan. They agreed. Weinstein recruited Kenneth Feinberg, a lawyer in his late thirties who had been Senator Edward Kennedy's chief of staff, to develop a plan to settle the case and distribute the proceeds. Feinberg was a shrewd choice on many counts. Weinstein knew and trusted him; both had been law clerks to Stanley Fuld, a distinguished former chief judge of the New York Court of Appeals and the two men had developed an excellent personal relationship. Feinberg was knowledgeable about toxic tort litigation, having represented corporate clients in connection with the abestos problem.[8] (This might have impaired his credibility with the PMC, but apparently it did not.) Also, he had a reputation as a mover, shaker, and conciliator.

Feinberg was an engaging, histrionic talker with a thick Boston accent. He combined the self-assurance of a senator, the mind of an intellectual, and the mien of a poker player. (Chomping on a cigar, his darting eyes diminished by Coke-bottle spectacles, the balding Feinberg reminded Yannacone, who bore no love for him, of "Groucho Marx imitating Woody Allen imitating Vaughn Meador imitating Jack Kennedy.")[9] Feinberg energetically set to work and by mid-March had drafted an eighty-page settlement plan, which the judge, after making some changes, distributed to the lawyers. Perhaps not coincidentally, the PMC itself broached the possibility of settlement discussions at about this time.[10]

Feinberg's plan, which did not state any dollar amount, consisted of three parts. The first focused on the elements for determining the aggregate amount of a settlement, especially the various sources of uncertainty and the nature and number of the claims. The second discussed alternative criteria—litigation costs, market shares, dioxin content of their Agent Orange, and voluntary agreement—for allocating any settlement amount among the defendants. The third part analyzed alternative criteria for distributing the settlement fund among the plaintiff class members; these included the likelihood that particular diseases were caused by dioxin, economic need, objective disability, and priority for children with birth defects. Feinberg, who claims to have drafted the document thinking that Weinstein would not divulge it, emphasized an especially divisive allocation formula, one based on market share adjusted to take account of dioxin content. When the defendants read it, some of them, especially Monsanto and Diamond Shamrock, were concerned; they assumed that Feinberg was representing the judge's views, and they opposed this formula.[11] Nevertheless, Feinberg's settlement plan, like his distribution plan a year later, succeeded in setting the terms for the intense debates that followed.

On Good Friday, April 20, 1984, Weinstein met in his chambers with the lawyers for both sides and introduced them to his two special masters for settlement—Feinberg and David I. Shapiro.[12] Shapiro's assignment from Weinstein (whom he had never met before) was to actually negotiate the settlement (in Shapiro's unvarnished words, to "get a deal done"). For this task, he was an ideal choice. In his mid-fifties, Shapiro was a feisty, shrewd, colorful man, given to scatological stories and deadpan humor. Corpulent but fastidious, he resembled a bullfrog in a pin-striped suit. He had begun his career in an office over a delicatessen on 91st Street and Broadway; "I got my first trial experience defending whores in women's court," he fondly remembers, "before going to work for the old CIO."

During the 1960s and early 1970s, Shapiro had been celebrated by many in the plaintiffs' bar as "the father of the consumer class action"; this reflected his ingenuity in engineering massive antitrust actions on behalf of state and local governments against the drug and other industries, winning enormous recoveries for his clients and lavish fee awards for himself. He knew little about toxic tort cases and had soured on plaintiffs' class action litigation in recent years (out of disgust, he claims, with the ways in which judges set fees and plaintiffs' lawyers often receive fee awards out of all proportion to their contribution). No one, however, was more knowledgeable than Shapiro about the design, trial, administration, and settlement of complex class actions. In addition, he was an exceedingly skillful, experienced negotiator and mediator. (His bookshelves are lined with works on the subject.) "What I do best and have done for twenty years," he says, "is to get a diverse group of people to march in the same direction."[13]

A third member of the team, Leonard Garment, was assigned by Weinstein to discover what the government might be willing to contribute to a settlement, especially through VA programs. Originally, Weinstein had tapped Garment (whom he knew from Garment's service on Senator Daniel Patrick Moynihan's judicial appointments screening committee) for a broader assignment, including settlement negotiations. But Garment, busy representing Edwin Meese in connection with his nomination as attorney general, suggested that his role be limited to gathering information about the politics of Agent Orange and seeking to maximize the VA's financial contribution to a settlement; he recommended that Shapiro, his partner and Brooklyn Law School chum, do the actual settlement negotiations. ("Shapiro," he told Weinstein, "has a great talent for backing a large truck into a small space, a skill requiring brute strength, intellectual agility, and a negotiator's resourcefulness.")[14]

As a Washington insider who had been an adviser to several Republican presidents, Garment possessed unusual political credentials for his assignment. White-haired, earthy, and soft-spoken, Garment was known as a troubleshooter, a sophisticated man of sound, moderate judgment who enjoyed excellent relationships with liberal groups as well as with the Reagan administration. If friendly persuasion could tease money and programs for veterans out of the federal government, Garment was the man who could bring it off.

At the Good Friday meeting, Weinstein told the assembled lawyers to regard Feinberg and Shapiro (Garment did not attend) as his agents; he was making the masters available to help the parties reach a settlement if they wished to do so. Shapiro then took over, with a cocky, irreverent, no-nonsense style that would have seemed inappropriate in a judge. He asked the PMC members to leave Judge Weinstein's chambers so that the masters could talk to the chemical companies' lawyers. He then turned to Weinstein, asking him to leave as well. Now alone with defendants' lawyers, Shapiro asked them whether they wanted to settle. They replied that they did but that the plaintiffs' lawyers were "crazy and unrealistic." Shapiro shot back, "They probably say the same about you." Suddenly, one of the Monsanto lawyers interjected: "We won't pay a penny more than $100 million, and only if the government kicks in the same amount." At that moment Shapiro became convinced that a deal would eventually be made.[15]

But although Feinberg and Shapiro met with both sides frequently for the next two weeks, enormous obstacles to settlement remained. First, the parties' initial positions were separated by astronomical distances. Prior to this conversation, the defendants had mentioned a maximum figure of $25 million, while the PMC, which had appointed Chesley and Locks to be its spokesmen in any settlement negotiations, was talking internally in terms of a minimum of $700 million. At the end of April, the parties were still more than $250 million apart; Chesley and Locks were still demanding $360 million, while the defendants had come up to $100 million. A second problem was the internal conflict within each camp. The chemical companies were at loggerheads over whether to settle, on what terms, and how to divide responsibility for any settlement amount among themselves. The PMC, a hastily organized "rump group" (as Feinberg later described it), was divided by egos and reputational concerns and was cautious lest talk of settlement prompt a rush by plaintiffs to opt out of the class.[16]

Third, the government's role was a sticking point. After the Monsanto lawyer's outburst about the government kicking in, Garment had investigated and learned that the VA programs were in fact doing most of what the defendants had claimed the government, as the "responsible party," ought to be doing. Several days later, when the masters reported Garment's information to the defendants' lawyers, the lawyers replied, "Oh, we knew all that already. We want the government to come up with *cash.*" When Shapiro countered that the VA programs serving Agent Orange claimants were the equivalent of some $60 million a year and that realistically the government could not be expected to spend more during a time of massive federal deficits, many of the lawyers seemed impressed, and some movement occurred among the defendants.[17]

To Shapiro, the defendants' emphasis on a government cash contribution was "a dead end. You can't do a deal with the feds. They always make everything an issue of principle and precedent." But Weinstein was determined to extract more from the government. He demanded that the Justice Department state its position on the settlement negotiations he had launched.[18] Arvin Maskin, the chief Justice Department attorney on the case, has insisted that up to that point the Justice Department had no idea that settlement negotiations were under way.[19] Still smarting from the denial by the Court of Appeals of the government's challenge to its joinder as a party, Maskin responded to Weinstein on April 24: "The United States declines to attend or participate in settlement negotiations or court settlement conferences because any settlement of this case that calls for contribution by the United States is not warranted. This is the United States' firm position, and we anticipate no change whatever in any aspect of it. In view of our position, we do not object to the Court's appointment of special masters for settlement."[20]

That same day, Garment reviewed the situation in an internal memorandum, which he shared with Shapiro. Up to that point, he wrote, the government "for good technical reasons . . . has not taken this case too seriously." Its position, Garment said, ignored the fact that a long trial with the government in the dock would be, as Weinstein had put it, "disastrous politics" internationally. "The Judge has made clear," Garment observed, "that questions of etiology and causation are less important to him than these general political considerations." Weinstein was "determined to settle this case and knows it can't be done without some form of contribution by the Government." Garment then reviewed the reasons why the government should settle: "The disadvantages of stiff-arming the case in the Summer and Fall of 1984 are obvious [referring to the election campaign].

A Government settlement would undercut support for pending Federal legislation" that would establish "statutory presumptions for cases of questionable etiology associated with Agent Orange" and would increase pressure to treat other toxic substances similarly. Finally, "The judge, to put it mildly, will not be sympathetic to the Government," and public protests and an adverse jury verdict would make dismissal of the government on technical *Feres* grounds a "troublesome prospect." What was desired, Garment concluded, was for the VA to assume the cost of medical treatment for the veterans, which he estimated at under $42 million per year; it would be left to the chemical companies to pay tort awards to them and perhaps their family members "in the range of $100 million."[21]

On May 4, Weinstein tried once again to dragoon the government into the negotiations, or at least to build a record of its intransigence. Feinberg had a letter hand-delivered to Maskin "formally notifying" him that negotiations were pending, that any settlement was unlikely to involve the release by plaintiffs or defendants of their claims against the government, and that Feinberg would welcome constructive participation by the government "in facilitating and implementing" a settlement. Although Maskin claims to have never received the letter (it was misaddressed), it would not have altered the government's position.[22] Weinstein also increased the pressure in other ways. On May 2, he had rejected Maskin's repeated request that the trial be bifurcated (to enable the government to protect its statutory right, which the chemical companies did not have, to a bench trial rather than a jury trial), and that the trial also be delayed so that the government could take discovery. Weinstein instead insisted that the cases would be tried together but with respect to the government's liability, the jury would only be "advisory," a tactic Weinstein had used in an earlier case. He also ruled that the government must conduct its discovery *at night during the trial*.[23]

Although the settlement masters continued to meet with the other parties during this period, the momentum generated by the need to gear up for trial now seemed irresistible. The veterans' lawyers were thirsting to go before the jury, and the chemical companies, while always concerned about their potential liability exposure, nevertheless felt confident that the plaintiffs' already fragile case would disintegrate under the pressures of trial. Barring some new development, settlement before trial now seemed out of the question.[24]

On Thursday morning, May 3—four days before jury selection was to begin—John Sabetta, Monsanto's lawyer, called Len Rivkin, Dow's lawyer. Sabetta said that Judge Weinstein's chambers had instructed all counsel to appear at the courthouse early Saturday morning and to bring whoever was necessary to authorize settlement on behalf of their clients. The judge, they were told, would provide each side with separate rooms and would be available to them at all times. They should "bring their toothbrushes" and be prepared to stay all night Saturday and Sunday, if necessary.[25] (During a fruitless midweek meeting with defendants' counsel, Shapiro had privately suggested to Feinberg that they try to break the logjam by requiring the lawyers and their principals to attend an around-the-clock negotiating marathon that weekend. Shapiro called Weinstein to ask his approval, but the judge was in court and unavailable. Shapiro then brazenly told the lawyers what was being required of them, assuring them that Weinstein had ordered it. He quickly telephoned the judge again, this time with some trepidation. "Don't get sore, Judge," Shapiro began, "but this is what I've done and you've got to cover for me." Weinstein burst out laughing. "You tell them that that's my order." Shapiro laughed even harder. "I already did," he said.)[26]

Dean also received a call when he arrived at the Ithaca, New York, airport on Friday evening. The night before, he had flown to Nitro, West Virginia, to examine Monsanto documents and had hurriedly returned to New York, where he practiced his opening before a mock jury. Having journeyed to Ithaca for a last, brief visit to his children before the start of what promised to be a marathon trial, he now was told to turn around and appear the next morning in Brooklyn. The summons was dramatic but not all that surprising. Judges were always anxious to settle cases, especially complex ones, and many settlements were concluded only on the eve of a trial after the judge had had an opportunity to "knock heads."[27]

When the lawyers arrived Saturday morning, they found that an entire floor of the deserted courthouse had been set aside for their use. Part of each contingent went off to continue their *voir dire* (jury challenges) with Magistrate Scheindlin that had begun on Friday. Judge Weinstein, ever the innovator, had approved Scheindlin's recommendation for an extremely detailed questionnaire for prospective jurors, one that probed for bias in unusual ways. (More than four hundred prospective jurors had been called in during that week to complete the questionnaire; at a cost of over $20,000, the clerk's office, now assisted by about a dozen temporary employees, had devised a random number system to protect the jurors from intrusive press inquiries.) When Dean and his colleagues reviewed the questionnaire with jury psychologists and polling experts, they were impressed by Weinstein's acuity but distressed that the prejudices of most prospective jurors, who they assumed would favor the veterans' cause, would now be revealed. The defendants' lawyers, who thought they discerned a pro-veteran bias in the responses of most of the prospective jurors, moved to strike the jury panel, which Weinstein firmly refused to do.[28]

The masters initiated the negotiation process by meeting with all of the lawyers together.[29] In the two weeks since April 20, Shapiro and Feinberg—the "strong-arm man" and the "fine tuner" (as some defendants' lawyers viewed them)—had already done some important spade work with both sides. Initial discussions centered on two issues: opt-outs and a "structured settlement." Weinstein previously had allowed class members to file opt-out forms by April 30; less than a week later, however, it remained unclear how many had actually done so. The defendants' lawyers feared that a settlement would be worthless if a large number of veterans decided to opt out and sue the chemical companies on their own. Shapiro suggested a simple solution: the parties could stipulate that if an unacceptable number of veterans opted out, the chemical companies could "walk away" from the settlement and the trial would resume.

Although the defendants' lawyers were attracted by the idea, the PMC initially rejected it, fearing that this would weaken their hand and also give Yannacone, who was watching from the wings and could persuade many veterans to opt out, the power to torpedo the settlement and thus perhaps dictate its terms. Shapiro expressed astonishment at the lack of sophistication on both sides:

> Settlement negotiations usually pit pros against pros. Here, neither the defendants' lawyers nor the PMC seemed to have any feel for the dynamics of class actions. They failed to realize that with a class action settlement, a defendant greatly reduces and puts a finite limit on its potential liability; even if a thousand veterans ultimately opted out, they would represent a very small percentage of the class, and defendants would have substantially limited their exposure. No defendant will walk away from that because for them, exposure limitation is what the game is all about.

Shapiro eventually persuaded the PMC to go along. In his long experience with class actions and opt-outs, he told them, he had never known a defendant to walk away from a settlement; the advantages of settlement were simply too great. Furthermore, he hinted, Judge Weinstein had ways to encourage the opt-outs to return to the class and join in the settlement.

The structured settlement issue was more complicated. When the masters had met with the defendants' lawyers in late April, Feinberg had indicated that a structured settlement was possible. The lawyers had understood him to be using that term in its conventional tort litigation sense: an arrangement under which a fixed settlement amount would be paid out over many years, beginning with the date the settlement order became final after appeals were exhausted. Under traditional tax principles, a defendant could deduct the total amount of the liability from its taxable income in the first year, even though it was actually paying out only a small fraction of that amount in cash during that year. As a result, a defendant, by writing off the total liability in the first year while continuing to invest the bulk of that money at a high return over a long payout period, could actually make a profit on the transaction. (This provision of the tax code was amended in July, only a few months later.)

Although this was the kind of structured settlement the defendants thought they were negotiating, the special masters had something very different in mind; they envisioned giving the defendants a choice between paying the full amount immediately and paying on the date the settlement order became final the full amount plus interest at the prime rate, running from the date of the settlement *agreement*. Shapiro emphasized this point to the PMC at his first meeting with them in the courthouse on Saturday. Shapiro listened to the PMC's demands, writing them on a blackboard. He urged the PMC lawyers to compromise on some items even as they insisted on others. He attempted to persuade them to lower their new settlement target, which he figured to be $250 million, to $200 million plus interest running from the date of the agreement. This, he argued, would really amount to $225 million or more by the time the settlement order became final.

The special masters' structured settlement approach initially encountered fierce resistance from both sides. It would of course be very expensive for the chemical companies. First, an immediate payout would mean that they could not enjoy the use of most of the settlement amount for years to come; the present value of these funds during the interim, however, was substantial. On the other hand, if they deferred payment, the additional cost could perhaps be even higher, depending on changes in interest rates. Second, even as they negotiated, Congress was rewriting the tax law to prohibit defendants in tort cases from deducting the entire amount of a settlement during the first year unless that amount was actually paid out. (As it turned out, the Agent Orange settlement was not completed in time to qualify for the more favorable tax treatment under the old rule.) Although some of the defendants' lawyers understood the financial implications of Shapiro's proposal before the final round of negotiations began, several realized it only during the weekend; indeed, one company's general counsel became quite agitated when he learned of it only on the morning of May 7, when the settlement was announced.

The PMC's resistance to Shapiro's approach was perhaps more surprising. "They were very worried about the veterans' reactions to a settlement figure," he recalled. "They seemed willing to accept a later date for triggering interest payments by the defendants in exchange for a higher initial settlement amount, even though the combination of an earlier trigger date and a lower amount up front could ultimately net the veterans a higher recovery. They figured that the up-front amount was what the media and the veterans would pick up on."

When Weinstein came to the courthouse Saturday morning, he first brought all the lawyers together for a pep talk about settlement, eloquently appealing to their patriotism. He then spoke to each side separately. Meeting with the defendants' lawyers late Saturday morning, he gave each an opportunity to speak, but Rivkin, representing Dow, did most of the talking. Rivkin enumerated ten elements of settlement that had to be addressed. First, the defendants wanted the judge to recertify the class as (b)(1)(B) mandatory (no opt-outs permitted), thereby ensuring that any settlement would be binding on all members. If the judge insisted on a (b)(3) class (opt-outs permitted), however, defendants wanted a walk-away provision. Second, Rivkin noted that defendants wanted protection against the "tail" of the case—claims by children yet unborn and by civilians. Third, they wanted a provision that if a settlement were reached but subsequently reversed, the ensuing trial would be nonjury; if not, they argued, the publicity surrounding a settlement would deprive them of a fair trial. Fourth, they wanted the class definition broadened to include all U.S. and Vietnamese civilians in Vietnam and all spouses and children of all U.S., Australian, and New Zealand soldiers. This would bind more potential claimants to the settlement. Fifth, they wanted the settlement agreement to stipulate that Agent Orange had not caused injuries. Sixth, they wanted the judge to make a "low, fair" fee award to plaintiffs' counsel in order to discourage such suits in the future. Seventh, they wanted the settlement agreement to take account of insurance coverage triggers by requiring that claimants against the settlement fund provide detailed information on exposure, manifestation of injuries, and so on. Eighth, they wanted no payment from the settlement fund to be made until the settlement had cleared final appellate court review. Ninth, the problem of numerous opt-outs must be resolved. Finally, plaintiffs' counsel must return all documents and agree not to use them publicly.

The judge, as always, had done his homework. He immediately responded to each of these demands. He indicated that he would insist on a (b)(3) class but that a walk-away provision was possible; that the tail problem would be addressed; that the nonjury trial contingency was a "good idea"; that he would not redefine the class by sending out a new class notice but in the notice of settlement would define it to include all veterans, whether claiming injury or not; that the settlement agreement would state that causation had not been proved; that the fee award would be "reasonable"; that insurance considerations would be respected; that no payments would be made until the settlement had cleared appellate review; and that he would approve whatever arrangements the parties could negotiate about documents.

Four additional points were then raised. First, the defendants argued that they should be indemnified from the settlement fund for any payments they might be obliged to make on Agent Orange claims as a result of judgments in other actions brought by veterans in *state* courts. Weinstein indicated that he had no objection. Second, they expressed concern about punitive damage claims, to which Weinstein replied that he was not allowing such claims. Third, Weinstein read to them Maskin's letter of April 24, indicating the government's unwillingness to participate in the settlement discussions, and Feinberg's May 4 letter to Maskin, informing him that unless the government negotiated the matter with the other parties, the court's settlement order would not release any claims against it. Fourth, Weinstein indicated that if no settlement was reached, he intended to adopt the theory, long advanced by plaintiffs, that any manufacturer that knew its product would be mixed with others that might contain dangerous levels of dioxin should be treated as if its product were identifiable by plaintiffs. This was an important point; it was tantamount to ruling that as a matter of law, all defendants were potentially liable if causation could be proved.

In the early afternoon, the judge met with the plaintiffs' lawyers. He talked to them like a Dutch uncle, sympathetic but pulling no punches. He began by saying that he understood the veterans' plight and that "my heart bleeds for deformed children." Nevertheless, he emphasized, their case on causation was very weak. Even if he was wrong about that, his rulings on their behalf, such as his decisions on choice of law and class action, might well be reversed on appeal, especially by the Burger Court. He predicted that they could go broke litigating the case for several more years and urged them to take what they could get now. The lawyers then caucused again and decided to hold firm at $250 million. But Musslewhite, sensing that important money decisions would soon have to be made, telephoned Schwartz and O'Quinn, two of the financiers on the PMC, to urge that they immediately fly up from Houston to join in the deliberations.

Meanwhile, Shapiro and Feinberg were meeting with the defendants' lawyers concerning how to allocate any settlement amount among each of the companies. This question had not previously been discussed by the group as a whole. As in most multiple-defendant cases, it proved to be exceedingly delicate, perhaps the most divisive issue of all. (As a practical matter, the real parties in interest here were the companies' insurers. But although several disputes had erupted earlier between chemical companies and insurance companies over coverage and legal defense, the liability amounts being discussed, now that punitive damages were out of the case, were well within policy limits. To the present time, unlike the situation in the asbestos cases, insurance disputes have had little effect on the case. As the primary insurers demand indemnification from reinsurers, however, this may yet change.)[30]

Three contending allocational criteria were discussed: dioxin content, favored by Dow and Hercules; product volume or market share, favored by Monsanto and Diamond Shamrock; and ability to pay, favored by the smaller companies. These criteria implied very different allocations. For a company that was part of a conglomerate, for example, a small market share might be linked to a large ability to pay. Although there was substantial agreement as to the facts—the product volumes were established by government records and there was no longer any real dispute over the general dioxin content of each product—no consensus on the allocation formula could be forged. To break the impasse, one of them said, "We'll never get agreement on this. Let's let the judge do it; he's fair." Each of the companies then argued its case separately to the special masters, who agreed to ask Weinstein to make a recommendation.

At 4:30 P.M., Weinstein called in the defendants' lawyers. He told them he was recommending that the allocation, based on a combination of product volume and dioxin content, be as follows: Monsanto (29.5 percent of the volume), 45.5 percent; Dow (28.6 percent volume), 19.5 percent; Hercules (19.7 percent volume), 10 percent; Diamond Shamrock (5.1 percent volume), 12 percent; T.H. Agriculture and Nutrition (7.2 percent volume), 6 percent; Thompson Chemicals (2.2 percent volume), 2 percent; and Uniroyal (6.5 percent volume), 5 percent.

Weinstein's statement brought squeals of pain and shrieks of delight from the lawyers. The economic stakes that these dry percentages implied were enormous, even for corporate giants like Dow, Monsanto, and Diamond Shamrock; each percentage point ultimately represented almost $1.8 million of liability. After hearing his recommendation, the lawyers left the judge's chambers to confer with their clients and insurers. Rivkin, who was influential with many lawyers in the group, announced to his colleagues that Dow was prepared to agree to Weinstein's suggested allocation if the total settlement amount did not exceed $150 million and if the "structure" of the settlement—the nonmonetary conditions—was satisfactory. Monsanto, however, strenuously resisted.

Shapiro and Feinberg then met separately with each of the defendants' lawyers. Shortly after nine o'clock on Saturday evening, the settlement masters again convened the group and announced that five of the seven companies had agreed to the recommended allocation and a settlement figure of $150 million. They then departed, saying they would meet again with the lawyers on Sunday morning. When they discussed the matter among themselves, however, the lawyers learned that in fact only three of them had agreed—T.H. Agriculture and Nutrition, Uniroyal, and Thompson Chemicals, all of whose allocations essentially conformed to their share of volume. The masters, in their zeal to generate momentum for a settlement, had decided to interpret "we'll think about it" as unequivocal assent.

On Sunday morning, the weary lawyers for both sides returned to the courthouse and caucused again. Monsanto, facing the possibility that it would have to litigate against the plaintiffs alone, fell into line. The defendants agreed to accept the Weinstein allocation up to $150 million, subject to their approval of the terms of the settlement structure, and they so informed the masters. They had surmounted their most difficult obstacle, the allocation formula.

Now it was the plaintiffs' group that began to fracture. When Shapiro met with them and the lawyers repeated their $250 million figure, Shapiro shook his head. "This case won't settle for $250 million. If you insist on that, you'll lose everything." To drive the point home, he told them about a case in which plaintiffs had rejected a $100 million class action settlement offer, then had gone on to lose the case. He also pressed once again for acceptance of the lower initial amount coupled with an early trigger date for interest. Moved by Shapiro's arguments, the PMC then decided to discuss a $200 million figure. Dean argued passionately for staying at $250 million and going to trial if necessary. "Let's hurt them in front of the jury for a few weeks," he urged. "Let's let *them* bleed, let *their* stocks go down. Let's go to work for a while and talk later." The lawyers then voted one by one and approved a $200 million counteroffer; Dean was the only dissenter. Shapiro said he would try to sell their proposal and left the room. Dean, keyed up for trial and overcome by feelings of frustration and betrayal, fled to an empty courtroom, where he sobbed. "There had not been one day during the last two years when I had not thought about my opening to the jury," he recalls. "I was a trial lawyer with blue balls. I was physically exhausted, and I felt that we would not be able to go out and face our clients."

At four o'clock on Sunday afternoon, after discussing the structural elements of the plaintiffs' position, Shapiro and Feinberg returned to the defendants' lawyers and reported on each of the elements of the PMC's counteroffer. The PMC would not agree to waive a jury trial under any circumstances; defendants' insistence on a waiver would be a "deal breaker." The PMC was firm at $200 million. It would agree to the "reverse indemnification" of defendants from the settlement fund in the event of adverse state court judgments, subject to a limit of 50 percent of the verdicts up to a total of $10 million. The PMC would allow the defendants to walk away if a substantial number of class members opted out. It wanted the defendants to assign to plaintiffs half of their claims against the government. It agreed to return all documents after retaining them long enough to sue the government. It agreed to broadening the class to include civilians. It agreed that the fund could not make payments until appeals were fully exhausted but wanted reimbursement for its expenses at an early date. Finally, the PMC demanded that interest be paid on the settlement amount from the date of the agreement.

After an hour of discussion, the defendants' lawyers authorized the masters to return to the PMC with a counterproposal. If the settlement were reversed, trial would be before a jury whose findings would be advisory, not binding, on the judge. Reverse indemnification must be for 100 percent of state court verdicts up to $25 million. Defendants would not assign their claims against the government. They wanted their documents returned in one year if the plaintiffs failed to sue the government. They wanted Judge Weinstein to certify an appeal immediately on any challenge to the settlement. They agreed to allow reimbursement of the lawyers' expenses even before appeals were final. They insisted that *all* parties release each other from future claims, including codefendants and corporate subsidiaries. They insisted on detailed, insurance-relevant information on all claim forms. And they demanded a ten-year reversionary interest in any moneys left unclaimed in the fund. Defendants agreed to negotiate in the $150–$180 million range; they would not go higher so long as they remained exposed to liability to American civilians, Vietnamese, foreign nationals, opt-outs, and after-born children. But they remained divided over the question of the trigger date for interest on the settlement amount, with Dow agreeable to the earlier date and Diamond Shamrock adamantly opposed.

Before returning to the PMC, Shapiro and Feinberg conferred with Judge Weinstein. The three men sensed that the time had come to make or break the settlement. At this point, the structural issues seemed readily resolvable; only the settlement amount really divided the parties. As Shapiro viewed the situation, it would be very difficult to move the PMC away from their $200 million figure. Several factors—their belief that they could damage the defendants at trial, Dean's opposition to even that amount, and the lawyers' fear that Yannacone would denounce such a settlement in the media as a sell-out and damage their reputations—together created political tensions within the group that made further compromise unlikely. Shapiro believed that the defendants, facing the specter of trial the very next day, could easily be convinced that $200 million would be a cheap settlement; indeed, he had heard that Dow had revealed to the other manufacturers a secret study it had commissioned indicating that a jury would award far more than that to the veterans. Moreover, he strongly suspected that defendants' insurance coverage would cover most or all of that amount.

The real obstacle to a $200 million settlement, Shapiro soon realized, was not the chemical companies but Judge Weinstein. Shapiro had tried to convince Weinstein that the defendants could be pushed up to $200 million, but the judge adamantly refused. He told Shapiro and Feinberg that he was very sympathetic to the veterans and that the injuries they and their families had suffered were enough to break his heart. He censured the chemical companies for their cavalier attitudes and failure to warn the government in the face of earlier indications about Agent Orange's effects on chloracne, and he deeply resented the government's stonewalling and detachment. Nevertheless, he reminded the masters, the veterans' case was shaky on the merits. He had an obligation, he said, to the legal system as a whole, and he did not want the settlement amount to signal that the case was stronger than it actually was, thereby encouraging groundless mass toxic tort litigation in the future. All things considered, he insisted, $180 million plus interest was the fair amount.

It is not clear where Weinstein's target figure of $180 million came from. Earlier he had insisted that he would not name a specific amount until the parties' differences were narrow, but Feinberg may have discussed it with him as early as March. In any event, he almost certainly had it firmly in mind well before the weekend negotiations began. As with his May 7 trial date and his insistence that the government be brought back in as a party, he never wavered from it. Shapiro saw the matter quite differently: "As a negotiator, I did not regard any particular figure as objectively 'fair' or 'right.' Instead I was guided by the principle that the parties themselves are the best judges of what is fair, and I asked myself, 'What is the most I can get defendants to agree to without squeezing them for every last cent?' At that point in the game, that figure was $200 million. After trial began, it might be higher. But the judge's perspective was different, more principled and I respect him for it. When I later explained to Len Rivkin why the judge stuck at $180 million when he could have gotten more, Rivkin said, 'The man's too much of an idealist.' "

The masters, having been given their marching orders, returned to the PMC. Shapiro remonstrated with the lawyers, predicting that they would never get the defendants to go above $180 million. He again pointed out that the class would in fact end up with more than

$200 million. This was not alchemy, he said, but economics. He re-
minded them that there would be a time lag of two years or so between settlement and payout, and that during that time interest on
the settlement amount would accumulate; this would occur whether
the defendants put up the $180 million immediately, allowing the
PMC to invest the funds at the prime rate, or whether defendants
instead retained the funds until the settlement became final subject to
an obligation to pay interest at the prime rate from the date of settlement. Either way, the PMC could point to a fund soon to be worth at
least $200 million. The lawyers agreed to think it over.

At seven that evening, after meeting with Weinstein, Shapiro and
Feinberg conferred again with the defendants' lawyers. The masters
began by telling them that the PMC was not about to go below $200
million. When the lawyers indicated that they might increase their
offer, however, Shapiro surprised them by urging them to "stay where
you are. Let the *judge* get them off the $200 million; then maybe we
can get them to $180 million plus interest, which we can probably sell.
If you move off the $150 million figure *now*, you'll never get them off
$200 million." Shapiro then transmitted Weinstein's reactions to de-
fendants' structural demands. Specifically, Weinstein rejected an advisory jury; again said that reverse indemnification must be
negotiated; indicated that the PMC would not insist on assignment of
claims against the government; said that the class would include only
veterans, not civilians; reported that the PMC agreed to return all
documents within one year; and refused to certify an immediate appeal. He left uncertain the date from which interest on the fund
would run.

Judge Weinstein then called in the PMC and the special masters. In
a sworn statement later filed as part of a challenge to the propriety of
the settlement, Benton Musslewhite described the judge's remarks at
that meeting:

> He would say: "Now, I am not going to hold it against you if you don't
> settle. I am not going to penalize you. I am going to conduct this trial on
> a fair basis to everybody," and then came the "but" . . . "But," he
> would say, "I have carried you plaintiffs all this time. I have decided a
> lot of questions in your favor that I could have decided the other way.
> And I want you to know that at nine o'clock Monday morning I am
> through carrying you. You are on your own. I will do my duty as a
> judge."
>
>   Then a little conversation would take place and then he would come
> back and say: "You know, remember, I just don't think you have got a

case on medical causation. I don't think you have a case on punitive damages."[31]

According to Musslewhite, he and the other lawyers understood these and other remarks to mean that if they did not settle for $180 million, the judge intended to direct a verdict against plaintiffs on the causation issue at least as to the "big-ticket" claims for birth defects and miscarriages, leaving at most only the cancer, chloracne, and liver disease claims. Musslewhite, echoing others on both sides of the case, also emphasized that Weinstein exploited their fatigue and other psychological factors.

> Not only were you tired and not your usual self in terms of resistance, of having control, you know, of what was going on, but it made you feel a kind of helplessness. I mean, you are there and you have got to stay in the negotiations . . . I could see how psychologically it was affecting all the members of the committee, particularly the ones who were going to have to try the case, to get to be ready to go on Monday. So many things that we had to do, and here we were down at the courthouse negotiating this settlement on an around-the-clock basis . . . the judge wore us all down with that tactic . . . the judge made us negotiate around the clock knowing that we had a difficult time being ready for trial, we were thin on manpower, and we were working night and day to get ready, and to lose the last 48 to 72 hours just before the trial was going to adversely affect us, and we knew it. You had to be dumb not to know that. Plus the fact that it tired us and made us less resistant to pressure, and he knew that, I think.

Musslewhite hesitated to call Weinstein's tactics "duress"; instead, he testified, the judge's statements "made it clear to us where we were headed in that litigation." Weinstein, many of the lawyers felt, had somehow fixed on $180 million as the right amount and was simply immovable.[32]

Even if he had been more tractable, however, the PMC was in a poor position to defend a higher figure, for the lawyers possessed little reliable information either about the number of class members who would actually claim against the settlement fund or about the nature of their specific injuries. In some ways, the PMC's lack of information was understandable. Until May 1983, litigation of the specific causation issue was, under Pratt's structuring of the case, "three trials away" (as Musslewhite later put it); at that time, it had seemed that the group's meager resources were best directed elsewhere. In May, Pratt had deferred the trial date indefinitely, and it was only in October, when Weinstein took over, that a firm, proximate trial date had been established; even then the projected trial was only to be on the claims of a handful of representative plaintiffs.

That said, however, the lawyers' ignorance concerning the number and type of actual claims, after six long years of litigation, was significant. In April 1984, the PMC had assigned Chesley, who was then conducting preliminary settlement discussions on its behalf with the special masters, the task of compiling that information. During the first week in May, he had reported that there were about 20,000 claims; of these he deemed 3,000 to 4,000 "serious" (which the PMC took to mean claims of cancers, birth defects, and deaths). There was considerable dispute about how conscientious Chesley had been in gathering his estimates (according to Musslewhite's sworn deposition, Chesley did not even contact some of the lawyers, including Musslewhite, Taylor, and Yannacone, who had the largest number of veteran clients) and about their accuracy (by February 1986, more than 244,000 claims had been filed).[33] In any event, it is clear that on the evening of May 6, in Musslewhite's words, "nobody really knew what the real numbers were. Nobody really knew what the true medical information was on the claim and the kinds of claims and the categories of illnesses."[34]

An even more important fact, which reveals much about the peculiar nature of this sort of mass tort litigation, is that even if Chesley had made a thorough claims investigation, it is by no means obvious how he should have defined a potential "claim." Beyond the few thousand individual veterans who had actually filed suit, should the more than 100,000 veterans who were listed in the Agent Orange Registry be considered claimants? Those who suffered from a disease alleged by the PMC to have been caused by Agent Orange? And how could the "seriousness" of a claim be evaluated in the absence of the kind of detailed individualized information on medical workup, family history, exposure, and other matters that had seldom been compiled on veterans? In Agent Orange and other mass toxic tort cases in which symptoms and causation are uncertain, the true claims universe is unknown and perhaps unknowable.

After Weinstein had explained his position to the PMC, he asked each of the lawyers to give their views. Several, including Locks, Chesley, and Schwartz, indicated that they favored settlement; the others resisted. When O'Quinn, one of the Houston financiers, expressed his opposition, Weinstein told him that although he respected

O'Quinn's views, he would hold him and the others "personally responsible" if they rejected the settlement and the case went to trial: "I don't care what the committee's internal fee agreement says, I will expect you to stay with this case until the bitter end, no matter what the cost." As the PMC left Weinstein's chambers, O'Quinn was visibly upset. "I am changing my vote," he told Musslewhite. "The judge is saying that I will be personally responsible for $180 million if we try this case and lose it. He won't sit still until we settle." Although some of the lawyers understood Weinstein merely to be reminding them of the obligations of being on the PMC, O'Quinn was taking no chances. When interviewed almost a year and a half later, O'Quinn remained convinced (despite a skeptical questioner) that Weinstein was threatening the lawyers with possible financial ruin through malpractice actions by the veterans if, after rejecting settlement, they then lost at trial.[35]

Here, as at other points during the negotiations, Weinstein exploited whatever leverage he could muster over the lawyers. While not actually threatening retribution if they refused to settle, he did use the ambiguity of his roles—as mediator and as ultimate decision maker—to play upon their fears, magnify the risks, and whittle down their resistance. In such a situation, the dangers of judicial overreaching and intimidation in quest of settlement are no less real for being subtle. A well-meaning but overzealous judge may occasionally go too far and "coerce" settlement, and Weinstein himself has been accused of this.[36] To avoid this risk, some lawyers and commentators recommend that the judge who orchestrates settlement negotiations not be the one who will preside at trial.[37] Weinstein did not adopt this procedure, perhaps because familiarizing a settlement judge with the details of so complex a case would have required a great deal of time, or perhaps because he sensed that no other judge could bring about an agreement. In any event, although the line between forceful persuasion and illegitimate coercion is a narrow, ill-defined one, Weinstein does not appear to have actually crossed it.

The PMC caucused. The resisters now switched sides, and after several hours of passionate debate the group approved the $180 million figure. Only Dean dissented. Emotionally and physically exhausted and literally in tears, Dean had gone to Weinstein's chambers, where the judge, Shapiro, and a law clerk were gathered. Dean told them he opposed what his colleagues were about to do and wanted to go home and get some rest. (A momentary break in the tension occurred when a messenger arrived with Chinese food that the defendants' lawyers had ordered. Laughing, the punctilious Weinstein refused it, saying, "Do you think I'm going to accept food from lawyers?") Meanwhile, at Henderson's suggestion, the PMC had assigned Locks to make one last effort to split the defendants, offering to settle with all but Monsanto and Diamond Shamrock at the already agreed-upon amounts and allocations. Locks's overture, however, was rebuffed; the defendants would deal with the PMC only through the settlement masters and would remain united. The PMC then reported to the masters its agreement on the $180 million.

Late Sunday evening, Judge Weinstein called in the defendants' lawyers. "Here is the deal," he began, "$180 million plus interest beginning this morning." When one of the lawyers protested that this would cost considerably more than $200 million, Shapiro responded that if they did not accept this, they would end up having to pay $200 million plus interest. The judge again emphasized the costs to defendants even if their case was strong—the vagaries of a trial, the risks to the defendants of trying the case before a Brooklyn jury, the uncertainties of appellate review, the damage to their reputations that intensive press coverage of the trial would inevitably cause. Impressed by these now-familiar arguments, the defendants agreed to the amount. (According to a Monsanto lawyer, the defendants also understood Weinstein to be hinting that he would not award substantial fees to the plaintiffs' lawyers, an understanding to which the defendants attached great importance, hoping that such a stand would discourage future mass tort claims.)[38]

Only David Gross, the lawyer for the smallest of the companies, Thompson Chemicals, now equivocated. Caught between his client's general counsel, who complained that the company might not be able to afford its share if its insurance did not cover it, and Weinstein, who was impatient to conclude the settlement, Gross pressed for an escape clause. Finally, under pressure from his annoyed colleagues and the special masters, Gross agreed to submit the issues of Thompson's ability to pay and insurance coverage to the judge and to be guided by his findings. Here, as with the sensitive allocation issue, the settlement hinged on the lawyers' perception that Weinstein was scrupulously fair and their willingness to be guided by his decision when internal negotiations reached an impasse. Weinstein expressed great pleasure at their cooperation and ushered them out.

At one in the morning, only hours before jury selection was to begin,

Weinstein called the defendants' lawyers back in. He confirmed that agreement had been reached on the amount and discussed the outstanding structural issues. After a further discussion with the PMC, he called both sides in to announce that a deal had been struck. He read a document that he had swiftly drafted, which enumerated the terms of the settlement, as follows: (1) Defendants would pay $180 million plus interest running from May 7; all codefendants would release each other, their subsidiaries, and parent companies from liability to one another. (2) The settlement fund would advance moneys to pay class notice and settlement administration expenses. (3) No other distribution of settlement funds would be made until appeals from a final settlement order had been exhausted. (4) Defendants could obtain reverse indemnification for veteran opt-out claims upheld by state courts up to $10 million until January 1, 1999. (5) The class definition would be interpreted to include service people whose injuries had not yet been manifested. (6) Plaintiffs could retain defendants' documents for one year. (7) All parties reserved all rights to sue the United States. (8) Defendants denied all liability. (9) Defendants reserved the right to reject the settlement if a "substantial" number of class members opted out. (10) Any class member who had previously opted out would have an opportunity to opt back in. (11) Unclaimed funds would revert to the defendants after twenty-five years. (12) The settlement agreement was subject to a Rule 23(e) "fairness" hearing. (13) Although after-born claimants were not included in the class and could therefore sue, the distribution plan would make special arrangements to address their needs. (14) The court would retain jurisdiction until the settlement fund was exhausted.

What Weinstein read, of course, was only a statement of settlement principles. Once the deal had been cut and the media had turned to other stories, it took two weeks of intensive, often around-the-clock negotiations to hammer out and agree upon the details. Disputes were numerous and sometimes rancorous. When would the money be deposited? Would it be in cash or securities, or if securities, what kind? How would defendants' walk-away option be triggered? How would the interest rate be calculated? How would the claims of after-born children be handled? On these and dozens of other issues, Shapiro and Feinberg (who, with their assistants, would receive approximately $85,000 and $750,000, respectively, from the fund in compensation through January 1986)[39] had to instruct and conciliate the lawyers and trace with them the potential impacts of alternative formulations of each clause. This required negotiating seven or eight draft agreements, during which time the impatient judge continually telephoned—and once even visited—Shapiro's office (where the negotiations took place) to demand the final agreement. The one dispute that the masters were unable to resolve, Thompson Chemicals' ability to pay and insurance coverage, was briefed and submitted to Weinstein, who found that the company could pay and was covered. Even then, Thompson's general counsel threatened to back out until Shapiro persuaded the other defendants to reduce Thompson's share slightly—what Shapiro calls a "fuckage factor."

But on May 7, only hours before jury selection was to begin, these problems seemed too distant and difficult for the exhausted lawyers to get excited about. What mattered was the settlement, and when the lawyers murmured their weary assents sometime after three o'clock in the morning, a grinning Judge Weinstein broke out several bottles of champagne to celebrate the agreement that he had sired. After a half hour of awkward conviviality, the bleary-eyed, punch-drunk lawyers straggled out of the room. The defendants' group met briefly to sign an internal agreement specifying the previously negotiated allocation among them and to discuss the Thompson Chemicals problem further. They then informed their clients.

Most were delighted with the outcome; according to Rivkin, Dow was pleased because "the amount they had to pay in the settlement was so small."[40] (One lawyer later indicated that his client, having studied what a jury might do to it, would have been willing to settle for twice the amount.)[41] One disinterested observer who was very knowledgeable about the case had believed that the case could settle for $400 million.[42] *Newsweek,* reporting on the settlement, wrote that the defendants' lawyers "privately chortled that they had walked away after paying only "ten cents on the dollar.""[43] With their long-standing concerns about massive potential liability dispelled, all of the major defendants immediately registered gains on the New York Stock Exchange.[44]

At 4 A.M., Schlegel telephoned the sleeping Dean to tell him he need not come to the courthouse for trial a few hours later. Weinstein, his energy and steely discipline seemingly undiminished by the ordeal, capped the long evening by going to a hotel to swim his customary laps before returning home to bed.[45]

On May 7, 1975, American troops had been evacuated from Saigon. Nine years later to the day, the Agent Orange case was settled. Although no one commented on the coincidence, it soon took on a haunting symbolic significance. Within hours of the settlement, many soldiers who had served in both conflicts bitterly concluded that the settlement was an even more abject and shameful retreat than the evacuation. Judge Weinstein's masterful achievement, which he fervently hoped would help heal the veterans' wounds, seemed only to open new ones.

9

A Question of Fairness

GREAT wars are not really ended by armistices or treaties, and the Agent Orange case was no exception. The settlement turned out to be but a pause in the hostilities, and then became one more occasion for intensifying them. Now, however, the struggle was no longer primarily between the plaintiffs and the defendants, for the latter had (in Len Rivkin's words) "bought their peace." It was a conflict among the veterans, and between them and their lawyers.

The ink on the settlement agreement had hardly dried when bitter recriminations began. Frank McCarthy, who had waited patiently for more than five years to see the trial of the case that had become his life's work, entered the Brooklyn courthouse at eight o'clock Monday morning. There he was greeted by Dean and Schlegel, who informed him that the case had been settled early that morning. McCarthy recalls,

> As they spoke, I could see the reporters and the TV cameras approaching. I knew I had to make a quick decision. Until yesterday, the veteran community had been essentially unified behind the case, but now it was sure to split, no matter what position I took on the settlement. I considered the poor shape that our case was in, the poor representation the vets were getting from lawyers we hardly knew, the way Weinstein was running the case. I was under heavy pressure, but my decision was easy. When asked, I had to come out publicly in support of the settlement.[1]

The next day, McCarthy and Yannacone were waiting in the CBS studio to be interviewed about the settlement. Yannacone turned to McCarthy and said, "The word is 'sellout.'" (Dean recalls with bitterness that Ralph Nader had made the same allegation to the *Washington Post*, which asked Dean to comment. "'I want to thank Mr.

Nader for all his help these past five years,' I told them. We had never even heard from him.") McCarthy, who still revered Yannacone for his efforts on behalf of the veterans, replied, "When they fired you, we had to go it alone. They are not our lawyers. But all I know is that there is $180 million there. It ain't much but it will help a lot of my people." It was then, McCarthy says, that he and Yannacone split. "We have fought ever since. Later on, I even exploded at him in court. He is 50 percent brilliant, but the other 50 percent is bullshit. When he was our lawyer, he only told us what he wanted us to know about the case. After he left the PMC, he was irreconcilable."[2]

Needless to say, Yannacone saw the matter rather differently, as did his loyal client, Michael Ryan. Although Yannacone's comments to the press on the morning of May 7 seemed mildly supportive of the settlement, and he later stated publicly that he favored it, McCarthy asserts that some of Yannacone's close associates orchestrated a campaign among veterans to vilify the settlement.[3] Yannacone, who of course had not participated in the settlement negotiations, became the symbol for their discontent. As the PMC had rejected their leader, they would reject the PMC's handiwork. Ryan's scorn for the settlement process, and for McCarthy's support of it, remains intense even today. He recalls how he heard of the settlement: "On Sunday afternoon, the day before the settlement was announced, Gene Locks called me and asked how many birth defect children we thought there were in the Agent Orange class. When I replied that we estimated 3,000 high-verdict children's claims out there, his answer was, 'That can't be.' The next thing I know, a reporter calls me at 7 A.M. Monday morning and tells me the case has been settled. We had no say in the settlement. Is it a lawyers' case or the clients' case? McCarthy's living with a pipe dream. The veterans got nothing. $180 million won't change anything."[4]

Gradually, Yannacone's own strategy emerged for dealing with the *fait accompli* of the settlement. It can be interpreted either as simple vacillation or as calculated ambiguity. Although he was constantly critical of the PMC after October and had often seemed on the verge of advising veterans to opt out of the class, he had in fact not recommended that course during the opt-out period that Weinstein had prescribed, which ended on April 30, one week before the settlement. Now that they were safely ensconced in the class (only 2,440 had filed opt-out forms),[5] he could have it both ways; as a nonparticipant he was free to heap vituperation on the PMC, the inadequacy of the settlement, and the litigation strategy that had led to it without having to recommend that his clients forgo its benefits. And he could quite plausibly argue that his earlier advice to remain in the class was perfectly consistent with his current denunciation of the settlement. On April 30, after all, who could have predicted that the veterans would not get their long-sought day in court, that within a week their lawyers would settle the case for so little?

By not launching a formal legal challenge either to the settlement itself or to his clients' continuing, postsettlement inclusion in the class, however, Yannacone relegated himself to a bit part in the case. His role, already reduced by the judge and the PMC in October, became that of scourge to Weinstein on behalf of those veterans who continued to denounce the settlement and demand a trial. Yannacone had become, by his own account, "Weinstein's 'golem' "—a Yiddish word that Yannacone, who grew up around Jews and learned their language, defines as "someone whom you create to help you and who then grows and grows until it is out of control."[6] (It is fascinating to speculate about what might have happened had Weinstein attempted to bring Yannacone, whose credibility among the veterans was legendary, into the settlement process. Would the PMC have negotiated with him? Would the defendants have been persuaded to agree to a higher settlement figure? Would Weinstein have accepted a higher figure? Would the discussions have broken down? Would Yannacone have supported the settlement more vigorously? Close observers of the case are divided on whether these possibilities were ever real ones.)

Yannacone was not the only one in an awkward, ambivalent position with respect to the court, the settlement, and the outstanding issues in the case. With the exception of Dean, all of the PMC members had voted to accept and sign the settlement agreement on behalf of themselves and their clients. They could hardly turn around now and repudiate it, although some future developments, notably Judge Weinstein's public denigration of the merits of their case, would sorely tempt them to do so. The settlement, after all, was practically a *fait accompli* and was probably the best that they could do for their clients. In addition, a concern for their professional reputations, not to mention their haunting knowledge that Judge Weinstein would soon be deciding how much money to award each of them in attorneys' fees, demanded that they support the settlement with as much enthusiasm as they could muster. Of the major players, Ashcraft & Gerel was in the best position to vigorously challenge the settlement and Weinstein's conduct in the case as legally invalid. Although that firm had served on the PMC for six months during 1983 and although approximately half of its clients remained in the class, it also represented most of the veterans and family members who had opted out, and it had not participated at all in the settlement negotiations. Concerning the opt-outs, therefore, the firm's fees would be governed by its contingent fee contracts with its clients, not awarded by the court.[7] Even so, as we shall see (Chapters 10 and 11), Weinstein was in a position to affect the firm's fortunes through his fee award and in other ways.

Many of the veterans found much in the settlement to complain about. First, it left the veterans' claims about the chemical companies' wrongdoing, dioxin's dangers, and its responsibility for their harms unheard and unresolved. According to the terms of the settlement agreement, "the defendants deny and disclaim any liability or wrongdoing whatsoever and believe that this action is without merit."[8] For many like the Ryans, as Yannacone continually proclaimed, this defeated the central purpose of the Agent Orange case, which had always been to publicize, palliate, and in some sense justify the veterans' sufferings by allowing them to tell their story, find an authoritative explanation for their conditions, and assign moral and legal responsibility. Compared to this goal, the prospect of monetary compensation, although important, was for these veterans decidedly subsidiary. "The settlement doesn't establish the truth," Michael Ryan complained. "How am I supposed to explain to Kerry what happened to her? Where was her day in court?"[9]

In addition, although $180 million was obviously a great deal of money, the largest settlement in any personal injury case up to that time, it seemed patently inadequate in several respects. This sum was but a small fraction of what a jury would have awarded them (or so many veterans had been led to believe) and an even smaller fraction of the chemical companies' profits that had been earned at the veterans' expense (or so Yannacone had told them). If the well-publicized "ten cents on the dollar" remark quoted in *Newsweek* was to be believed, the settlement was also insufficient to deter the chemical companies from manufacturing such a product in the future. After their lawyers had taken their share (which many veterans expected to be as much as half of the settlement) off the top, what remained must then be divided among a flood of claimants far larger than anyone, including their lawyers, had predicted. And no veteran or family member would receive a penny of it until all appeals had been exhausted,[10] which could easily take more than two years. Of course, the delay in payment would probably have been at least as long even if they had won a jury verdict at trial, because of the inevitable appeals.

The settlement also threatened the organizational health of some of the Vietnam veterans' groups. "More [was] at stake here," one commentator later wrote, "than the amount of money available to compensate alleged Agent Orange victims. There [was] the symbolism of a settlement which, once again, resulted in something less than an unconditional victory for the Vietnam veterans. And there may also be a sense that with the settlement of the case there [were] no more issues to keep the Vietnam veterans' movement alive."[11]

There were other objections to the settlement, objections that might support a legal challenge to its validity. Musslewhite and Taylor, who, with the exception of Yannacone, represented the largest number of individual veterans (more than 3,000 between them), insisted that if they had known on April 30 (the deadline for filing opt-out requests) what they learned on May 7—that the class would settle for only $180 million—they would have advised their clients to opt out, many would have done so, and the settlement (which gave the defendants the right to walk away if that number was "substantial") would have collapsed of its own weight. The lawyers had not recommended that course, they said, because they had assumed they would be going to trial in a week. (Musslewhite even claims that Weinstein established the April 30 deadline knowing that a settlement might be in the offing and that once the veterans knew about the settlement figure he had in mind, a large number would opt out.)[12]

Moreover, the settlement agreement gave no indication how the fund would be distributed, other than a provision that "arrangements will be made to assist" after-born children.[13] Given the enormous range of possible distributional criteria, each with very different effects upon particular veterans (see Chapter 10), it was difficult for anyone to know how to evaluate the settlement. As Ron Deboer, a veteran allied with Yannacone, put it: "Who does the settlement affect? Veterans yet to be defined, children yet to be defined, widows yet to be defined, and compensation yet to be defined."[14] Until the distribution plan was revealed, the settlement would be little more than a pig in a poke. Shapiro, writing to Weinstein three days after the settlement, anticipated this uncertainty and counted it a virtue.

The wily lawyer therefore strongly urged the judge to say as little as possible about allocation and distribution questions until after he had held hearings on and approved the settlement. "While it is conceivable that some elements of a skeletal plan could be articulated with safety, in this case particularly 'less is more.' "[15]

Finally, Judge Weinstein and special master Feinberg began to use the postsettlement court hearings to disparage the plaintiffs' causation case publicly.[16] These remarks, which echoed what Weinstein had already told the PMC during the settlement negotiations, not only infuriated the veterans, who had a great deal of emotional energy invested in the causation thesis, but placed their lawyers in the awkward position of having to continue their initial support for the settlement despite their profound disagreement with the judge's chief reason for thinking it fair—their inability to prove causation.[17] Henderson, who was responsible for preparing the PMC's causation evidence, particularly resented Weinstein's words. The judge, Henderson points out, could easily have justified the settlement on the basis of the government contract defense or other legal obstacles to recovery, without disparaging causation. "His tactic was political," Henderson maintains, "in that it made the settlement understandable to the veterans while appeasing the defendants who demanded 'no causation' as part of the settlement."[18]

Although a settlement agreement had been signed, the class action, technically speaking, was not yet at an end. Under Rule 23(e) of the Federal Rules of Civil Procedure, no class action may be settled until the class members—who by definition are bound by its terms—are notified of the proposed settlement and given an opportunity to be heard about it, and until the court finally approves the settlement. In order to approve the settlement, the court must find that it is "fair, reasonable and adequate" in light of all the circumstances; the Second Circuit had reduced this vague standard to nine general criteria, leaving the trial court with virtually unlimited discretion.[19]

The "Fairness Hearings"

In August 1984, an extraordinary series of fairness hearings—the first nationwide hearings ever held in a class action—was conducted by Judge Weinstein in Brooklyn, Chicago, Houston, Atlanta, and San Francisco.[20] Vietnam veterans, their family members, some Red Cross civilians who had been exposed to Agent Orange, and representatives from veterans' organizations, state Agent Orange commissions, and New Zealand and Australia—in all, more than a thousand class members—came to testify, often dressed in camouflage fatigues and exhibiting severe disabilities. Hundreds more submitted their views in writing. The flavor of the testimony was captured by Judge Weinstein in a section of his September 25 "fairness opinion," in which he sought to convey "the moving sights and sounds of the hearings":

> Broken-hearted young widows who have seen their strapping young husbands die of cancer, wives who must live with husbands wracked with pain and in deep depression, mothers whose children suffer from multiple birth defects and require almost saint-like daily care, the strong men who have tears welling up in their eyes as they tell of fear that their families will be left without support because of their imminent death, the man whose mind is so clouded he must be prompted by his wife standing by with his defective child in her arms to go on with his speech, the veterans trying to control the rage that wells up within them, the crippled and diseased with running sores and green fungus growths, and the women who volunteered for field or Red Cross duty and now feel themselves rejected and sick with what they believe are Agent Orange related diseases.[21]

A variety of themes emerged from the testimony, but three stand out as especially important and expressed by almost all. First, a considerable number of witnesses bitterly denounced the insensitivity, inaccessibility, and incompetence of the VA, as well as the poor treatment dispensed in its facilities. Second, nearly every witness, including those who supported the settlement, agreed that the amount was very inadequate. For some, this was an indignity, a slap in the veterans' faces, and constituted reason enough to reject it. Others expressed the view that no amount would be adequate; some took this to imply that the agreement should be supported because the money was in hand, was better than nothing, and was perhaps a first step toward a more generous social response to the Vietnam veterans. Others saw money as no substitute for the need to expose the truth by having their day in court. Third, numerous witnesses, especially the attorneys representing veterans, emphasized that they lacked sufficient information about the settlement and about the claims of medical problems associated with Agent Orange exposure to evaluate the fairness of the settlement. More time, research, and analysis were required, they maintained, before a just settlement could be assured. A fourth theme, implicit or explicit in the comments of many veterans, was that Agent Orange had indeed caused their conditions; the only question was whether they would have the opportunity to demonstrate this verity at trial.

Those witnesses who supported the settlement, most notably members of the PMC, stressed the pitfalls that could await plaintiffs if they proceeded to trial, creating a significant risk of losing altogether. Even if the jury rendered a verdict in their favor, the litigation process would be a protracted one; many veterans could not endure such a wait, it was pointed out, and the afflicted children needed help immediately. In addition, some speakers viewed the settlement as an entering wedge in the campaign to pry open the government's coffers and assign its responsibility for the victims of Agent Orange, a strategy that Weinstein actually urged them to pursue: "Let somebody else pay the daily medical bills which will run into the billions of dollars while you use [the settlement fund] to give you leverage to make sure you get what you're entitled to."[22]

The great majority of witnesses, however, opposed the settlement. Many expressed deep distrust of the PMC's motives and maneuverings. Yannacone echoed the statements of many veterans when he testified that by settling, the PMC had missed the whole point of the litigation. Dramatizing the veterans' plight, not gaining money, had been the principal motive for bringing the case, he said, and he frequently alluded to his earlier triumph in the DDT case. Only a trial could accomplish that goal. By selling their only opportunity to tell their story to the American public, the PMC had betrayed their cause. Equally important, a trial was necessary to establish the "accountability" (or "guilt" or "responsibility") of the chemical companies and/or the government. Some of the testimony that articulated this theme— the denunciation of "sellout," "coverup," and "conspiracy"—resembled the populistic, often paranoid rhetoric of earlier periods in American history. Many felt they had been victimized by corporate greed, human experimentation, and Hitlerian cruelty, with the connivance of their lawyers and their government.[23]

By implication, at least, many posited a world in which harm of the kind that had befallen them could not possibly occur without someone being culpable; from this assumption of culpability, it was but a short step for the angry veterans to conclude that someone had intended the tragic results or were indifferent to them. For them, Agent Orange provided the crucial link that could connect this understanding of the moral structure of the world to their present sufferings. The chemical had become a scapegoat for their manifold ills, the material embodiment of their government's and society's neglect of them.

Their evocative imagery was that of innocent, unwitting victims whose honorable self-sacrifice was grotesquely mocked and debased by the self-seeking, unfeeling ambitions of the corporations and lawyers, the rich and the powerful. One witness, the anguished mother of a neurologically damaged child, warned, "Our sons and daughters shall join their mutated and damaged chromosomes with those perfect and pretty little offspring of you who went to law school or into corporate employ instead of to Da Nang, An Khe, and Quang Tri, and we shall then be vindicated when our daily existence becomes your greatest nightmare."[24] The refusals of the chemical companies to admit their guilt, of the government to admit its responsibility, and of the court to unseal the damning documents before their return to the defendants were galling confirmations of such bitter views. (As we shall see in Chapter 11, Weinstein eventually ordered the documents to be unsealed but stayed that order pending appeal.)

Virtually all the witnesses, whether favoring or opposing the settlement, expressed certain specific concerns as variations or applications of the more general themes. As summarized by Judge Weinstein, these included the need for medical and financial help for veterans and for their children born with birth defects, the need for information on possible genetic damage to veterans and their children, the inadequacy of the settlement relative to defendants' massive resources, the need for more time to file claims, and the need for further medical research on Agent Orange poisoning.

Many witnesses seemed to have a distinctive, almost religiously reverential conception of the role of courts in American society. For them, the Agent Orange case was a kind of elaborate morality play staged by the judicial system, a highly stylized contest between good and evil in which witnesses would step forward to tell their tragic stories, and the judge and jury, a modern Greek chorus, would certify the truth. The jury (to change metaphors) would dispense the justice that had so far eluded them, equalizing the odds in a world of loaded dice. Many charged that the legal system had broken its solemn promise of "a day in court." As the wife of a leukemia-stricken veteran put it, "12 objective Americans would be examining these chemical giants."[25] For them, the opportunity to tell those stories to people who would listen carefully and respond morally was what a trial was chiefly about. (Significantly, many of the veterans testifying at the fairness hearings became so engrossed in their own stories that they never got around to discussing the settlement unless prodded by Weinstein.) Later, in his fairness opinion, the judge alluded to this mythic, symbolic view of the trial. Noting that many Agent Orange plaintiffs had sued "not for money but for public vindication," he expressed the hope that the case had fulfilled a cathartic function similar to that in James Frazer's classic account of ceremonies in *The Golden Bough:* "To effect a total clearance of all the ills that have been infecting a people."[26]

Weinstein's reaction to this widespread conception of the Agent Orange case was complex, proceeding at several levels. Evincing a deep, sincere respect and sympathy for the many veterans who came before him to denounce the settlement and to demand far more radical, systematic solutions to their problems, he seldom sought to dispel their evident illusion that he was situated at some Archimedian point outside the conventional legal system, capable of effecting far-reaching changes in their lives. When their lawyers attempted to make similar points, however, he had little patience for such grandiose ambitions. For example, a lawyer who represented some 120 veterans in the San Francisco Bay area criticized the settlement for failing, among other things, to achieve the injunctive relief against the distribution and use of dioxin-contaminated herbicides that Yannacone had originally sought. Weinstein interrupted to remind her of "the limited nature of the court. It's all right for a veteran to make a statement such as that, but I don't understand how a practicing lawyer can take that position with respect to the particular litigation before me . . . It seems to me that I am entitled to a candid recognition of the limited power of the court in dealing with a matter under Article III of the Constitution."[27]

Such a response by a man with the deserved reputation of being one of the most innovative and activist district judges on the federal bench is not without irony, of course. Nevertheless, it testifies eloquently both to Weinstein's desire to hear the veterans out and his frustration at the impossible position in which their poignant but unrealistic expectations placed him. Alone among the participants, he was legally and morally obliged to be rational and hard-nosed concerning probable outcomes, even when his emotions and humanity inclined him in other directions.

The "Fairness Opinion"

On September 25, Weinstein issued his fairness opinion. His law clerks had drafted portions of it as early as February or March with the intention of issuing them as separate opinions,[28] and he had often expressed his views in open court. His conclusion was never really in doubt.

The settlement, after all, was not an agreement that the lawyers had negotiated and drafted by themselves and brought to the court for its evaluation and approval. It was in fact Weinstein's own creation in every sense of the word. If he had not contrived the settlement, by all acounts it would not have occurred when and in the form it did; indeed, it might not have occurred at all. His hand (and those of his special masters) appeared in every provision, every detail, of the document. His broad conception of the lawsuit's structure and significance, and his architectonic strategy for settling it, had guided every action and decision since October 21, 1983. He had staked a great deal, including numerous possibilities for appellate court reversal of his many innovative rulings, upon his ability to craft a settlement that would terminate the case and foreclose an appeal.

Weinstein had also invested an enormous amount of the court s resources in the effort; the special masters' fees alone already totaled hundreds of thousands of dollars and would exceed one million before the case was over.[29] He had devoted a great deal of his own time and energy to the search for settlement and had placed his considerable personal and judicial reputation on the line in extracting concessions and accommodations from both sides in the interests of securing an agreement. (Few other judicial settlements have produced a multipage spread in the *New York Times* and articles in *Time, Newsweek,* and most other major news outlets in America and abroad.)[30] He had quite literally dictated the principal terms of the settlement—the amount, the trigger date on interest, the walk away provision, the preservation of claims against the government—and had cajoled the lawyers into accepting them.

Given these firm commitments to a settlement almost entirely of his own construction, it was inconceivable that Judge Weinstein would fail to find the agreement "fair, reasonable, and adequate." In effect, he was acting as judge in what had come to be his own case insofar as the settlement was concerned. As to that issue, at least, he was plainly interested in the outcome. For this reason alone, he should have left the Rule 23(e) evaluation of the settlement to another, more detached judge. His failure to do so was a serious error in judgment, although it is difficult to imagine that another judge would not also have approved it.

In the fairness opinion, Weinstein did not attempt to appraise the settlement's popularity on the basis of the overwhelmingly negative views of veterans as reported at the hearings;[31] he stressed that "only a small fraction of one percent of the class" had testified and that "the silent majority remains inscrutable."[32] Instead, he decided to take a different tack. Enumerating the advantages of the settlement for each side and for the public, he articulated most of the same considerations he had emphasized to the lawyers in the hectic hours before May 7. From the plaintiffs' perspective, he argued, there were five crucial realities: "it was highly unlikely" that they could prove that Agent Orange caused any injuries (other than chloracne); the law applicable to the dispute was "unique" and would therefore be subject to the uncertainties and delays of appeals; there were "serious doubts about the plaintiffs' attorneys' ability to finance the litigation properly"; any recovery would not reach plaintiffs "for many years"; and an unfavorable outcome might jeopardize their position in Congress and the executive branch "which, in the final analysis, must take responsibility for the medical and other care of servicepersons and their families."

For the defendants, the settlement would curtail their enormous legal and corporate costs, relieve them of the "slight" risk of liability "with claims totaling billions of dollars," and bespeak the companies' compassion and respect for Vietnam veterans and their families. And the settlement would serve the public. In a statement that was striking in its calculated ambiguity concerning causation, Weinstein asserted that the public could now "justifiably assume, for perhaps the first time, that there is some merit to the claims of those exposed to Agent Orange that they are suffering because of their war and postwar experiences." By avoiding a protracted litigation, he maintained, the settlement would free public energies to be used in more positive ways and would economize on scarce judicial resources.[33]

If the conclusion of the fairness opinion was predictable, Weinstein's analysis was not. In some 150 pages of single-spaced, double-column pages, he reviewed each major factual and legal claim in the case.[34] Laying bare their complexity and exploring their nuances and contingencies, he went on to suggest how he would probably have decided the claims had the case gone to trial. He was persuasive that plaintiffs' case was highly vulnerable on many counts and that the case's unprecedented character created risks for defendants as well, thereby justifying both sides in preferring a settlement to the vagaries of continued litigation. But what Weinstein did not even attempt to do was to justify the specific terms of *this particular* settlement, especially the $180 million amount, which, as some defendants privately conceded and as Weinstein's special masters had informed him, was far below what key defendants were prepared to pay.

Weinstein began the opinion with a procedural history of the case. Noting his earlier choice-of-law ruling that "the states would look to federal or national consensus substantive law," he acknowledged the novelty of this ruling and the "substantial probability" that it would have been appealed and possibly reversed. As to class certification, he noted that individual class notices had been mailed on March 9, 1984 (less than two months before settlement). He failed to mention, however, allegations of serious deficiencies in his class notification order which, if true, might well have led an appellate court to invalidate his class certification and hence the settlement itself. (There was evidence, for example, that individual written notices—generally required as a constitutional matter in most previous (b)(3) class actions—were mailed to only a small fraction of the class and that at least one-third of these were never delivered; that many Australian and New Zealand class members did not receive notice before the opt-out deadline; that relatively few radio and TV stations apparently broadcast the notice; and that in many cases publication of the notice in periodicals was late, geographically confined, and ineffective. These allegations, advanced by the lawyers for the opt-out veterans, are being controverted by the defendants and PMC on appeal.)[35]

Weinstein's silence about these problems, which the PMC not only acknowledged but had stressed,[36] made his emphasis on the fact that only about a tenth of one percent of the class had filed opt-out requests seem disingenuous and misleading. In the same vein, Weinstein noted that the defendants' claims against the government were to have been tried on May 7 along with the plaintiffs' claims and that the government would have had to continue to conduct discovery during trial. But he failed to explain how the government, so recently restored as a party and having conducted *no* discovery, could fairly have been expected to defend itself under those extraordinary circumstances.

Weinstein next turned to the factual problems with plaintiffs' claims, especially the crucial question of causation. The data demonstrated that dioxin "may be highly toxic to humans," he acknowledged, but he emphasized the "[fundamental] distinction between avoidance of risk through regulation and compensation for injuries after the fact." In the latter case, "a far higher probability (greater than 50%) is required since the law believes it unfair to require an individual to pay for another's tragedy unless it is shown that it is more likely than not that he caused it."

He then reviewed the causation evidence on which the parties would have relied at trial. On August 24, 1984, at Weinstein's urging, the chemical companies had filed their fairness brief, a 300-page tome, almost all of which was devoted to the first detailed analysis of the scientific data on causation that the companies had ever submitted in the case. In view of this data and in light of subsequent events, the companies' failure to move for summary judgment on the causation issue prior to May 7 is especially striking, intriguing, and significant. After all, if the evidence negating causation was so overwhelming, why should the companies put themselves through an unpleasant, costly, and unnecessary trial? The answer, according to a lawyer for a major defendant, is that even the companies believed that such a motion would have been utterly futile because the causation issue must be submitted to the jury.[37] (That prediction by the companies makes Weinstein's decision granting them summary judgment in the opt-out cases, discussed in Chapter 11, quite extraordinary and even more doubtful.)

He began by noting that two recent epidemiological studies, the "Ranch Hand II" study of veterans who had participated in the fixed-wing spraying program, published in February 1984, and the CDC Birth Defect Study, published in August (only a month earlier), had produced generally negative findings and must be regarded as inconclusive at best. "This is not sufficient to support a recovery in tort law." As to specific causation evidence on the five representative plaintiffs, Weinstein observed, "It cannot be said without hearing the evidence that the plaintiffs could not possibly recover . . . How effective the testimony would be at trial is not clear." Nevertheless, plaintiffs had a strong incentive to settle because even if the case were sent to the jury and resulted in a favorable verdict, "it appears doubtful whether the verdict would have withstood a post-trial motion of judgment notwithstanding the verdict in the trial and appellate courts."

Weinstein then turned to what he termed the "powerful" factual evidence in support of the government contract defense; this evidence, now even stronger than when Judge Pratt had ruled on the summary judgment motions back in May 1983, persuaded Weinstein that it was "not unlikely [that] the information necessary for an informed decision on Agent Orange was readily available to the government while it was ordering and using [it]." (Here Weinstein's undeniable conclusion—that this evidence constituted a strong incentive for plaintiffs to settle—was less interesting than his subtle transformation and facilitation of the defense. According to his new formulation, the chemical companies did not need to show that the government actually knew as much as they did. Rather, they only had to show that "information necessary to an informed decision on Agent Orange" was available to the government.)

The bulk of Weinstein's fairness opinion, however, delineated the *legal* problems with plaintiffs' claims, other than those relating to class certification, *Feres* immunity, and choice of law, which had already been explored in his published opinions. He began with a very lengthy technical analysis of the numerous statute of limitations issues; for example, he considered which statute or statutes would apply to which claims during which periods, how it would be interpreted, and whether that interpretation would be constitutional. This discussion led him to conclude that the "uncertainties . . . could not finally be resolved until after trial and appeals," yet another justification for the settlement.

It is of considerable interest that after indicating that he would have applied New York's "Special Agent Orange Statute" of limitations, one that is very generous to veterans' claims, to suits by non–New Yorkers as well as New Yorkers, Weinstein added (without citing any authority or reason) that this ruling, so crucial to the veterans' hopes, "would not apply to servicepersons who have chosen not to participate in the class." Opt-outs would instead be bound by their individual state statutes of limitations, even though their cases had been consolidated in New York. This was a legally defensible position, to be sure, but seemed strikingly wooden when compared to Weinstein's decidedly flexible approach to choice-of-law doctrine only months earlier. In this move, and even more in his "classwide solution" to the indeterminate plaintiff problem (discussed below), one can discern an important, distinctive aspect of Weinstein's handling of the case: he advantaged class action claims over otherwise identical opt-out claims, apparently in the hope that this might encourage the latter to return to the class. As these examples suggest, however, Weinstein's preference went beyond merely affording the procedural advantages that Rule 23 created for class actions. He was also prepared to differentiate certain more *substantive* rights of individuals depending upon whether they joined the class or not, a move the Federal Rules of Civil Procedure explicitly warned against.[38]

He next turned to the problem of the indeterminate defendant—the inability of any veteran, because of the way in which the government had mixed the herbicides, to identify the particular manufacturer to whose herbicide he was exposed. The judge considered two possible theories for overcoming this obstacle. In his innovative *Hall* decision, he had held that "joint or parallel action" of an industry's members in creating a risk might suffice to shift to those members the burden of proving which of them had or had not caused the injury. In his fairness opinion, Weinstein stated that although the chemical companies' failure to eliminate dioxin would not create such "enterprise liability" (because that failure was not a concerted one), it might be triggered as to a particular defendant if plaintiffs could show that that company had known of the danger and had failed to warn the government.

The second theory for overcoming the indeterminate defendant problem, "alternative liability," was based on the California Supreme Court's important 1980 *Sindell* decision. This still-controversial theory imposed liability, notwithstanding plaintiffs' inability to identify the particular manufacturer whose product injured it, if plaintiffs could show that most or all of the manufacturers of a fungible product that caused their harm were before the court and that some rational basis, such as market shares, existed for apportioning damages among them. Although this theory left many questions unsettled, Weinstein correctly pointed out that Agent Orange was "a far more appealing case for the application of some form of alternative liability than are the DES cases." Here, because virtually all producers of the herbicide and all of its putative American victims were before the court, because the producers knew that their herbicides, albeit not identical in dioxin content, would be mixed together, and because each producer's market share was readily established, the theory's major disadvantage—the risk of holding an innocent defendant liable or taxing a guilty one for more of the damage than its activities warranted—was minimal.

Weinstein, however, was troubled by how these two liability theories might interact with several distinctive aspects of the Agent Orange case, especially the government contract defense, plaintiffs' duty-to-warn arguments (claiming that the chemical companies had violated a duty to warn the government of the dangers not only of their own product but of their competitors' products), and the causation problem. He did not want to adopt a liability rule that would prevent an innocent defendant, either in principle or as a practical matter, from extricating itself from the broad net that these liability theories would cast.

He solved the problem with characteristic ingenuity, modifying and melding the two theories into a new burden-shifting rule. If plaintiffs could show that any particular defendant to whose Agent Orange they might have been exposed "knew or should have known about the danger of Agent Orange, whether manufactured by it or by a comanufacturer . . . and failed to warn the United States of those dangers," then the burden would shift to that manufacturer to show that (1) its Agent Orange could not have caused the injury, or (2) the government knew as much as that manufacturer knew or should have known about those dangers, or (3) even if the government had known that much, it would nevertheless have produced or continued to purchase Agent Orange of the same toxicity as that manufacturer had supplied and would not have taken steps to reduce its hazards to the plaintiffs. If the manufacturer failed to sustain that burden, it would be jointly and severally liable with all other similarly situated manufacturers, unless it could show that it should be liable for only a portion of the damages. This novel solution to the indeterminate defendant problem differed from the solution Weinstein had devised in *Hall* and from what courts had fashioned in *Sindell* and other DES cases. The distinctive facts of the Agent Orange case demanded a burden-shifting rule "unique to this case," and Weinstein had supplied one.

The problem of the indeterminate *plaintiff*, however, could not be solved with a case-specific rule. Weinstein defined the problem as follows:

It is likely that even if plaintiffs as a class could prove that they were injured by Agent Orange, no individual class members would be able to prove that his or her injuries were caused by Agent Orange. For example, plaintiffs as a class may be able to show that statistically, X% of the population not exposed to Agent Orange could have been expected to develop soft-tissue sarcoma, but that among those veterans who were exposed to Agent Orange, X + Y% suffer from soft-tissue sarcoma. If Y is equal to or less than X and there is no meaningful "particularistic" or anecdotal proof as to the vast majority of plaintiffs, virtually no plaintiff would be able to show by a preponderance of the evidence that his or her cancer is attributable to the Agent Orange rather than being part of the "background" level of cancer in the population as a whole. The probability of specific cause would necessarily be less than 50% based upon the evidence submitted.[39]

Here Weinstein crystallized the most troublesome, least tractable feature of mass toxic tort cases like Agent Orange—the difficulty of proving specific causation of injuries that are not substance-specific.

This problem, which is considered in detail in Chapter 11, has several different aspects. First, traditional tort law doctrine requires a plaintiff to prove, by "a preponderance of the evidence" (that is, with a probability of greater than 50 percent), that defendant actually caused plaintiff's harm. Second, that "preponderance rule" is an all-or-nothing one. A plaintiff who has satisfied that standard is entitled to recover 100 percent of the damages from that defendant; a plaintiff whose proof fails to meet that standard recovers zero. In mass exposure cases in which a plaintiff's condition may have been caused not only by defendant's substance but by other sources for which defendant is not responsible (including Mother Nature), plaintiff may be able to prove, by a preponderance of the evidence, that defendant increased plaintiff's probability of contracting that condition by some amount. But unless the defendant more than doubled the risk (that is, the probability that defendant caused the harm is greater than 50 percent), plaintiff can recover nothing. These two features of the rule, the preponderance requirement and its all-or-nothing character, are aggravated by the fact that the scientific evidence required to prove causation in mass exposure cases is often inconclusive and controversial. Taken together, these features imply that tort damages will often be either greater or less than is justified by the actual risk created by the defendants, especially in mass toxic exposure cases involving conditions that may have multiple causes. If the damages are greater, then the rule will overdeter defendants' activity; if they are less, it will underdeter. Either way, society suffers—in the one case, from too little risky activity; in the other, from too much of it.

Several commentators had discussed these problems and proposed various solutions, but no court had squarely faced it before.[40] In the DES and asbestos cases, both substances caused specific, distinctive injuries, although asbestos-related lung cancer claims raised similar difficulties; the *Allen* case (decided only three days after the Agent Orange settlement), which involved soldiers' claims of nuclear radiation–caused cancers, managed to avoid the difficulty, at least on Weinstein's reading of it.[41] This problem, in short, awaited dissection by Weinstein's fertile, analytically powerful mind.

He began by distinguishing two versions of the preponderance rule in tort law. These versions differ, however, only as to the type of evidence that will support recovery. The "strong" version demands not merely statistical correlations showing a probability of more than 50 percent—that is, a showing that the observed disease rate in the exposed population was more than double the rate in the nonexposed population (the expected or background level). It also demands "particularistic" evidence that could provide direct knowledge of the causality—for example, a physician's testimony that clinical examination of the plaintiff indicates that his disease was caused by exposure to the suspect chemical or that he was exposed to unusually high concentrations of it. The "weak" version, in contrast, can be satisfied with statistical evidence alone.

Weinstein stated that the weak version of the preponderance rule should apply in mass exposure cases. This was an extremely controversial preference, for which Weinstein presented no detailed justification. Instead, he merely cited a recent law review article that asserted that particularistic evidence, because "it rests on intuitive or more rigorously acquired impressions of the frequency with which similar events have occurred in like circumstances," is no less probabilistic than statistical evidence; the article suggested that both forms of evidence are therefore equally probative. This article and argument are considered in Chapter 12.

Having embraced the weak version, Weinstein then considered a burden-shifting approach to the indeterminate plaintiff problem analogous to his solution to the indeterminate defendant problem: once plaintiffs showed, through statistically significant correlations, that the defendants had created an increased risk of injury to an identifiable population of which they were members, the burden would shift to defendants to show that they did *not* cause the injury. If defendants failed to sustain that burden, plaintiffs could recover, although their damages would be reduced proportionally to reflect the statistical probability that they, as individuals, had been injured by defendants. (This last point was not mentioned by Weinstein but seems logically required by the approach.) Here too, however, Weinstein worried about the potential sweep of such a rule. With indeterminate plaintiffs, he pointed out, a burden-shifting rule could impose disproportionate liability; for the same reason that plaintiffs could not prove specific causation (except statistically), defendants could not prove specific *non*causation and would thus be liable for all the harm.

Although Weinstein used this reasoning as the basis for moving to a classwide solution, as we shall see, his justification, the danger of disproportionate liability, is questionable. In Agent Orange even more than in the DES and asbestos cases, liability-limiting criteria—market shares, dioxin content, and the like—*were* available to protect defendants held under such a burden-shifting rule. Weinstein had, after all, used these very criteria to fashion the allocation system for defendants that led to the settlement. Nor was this merely an academic quibble; what was at stake was nothing less than the viability of *individual* actions to recover for mass toxic harms.

It is true that burden-shifting might be objectionable on a different ground—if defendants were thought to be systematically unable to discharge such a burden. But assuming the appropriateness of relying wholly on *statistical* causation evidence (an assumption that Weinstein endorsed but that I question in Chapter 12), defendants would be no less capable than plaintiffs of adducing it. By rejecting the burden-shifting approach to the indeterminate plaintiff problem and insisting instead on a classwide solution, Weinstein was not only being inconsistent. In the guise of a procedural analysis, he was making social policy of the most fundamental and, as we shall see, dubious sort.

Weinstein's classwide solution was quite straightforward, given his previous analysis: "Try all plaintiffs' claims together in a class action thereby arriving at a single, classwide determination of the total harm to the community of plaintiffs . . . The defendant would then be liable to each exposed plaintiff for a pro rata share of that plaintiff's injuries." To illustrate, he posited a case in which 10 million people are exposed to a fungible product made by ten manufacturers; the expected number of cancers of a particular type in that population is

1,000; in fact, the number of those cancers is 1,100, a statistically significant increase; and the damages average $1 million per cancer. Although the probability that the product caused any particular plaintiff's cancer is only about 9 percent (100/1,100)—far too low to support recovery under either version of the preponderance rule—a class action on behalf of all 1,100 victims, resulting in a recovery of $100 million (100 excess cancers × $1 million) would be justified under Weinstein's classwide approach, which incorporated the ideas of proportional liability and probabilistic causation. That liability would then be allocated among the ten defendants according to market shares or toxicity, and the damages fund then would be divided equally among the 1,100, giving each a recovery of about $90,000.

Complications were to be expected, of course, and Weinstein noted some of them. For example, some of the 100 excess cancers might be attributable not to defendants but to random variation; moreover, the administrative costs of proving damages might be very high. But "rough justice" was all that could reasonably be demanded in so complex an area: "We are in a different world of proof than that of the archetypical smoking gun," Weinstein insisted. "We must make the best estimates of probability that we can, using the help of experts such as statisticians and our own common sense and experience with the real universe." Furthermore, he added, the classwide solution might in fact be "the only practicable way to secure a remedy" for plaintiffs because of the high administrative costs, risk of inconsistent verdicts, and other incidents of individual litigation. "Particularly during this period of rapidly changing scientific approaches and increased threats to the environment," he concluded, "we should not unduly restrict development of legal theory and practice" by dismissing the class action.

With this analysis, Weinstein had thrust forward the frontiers of mass toxic tort law. At each point, he had manifested a general readiness, even eagerness, to abandon or adapt traditional tort rules that would otherwise bar "statistically injured" plaintiffs from recovering. Because particularistic evidence was hard to come by in mass exposure situations, he had opposed placing "too heavy a burden . . . on plaintiffs by requiring a high percentage or incidence of a disease to be attributable to a particular product." This led him to endorse the weak version of the preponderance rule, another innovation. And to overcome the indeterminate plaintiff problem, he had both rejected an individualized burden-shifting solution in favor of a classwide one and endorsed the previously untried ideas of proportional liability and probabilistic causation. Under his novel approach, not only were class actions permissible in mass exposure cases, notwithstanding Rule 23; they must henceforth be regarded as *indispensable,* at least in indeterminate plaintiff situations.

This was a pathbreaking analysis, a genuinely radical step designed to equip the tort system for service in a new, decidedly different kind of campaign. Whether Weinstein was correct or not, whether his classwide solution was truly necessary and whether it would so transform that system that it could no longer properly perform its traditional functions, are important questions, to which I shall turn in Chapter 12. For the moment, however, two points are of particular interest. First, Weinstein's flexibility and openness to change on the fundamental question of how to prove specific causation, so striking in the fairness opinion, were equally conspicuous by their absence when he later came to decide that question in the individual opt-out and civilian cases that remained. As to those cases, he now ominously predicted, "like inhibitions against dismissal . . . do not exist." Those cases are discussed in Chapter 11. Second, as with some other innovations, he took this momentous, controversial, and unprecedented approach (at least for tort law) in a *fairness* opinion. The only issue he really needed—or was supposed—to decide in that opinion was whether legal uncertainty and other factors made settlement reasonable.[42] That issue, of course, was not really in doubt (although the reasonableness of the *amount* of the settlement might be). Moreover, his approach was based on the supposition (which he had already expressly rejected) that general causation could be proved. His now-familiar gambits—making new law gratuitously and without appearing to do so, while effectively shielding his bold move from appellate court reversal—were thus very much in evidence.

The remainder of Weinstein's fairness opinion is of considerable interest, but it can be briefly highlighted. He ruled that the government contract defense must be governed by federal law, and he modified it to increase the burden on manufacturers to inquire into the dangers of their products. Also he rejected all claims of punitive damages, grounding his decision on the lack of evidence of causation or "evil motive or reckless indifference" (the showing generally required as a precondition for punitive damages). His characterization of the evidence bearing on reckless indifference, however, seems curiously misleading: "Construing the evidence in the light most favor-

able to the plaintiffs, it at best shows that the defendants should have
been aware of the dangers to servicepersons posed by the spraying of
Agent Orange in heavy concentrations and that they did not pass on
to the government information they did have." As Weinstein well
knew, however, some of plaintiffs' evidence was potentially more
damning, suggesting more than a mere failure to pass on data. Indeed, earlier in his opinion he had cited the smoking gun memorandum, observing that "plaintiffs may be able to show that there was an
understanding among the manufacturers to keep the government 'in
the dark' about the dangers." Under the law of most states, a jury that
found this kind of conspiracy of silence could properly make a punitive damage award, assuming causation was proved. (Dean claims
that according to the jury study he had commissioned, 50 percent of
the jurors would have awarded punitive damages even if that would
force the defendants out of business, and the award would have
exceeded $1 billion.) Finally, Weinstein reviewed the various existing
and proposed government programs potentially available to class
members and their families, demonstrating that program benefits
were inadequate and largely dependent upon a showing of causation.

   Weinstein concluded that based upon all of the considerations and
uncertainties he had canvassed, the settlement was reasonable and in
the public interest. Although unnecessary, even inappropriate to his
decision, the judge decided to use the occasion to moralize *ex cathedra*,
instructing the society outside the courtroom concerning its ethical
obligations to the veterans. "The government must be considered the
source of ultimate protection whether or not" causation was ultimately proved, because of its responsibility for the Vietnam War and
for the disproportionate burdens it had obliged the veterans and their
families to bear. And "the veterans' peer group that substituted school
or other activity for service in the armed forces"—many of whom
were now successful men whose "careers might have been retarded
or ended had they served in Vietnam"—should now "volunteer some
of their talents, resources, and influence" to aid the veterans. These
personal sentiments, although admirable as an expression of one's
political and moral convictions, have no place in an authoritative legal
decision.

   At the end of his opinion, he turned to the "bottom line" issue—
how the $180 million settlement fund would be distributed among the
class members. Earlier in the opinion he had sought to explain why
he was deferring preparation of a final distribution plan, and now he

laid down some general but controversial guidelines for that plan, which special master Feinberg had been assigned to develop.

In issuing his fairness opinion, Weinstein raised the curtain on the final act of the Agent Orange class action drama. Much that followed was anticlimactic. But the judge still had many surprises in store, and several important questions, especially with regard to attorneys' fees and the distribution plan, remained to be decided before the court's approval of the settlement would become final. In addition, other Agent Orange litigation outside the class action, opt-out cases that the settlement therefore could not terminate, would proceed.

10

Compensations

COMPLEX class action litigation does not arise just because a perceived injustice has occurred and a legal remedy exists. If we use a crude biological metaphor and think of such a case as an organism, we recognize that to survive and flourish, it must ingest nutrients and distribute them to the organs that need them. In the class action, this nourishment takes two forms—compensation to the lawyers, who often conceive and always direct the litigation, and compensation to the class members, in whose names the lawyers must act. Both forms are distributed by the judge, the first through his award of a "reasonable attorney's fee" and the second through his adoption of a distribution plan for the class. Characteristically, Weinstein performed these essential functions in extraordinary, even unprecedented, ways that will profoundly influence mass toxic tort litigation in the years to come.

The Attorneys' Fee Awards

Needless to say, the lawyers for the plaintiff class—the PMC, Yannacone & Associates, and the local attorneys with whom the latter had originally entered into associated counsel agreements—were vitally concerned about the counsel fees that Weinstein would award. Yet the question was of far broader significance.

Like many, perhaps most, class actions in which the plaintiffs are diffuse and poorly financed, the Agent Orange litigation was essentially a lawyers' case. To be sure, individual veterans like Paul Reutershan, Frank McCarthy, and Michael Ryan had been essential to the case's legal standing, organizational effectiveness, and moral legitimacy. But as Weinstein insisted in response to Yannacone's charge that the PMC had failed to inform the named plaintiffs about the settlement negotiations, "the nominal representative plaintiffs in a class action are only names." When Yannacone protested that "Michael and Kerry Ryan are not just names," Weinstein disagreed. "This is what Rule 23 envisions," he said. "There is no possible way for the named plaintiffs to participate in the details once the case is turned over to the lawyers." Yannacone denied this, asserting that "from January 7, 1979, to October 21, 1983, the named representative plaintiffs were apprised of every step of the litigation," an assertion that Michael Ryan now supports. (When Yannacone said this, Frank McCarthy—who was not a plaintiff but had followed the case as closely as anyone—shouted from the audience, "Victor, that's bull and you know it. That's a blatant lie.")[1]

In fact, although Yannacone *had* tried to keep Ryan generally informed, the lawyers had financed the litigation on their own—to the tune of millions of dollars in disbursements and even more in unreimbursed time[2]—and made all of the important decisions about its form and direction with little constraint or input from their class clients, almost all of whom they would never meet. As Weinstein noted in the exchange with Yannacone, this was probably an inevitable feature of complex class action litigation.

Legitimate questions can be raised about lawyers' cases of this kind, and I consider some in Chapter 12. But there can be no doubt that if mass tort (or indeed conventional tort) cases are to be brought, the chief incentive animating the private bar—the prospect of a profitable fee—must be adequate. And because plaintiffs' lawyers take such cases only on a contingency basis, the fee, if it is to produce adequate incentives for plaintiffs' lawyers, must be great enough to compensate them not only for the ones they win but also for the nonfrivolous cases they will ultimately lose. Bound up in the fee question, then, is the far larger social issue that the Agent Orange case as a whole illuminates: the role that we want private mass toxic tort litigation to play in our overall strategies of risk control and compensation.

In July 1984, Magistrate Scheindlin had invited detailed fee applications from plaintiffs' lawyers, and more than a hundred filed them.[3] Most, of course, had not served on the PMC and had played at best a marginal role. But for some, such as Yannacone and Dean, the case had demanded an enormous expenditure of time, money, and energy, had consumed a sizable portion of their professional careers, and had taken an extraordinary personal toll. For others, like the financiers on the PMC, the case had been a calculated investment, requiring their risk capital but little more. Still others, like Henderson and Schlegel, had invested much time or money or both, but only for a relatively limited period of time. For all of these men, the stakes were extremely high; their professional reputations as well as their financial well-being were on the line.

The day after Judge Weinstein issued his fairness opinion, he began hearings on the fee question.[4] Frank McCarthy, who brandished a sign reading "Not a dime! Winning is enough," urged that the attorneys receive no fee in view of the low settlement amount. Laughing, Weinstein observed that "lawyers make laws and the first law that lawyers make is that lawyers get paid first." When the judge indicated that fees would be awarded, McCarthy requested that the award be deferred until after the number of claims was known and a distribution plan was adopted. Stan Chesley, renowned among some trial lawyers as the "master of disaster" for his skill in extracting large settlements in mass tort cases, urged the court to award a "multiplier" (above and beyond an award based on time spent on the case) to reflect the "monumental result" they had achieved. Although Weinstein did not characterize plaintiffs' case as "legal blackmail" (Rivkin's epithet) of the defendants or "orangemail" (the *New York Times* editorial writer's phrase),[5] his response to Chesley chilled and astonished the assembled plaintiffs' lawyers:

> This result was not, with all due respect, due to your great legal or factual work . . . It was due to the basic problem that the defendants had in trying to get rid of a case. Had you been permitted to go forward with all your work, in my opinion, you would have gotten nothing from the case . . . Given the fact . . . that you've shown no factual connection of any substance between the diseases and the alleged cause, I do not believe it desirable to encourage cases like this with very large multipliers.

Testifying as the PMC's expert on fees, Arthur Miller, a prominent Harvard Law School professor and a friend of and scholarly collaborator with Weinstein, disagreed. "It seems to me," he said, "that this case is about as risky or riskier viewed as of July '83 [when Yannacone left the case and the PMC began to reorganize] than any case you could possibly imagine." At that time, Miller emphasized, "the game [was] going rather badly . . . two defendants were gone, depositions were not very far advanced, the group was financially overwhelmed, they could not sustain themselves . . . The case was completely shaped by the defense, so it was worse than starting at zero."

Yannacone, whose former associates were seeking an award for 44,000 hours of work plus expenses, was anxious both to dispel any suggestion that he had left the case in a shambles and to discredit the PMC's efforts. Their fee request of $26 million, he proclaimed, was "outrageous," they had taken a case that was "unique, different, unprecedented and unheard of and . . . tried to make it fit into a conventional mold," they had agreed to an "inadequate" settlement, they had failed to understand that the Agent Orange case was "public interest litigation," and hence they did not deserve any multiplier. He then lauded his own heroic exploits and those of his clients:

> Who would have expected an uneducated-in-chemistry waist gunner— door gunner, it shows you how old I am—to have guessed that 2,3,7,8 Tetrachlorodibenzoparadioxin was as big a problem as it is? Who would have expected a group of grunts from the jungle to have taken on five of the largest chemical companies in the world and beaten them? Who would have expected a country lawyer from Patchogue to have stood up in this Court four and a half years, and other country lawyers from Long Island, to have taken on the best of the Wall Street and corporate bar and held them off without any money? . . . We brought one of the largest lawsuits in the world for under a million dollars. And we accomplished our basic objective [using the court to reach "the conscience of the community"], and that's what public interest litigation is all about.

Tom Henderson testified that the PMC members took "umbrage" at Weinstein's view of their causation case and his earlier observation that they had "drilled a dry hole," to which Weinstein responded that precisely because he had the highest regard for their professional skill, "I have the absolute sense that you have done as much with this case as anyone could . . . You did an extraordinary job, but that has nothing to do with the result." (In an effort to persuade Weinstein and demonstrate the strength of the veterans' causation evidence on the record, Henderson later submitted a brief laying out the PMC's planned causation case. Here, the PMC had to walk a fine line between representing the interests of the class action clients, which now required them to support the settlement, and bolstering the claims of the opt-out veterans, which were still to be litigated.)[6]

To Irving Like, who argued that the causation case had not been in a shambles and that the court should have shifted the burden of proof on that issue to the chemical companies, the judge replied that burden-shifting would be irrelevant unless the proof of probabilities were near equipoise (fifty–fifty) and that plaintiffs' case was "not in the ball park in my opinion." Al Fiorella and his colleagues in the original Long Island consortium emphasized that their efforts had produced the foundation on which the final PMC was able to build and that most of them had continued those efforts when the new group took over. Finally, Weinstein made it clear that he would not award fees to the local lawyers whose work had not benefited the class as a whole and would not enforce contingent fee arrangements that those lawyers had with members of the class.

Although each defendant's share of the settlement obligation had long ago been fixed, and the chemical companies thus had no immediate stake in the fee award, their clients had an interest in weakening the plaintiffs' bar, and they could not resist getting in their licks. Townley & Updike, the law firm representing Monsanto, filed a combative brief attacking the veterans' lawyers, the case they had developed, and their fee petitions.[7] It was predictable that Dean and his colleagues would regard Townley & Updike's action as reprehensible, but at least one defendants' lawyer shared their view. Len Rivkin insisted that Dow had not joined in Monsanto's filing and did not agree with the *ad hominem* character of its argument. "The Wall Street boys," the Long Island lawyer said, "don't know what they are doing in trying a case."[8]

On January 7, 1985, Judge Weinstein issued his attorneys' fee decision.[9] Like so many of his rulings in the case, it was highly unconventional, bitterly controversial, and in its way courageous. He was guided by a number of convictions, some of which he had articulated in the hearings. First, he obviously felt that the Agent Orange case was not simply a high-risk case, which under conventional fee analysis would have suggested that he reward the lawyers by adding a "risk multiplier" to their time-based award; to Weinstein, its probability of success was so low that it bordered on the frivolous. Generally speaking, he wished to encourage "the legal profession . . . to think at least twice before initiating sprawling, complicated cases of highly questionable merit that will consume time, expense, and effort on the part of all concerned, including the courts, in a degree vastly disproportionate to the results eventually obtainable."

There were several problems in applying this sensible principle to the Agent Orange case. The "results" obtained, after all, had included a settlement fund whose value was approaching $200 million even as he wrote, the largest personal injury recovery ever up to that time. While it was certainly true that this figure reflected a number of factors—defendants' potential exposure to massive liability, high litigation costs, the novelty of the legal issues, defendants' concern about their public image, and especially uncertainty—that were somewhat independent of the merits of the veterans' claims, it still was not obvious how he could regard as wholly unsubstantial a case that the defendants were willing to pay an unprecedented sum to settle—indeed, a sum that some companies apparently regarded as a *bargain.* Weinstein had also conceded in his fairness opinion that, although he found the causation case unconvincing and might even have rejected a jury verdict for plaintiffs, "it cannot be said without hearing the evidence that the plaintiffs could not possibly recover."[10] Even some of the defendants' lawyers agreed that they had seen tort cases in which plaintiffs had obtained verdicts on less evidence than this, and several of his own special masters privately doubted whether he could legally take the case away from the jury.[11] Without addressing these facts directly, Weinstein asserted that "in marginal cases—particularly those in which a comparatively modest compromise settlement has been reached—many courts would conclude that" no risk multiplier was warranted.

Second, contrary to Miller's testimony, Weinstein was convinced that his policy on fees would not discourage lawyers from taking on risky cases. "There are a thousand bright lawyers out there who would jump into such a case in hopes of a one million dollar award," he would say a month later. The plaintiffs' lawyers' frantic efforts to sign up clients in the Bhopal case, he maintained, showed that his opinion had had no chilling effect. Instead, it simply meant that lawyers should consider a case carefully before jumping in. "Wouldn't you still take the case?" he asked the lawyers rhetorically. "Here you have a chance to be a hero, take on the chemical industry, make a name for yourself." Praising the American plaintiffs' bar, Weinstein asserted that it had "fully equalized the contest" and that defendants did not have any special advantage. (When Henderson, seeking a higher award, noted that he would like to know what his opponents charged "when they trudge over here from Manhattan," Weinstein responded, "They didn't trudge over here. They came in a limousine.")[12]

Third, Weinstein believed that the settlement had not come about through the PMC's lawyering skills in developing a meritorious case, which might have entitled them to a "quality multiplier." Rather it reflected other factors—the defendants' dilemma (to which he had alluded in the fee hearing) and his own and and his settlement masters' extraordinary efforts (to which he did not allude). On this point, he was almost certainly correct. Few participants in the case believe that it could have been settled before trial except by Weinstein's unique intervention; Yannacone, speaking not in admiration of Weinstein but with contempt for the PMC, said that the settlement "only reflects the judge's masterful skill in extracting money from defendants," and many subscribe to the view of one lawyer (himself a former judge) that "we'd still be in discovery if Weinstein had not taken the case over."[13] Whether it would have been settled once trial began is of course a different question.

Weinstein also believed that fee award procedures consumed a great deal of time, for which the class should not have to pay. "We're forcing lawyers to be paper shufflers and record keepers," he said, "instead of solving problems."[14] Nevertheless, Weinstein did award a 1.5 quality multiplier for several PMC members and for Like and the law professors who had assisted plaintiffs, a 1.75 multiplier for Schlegel, and (eventually) a 1.25 multiplier for Yannacone. (The chemical companies' lawyers, PMC members quipped, had already received their multipliers—to the tune of the estimated $75–$100 million or more that they had already billed their clients.)[15]

Finally, he knew that the settlement fund was woefully inadequate to the needs of the veterans and their families, and he took very seriously his fiduciary obligations to protect the class's fund, from which the fees would be paid, from the now-conflicting claims of their lawyers. He therefore scrutinized the lawyers' fee petitions with exceptional care, refusing to recognize time spent on certain activities that did not in his view "directly benefit the class as a whole." For example, time spent on PMC management and financing—activities without which no case of this magnitude could possibly be maintained—was not reimbursed. He pointedly criticized Benton Musslewhite, denigrating the quality of his work and disallowing many expenses that were "unnecessarily high in relation to their utility to the class," especially his use of "first-class restaurants and hotels and . . . courier services." (Weinstein later apologized to Musslewhite— although adding that he thought much of Musslewhite's work was unnecessary—and agreed to modify his words in the published opinion.)[16]

But it was Victor Yannacone who suffered most at the judge's hands. To a considerable extent, the wound was self-inflicted. Instead of simply submitting the required breakdown of hours and detailed description of activities, Yannacone used the occasion to settle old scores by filing confidential memoranda that had flown between him and the old consortium members, revealing the personal animosity, organizational disarray, and financial desperation within the plaintiffs' lawyers' camp.[17] In his fee opinion, the judge noted that "the greater part of his time appeared to have been spent organizing veterans." Acknowledging that "perhaps no other person has done as much as Mr. Yannacone to publicize the needs of the veterans," and that "this *pro bono publico* work was in the highest tradition of the bar," Weinstein concluded that "most of it did not directly further the class action."

Although this assertion must be understood as reflecting Weinstein's view of the merits, it nevertheless was a shocking assertion, almost a contradiction in terms. Indeed, even some defendants' lawyers disputed it.[18] Whether or not Yannacone was "a skillful litigator and orator" (as Weinstein put it), there probably would have been no Agent Orange class action to settle had Yannacone not organized the class, assembled the initial litigation team, sustained the veterans' morale, and helped his colleagues overcome the defendants' early motions to dismiss. If Weinstein meant instead that the class's interests would have been better served if no action had been brought, it is difficult to see how he could justify *any* fee award to *anybody*.

But Yannacone's hauteur in refusing to document his activities had left the judge with little choice; in that sense, Weinstein's allowance of 2,000 hours (albeit without any quality multiplier) was appropriate, if not generous. As for the $329,123 in litigation expenses for which Yannacone seemed to be seeking reimbursement (his submission was ambiguous), his documentation "range[d] from nonexistent to grossly inadequate," and Weinstein disallowed all of it, subject to reargument before Magistrate Scheindlin if Yannacone could furnish the necessary documentation. (Dean claims that he begged Yannacone to submit time records but that the vainglorious Yannacone exclaimed, "I have a quarter million slips of paper in my house and I'm not going to be subjected to this kind of abuse." When Dean retorted that Yannacone had a "death wish" and should at least do it for his deceased, beloved partner, Keith Kavanagh, Yannacone said, "I'll think about it," but failed to prepare the documentation.[19] Apparently, some others were even more distressed than he by Yannacone's inattentive behavior, albeit for different reasons; this was particularly true of lawyers whom Yannacone retained to help prosecute his fee claim.)[20]

Yannacone's explanation is more sinister. He claims that Weinstein sent Feinberg, who was then developing the distribution plan, to meet with Yannacone on the evening before the Chicago fairness hearing to persuade him to use his enormous influence with the veterans (whom Yannacone met with in each of the five hearing cities) to win their support for the settlement. "Victor," Yannacone reports Feinberg to have said, "we need your help. All you have to do is cooperate and you can become executive director of the settlement fund." Yannacone also claims that Feinberg, with the judge looking on from only fifty feet away, indicated to Yannacone that he would be rewarded or punished for his position when the judge came to award fees.[21]

Yannacone's allegations seem implausible, and Feinberg insists that he merely implored Yannacone for his help in getting the veterans' approval.[22] Yet these conflicting claims reveal a harsh reality about complex class actions, especially suits involving the kinds of issues, personalities, and political or strategic disputes that bitterly divide class members and their lawyers. In a case like Agent Orange, the judge, because he has staked his credibility on a difficult settlement or for some other reason, may acquire a strong interest in a particular outcome. It is often easy for dissidents to portray the judge in such cases as having used the formidable powers that the law entrusts to him for the protection of the class—especially control over appointment and discharge of the PMC and over fees—as instruments to gratify his desire. Such suspicions, even when unfounded, can contaminate the case, mocking the court's pretensions to justice. The significance of innuendo like Yannacone's, therefore, transcends its truth or falsity; so long as it is even entertained, it will blight the Agent Orange case.

Weinstein initially awarded fees of $7.9 million and reimbursed expenses of $1.4 million, for a total of $9.3 million, only 5 percent of the settlement amount. This percentage was far below both what the lawyers had requested and the customary contingent fee arrangements in tort cases (usually one-third recovery after trial, or a smaller percentage for pretrial settlement). It was also far below the $25.9 million ($23.5 million fees, $2.4 million expenses) that Miller had recommended for the PMC. To interested parties like Tom Henderson, Weinstein's fee award would have a "devastating" effect on lawyers' willingness to bring future toxic tort cases. He bitterly compared it to the $2 million per *week* that, according to his calculations, the chemical companies' law firms were spending on the case just prior to the settlement.

By conventional class action standards, Weinstein's fee award was in fact extremely low. This reflected, however, not the vindictiveness attributed to him by some of the lawyers but his conviction that plaintiffs had no case, that such cases should be discouraged in the future, and that he, and not the PMC, had really effected the settlement. The *New York Times*, in an unusually hard-hitting editorial, applauded Weinstein's low fee awards as a needed stand against the lawyers' tactic of "orangemail."[23] (The "lowness" of the award, of course, is in the eye of the beholder. Yannacone contended that it was more than the PMC deserved.[24] And Dean, who came out relatively well, complained good-naturedly several days after having been awarded $1.34 million in fees, $128,000 in disbursements, and, rarer still, a commendation by this most demanding of judges for his "extraordinary level of skill and excellence." Dean, pointing out that he had lost his marriage, his health, and at least $40,000 in undocumented expenses, remarked, "But how can you tell the man on the street that $1.34 million isn't a lot of money?")[25]

Weinstein indicated that any disgruntled attorneys might present their fee grievances, with additional documentation, to Magistrate Scheindlin, and many of them did so. On May 30, 1985, Scheindlin submitted her report to Weinstein recommending a number of changes, and on June 18 Weinstein issued his final fee opinion. Two decisions were of particular interest. First, Scheindlin recommended that Ashcraft & Gerel receive a *negative* quality multiplier, and Weinstein agreed, stating that the firm's "refusal to participate in the case except on its own terms and withdrawal from an active role adversely affected the interests of the class." Against that reduced fee, he now decided to offset the "free rider" benefits on discovery materials that the firm had enjoyed at the expense of the lawyers for the class, leaving it with no fee award. (The firm was granted reimbursement for expenses.) Second, while recognizing that Yannacone had spent far more on the case, he allowed him an additional $100,000 in expenses—"the minimum sum that must have been expended to benefit the class"—"despite his failure to submit organized documentation in a form permitting effective review by the court." Scheindlin also recommended a 1.25 quality multiplier on Yannacone's fee award and a small increase in his allowable hours, which Weinstein affirmed without discussion. As a result of all of the changes, the total amount awarded to plaintiffs' lawyers was $10.7 million, still a very low award by conventional standards.[26]

A final significant aspect of Weinstein's initial fee opinion concerned his review of the PMC's internal fee-splitting agreement.[27] The initial arrangement, signed during the group's most financially desperate hours, was described in Chapter 7; under its terms (in Weinstein's words), "those who advanced money would be advantaged to an extraordinary degree over those who gave their time and skill to the enterprise." The arrangement raised a number of important and little-explored legal and ethical issues. First, this "banker's approach" (as Sol Schreiber calls it) might amount to champerty (the fomenting and maintenance by lawyers of litigation in which they have a proprietary interest), a practice that the courts have long regarded as unethical and illegal.[28]

Second, as noted in Chapter 7, the arrangement created the potential for serious conflicts of interest between the financiers and the litigators on the PMC and exacerbated similar conflicts between the lawyers and their clients. A financier who knows that he will receive a profitable return on his investment "off the top" of any fee award has a strong incentive to settle the case quickly, even if the settlement amount is far below what might be obtained by holding out for a higher figure or by proceeding to trial (at the risk of losing everything). By the same token, a litigator who knows that such a settlement will siphon off the bulk of the fee award for the financiers, leaving relatively little to be divided up among the litigators, has a strong incentive to resist such a settlement. The clients' interests may well be lost in the crossfire. In such a situation mistrust flourishes; for example, some saw Chesley's eagerness to lead the settlement talks, his readiness to compromise at the $180 million figure, his assurance that even with a very small fee award he would receive a quick $600,000 on his $200,000 investment, as predictable signs of this logic at work. (Also contributing to these suspicions was Chesley's well-established reputation for settling huge class action cases, securing handsome fees in the process, and Musslewhite's allegation that Chesley had represented one of the defendants' excess insurance carriers.)[29]

Third, the PMC agreement placed the court in the awkward position of awarding fees that it knew would actually be allocated among the lawyers in an entirely different manner and without regard to the traditional, legally sanctioned criteria—work performed, professional value conferred, or responsibility assumed.

Weinstein, who learned of this agreement in the late summer of 1984, was mindful of these problems. He informed the PMC members through Chesley that unless they amended their fee agreement, he would nullify it. The financiers, who desperately wanted to preserve as much of it as possible, persuaded the others to modify it, and on December 13, 1984, the PMC executed an amended agreement, which was to be retroactive to October 1, 1983. The "off the top" provision was retained—indeed, the amount that each financier might receive was increased to $750,000 (his $250,000 expenses contribution multiplied by three)—but this advantage was extended to the others (Dean, Schlegel, and Musslewhite), albeit at a lower amount ($50,000 expenses each, multiplied by three). And instead of the percentage allocation specified for the remainder of the award, the new arrangement would divide the fees remaining after the off-the-top deductions according to the proportion that each lawyer's fee award bore to the total fee award.[30]

In his initial fee opinion, Weinstein, although clearly troubled by this renegotiated agreement, decided not to disturb it. The class would not be affected, he reasoned; only the litigators would be taxed. Furthermore, "law is a business," and lawyers should not ordinarily look to the courts to second-guess their financial decisions, especially when the litigation might not have been funded without such an agreement. Finally, no one had yet challenged it, and the judge was not going to decide so novel a question on a hypothetical basis.[31]

This last reason was obviated in May 1985 when Dean moved to invalidate the new agreement. Conceding that he had not signed it under duress or ignorance, he pointed out that under its terms he would receive $331,000 rather than the $1.34 million that the court had awarded him, a diminution of more than $1 million, or 75 percent of his fee; Schlegel's reduction would be more than $530,000 and Musslewhite's more than $150,000. In contrast, Schwartz and O'Quinn would receive $475,000 more and $426,000 more, respectively, than the court had awarded them. Dean, the PMC's chief counsel, would receive an effective hourly rate of $55.62, while Schwartz, essentially a passive investor, would receive more than $1,700 per hour. This arrangement, Dean argued, constituted unethical fee-splitting, disproportionate to the services performed and responsibility assumed, and champerty; it almost amounted to a usurious loan.[32]

Dean's arguments have some force, yet the ethical strictures they embody seem curiously anachronistic, quaint reminders of bygone attitudes toward the social functions of adjudication. The legal system cannot have it both ways. If it desires the end, then it must desire (or at least accept) the only practical means to that end. If it wishes to encourage so-called public interest tort litigation on behalf of diffuse, poorly financed interests over extremely complex issues of scientific or technical uncertainty, then it must either transform the government into a tort litigator on behalf of these interests (a solution with enormous problems of its own), or it must countenance, indeed welcome, private arrangements for securing the resources necessary for effectively prosecuting such cases. The truth is that in the fall of 1983, if the Agent Orange litigation was to go forward, the resources of the financiers were desperately needed; it is no exaggeration to say that at that critical moment and thereafter, they were needed far more than the services of the chief trial counsel, valuable as his services were.[33] The otherwise grotesque imbalance revealed by Dean's comparisons reflected the relative value that their money and his services had for the survival of the case at that point, a value Dean obviously appreciated when he signed the agreement. Although the opportunism of investors is not a pretty or edifying sight, the prospect of meritorious cases failing for want of resources is even less appealing. Any set of principles that affirms the importance of litigating very costly cases while denying the means for doing so seems more hypocritical than ethical, more delusive than just.

On June 27, Weinstein rejected Dean's challenge to the agreement. After discussing the competing considerations, the judge chose to address the ethical problems case by case rather than announce any general rule. In this case, he observed, any conflict of interest and incentives to settle prematurely were purely hypothetical, for he had found the settlement to be fair and in the best interests of the class. In the future, however, lawyers would be required to disclose to the court the existence and terms of such a fee-sharing arrangement, so that the court could protect the class—perhaps by requiring modifications, reconsidering class certification, or notifying the class—and the lawyers could proceed accordingly.[34]

Weinstein's initial fee opinion had brought the Agent Orange class action to a close at the trial court level. He wrote there that although no distribution plan had been issued, preliminary discussions persuaded him that "a viable plan for distribution of the fund is possible. Accordingly, the settlement is approved now. This action will permit prompt appeals from this judgment while a final plan for distribution, after hearings, is developed."[35] Musslewhite and Taylor each filed lengthy motions asking Weinstein to reconsider his approval of the settlement. (Musslewhite, having decided that no PMC member could attack the settlement without triggering a conflict of interest, had resigned from the PMC in late January.) They supported their arguments on the basis of, among other things, sworn depositions by Yannacone and Musslewhite. There, the lawyers alleged the class members' ignorance about the settlement negotiations, the incompetence and conflicts of interest of certain PMC lawyers, overreaching by the judge, a possible conflict of interest on Chesley's part, and misunderstandings and mistaken assumptions concerning the settlement that had distorted the judgments of all parties. These errors especially concerned the number and nature of potential claims and the likelihood that plaintiffs could have prevailed at trial and on appeal.[36] But the judge had heard and rejected these arguments before, and the motions were doomed. On March 18, 1985, Weinstein denied them from the bench.[37]

Nevertheless, the farrago of criticisms of the settlement process leveled by Musslewhite and Taylor contained several that should have been genuinely troubling. Two, relating to alleged deficiencies in the class notice and the substantial opposition to the settlement among the veterans, were discussed earlier. Another concerned the allegation that the settlement had been concluded with little knowledge of how many claims existed and what types of injuries were alleged. Because of Chesley's superficial inquiries (see Chapter 8), Musslewhite and Taylor maintained, the only firm figures that the PMC and court possessed were the number of persons named in the 600 or so individual lawsuits that had been filed and consolidated into MDL 381 and the number who had filed opt-out forms (2,440). Taylor and Musslewhite questioned how the reasonableness and adequacy of a settlement could possibly be evaluated, much less certified, without some basis for knowing how many people would be claiming against the fund, even if it turned out that many of those claims were unrelated to Agent Orange. (In fact, the number of claim forms, many containing more than one claimant, exceeded 244,000, more than four times the number that the judge and his special masters had assumed at the time of settlement.[38] These forms included claims of more than

10,000 cancers, 67,000 families having one or more children with birth defects, and 40,000 wives with miscarriages or stillbirths.)[39] A similar criticism applied to the absence of a final distribution plan. How could a settlement be rationally evaluated either by the class members or by the court without anyone knowing who would get what?

To each of these criticisms, which defendants and the PMC are disputing on appeal, Weinstein made specific rejoinders, some more convincing than others. As we saw earlier, the very notion of a "claim" was undeniably difficult to define in the context of the Agent Orange case. His overriding argument, however—his frequently played trump card—was that plaintiffs' case, particularly with regard to causation, was so weak that it would not have been entitled to go to a jury. Plaintiffs, that is, were legally entitled to zero. In that view, *any* settlement amount (even one for subway fare) covering *any* number of claims and *any* distribution of that amount (even one that excluded the vast majority of claimants) were more than they were entitled to. Such a settlement therefore would have been reasonable within the contemplation of the law.[40] This argument was Weinstein's ultimate conversation stopper. Only an appellate court could compel him to resume it.

The Distribution Plan

The settlement, of course, only created a fund; it did not put a single dollar in any veteran's pocket. The crucial question of how the fund should be distributed remained, and it was an extremely vexing one. Before one could even grapple with the host of legal, administrative, and programmatic details that any compensation scheme entailed, some bedrock philosophical and structural decisions had to be made.

First, $180 million plus steadily accumulating interest seemed like a great deal of money until one considered the number of individuals competing for it and their compelling, and costly, needs. Which group should receive priority—totally disabled veterans? the widows of veterans whom illness had already felled? children with birth defects? Second, the Agent Orange case had been brought and litigated under tort principles, according to which proof of causation and harm were both legally required and morally essential to recovery. Should the fund, then, be distributed according to tort principles? Or should the court regard these as unworkable, leaving it free to use other distributive criteria, such as administrative efficiency, political consensus, or maximum number of individuals helped? Third, the fund could be used for direct payments to individual class members or for support of veterans' organizations whose activities might be used to multiply the limited settlement funds into far greater assistance from the VA or Congress or might create other "collective goods" for the benefit of the class as a whole. Should the fund assist only individuals, or should it support organizations as well? If the latter, how much money should go to each type of recipient? Finally and most generally, could the court hope to answer these high-stakes questions by invoking established judicial principles or socially agreed-upon norms? Or was the court actually engaged in a process of willful, political choice? And if so, might its distribution decision not leave the veteran community more fragmented, embittered, and cynical about the rule of law than before?

These were large and daunting questions. To begin answering them, the court needed to obtain some basic information and expertise concerning the VA's existing programs, compensation methods, and treatment criteria. Even before the final settlement agreement was signed, Feinberg urged Len Garment to persuade the government, especially the VA, to help Feinberg develop the plan. Because the government "technically remains in a litigation posture" with the parties who had settled, Feinberg reminded Garment that the special masters must be both candid and careful in seeking its cooperation on the plan. "What we are seeking," Feinberg emphasized, "are Government ideas, not Government funding."[41]

Garment immediately set up a meeting on May 22 attended by himself, Feinberg, Maskin (the Justice Department lawyer), Harry Walters (the VA administrator), and his general counsel. The special masters requested certain information and assistance and urged the VA to take certain actions that might weaken support for provisions in pending legislation opposed by the administration, provisions that would extend VA benefits to categories of veterans who claimed certain Agent Orange–related disabilities. Walters listened quietly, and his responses were noncommittal and (so Garment thought) unfriendly.[42] After reporting to Judge Weinstein about this meeting, Garment followed up with Maskin, requesting some VA statistical information and an opportunity to meet with certain VA personnel. Maskin sent Garment most of the requested information, but pointed out that some (including data on certain troop locations at least twelve years earlier) contained "sensitive information" and could not yet be revealed. He added that the government, as a continuing Agent Orange litigant, would neither "participate in the structure and implementation of the compromise agreement . . . [or] now provide special assistance in your effort" to develop a distribution plan.[43]

Relations with the government soon turned from bad to worse. In July, one month before the Atlanta fairness hearings were to begin, Feinberg wrote to Maskin suggesting that Judge Weinstein use that visit to meet with experts at the Center for Disease Control (CDC) and the National Institute for Occupational Safety and Health (NIOSH) to discuss technical criteria for determining eligibility for compensation, the form of a health delivery system, and issues relating to services for children with birth defects. On July 31, Maskin responded, rejecting Feinberg's request. The CDC and NIOSH, he wrote, were "not suited" to render that kind of advice; moreover, it would be inappropriate for the government "to participate now in the structure of a settlement arranged by parties who are currently pursuing claims against it," especially since Weinstein would be sitting as trier of fact on the pending birth defect claims.[44]

Maskin's and Walters's frosty responses to the pleas of the special masters for help may have been more than mere bureaucratic reflexes. In October 1984, shortly after Judge Weinstein issued his fairness opinion in the class action and the PMC filed a $10 million lawsuit against the government on behalf of the veterans and their families, Garment decided to try again. With one eye on the veterans' new lawsuit and the other on the approaching presidential election, he went over Maskin's head and contacted Tex Lezar, counselor to the attorney general; Michael Horowitz, the general counsel of the Office of Management and Budget (OMB); and Fred Fielding, counsel to the president. He told them that Weinstein wanted to settle all of the Agent Orange cases and that a contribution from the government might make this possible. Garment tried to persuade these conservative Republicans of the precedential risks of protracted litigation in a Brooklyn courtroom before a very liberal judge, the fiscal danger of a large potential liability at a time of deep federal deficits, and the political advantage to the president in making some sympathetic gestures to the veterans concerning their Agent Orange claims. Garment proposed that in anticipation of the Veterans' Dioxin and Radiation Exposure Compensation Standards Act of 1984, passage of which was imminent, the VA should adopt some conciliatory gestures.[45]

The proposed steps, which Feinberg had drafted in consultation with the judge, were innocuous enough: publicity and educational activities, a task force to examine the problems of Vietnam veterans, encouragement of Agent Orange research, review of VA procedures in light of criticisms aired at the fairness hearings, and permission for government experts to help the court develop a distribution plan. Only one proposal required the government to commit funds—up to $5 million to assist in the processing of claims under the distribution plan or, alternatively, up to $2 million to analyze the so-called HERBS tapes, which contained data on soldiers' Agent Orange exposure levels at different locations in Vietnam. If the VA took these steps, Garment noted, the president could ostentatiously announce them in his message accompanying the signing of the legislation, and the plaintiffs might agree to drop their case.

Horowitz, a feisty, combative, liberal-turned-conservative lawyer who in 1985 was nominated to a prestigious federal appeals court judgeship, would have none of it. In a telephone conversation, Garment remonstrated with Horowitz, arguing for "a symbolic statement of support for the vets who think they suffered Agent Orange injury." When Horowitz voiced the suspicion that Weinstein wanted to use the settlement fund to lobby for the veterans and was manipulating Garment, Garment replied that his proposals were "a sensible way of dealing with the remaining pieces of the litigation" and that Horowitz was wasting government funds by refusing to help. Horowitz responded acidly that "I truly don't care how much money is spent resisting Weinstein. That's why we have Justice Department lawyers. It's unseemly to ask me to negotiate the language of a presidential statement to help settle a lawsuit." Garment decided to use the opportunity to lecture Horowitz on special-interest politics, angrily reminding him, "It's done all the time with Congress and constituent groups, and this is not just a lawsuit. Your position is as arrogant as the worst of the big government bureaucrats that you're always caricaturing and carrying on about. Remember your power is conferred and temporary. Smarter people than you have forgotten that fact."[46]

The conversation ended abruptly, but Horowitz prevailed in the end. When President Reagan signed the legislation just before the election, his message excluded Garment's draft language and made no reference to Agent Orange. (Several months later, when Horowitz sent Garment an article reporting an epidemiological study that showed no increased incidence of soft-tissue sarcomas among veterans exposed to Agent Orange, he attached a note saying simply "What's left?")[47]

But Garment's defeat at the hands of the bureaucracy, which frustrated and further angered Weinstein, was still not complete. At Feinberg's urging, Garment wrote to Maskin in mid-November asking that four low-level government employees (three from the VA) be permitted to serve on an advisory board of veterans that Weinstein wished to establish to help the court design the distribution plan. The board, Garment emphasized, was a *pro bono* effort; the fund would reimburse all expenses, and the occasional meetings would be held on weekends. Even this involvement proved too "compromising" for the government; Maskin, who claims that the special masters had already met with the nominees before making the request, firmly "decline[d] permission for any of its employees to participate in any way" in the board's activities.[48] But the special masters had the last laugh. The court eventually appointed the four employees anyway, and Feinberg gleefully issued a press release announcing the creation of the board.[49]

Meanwhile, Feinberg was busy drafting his plan. Weinstein, in the fairness opinion, had set certain parameters that must be respected. Key decisions on the plan should, subject to the court's final authority, "be made primarily by veterans, not by nonveteran lawyers," and the decision-making process should be organized so as to "unite the class rather than promote division and discord." The government, not the fund, must assume primary responsibility for the costs of medical treatment and research. "Transaction costs in distributing the settlement must be kept to a minimum. Complex fact-finding should be avoided to reduce the need for attorneys' fees, experts' fees, and time-consuming adjudication of individual claims." Simple eligibility criteria and ease of proof should be emphasized. The plan should provide for those who may manifest their illnesses only in the future. A national center should be funded as "a visible, central source of legal and political power" for Vietnam veterans, one that would not sap the vitality of current volunteer efforts. Genetic and family counseling services should be provided to exposed veterans, and children with birth defects should receive special assistance. Legislation should be adopted to make fund benefits nontaxable and to ensure that they were not simply offset by reductions in other governmental or private benefits. (Two weeks earlier, the judge had been angered by a newspaper report that a local welfare agency had terminated the welfare, Medicaid, and food stamp benefits of a disabled Vietnam veteran from New Jersey because he had refused to assign his right to a possible recovery in the class action. Weinstein wrote that this was a "misunderstanding" of the status of the litigation and should be rescinded.) Perhaps most important, Weinstein stated, individual benefits must be restricted in amount:

> The limited size of the fund, the near impossibility of proving scientifically which adverse health effects are compensable and which are not, the persuasive evidence of need likely to accompany many individual applications, the danger that large compensation awards will further divide rather than unite the Vietnam veteran community—all of these considerations call into question the idea of providing substantial compensation for individual exposed veterans.
>
> Various options might be considered as alternatives. A limited portion of the fund might be earmarked for all class members filing claims who demonstrate both exposure to Agent Orange and the existence of adverse health effects. An additional lump sum amount might be targeted to those veterans suffering from total physical disability or death from a disease such as cancer. A decreasing term life insurance program for all class members filing valid claims should also be considered. Compassion—not scientific proof—would be the underlying principle of such a program.[50]

As Feinberg saw it, there were, broadly speaking, really three possible plan designs.[51] The first was the tort approach, and its chief advocates were the PMC lawyers. In November, the PMC had submitted a proposed plan emphasizing that the veterans' case had been brought in tort and settled on the assumption that tort principles would control the distribution. To the PMC, a tort approach implied that benefit levels should be "deriv[ed] . . . to the extent possible, from the relative values of various claims" rather than from claimants' "needs." During the late summer of 1984, the PMC, with $100,000 released from the fund by Weinstein, over defendants' protests, had hired five of their expert witnesses to prepare a schedule of diseases "considered to be Agent Orange–related" for eligibility purposes, along with diagnostic criteria for each. The value of each claim would be individually discounted by a number of legal obstacles that might have defeated the claim at trial or on appeal, and each claimant, to whom a lengthy questionnaire would be sent, would then have to prove "a multitude of factors," including exposure levels, individual and family medical backgrounds, life style, "various confounding factors," specific causation, proximate causation, and damages. Each award would be adjusted to reflect certain additional individual factors, including collateral sources (such as insurance), number of dependents, "total need of claimant," ability to receive gratuitous services, and predicted life span. The PMC's plan concluded with fourteen pages devoted to claims-processing procedures and criteria.[52]

To describe this proposal, of course, is to understand why Feinberg (and ultimately Weinstein) rejected it. By recreating the very tort system that the settlement had been designed to avoid, it would have quickly consumed the fund with immense transaction and administrative costs. Henderson insists that the PMC's questionnaire and criteria would have weeded out most of the undeserving claims, leaving an estimated 30,000 to be processed more carefully, and he contrasts this to the far greater volume of claims filed under the court's distribution plan.[53] However, he does not indicate the accuracy of such self-reporting or the cost of proving, under tort principles, the large number of claims that would remain.

Feinberg's second possibility was to use the fund to provide classwide benefits, including research on Agent Orange, information, lobbying, and special services. This approach had been advocated by, among others, the Vietnam Veterans Agent Orange Committee of Texas, which remained unalterably opposed to the settlement, to the PMC's role in the case, and to a tort-based distribution. Instead, they favored creation of a foundation to support these classwide activities, especially a "National Health Service" that would fund treatment for a list of herbicide-caused diseases, to be developed over time.[54] Although this proposal embraced several ideas that Weinstein had endorsed in his fairness opinion, including an organizational advocate for veterans' needs, it neglected his central purpose—compensation focused on the most seriously disabled.

The third possibility would look to the workers' compensation model, and it was around this approach that Feinberg, receiving "constant guidance" from Weinstein, built the proposed plan that he submitted to the judge on February 27, 1985. The Feinberg proposal, more than 600 pages long, contained two essential features, supported by an immense array of consultants' reports and detailed analysis. First, it would create three separate funds—$130 million to provide cash payments to eligible veterans or family members, $30 million to provide services for children with birth defects and their families, and $30 million to provide grants to veterans' organizations and other groups for legal, medical, and social services. These two endowments would be administered by a nonprofit foundation run by a board consisting primarily of Vietnam veterans, with the court retaining "overall authority," particularly concerning budgets. Second, eligibility for cash payments would extend to all veterans suffering nontraumatic death or long-term total disability, *regardless of cause,* so long as they were among the 50 percent of veterans most heavily exposed to Agent Orange. Feinberg estimated that this exposure test (which he said was intended not to indicate causation but to limit the number of eligible claimants) would qualify some 3,000 deaths and some 7,000 disabilities for compensation at present, with the number increasing during the ten-year life of the compensation program. Disability benefits would be paid under a decreasing-term insurance system, with lower awards for more recently manifested disabilities.[55]

Feinberg's plan was ingenious in many respects. He had started (as he put it) "backwards—not with what would be fair eligibility criteria but with how much money we wanted each veteran to end up with." Two-thirds of the money would be used to compensate the most seriously affected under a system that, because of the relatively clearcut objective eligibility criteria, promised to be cheap to administer. "Twenty-five thousand dollars seemed like a good, Solomonic figure for total disability," Feinberg explained. "This would be more than a mere symbol but not enough for the lawyers to get into it. Twenty-five thousand was the most we could award and still compensate a substantial number of claimants." The two endowments for classwide services, he hoped, would take some of the sting out of the narrow eligibility for cash payments and satisfy the legal requirement that the plan benefit a substantial number of class members.

In rejecting specific disease-based eligibility, Feinberg had been guided by more than concerns about administrative costs and scientific uncertainty. Beyond that, he believed, distinctions among veterans that they *perceived* as unfair would be corrosive and divisive. "This was a volatile class in a volatile case during a volatile period," he noted. "If we failed to come up with a fair test, we could have a riot." Means testing had been rejected by Weinstein early on; the whole class was needy, he believed, and it would be administratively costly to determine need individually. Other criteria, such as limiting eligibility to those with dependents, were thought to be too divisive.[56]

Finally, his plan would implement several principles on which most veterans seemed to agree—that children with birth defects would receive benefits, that the disabled would receive more than the dead, and that veterans would control the distribution process. And the fundamental problem of proving exposure had been addressed by a team of consultants who had developed a methodology for determining probable Agent Orange exposure, based on the HERBS tapes but augmented by other criteria.

Still, Feinberg's proposal was bound to be controversial, and at the March 5 hearing on his plan, the criticism of it and of the process by which it was developed was harsh. As Feinberg shuttled back and forth between the courtroom and Weinstein's chambers, alternately making phone calls and listening to the testimony, a parade of witnesses strode to the rostrum to address the judge—and the media. That very morning, the New York Times had reported that a Vietnam veteran in Yonkers had fatally shot himself and his wife and child, and many of the veterans at the hearing, linking this tragedy to Agent Orange, were extremely agitated. (The Times reported that he "apparently thought he was suffering from the effects of Agent Orange contamination.")[57] Several disabled veterans in wheelchairs lined the courtroom aisles, while their comrades, many dressed in army fatigues and orange T-shirts labeled "Sprayed and Betrayed," grimly watched the proceedings from their seats, their concentration occasionally punctuated by applause for a speaker.[58]

Frank McCarthy, neatly dressed in a dark, vested suit, was the first speaker. Although unable to fully digest Feinberg's plan in the few days since it had been released, he opposed basing awards on total disability. He pointed out that those veterans would already be receiving compensation under government programs, and urged that payments instead be income-related. He predicted that the veteran community, already politically fragmented, would be further divided as their organizations competed for grants from the new foundation, and he therefore opposed distributing funds to veterans' organizations, including his own. (Privately, McCarthy was optimistic about the potential effects of the distribution on "the war for the veterans' futures. In the Agent Orange case, we have lost the battles but can still win the war. In Vietnam, it was just the opposite; we won the battles and lost the war.")[59]

When Lawrence Smith, the leader of the black veterans' organization, complained that blacks had received little information about the case, Weinstein resisted any suggestion of discrimination, and when Smith demanded genetic research, Weinstein said emphatically that he would not use any of the settlement funds for research: "That is the government's responsibility."

Few speakers had specific suggestions concerning the plan; instead, self-pity and claims of betrayal abounded. A black soldier, his voice nearly breaking with emotion, said that his son had died recently of birth defects; he demanded to know "what kind of study you did to deny Agent Orange was responsible," and accused Weinstein of "destroying these men even today with this decision." Most speakers used the occasion to denounce the settlement—several described it as a "rape"—and those who supported it, such as McCarthy. (One accused McCarthy of cutting and running. "We didn't do that in Vietnam," the accuser bitterly said.) Many warned that the settlement would not lay the Agent Orange issue to rest. "This too shall *not* pass," one concluded, and another told the judge, "We will still be here to haunt you." When Weinstein, after hearing a wife describe her husband's long bout with Hodgkin's disease, gently said, "I'm not in a position to respond. I feel very badly about your situation," the woman simply stared at him and slowly walked away. Some soldiers saw in the litigation poignant parallels to the war. "I don't want this case to be inconclusive like the war was," one physically wasted veteran said. "I have never seen lawyers lose. I still don't know whether Agent Orange was responsible." (One veteran, after getting Weinstein to confirm that no chemical company representatives were present, asked, "Why do they never come to these hearings?")

Feelings almost reached the kindling point when a veteran named James Tower, wearing a bright orange coat, walked to the microphone and urged that the veterans "take the money, give it to the kids, go buy guns." As he turned and left the room, he shouted "Everybody has a book of matches in his pocket, burn everything down" and warned Weinstein that "somebody, sometime is going to get to you," adding that this was not a threat. Cool and unruffled, the judge slowly repeated Tower's words to the court stenographer "for the record." The next speaker, a Mexican American man from Houston, wearing a fatigue jacket covered with battle ribbons and medals, apologized for Tower and told Weinstein, "Dogs that bark don't bite; it's the dogs that don't bark that will get you."

Finally, the plaintiffs' lawyers testified. Rob Taylor, who represented the opt-outs, criticized Feinberg for having abandoned tort principles (as he saw it, under the Feinberg plan the wives and children would receive no compensation, and under tort principles they would have recovered something). Taylor also rebuked Feinberg for having said publicly that there was no proof of causation, which was unfair to the opt-outs and to the class should the settlement be vacated on appeal. It was the inadequacy of Weinstein's settlement, Taylor charged, that had forced the judge to devise a "welfare distribution scheme."

Dean praised the plan's "scholarliness," calling it "fair but flawed." He opposed giving any money to veterans' organizations, which had not been plaintiffs in the lawsuit. The main problem with the plan, Dean said, was that it failed to make distinctions among disease based on causation; veterans with soft-tissue sarcomas, for example, would not be compensated without proof of exposure and total disability, while those who died of Rocky Mountain spotted fever or heart attacks would be. (Weinstein acknowledged that the plan would indeed have these results.) Dean also worried about the politicization of disability determinations; even though neither the VA nor Social Security would be making the decisions, Dean argued, their criteria would be used. Instead, he stated, compensation should be automatic for listed diseases, as the PMC had urged, thereby extending eligibility beyond the 7,000 that Feinberg had predicted. When Weinstein pointed out that with a limited fund, this would reduce the award for each covered veteran, Dean responded, somewhat lamely, that he would augment the fund with the $30 million that Feinberg would allocate to organizations. (Watching the boyish Dean, a woman in the audience leaned over to Yannacone and asked, "Is he a vet?" to which Yannacone replied, "No, he's your lawyer. He took over the case from me.")[60]

It was fitting, perhaps, that Yannacone, who had really conceived the Agent Orange class action and who for most veterans truly embodied the case, should be the final speaker at its final hearing. (The remaining hearings concerned only the opt-out cases and the claims against the government.) (Earlier, talking privately as he waited to testify, Yannacone had focused his anger and derision on the PMC. Except for Schlegel, he said, its members had virtually no clients who were actually veterans, while he, Yannacone, represented almost 8,000; they had taken the lawsuit away from the veterans. They had completely mishandled the scientific aspects of the case by failing to consult with him or his wife and by failing to depose Dow's experts. They had adopted an "asbestos strategy" of seeking to prove causation by proposing simply to use an expert medical witness in the hope of getting to a jury, obtaining a favorable verdict, and settling the case before defendants appealed; they had refused to adhere to his original strategy of accepting 1 ppm of dioxin as the industry standard established by Dow and Hercules, and using that to indict the others and get punitive damages against Monsanto and Diamond Shamrock.)[61]

Round and dapper in his gray, vested suit and speaking eloquently and without notes as he leaned back with crossed arms against the empty jury box, Yannacone launched into a denunciation of Feinberg's plan, Weinstein's judging, and the PMC's handling of the case after his own ouster in October 1983.[62] During the Vietnam War years, Yannacone began, when riots broke out and certain lawyers chanted "Burn, baby, burn," he told students that "litigation is civilization's answer to revolution. As long as the door to the courthouse is open, the door to the streets is closed." Today, Yannacone intoned, his eyes sweeping across the courtroom, "I look at many here who have been in it since 1979, and I see the last days of what was a noble crusade, and I hear [Judge Weinstein] ask David Dean, 'What is the incidence of disease among Vietnam veterans?' " He continued, "I have asked the present PMC, my former colleagues, and this court to do a simple thing—count the number of sick veterans in America. Don't get excited about them, just count them." There was now no reliable basis, he said, for statements by Weinstein and others about the percentage of children born with birth defects (since we do not know the number of such births) or about exposure to Agent Orange (since the HERBS tapes, which logged only Ranch Hand missions, were "about as reliable as General Westmoreland's order of battle"). The PMC's disease-listing approach was feasible, Yannacone observed, but was beside the point. "The purpose of the Agent Orange lawsuit, the reason we knocked on the door of this Courthouse and brought you a case that [had] never been seen [before], . . . and the reason . . . I told the veterans who call me to stay together with this lawsuit," Yannacone proclaimed, was that "no matter how badly the lawyers screwed it up, the Court would eventually see to it that justice was due."

That prediction, he lamented, had not been fulfilled. The "vast majority" of the combat veterans who had supported the litigation "are not interested in the kind of distribution that the Feinberg plan proposes." It might be a proper distribution for Bhopal or other mass disasters but not for Agent Orange. He had originally estimated the cost of treating and caring for the veterans and their children at between two and eight billion dollars and knew that only the VA disability program could provide that kind of money. He had expected the chemical companies to devote all their resources to fighting the veterans' claims, and they had. In doing so, however, the companies had also had to divulge previously secret information about other toxic chemicals used in Vietnam, information that Yannacone had planned to use "to literally compel the Government, the Congress and the VA and the Executive, which can do it by fiat" to compensate the veterans.

But the children, Yannacone passionately stated, "represented a dramatically different problem. The children have not even begun to be addressed in the Feinberg plan." It was imperative, then, that the children's birth defects be identified and made eligible for some "derivative" form of service-connected disability compensation. Kerry Ryan, he noted, "is just as much a Vietnam veteran as Michael although she did not go there, she came later."

Yannacone then proposed that the court get congressmen to use their franking privilege to send out postcards on which sick veterans could respond with information about their conditions; the postcards would be processed and followed up, and a profile would be developed. "Stop this rush to distribute a few dollars to a few people," Yannacone pleaded, "and first find out how many there are out there." Weinstein interjected to say that he was not going to ask Congress, which had already provided tens of millions of dollars for studies, to do anything more. Yannacone had had the case for many years, he added, and the time had come to "complete the litigation. The distribution will be deferred as it is because appeals will be taken. I can no longer put off a decision. This court exists to decide matters." Yannacone, respectful but obviously exasperated and angry, reminded Weinstein that the court had already awarded a consultant contract for "more money than we ask for to count the veterans and find out how sick they are . . . [so that] when the CDC comes out with its study [in 1989], we can refute it before the VA and Congress."

Thus ended Victor Yannacone's role in the Agent Orange drama. Almost seven years after he had entered and taken center stage, he was left to haunt its margins. Still attended by a retinue of admirers and invariably surrounded by a phalanx of loyal, fatigue-clad veterans, he was reduced to being a self-styled conscience of the court and grand kibitzer. In those roles, he invoked the pristine clarity of their early vision, rehashed previously rejected proposals, and sniped at his successors. Yet his devotion to his clients had never waned, and his moving denouement, redeemed only by his inexhaustible energy, humor, and dignity, conjured up many warring images—the spurned but still ardent suitor, the perennial crusader always ready for another fight, the shipwrecked dreamer clinging to his illusions, the irresponsible child who clasps success to his own bosom but flings failure at everyone in sight. Yannacone had given much to the cause, but in the end he had little to show for it but his battle scars, his seething resentments and the gratitude of his embittered veterans.

Despite the chorus of criticism of the Feinberg plan at the hearing, there was never much doubt that Weinstein would adopt it substantially. For one thing, Feinberg's plan was crafted to stay within the guidelines that Weinstein had established in the fairness opinion. Given those guidelines, Feinberg's approach was more or less inevitable. Beyond that, Weinstein constantly instructed Feinberg about the elements he wanted it to contain.[63] And the veterans' organizations had largely been co-opted by the process. Weinstein had appointed a twenty-nine-member advisory board, selected by Feinberg with some political care, which met several times between November 1984 and February 1985 to discuss the evolving plan. Feinberg and Weinstein had endorsed several of their suggestions, including focusing compensation on the totally disabled.

In addition, the plan provided for $60 million in funds for services, half of which would go directly to the veteran-related groups themselves. The representative of the Agent Orange Children's Fund had begun her testimony by expressing "100 percent" opposition to the settlement, only to urge that her group receive a portion of the $30 million endowment.[64] According to Michael Ryan, McCarthy and other veterans' groups that supported the settlement will "use the money to set up little kingdoms to perpetuate themselves. They will piss it away."[65] The prospect of organizational funding had not stopped many of the veterans and groups from expressing opposition to the plan, of course, but the fairness hearings had shown that Weinstein did not take their sentiments to be either representative of the "silent majority" or determinative of the legal question before him. (Feinberg probably echoed the judge's view in asserting that the bulk of the Vietnam veterans were "indifferent.") The other source of opposition, the plaintiffs' lawyers, had an ideological objection to the plan—its rejection of tort principles—but their direct financial interests were unaffected, and their criticism seemed somewhat muted and perfunctory. Finally, as Feinberg had predicted, "the weariness factor" worked in favor of his plan.[66]

It came as no great surprise, then, when Weinstein, on the day after Veterans' Day, 1985, issued the final distribution plan adopting Feinberg's proposal "with slight modifications." Weinstein changed the form of the maximum death benefit from a ten-year payout to an immediate, time-discounted lump sum payment, which (along with a slight adjustment required by allowing late claimants to file) necessitated a reduction in the death benefit amount from $5,000 to $3,400. He also jettisoned Feinberg's proposal that a veteran, to be eligible, must have been among the 50 percent most heavily exposed. Responding to objections voiced by veterans' groups and to the lack of scientific consensus concerning the correlation between *degree* of exposure to dioxin and adverse health effects, Weinstein tied eligibility to *any* exposure. By substantially enlarging the number of valid claims, this change required that the disability benefit be reduced by almost half (to $12,800), narrowing considerably the difference between a death benefit and a disability benefit. In addition, Weinstein merged the two $30 million endowments that Feinberg had proposed into a single $45 million fund with a twenty-five-year life span, emphasizing future needs of the class, especially those of children with birth defects. He also insisted that cash payments not be treated as offsets to benefits payable under other government or private programs. Finally, he eliminated Feinberg's separate fund for administering the payment program, collapsing it into the $150 million available for eligible claimants.[67]

Several features of the final plan, and Weinstein's defense of it, are significant. First, he repudiated as distributive criteria the very tort principles on which plaintiffs had originally sued. Although eminently defensible on policy grounds—tort-based awards would have been eaten up by the immense costs of determining and distributing them— this move was of doubtful legality. Like so much else that Weinstein did, it was premised on his conclusion that causation could not be proved, yet no formal finding on causation had ever been made in the class action. Indeed, this settlement (like many) was intended to *avoid* just such a determination, and appellate courts had warned trial judges against resolving sharply contested fact issues (like causation) in passing on settlements, a stricture that seemed to apply even more strongly to distribution plans.[68]

Second, Weinstein's notice of proposed settlement had not contained a distribution plan but had simply outlined the basic elements of the plan the PMC had indicated it would propose, which proposal Weinstein subsequently rejected. And it was only in May 1985, more than four months after he had finally approved the settlement, that he issued the plan. As Musslewhite had argued, however, class action law views the plan as an integral part of the settlement, something class members must be notified of before they can evaluate the reasonableness of the settlement at the fairness hearing. Thus it is difficult to see how a court can properly approve a settlement without first having specified at least a tentative distribution plan on which the class can comment; if the court instead approves the settlement, without adequate notice, that approval may be void, and the settlement may be vacated.[69]

This much was not simply common sense; it was also established law. In the *Chicken Antitrust* litigation, for example, the appellate court, ruling on a closely related procedural point in a case in which the lower court had approved a settlement before finalizing the distribution plan, noted that "no overall settlement can be adjudged fair or unfair unless the allocation scheme is also examined." Moreover, the official *Manual for Complex Litigation*, which applies to federal court cases like Agent Orange, recommends that judges include, in the proposed settlement notices that they must send to class members before the fairness hearing, information describing "the procedures for allocating and distributing the settlement funds."[70]

Weinstein never gave a good reason for ignoring this basic requirement. He cited *Chicken Antitrust* for the proposition that he was entitled to *not* specify a plan, even though that case actually demonstrates the very opposite: there, in contrast to Agent Orange, a tentative distribution plan had been developed prior to the proposed settlement, the class was notified about it prior to the fairness hearing and in fact the class voiced objections to it at that hearing. The only justification Weinstein gave for reversing this sequence was a wish to finalize the settlement quickly so that appeals could begin. But this gained him only four months, hardly worth denying class members the *meaningful* right to be heard, a right that the law has created for their protection and that exists regardless of the particular distribution being proposed.[71]

To effect the particular kind of distribution he desired, Weinstein needed to avoid these restrictions and further enlarge his discretion. He did so by invoking the *cy pres* doctrine. This doctrine holds that if a testator makes a charitable bequest in a will and that bequest becomes impossible to implement, the court may distribute the funds in a way that it believes will best serve the testator's original purpose. Arguing that a tort distribution was neither feasible nor desirable, Weinstein claimed the same kind of discretion concerning how to distribute the settlement fund that the *cy pres* doctrine conferred as to bequests. But this gambit posed several difficulties. If the settling parties (analogous to the testator) had any distributive purpose in mind, it was presumably tort-based. And in the precedents that Weinstein cited, *cy pres* was used not to free the court to distribute an entire fund (as Weinstein was doing) but simply to liquidate a relatively small surplus that remained after all individual claims had been satisfied under an approved plan—a very different matter. Weinstein was turning the doctrine on its head in order to obtain total discretion over the entire fund.[72]

How Weinstein used this discretion is perhaps most vividly revealed in his decision, announced in only a few sentences, to exclude the veterans' wives and children with birth defects from the compensation program (except as the veterans' heirs).[73] Recall that they were equal members of the class that Weinstein certified, on whose behalf the case was settled, and whose interests he was equally bound to protect; that their claims were independent of the veterans'; and that the class wanted them to receive priority in the distribution plan. Yet Weinstein depicted his decision to exclude them not as the controversial, fundamental political choice that it clearly was, but as merely a straightforward implication of what he insisted on treating as an established fact—that the miscarriage and birth defect claims, although not frivolous, were even weaker causally than those of the veterans. This decision presumably reflected his policy judgment that given the limitations of the fund, the veterans' already low benefit levels should not be reduced even further. But it implemented that judgment by reintroducing a quintessentially tort criterion (relative strength of causation evidence) into a distribution scheme that had flatly repudiated it, thereby undermining the analytical integrity of his plan.

By ignoring the mandatory temporal sequence of distribution plan and settlement, using lack of causation as a "factual" predicate for claiming the power to distribute the entire fund according to his own criteria, and finally adopting a modified workers' compensation distribution, Weinstein managed to accomplish several remarkable things. First, he made his approval of the settlement far less controversial than it would have been had it incorporated the plan that was ultimately adopted. Second, he freed himself from the law's procedural and substantive constraints concerning the nature of class distributions. Most important, he established precisely what Congress had rejected just prior to the 1984 elections—a large new federal benefit program for Vietnam veterans. Unlike legislated benefit programs, Weinstein's was drawn to his personal specifications and was not vulnerable to modification or repeal, budgetary review, administrative oversight, public control through the representative organs of government, or any other mechanism of political accountability. In effect, Weinstein had fused in himself legislative, administrative, and judicial powers, subject to no checks and balances and no higher authority than his own conscience and the unlikely intervention of the appellate court. Like so many of Weinstein's other decisions in the Agent Orange case, his distribution plan represented a sound (or at least defensible) exercise of policy discretion masquerading as the rule of law.

11

The Final Act

ALTHOUGH the class action was over, the Agent Orange litigation continued. First, the Vietnam Veterans of America sought
to unseal (make public) all documents in the Agent Orange case, a
move that the chemical companies vigorously resisted. Second, about
350 of the veterans and family members who had opted out of the
class maintained individual actions against the chemical companies.
With the class action settled, these opt-out cases, joined by a handful
of similar cases brought by civilians exposed to Agent Orange in
Vietnam, could now proceed toward trial. Third, the plaintiffs and
the chemical companies had claims against the United States, claims
that the settlement had expressly preserved. By mid-1985, Weinstein
had resolved all of these issues, and the Agent Orange litigation
moved to the appellate court.

Unsealing the Documents

Many Agent Orange documents are claimed to be sensitive.[1] Some
involve the chemical companies' commercial, financial, or trade secret
information, and others may concern national security. In February
1981, Judge Pratt permitted defendants to designate discovery documents as confidential, and in May 1982 Pratt upheld Schreiber's blan-
ket protective order imposing sealing and secrecy requirements on *all*
documents in the case, although some exceptions were subsequently
recognized. Protective orders relating to government documents had
also been entered. Shortly after Pratt's summary judgment ruling in
May 1983, he permitted disclosure of the documents referred to in the
parties' summary judgment briefs. Several months later, the govern-

ment agreed to disclose most of its documents and depositions, and when it filed its August 1984 brief attacking the chemical companies' government contract defense, the government moved to unseal the underlying documents. Apart from these three instances, however, all other documents remained under seal.

When many veterans charged during the fairness hearings that the settlement was a "coverup,"[2] Weinstein invited a motion to unseal the remaining documents. The Vietnam Veterans of America, with Yannacone's support, later intervened to make such a motion, which eventually included all documents and depositions. The chemical companies opposed it, arguing that they had relied on the protective orders when they agreed to produce the documents, and that the agreement settling the case stipulated that plaintiffs would return all documents to them after a specified period of time. After hearing these arguments, Magistrate Scheindlin recommended to Weinstein that the protective order be lifted. While rejecting any legal right of public access to discovery documents, she found a statutory presumption favoring disclosure, which defendants could overcome only by showing the need for continued confidentiality on a document-by-document basis. Also, the protective order should not apply to government documents disclosed by agencies pursuant to a Freedom of Information Act request.[3]

At a hearing on February 6, 1985, Dow's lawyer, Leonard Rivkin, protested heatedly to Judge Weinstein that Scheindlin's recommendation meant that the Agent Orange controversy would "not be ended but will resume in the newspapers" and that it violated the settlement agreement.[4] (Here he invoked a 1981 decision by Weinstein that had refused public disclosure of the terms of a settlement agreement.)[5] Weinstein responded that the PMC did not represent all of the relevant interests and that the documents were of interest to millions of people, far more than in the earlier case. Rivkin, in retreat, urged that the protective order be retained at least until the Agent Orange litigation ended. This immediately brought Yannacone to his feet. Obviously agitated, Yannacone shouted that the PMC had already denied the veterans their day in court, some of the documents showed "collusion between the chemical companies and the government," and "you have just disenfranchised the veterans." When the burst of applause from the veterans in the audience died down, Weinstein replied playfully with a mock Jewish accent, "Don't holler on me!" He then affirmed Scheindlin's decision but barred disclosure until after

appeals on the settlement were exhausted. (The defendants subsequently appealed this disclosure order, their only remaining challenge in the Agent Orange case.)[6]

The Opt-Out Cases

The opt-out cases had languished pending the settlement of the class
action; indeed, the deadline for opting out (April 30, 1984) expired
only days before the agreement was reached. Thereafter Judge
Weinstein permitted (according to Rob Taylor, the opt-outs' principal
lawyer, he *pressured*) the opt-outs to return to the class and share in its
benefits.[7] By mid-July, some 600 had rejoined; many of these had
apparently filed opt-out forms in the mistaken belief (which the poorly
drafted form may have encouraged) that they were opting *in*.[8] Of the
remaining opt-outs, about 350 others decided to resume the litigation.
On July 24, the chemical companies moved for summary judgment
against all of them as a group, advancing the principal defenses used
in the class action: no liability of particular manufacturers, no causation, and the government contract defense.[9] Ashcraft & Gerel represented almost all of the opt-outs. (The firm also continued to represent
many class members; its class action clients even included two of the
five "representative" plaintiffs upon whom the trial was to have focused. Although Weinstein viewed this dual representation a "substantial" conflict of interest, he permitted the firm to continue the
representation because of the exigent circumstances.)[10]

In view of Weinstein's subsequent decision, it is important to emphasize the precise procedural posture in which the causation issue
now came to the court. By moving for summary judgment, the chemical companies were seeking final judgment on the basis of documents, depositions, and affidavits. Because summary judgment
precludes any opportunity to try factual disputes to the jury, it may
be granted only when trial is clearly unnecessary—in this case, only
if the opt-out plaintiffs failed to raise a "genuine issue as to any
material fact."[11]

The kind and probity of evidence that suffices to raise an issue
of material fact and defeat the motion, of course, are difficult to for-
mulate in the abstract. But the general rule is that any doubts must be
resolved *against* summary judgment. Several considerations support
this universally accepted rule: the plaintiffs' constitutional right to

have a jury decide all material factual issues; the desire to avoid deciding factual issues before the evidentiary record is fully developed; the importance of judgments about witnesses' credibility and demeanor that can come only from live testimony and cross-examination before the jury; and the danger that judges will use summary judgment to arrogate the fact-finding function that the legal system confers upon juries.[12]

The judge is obliged to ensure that only *genuine* issues of fact go to the jury. But that qualification has been taken to mean that plaintiffs should not be allowed to reach a jury solely on the basis of "purely conclusory" factual allegations. In the past, summary judgment has been confined to cases in which there was no dispute about facts or in which plaintiffs produced no evidence or produced evidence that was significantly incomplete when more was available or produced evidence that contradicted known and incontrovertible facts or was internally inconsistent.[13] Even then, the courts have insisted that plaintiffs are entitled to all favorable inferences, and that the interpretation of evidence remains the jury's responsibility, not the judge's.[14] These strictures against summary judgment are probably strongest in the Second Circuit, where the Agent Orange case was to be tried; indeed, a district judge in New York noted in 1984 that "motions for summary judgment in this circuit are usually a waste of time and should be discouraged."[15]

These are generalizations, of course, and do not tell us (or the judge) how a close case should be decided. It can be difficult to draw the line between evidence that is so weak and improbable that it amounts to "no" evidence (thereby justifying summary judgment) and the only marginally greater quantum of evidence that raises an issue of fact that a jury must decide. In cases like Agent Orange, which turn on scientific propositions that are often controversial and inconclusive, this line drawing is further complicated by the Federal Rules of Evidence, which require the judge to decide whether technical studies and expert testimony are admissible or not. Under the Rules' vague standards, admissibility turns on several factors, including the relevance of the testimony, its capacity to assist or mislead the jury in fact finding, and the putative expert's qualifications.

In such cases, however, the testimony of qualified experts that is favorable to plaintiffs, unless wholly implausible, generally suffices to send the case to a jury. The usual approach is exemplified in the *Ferebee* case, decided only three months earlier and involving lung disease allegedly caused by occupational exposure to the herbicide paraquat. There the influential District of Columbia Circuit rejected a chemical company argument that plaintiff's case should never have been permitted to reach the jury: "Judges, both trial and appellate, have no special competence to resolve the complex and refractory causal issues raised by the attempt to link low-level exposure to toxic chemicals with human disease. On questions such as these, which stand at the frontier of current medical and epidemiological inquiry, if experts are willing to testify that such a link exists, it is for the jury to decide whether to credit such testimony . . . The case was thus a classic battle of the experts, a battle in which the jury must decide the victor."[16]

When Rob Taylor argued against the defendants' summary judgment motion on September 18, then, the question for the court was not which experts, with their differing interpretations of the scientific evidence, the jury ought to believe. Instead it was the more limited, threshold question of whether plaintiffs' causation evidence raised a genuine issue of fact. Just before the hearing, Taylor had filed (belatedly) a lengthy memorandum summarizing the three types of evidence with which the opt-outs would prove specific causation of the veterans' diseases, the wives' miscarriages, and the children's birth defects. Taylor argued that animal studies demonstrated the mechanism by which dioxin could cause the observed conditions in humans, that epidemiological studies demonstrated that exposure to Agent Orange placed the veterans and their families at increased risk of those conditions, and that expert medical testimony interpreting those data could provide the causal link to the individual plaintiffs' conditions. No single element standing alone could prove causation, he argued, but these three—animal studies, epidemiology, and expert medical testimony—taken together raised a genuine question of fact for the jury. (The PMC had already presented most of his evidence in the class action, but some of it, including expert witness affidavits, was new.)[17]

Taylor had hardly begun his presentation when Judge Weinstein demanded to know "what animal study you have that shows male-mediated birth defects." Yannacone, who sat by Taylor's side, quickly cited several. Taylor conceded that they showed only the mechanism by which dioxin "could" cause genetic damage. Weinstein acknowledged an "indication of mechanism" but insisted on "studies . . . showing statistics." Taylor cited human exposure data from the CDC birth defects epidemiological study, emphasizing that the study had found statistically significant increases in certain rare birth defects and tumors (a finding that the study's authors had downplayed). Weinstein interrupted to say that this evidence was "not sufficient in my opinion to warrant letting the case go forward." Taylor, insisting that epidemiology was "simply one component," moved to the affidavits of plaintiffs' experts, especially Dr. Maureen Hatch and Dr. Ellen Silbergeld, a former research scientist at Johns Hopkins and now chief toxicologist for the Environmental Defense Fund. Hatch said that data indicated that parental exposure to Agent Orange "may" cause birth defects in offspring, and Silbergeld said that data showed an increased risk of certain diseases in the exposed fathers and provided "very strong evidence" that Agent Orange had caused plaintiffs' conditions.

Even this, Weinstein insisted, could not defeat summary judgment. He had no doubt that "dioxin can cause serious harm," but he dismissed the animal and occupational studies cited by Taylor because they used much higher dosages than the veterans had been exposed to; moreover, even an increased risk of the disease could not prove specific causation. At the very least, Weinstein said, Taylor must obtain an expert's affidavit stating *as to a particular plaintiff* that "in her scientific opinion, there is more than 50 percent probability that their particular diseases were due to exposure to Agent Orange in Vietnam. You could have twenty days to do that."

Taylor was now faced with two serious problems of an evidentiary and logistical nature. First, it was virtually impossible for him to prove the degree of any individual veteran's exposure to dioxin. The HERBS computer tapes and data on troop locations could be made to yield some very rough estimates of which individuals had been exposed. But the *degree* of exposure, so crucial to the proof of individual causation, depended upon variables such as the dioxin contamination of particular supplies of Agent Orange, the incidence of ground spraying, and the dispersion of groundwater, for which little reliable data existed. This problem had not figured prominently in the class action because of the pretrial settlement, but it could hardly be avoided in the individual opt-out cases. Second, even apart from the proof-of-exposure problem, it seemed most unlikely that Taylor could obtain individual affidavits for each of the 340 plaintiffs in less than three weeks.

Taylor emphasized this second problem, arguing that his generic proof of causation was appropriate because the defendants' motion was generic and not addressed to particular plaintiffs. By ignoring this fact, he continued, Weinstein was in effect shifting the burden of proof on the summary judgment motion to plaintiffs. Taylor then cited Dr. Marvin Schneiderman's deposition. In response to a question about whether Agent Orange had caused Danny Ford's condition, Schneiderman had said that Ford's cancer "in a person who has been exposed, and in the absence of any other knowledge of the cause . . . in that individual is more likely, in my opinion, to have been related to that exposure than to some other not known, ill-defined set of causes." This qualified statement failed to negate other causes, and Weinstein dismissed it, noting that Taylor was no longer representing Ford and that Schneiderman had not personally examined him. The judge gave Taylor thirty days to submit additional evidence on specific causation or suffer summary judgment.[18]

One month later, on October 17, Taylor complied. His new evidence included an affidavit by Dr. Bertram Carnow, a professor of environmental and occupational medicine at the University of Illinois who had testified for plaintiffs in the 1982 trial resulting in a $58 million verdict for railroad workers exposed to dioxin. Carnow's affidavit stated that the lymphosarcoma of John Lilley (an opt-out) "was, in my opinion, caused by his exposure to . . . [Agent Orange] . . . His exposure to Agent Orange is the likely cause of his malignancy and death at well above the '50 percent level.' "[19] The evidence also included other experts' testimony stating—in the very words that Weinstein had demanded—that Agent Orange caused the lymphoma of David Lambiotte (another opt-out, who had been cast as a representative plaintiff in the class action).[20] In response, the chemical companies failed to file any particularized affidavits negating causation and instead challenged Carnow's credentials and credibility.[21]

On December 10, the summary judgment motion was again argued. Seeing Weinstein's handwriting on the wall, Taylor was anxious to have the individual opt-out cases returned to the courts in which they had originally been filed for trial of the specific causation and damages issues. Beginning with Judge Pratt's case management plan four years earlier, it had always been assumed that the cases would be remanded once the generic issues were resolved. More important, Taylor believed that local law in those jurisdictions was more favorable to the veterans on the question of whether their causation evidence sufficed to defeat defendants' motion for summary judgment than Judge Weinstein apparently was going to be. For example, the courts in Maryland, where many of Taylor's clients had originally sued, would probably apply the pro-plaintiff *Ferebee* standard. And even if Weinstein held on to the cases, Taylor argued, local law should control in a diversity case like Agent Orange.

Weinstein, however, decided to finesse this question; if he dismissed the cases, he said, transfer would become a moot point. (This was circular reasoning, as the very issue that Taylor had raised was whether Weinstein *could* dismiss them on this particular ground, that is, specific causation, or whether, as Taylor urged, that action could be taken, if at all, only by the original court.)[22]

When Taylor resumed his argument, the judge suddenly interrupted to say that he was inclined to deny Taylor's firm a fee for its work in the class action because it relied to some extent on the PMC's discovery materials. Taylor was startled by this observation; it seemed to come out of left field for the purpose of intimidating him. Rivkin then rose to bitterly attack Dr. Carnow, accusing him of failing the internal medicine boards five times, committing perjury, and being a "professional testifier" whose testimony "demeans the veterans." Even the PMC, he said, had not stooped so low as to use Carnow, and Taylor was desperate to have at least one doctor's affidavit in a hurry.[23]

Carnow's affidavit nevertheless placed Weinstein in a serious bind. While unwilling to concur with Rivkin's slashing criticism of Carnow on the record, the judge obviously gave no credence to the doctor's testimony. He seemed determined to grant summary judgment in the opt-out cases, but to do so in the face of Carnow's testimony would probably be reversible error. Weinstein cleverly maneuvered around the problem. Conceding that the Second Circuit would not permit summary judgment in view of Carnow's affidavit, the judge sought to discredit the affidavit without appearing to pass on the doctor's credibility, a jury question. Carnow, he said, went "far beyond" the testimony of Silbergeld and Taylor's other experts: "Their opinions are at least the opinions of reputable scientists who qualify their opinions in a variety of ways . . . His testimony . . . is so out of line with the general materials that it seems to me to provide a Second Circuit basis to reanalyze its position with respect to summary judgment."[24]

Weinstein therefore granted summary judgment as to the wives' and children's claims, but in light of Carnow's affidavit, he denied it as to *Lilley*. He gave Taylor only forty-five more days to produce the kind of evidence in the 350 other veterans' cases that Taylor had produced in *Lilley*. (Taylor insisted, to no avail, that he needed at least six months.) Then, acting *sua sponte* (on his own motion), Weinstein decided, for probably the first time since he took over the Agent Orange case, to certify a question to the Second Circuit—here, the issue of admissibility of Carnow's testimony. (This allowed Rivkin an immediate appeal, which would force the already overextended Taylor to litigate on yet another front. Rivkin, however, decided not to appeal this issue separately, and thus it was never certified.) In addition, Weinstein later stayed the certification to permit the defendants to depose Carnow and even indicated that he might require Carnow to testify at the next court hearing on the summary judgment motion.[25]

On January 11, Taylor asked Weinstein to recuse himself from hearing the other opt-out cases. He argued that the judge's behavior—among other things, his need to justify an unfair settlement, his belittling of the veterans' causation evidence, his conversion of the summary judgment motion from defendants' generic motion to a particularized one, his shifting of the burden of proof, his certification of Carnow's credibility, his Draconian time limits on proof, and his threat to deny Ashcraft & Gerel its class action counsel fees—demonstrated bias and "a clear attempt to place improper pressure on plaintiffs to return to the class action."[26] A week later, Weinstein expressed his appreciation to Taylor for giving him an opportunity "to escape from the toils of the Agent Orange litigation," but he refused recusal, and when Taylor appealed, the Second Circuit summarily affirmed.[27]

Meanwhile, Taylor struggled to meet Weinstein's forty-five-day deadline for specific causation proof in the 350 other opt-out cases. On January 24 he filed Dr. Barry Singer's affidavit. Singer had examined individual affidavits from 189 veterans exposed to Agent Orange, and although he had not examined their medical records, Taylor had given him the factual summaries of those records. He stated that after reviewing the scientific evidence, assuming the truth of the veterans' affidavits and lacking any evidence of other cases of their conditions, "it is my opinion to a reasonable degree of medical probability (that is, more likely than not) that" those conditions were "proximately caused by exposure to Agent Orange." Like Schneiderman's testimony, this qualification ("absent any evidence of other causes") deprived Singer's affidavit of much value on the specific causation issue. Singer's subsequent affidavit, virtually identical to the first, covered ninety-three additional veterans.[28] Other doctors' affidavits stating that Agent Orange caused harm to a number of civilian plaintiffs were also filed.[29] Some of these seemed perfunctory, conclusory, and (even to the lay eye) debatable; one, for example, attributed the individual's lung and bladder cancer to Agent Orange despite a history of heavy smoking and alcohol consumption.[30] They had obviously been tailored to meet Weinstein's specifications.

But the most serious challenge to Weinstein was yet to come. On March 11, Taylor filed a sixty-five-page affidavit by Dr. Samuel Epstein. Despite Epstein's controversial reputation, his expertise was widely recognized, and his testimony, far more than Carnow's, had to be taken very seriously. Epstein's affidavit began by taking exception to Feinberg's public statements about the weakness of the causation claim. It also criticized the PMC for failing to present a comprehensive literature review on causation, which Epstein then proceeded to provide. After summarizing the views of "a wide range of scientific authorities" including Singer, Silbergeld, Schneiderman, Bogen, and Carnow, who believed, as Epstein did, that "a causal relationship exists between exposure to Agent Orange and a wide range of toxic multi-system and multi-organ effects," he turned to specific causation, appending fifteen affidavits on individual opt-outs. For each, he said, he had reviewed the veteran's medical records, interview materials, affidavits, family history, and questionnaire data on exposure, and he had considered the temporal pattern of the disease and the possibility of other risk factors or etiologies. And for each, he concluded "to a reasonable degree of medical certainty" that the veteran's conditions "are much more likely than not to have been caused by exposure to Agent Orange."[31]

Epstein's affidavit threatened to break the case wide open. It was not that his testimony was incontrovertible; indeed, defendants quickly took Epstein's deposition and used it to attack his consistency, methodology, and conclusions.[32] Rather, it was that these objections seemed to go to the weight and credibility of his testimony, which were clearly *jury* questions. Weinstein seemed to recognize this at the final hearing on April 15. After listening to the Dow lawyers criticize Epstein, the judge replied, "Don't knock Epstein. He is a well-recognized expert," to which Rivkin immediately rejoined, "A well-recognized *plaintiff's* expert." Weinstein reserved decision on the summary judgment motions.[33]

On May 8, only days after the Second Circuit upheld his refusal to recuse himself, the judge issued his eagerly awaited decision. His conclusion appeared on the very first page of his long opinion. Although the veterans did suffer, and many deserved government help, he wrote, "they cannot obtain aid through this suit against private corporations." His reason was equally unequivocal: while summary judgment "is somewhat unusual" in a negligence case (in which the jury passes on the "reasonableness" of defendants' risk-creating behavior), "all reliable studies of the effect of Agent Orange on members of the class so far published provide no support for plaintiffs' claims of causation." (Two months later, he also granted summary judgment in *Lilley*, employing the identical reasoning but buttressing it by pointing to a number of serious gaps and inconsistencies in Carnow's testimony.)[34]

Weinstein's refusal to submit the opt-outs' causation claims to a jury was probably his single most far-reaching ruling in the Agent Orange case and will exercise a profound influence over future mass toxic tort litigation. The grant of summary judgment against the veterans is especially remarkable, given that the defendants had already agreed to pay $180 million to settle essentially identical claims, a settlement that Weinstein had pronounced fair and reasonable. Although, strictly speaking, the class action settlement was legally irrelevant to the decision in the opt-out cases—the class action defendants had "bought their peace" while the opt-outs had chosen to litigate—Weinstein's ruling seems highly questionable. The crucial elements of his opinion, therefore, deserve to be scrutinized in some detail.

The assumption driving his analysis appeared in his initial discussion of the causation evidence. The human epidemiological studies on the effects of Agent Orange, he asserted, "are the only useful studies having any bearing on causation. All the other data supplied by the parties rests on surmise and inapposite extrapolations from animal studies and industrial accidents." Weinstein's desire for epidemiological evidence is understandable, especially in a mass toxic tort case in which direct proof of specific causation is weak. Other things being equal, one would obviously prefer to base scientific conclusions on data drawn from the plaintiffs' actual experience with the exposure in question rather than rely solely on laboratory experiments or on human exposures at higher or more sustained levels.

Other things, however, are not equal. Epidemiological studies are notoriously subject to methodological difficulties not encountered in the laboratory. First, although epidemiology can reveal a correlation between an exposure and a disease, that does not prove causation; as Weinstein recognized, causation requires something more. Second, epidemiology typically must rely on incomplete and perhaps unreliable data, often using records compiled by nonscientists for other purposes usually long before the study was even planned. Third, the control group may be inadequate, and it can be misleading to extrapolate from the test population to another population with different characteristics, different exposure routes or levels, and so forth.[35]

For these reasons, epidemiologists consider their studies to be useful only when high exposure levels (as with sustained occupational exposures) produce at least a 25 percent increase in the disease risk over the background risk; any smaller excess is swallowed up by statistical variance, methodological flaws, and other problems.[36] Clearly, epidemiology may produce valuable evidence, but it is not the philosopher's stone for which Weinstein searched. Animal studies, of course, have their own characteristic disadvantages for demonstrating causation and measuring dose-effect relationships. The most important are the needs to extrapolate from test animals to humans and to use doses high enough to produce a statistically significant effect during a reasonable time period in a necessarily small (because of resource constraints) population of test animals.[37]

Thus neither clinical studies nor epidemiological studies can be viewed as sufficient, standing alone, to "prove" causation in a case like Agent Orange. Scientists recognize the limitations of each and regard them as complementary methods. To understand why, consider that the typical pattern of toxicological investigation (as with the research on Agent Orange) begins with crude epidemiological observations (for example, numerous babies are being born in Vietnam with birth defects), which lead to animal testing of suspect chemicals in the laboratory (for example, the Bionetics study). If those tests prove positive or are otherwise suggestive, one or more refined epidemiological studies may then be conducted (such as the CDC Birth Defects Study). By using the two methods in this way, it is possible to strengthen the inference that the substance—shown clinically to be hazardous to test animals under certain carefully controlled laboratory conditions and shown epidemiologically to be correlated with changes in the disease rate of human populations—did (or did not) actually *cause* the disease. Without initial epidemiological observations, scientists would have little reason to select particular substances for further study. Without laboratory studies, they could not estimate the substance's risks under conditions to which the human population may have been exposed, but for which epidemiologists have not and perhaps cannot control and for which epidemiological methods may lack the required sensitivity. And without more refined epidemiological studies, especially in heavily exposed populations, scientists would have less confidence in their estimates concerning how the substance might affect human populations exposed to low levels over long periods of time.[38]

The interdependence of the methodologies casts serious doubt on Weinstein's decision to accept only epidemiological data. That decision effectively excluded most of plaintiffs' evidence and the only evidence actually capable of proving causation. (Indeed, Weinstein later speculated that had the epidemiological studies not been available, he probably would have had to send the Agent Orange case to the jury.)[39] A related error was Weinstein's overreliance on the negative epidemiological findings on causation. Negative findings, of course, can indeed reflect an absence of any underlying correlation. But they may result from methodological problems, especially insufficient "power" (for example, inadequate sample size) or misclassification (erroneous assignment of values, such as exposure levels or disease outcomes, to individuals). To the extent that these problems exist, a study is less capable of proving that a correlation does or does not exist; false negatives are as likely in such cases as false positives.[40]

The Agent Orange studies exhibited some of these problems—especially poor data on exposure, some self-reporting of outcomes, and high background levels of, and other potential causes for, the diseases under investigation. These problems have led one leading epidemiologist to state that no convincing epidemiological study of the effects of Agent Orange on Vietnam veterans can be conducted at *any* cost.[41] Most epidemiologists, then, would interpret the results of the studies as inconclusive, rather than negative. They would look to animal studies to provide evidence that could more conclusively confirm or rebut the no-effect hypothesis suggested by the epidemiology.[42] They would be especially likely to do so because animal studies have shown dioxin to be a potent carcinogen in some species.[43] For this reason, the fact that the plaintiffs bore the burden of proving causation yet had inconclusive epidemiological evidence did not in itself warrant dismissing their case.

Three other factors strengthen these doubts concerning Weinstein's evidentiary approach. First, only very recently have courts been willing to accept epidemiological evidence *at all*.[44] Prior to the 1970s, such evidence was apparently not used to prove causation in tort cases, and until the swine flu litigation growing out of the 1976 mass vaccination program, it was apparently used only in an ancillary manner, to confirm individualized evidence on exposure and injury. (In some asbestos and DES cases, for example, epidemiological evidence was used to show simply that a disease was not unique to the plaintiff but also afflicted others. In those cases, moreover, the epidemiological studies were highly consistent with relevant medical and clinical evidence and did not purport to stand independently of them in any sense.) Even in the swine flu cases, in which epidemiological evidence was used to prove causation, the courts were careful not to rely on it exclusively.[45] Indeed, in a 1984 toxic radiation case, the court appeared to reject such evidence altogether.[46]

Second, in emphasizing that animal studies could at best show only that Agent Orange "may be" a cause of particular diseases, Weinstein overlooked the fact that epidemiology is no more (and perhaps less) probative; at most, it can demonstrate a statistical correlation (typically with a high standard error), not the causal relationship to a particular veteran's injury that Weinstein demanded.[47] Finally, he excluded more than a hundred nongovernmental epidemiological studies that plaintiffs had cited. Although it is true that such studies are often of little or no value,[48] Weinstein rejected them categorically; all, he said, were "irrelevant" because "most" relied on "inapposite data" and "some" were flawed. But he did not elaborate.[49] Nor did he explain why he should not consider those studies (presumably "some") that were *not* flawed or inapposite, why the flaws in the others were on balance more serious than the flaws in the epidemiological studies on which his opinion relied so strongly, or why flaws, where they did exist, were matters to be resolved by the judge at the threshold rather than explored on cross-examination at trial.

This last point especially bears emphasizing. Recall that the opt-out cases were before Weinstein on motions for summary judgment. The issue before him, therefore, was not how he would evaluate the evidence were he the trier of fact. It was whether, after resolving all uncertainties and inferences in favor of the veterans, a genuine issue of causation remained for the jury. Here the legal standards governing summary judgment converge with the legal standards for excluding evidence.[50] This being so, Weinstein's refusal to admit the testimony of the veterans' qualified medical experts, especially Epstein, was the linchpin of his decision. It therefore merits particularly close examination.

Under Rule 703 of the Federal Rules of Evidence, the key question was whether the data on which the medical experts had relied was "of a type reasonably relied upon by experts in the field" and therefore admissible. Weinstein suggested that the Second Circuit would allow a trial judge to deny admissibility if the judge determined that although the data were of a type reasonably relied on by experts, the particular expert had—in the judge's view—acted unreasonably in basing the opinion on underlying data or assumptions that the judge regarded as untrustworthy. This "rigorous examination" of the underlying data or assumptions, Weinstein added, was "especially important in the mass toxic tort context," in which causation evidence depended almost entirely on expert testimony.

Weinstein then proceeded to exclude Singer's and Epstein's testimony for a number of related reasons: Singer and, to a lesser extent, Epstein had relied on personal affidavits by veterans (or by their attorneys after conversations with them), affidavits that appended checklists of symptoms to compile their medical histories; they had failed to consider and discuss the epidemiological evidence on Vietnam veterans; and they had failed to exclude other possible causes of the veterans' illnesses. (Here Epstein was hoist by his own petard. Weinstein, borrowing almost verbatim from the chemical companies' brief filed nine days earlier,[51] quoted extensively from Epstein's recent book, *The Politics of Cancer*—with devastating effect. Although the book emphasized that cancer has numerous environmental causes, including chemicals, drugs, alcohol, smoking, and radiation, Epstein's testimony failed to exclude these as possible causes of the veterans' diseases.)

Presenting and rebutting Singer's and Epstein's testimony, Weinstein said, would consume substantial time at trial and would probably "mislead and confuse" the jury. It must therefore be excluded not only under Rule 703 but also under Rule 403, which applied to evidence whose probative value was "substantially outweighed" by these disadvantages. By excluding the veterans' expert testimony on causation, Weinstein in effect ended the case; without that evidence, summary judgment, which was (as he put it) "a drastic procedural device," became inevitable.

It is extremely difficult to evaluate Weinstein's decision, for it proceeds at several levels. In addition to his overreliance on negative epidemiological results and his refusal to consider animal test data (or, more precisely, to allow expert witnesses to do so), his "rigorous examination" of the underlying data relied on by experts seems questionable. First, it inescapably amounts to a judicial second-guessing of scientists' substantive judgments—a perilous enterprise given the scientific ignorance of most generalist judges, the distortions of the adversary process, and the absence of objectively "right" answers to some of the most important questions at issue.

It is true that Weinstein personally read an enormous amount of the technical literature on toxicology, statistics, and other relevant disciplines; he even devised a form, indicating outside readings he would take judicial notice of, which he gave to the lawyers in the case.[52] But even so, he remained self-taught and incompletely informed, lacking in the intuition and finely honed technical judgment of the experienced scientist. His critical perspective, clarified by extraordinary diligence and self-confidence, tempted him to jump in boldly where even specialists feared to tread. Were all judges as incisive as Weinstein, there might be much to be said for this intervention. Even then, of course, intelligence is not the only, or perhaps even the most important, factor in deciding how society wishes to allocate authority between judges and juries. In any event, few judges are his intellectual peers.

Second, none of the cases Weinstein cited to support his evidentiary ruling clearly compelled exclusion, much less summary judgment. Some involved disputes in which definitive evidence on one side was met only by expert testimony that was biased, wholly unsupported, inconsistent with known facts, or seriously incomplete.[53] Other cases involved methodologies of recognized unreliability or techniques applied with bias or clear incompetence. The only mass toxic tort case cited, *Swine Flu*, fell into the latter category.[54] In Agent Orange, however, the epidemiological evidence against causation was at best inconclusive, and the expert testimony favoring causation, although arguably weak, was not found by Weinstein to be biased. Moreover, it relied largely on animal and industrial studies that, although inevitably imperfect and of controverted significance, were in fact the most common, accepted bases for drawing scientific inferences about causation. In some cases cited by Weinstein, expert testimony had been excluded so that the jury could decide a factual question unencumbered;[55] in Agent Orange, however, exclusion meant that the question would never even reach the jury.

Significantly, none of the cases Weinstein cited to support excluding misleading evidence involved a situation like Agent Orange, in which the problem was to decide between conflicting scientific hypotheses and inconclusive data on both sides of the issue. (Indeed, Weinstein cited several toxic shock syndrome cases that actually contradicted his position; they emphasized that where causation was the central issue, even arguably conclusory or potentially confusing or unreliable evidence should be admitted.)[56] This does not mean that Weinstein's use of precedent was illogical. The strength of a particular analogy is infinitely arguable, especially when used in a novel area of litigation, and Weinstein genuinely believed that in mass toxic tort cases, the courts' generally uncritical acceptance of expert testimony must be replaced with a more critical view. It only means that the cases he cited were not persuasive and did not preclude a contrary decision.

Third, Weinstein's "rigorous examination" manifested a certain niggardliness in summing up the veterans' evidence. One example, already mentioned, was his unexplained rejection of their epidemiological studies. Another was his treatment of the evidence of specific causation in the case of veteran David Lambiotte, one of the representative plaintiffs in the original class action. Weinstein simply dismissed it, observing only that Lambiotte was not an opt-out plaintiff. In a different spirit, he might instead have viewed this evidence as relevant to the key issue of whether Agent Orange, at the exposure levels experienced by Lambiotte, could have caused the diseases of other veterans.

Yet another example was Weinstein's sharp criticism of their experts' reliance on the veterans' subjective affidavits and checklists rather than on personal examinations. Again, although he was certainly correct in viewing this evidence as weak, a less censorious mood might have led him to inquire into the question of necessity. Taylor had argued, after all, that a number of factors—among others, the inconclusiveness of the epidemiology; the large number of individual plaintiffs; the inherent difficulty of proving dioxin's diffuse, latent toxicity; and especially the unusual sequence of events in the litigation that made it reasonable for the opt-outs not to develop their causation proof until very late in the game—left them with little time and no practical alternative. Moreover, several court decisions (including some that Weinstein cited) indicated that necessitous circumstances might require admission of otherwise excludable evidence.[57] For that matter, had not Weinstein himself often cited unusual features such as these to justify cutting procedural corners in the interests of substantial justice, as in his handling of the choice-of-law and class action questions?[58] Thus it was arguably wrong and certainly ungenerous for Weinstein to dismiss the veterans' claim of necessity by simply observing that "after six years of litigation, it does not seem too much to expect plaintiffs' counsel to have obtained more persuasive medical and other records."

Still, when all is said and done, the propriety of Weinstein's grant of summary judgment remains a close question—probably wrong, but not clearly so. (It is interesting in this regard that, as noted earlier, even the chemical companies had assumed prior to the settlement that a summary judgment motion would be futile. In addition, Feinberg and some other neutral observers who were close to the case and who generally admire Weinstein's handling of it privately assert that summary judgment should not have been granted and may even constitute reversible error.)[59] The key elements in Weinstein's approach to the evidentiary issue—and hence to summary judgment—turn upon arguable questions that can be resolved only by a nice balancing of delicate judgments. In such a situation, a great deal depends on the presumptions, the underlying attitudes, that one brings to these judgments.

Weinstein articulated his with characteristic clarity. One—that epidemiological studies were the only probative evidence of causation—has already been criticized. A second presumption—that "the uncertainty of the evidence in [toxic tort] cases, dependent as it is upon speculative scientific hypotheses and epidemiological studies, creates a special need for robust screening of experts and gatekeeping under Rules 403 and 703 by the court"—is also doubtful. Ultimately, one's evaluation of what Weinstein did must turn on one's appraisal of this statement.

The only reason Weinstein advanced to justify this "special need" involved the costs of protracted litigation in such cases. But that consideration alone can hardly be determinative. Society does have a stake in reducing the social costs of litigation, and strong arguments can be made that litigants should bear more of those costs than they now do.[60] On the other hand, the justice system is a public good conferring broad social benefits. Courts sit to decide cases, and so long as the parties are prepared to pay what society has decided to charge them for litigation, the existence of those costs cannot alone constitute a sufficient ground for denying them their constitutionally protected right to go to trial on genuine factual issues.

Also dubious is the argument that the scientific character of toxic tort disputes implies greater judicial screening of evidence and easier summary judgments against plaintiffs. It might actually suggest just the opposite. First, we must consider the quality of evidence available in such cases. Here we do well to recall two of Weinstein's observations in his fairness opinion. In mass toxic tort cases, he stressed, "We are in a different world of proof than that of the archetypical smoking gun. We must make the best estimates of probability that we can using the help of experts such as statisticians and our own common sense and experience with the real universe." And in such cases, "available data and statistical studies are rarely as reliable and complete as they ideally could be."[61]

In short, certain weaknesses of proof of causation are inescapable; they are not failures of proof in the ordinary sense but *inhere in the nature of the problem being litigated*. This may constitute an argument for litigating such problems in different ways or for taking them out of the tort system altogether, issues I consider in Chapter 12. But so long as these cases remain in the tort system, it seems imprudent and illogical to treat them as if they were simply garden-variety slip-and-fall cases, subject to the same evidentiary requirements.

In his fairness opinion, Weinstein seemed to recognize this, at least insofar as class actions were concerned. Because "it would be impossible in most cases to identify the individual class members who were injured by Agent Orange," he argued, the legal system must adapt its proof requirements:

> Given the desirability of resolving the indeterminate plaintiff problem using a form of proportional liability or some other acceptable method, a dismissal of the class action would be unwarranted. The statistical theory, available data, and public policy are far from settled. Particularly during this period of rapidly changing scientific approaches and increased threats to the environment, we should not unduly restrict development of legal theory and practice—both substantive and procedural—by dismissing a class action such as the one now before us.[62]

Why should this caution against premature dismissal not apply equally to individual actions? Weinstein's answer to this question (earlier in the fairness opinion) was quite unsatisfactory. Using his numerical example, discussed in Chapter 9, of a substance that causes 1,100 cancers, 100 more than "expected," he had correctly stated that as to any one of the 1,100 victims, there was only a 9 percent probability (100/1,100) of causation and that "under traditional tort principles no plaintiff could recover." He then considered the possible solution of shifting the burden of proof to defendants at this point in indeterminate plaintiff situations, only to reject it because defendants would be unable to sustain that burden and would thus incur disproportionate liability.[63]

These reasons for rejecting burden-shifting, however, are inadequate in the Agent Orange case for at least two reasons noted in Chapter 9. First, Weinstein himself had devised liability-limiting allocational criteria (market share and dioxin content) that would limit each defendant's liability to approximately the damage it had probably caused. Second, a statistically based, proportionate-damage rule (in the hypothetical case, 9 percent) could readily be applied to reduce an individual plaintiff's recovery, at least in cases in which, as in this hypothetical case, epidemiological evidence had established the number of "excess" diseases, in the population of which plaintiff was a part, that defendants as a class had caused with the requisite certainty. Assuming that such evidence existed and could be relied upon, all of the reasons justifying Weinstein's "classwide solution" would seem equally to support a solution to the problem of proportionate damages for *individual* plaintiffs like the opt-out litigants.

The point, I hasten to add, is *not* that this is a desirable solution, although some commentators have found it so.[64] Nor is it that individual actions are superior to class actions in all respects. Certainly, there are substantial, perhaps even compelling, arguments against an individual plaintiff approach—for example, arguments based on excessive litigation costs, the vagaries of juries, or the unreliability of epidemiological evidence. The point, rather, is that some of the arguments against the "individual plaintiff solution," including that most prominently advanced by Weinstein in his opinion, also cast doubt upon the "classwide solution" favored by him; yet he did not explain why the former should be dismissed on causation grounds so much more readily than the latter.

The analysis in these last few pages has been designed to show that the quality of evidence available in mass toxic tort cases like Agent Orange might not imply easier dismissal than in conventional cases.

But there is a final reason to question Weinstein's approach. It involves the role of the jury, an institution for which Weinstein often evinces a high regard.[65] (Indeed, a lawyers' reference service reports that Weinstein "almost never grants a summary judgment.")[66] Just because the kind of evidence typically adduced to prove causation in mass toxic tort cases is scientific, uncertain, and controversial, it does not follow that a judge is more competent to evaluate its significance and weight than a jury. As Weinstein himself recently quipped, "I can't even pronounce the words. I'm going to decide whether the jury can hear it?"[67] (A third possibility, considered in Chapter 12, is that in this area, neither judge nor jury is as competent to do so as an agency.) For better or for worse, our legal system has placed its faith in juries, even in cases, like some antitrust disputes, that are as technical and complex as toxic tort litigation.[68] Although respectable arguments can certainly be made that this faith is misplaced in such cases, Weinstein did not even attempt to make them.

On the other side, a common argument against letting juries decide—that plaintiffs' lawyers can always come up with an expert who will claim causation and that juries will almost always resolve causation issues in their favor in mass toxic tort cases[69]—appears highly questionable. In April 1985, a West Virginia jury, after a ten-month trial, found that dioxin in Agent Orange had not caused the cancers and nervous disorders of a group of Monsanto employees. In the *Bendectin* case, a jury hearing 1,000 consolidated birth defect claims found for the defendant on causation grounds.[70] Many asbestos suits failed for the same reason. As trial lawyers well know, juries are simply unpredictable.

But the real point is more fundamental. If judges are to supplant juries in such cases, that should reflect a basic policy decision by Congress and state legislatures (assuming no constitutional inhibitions against it). It should not result from a sub rosa (or even explicit) judicial tinkering with the standards for summary judgment and admissibility of evidence, especially in a case in which the best explanation for the judge's decision is simply that he disbelieved plaintiffs' experts.

In the end, then, Weinstein's grant of summary judgment in the opt-out cases raises serious questions of legal process and public policy, questions that his analysis—and perhaps any analysis conducted in the context of an isolated tort case—could not really lay to rest. I shall return to these questions in the final chapter, where they can be addressed in a broader context.

The Claims against the Government

After the class action settlement was concluded, Judge Weinstein often expressed the conviction in open court that specific causation could not be shown.[71] If that was so, and if he granted the chemical companies summary judgment on causation grounds in the opt-out cases, the United States government had every reason to expect that the claims against it must also be dismissed.

These claims were of five kinds. First, shortly after the settlement was signed, the PMC lawyers filed another class action, this time against the government, seeking $10 billion in damages on behalf of the veterans, wives, and children.[72] Second, the chemical companies, having incurred a $180 million liability by settling, now sought to recover most of it from the government by arguing that the United States owed them a duty to indemnify them.[73] Third, a few civilians asserted claims against the government that were not barred by the *Feres* doctrine.[74] Fourth, Musslewhite filed a $1.8 billion action in the Court of Claims arguing that the government had taken veterans' property without just compensation.[75] Fifth, Yannacone filed an action, essentially identical to the earlier one against the VA that Judge Pratt had dismissed, against other federal agencies claiming governmental failures to warn, treat, and distribute program benefits to the veterans and their families. (This was quickly dismissed as having been previously resolved.)[76] Weinstein's treatment of the first two types of claims, which essentially disposed of them all, are discussed below.

Claims by Veterans and Family Members

Only days after the settlement was announced, Dean buttonholed Maskin, the lead Justice Department lawyer, and warned him, "We are coming after you now, especially on the wives' and kids' claims."[77] The PMC's new class action presented two groups of claims—those of the veterans and the independent claims of their wives and children. Each of them presented different obstacles to recovery. Because both Pratt and Weinstein had earlier held the veterans' own claims to be *Feres*-barred, the PMC was now forced to argue that those rulings covered only injuries incurred during service and did not apply to other harms. Specifically, *Feres* did not bar harms resulting from the government's negligent failure to warn about Agent Orange's dangers during the preinduction period, from its negligent failure to warn about, monitor, and treat Agent Orange's effects during the postdischarge period, or from intentional torts by the government.

Weinstein expressed his doubts about the claims in several ways. First, Pratt had already rejected these preinduction and postdischarge theories as mere "artful pleading."[78] Although Weinstein indicated that he did not feel that Pratt's decision bound either these plaintiffs or him (because no class had yet been certified when Pratt ruled), he doubted that these claims could be squared with *Feres*.[79] Moreover, he refused to certify the class, ruling that the costs of providing class notice under Rule 23 would be too great given "the almost nonexistent possibility of recovery against the government on the merits."[80] Furthermore, the PMC's causation affidavits were even more general and equivocal than those that Taylor later produced, and Weinstein rejected, in the opt-out cases. Finally, although Weinstein had ruled (contrary to Pratt's earlier decision) that *Feres* did not bar the independent family members' claims (see Chapter 7), the causation obstacle to those claims remained.

When the veterans' and independent family members' claims were heard on December 10, 1984, it quickly appeared that the PMC had an additional problem: it had no clients. The government had filed Frank McCarthy's declaration that AOVI had not authorized the PMC to sue the government and that "the overwhelming majority" of the more than 100,000 Vietnam veterans with whom AOVI was in contact "are opposed to any suit which claims the Government was responsible for injuries to" them and their families from Agent Orange.[81]

As Neil Peterson, the PMC's spokesman, presented the family members' arguments, Weinstein suddenly interjected and asked the lawyer to name a single wife or child who had brought an individual suit against the government. Since class certification had already been denied, individual claims were the only possible remaining basis for suit, and the judge was demanding to know whom the PMC claimed to represent. The assembled PMC lawyers blanched, hemmed, and hawed.[82] Even Taylor, who did have several individual wives and children as clients and thus had standing to assert the claims, fared no better in the end, as we have seen. Indeed, the judge's intention to throw out all the claims was so unmistakable that Taylor, deciding to salvage what he could, requested Weinstein's leave to dismiss the children's birth defect claims against the government voluntarily and without prejudice to their right to sue again in the future. Maskin opposed voluntary dismissal, insisting that if the causation evidence was as weak as Weinstein said, the judge was obliged to dismiss the children's claims along with the others—on the merits, once and for all.[83]

On February 11, 1985, Weinstein formally dismissed all claims against the government by the veterans, wives, and children. As he had ruled a year earlier in the original class action, *Feres* barred the veterans' claims (as well as the dependent, derivative claims of family members), and he also applied this principle to bar those claims based on postdischarge failure to warn, which he (like Pratt earlier) described as "artful pleading."[84] Earlier he had emphasized the practical objections to a governmental warning,[85] but he now confined himself to legal considerations, seeking to differentiate earlier cases that had upheld postdischarge claims despite *Feres*.

Although his decision was defensible as a buttress for *Feres*, his distinctions of those cases were unconvincing. He began by using a common judicial technique for distinguishing inconvenient cases. He chose to emphasize one particular fact in the earlier case—the government's conduct of an LSD experiment involving the soldier—that was absent in the case before him. Had he instead characterized the facts more broadly (and no less accurately), he would have strengthened the analogy between the two cases—for example, by emphasizing that in both cases the government had knowingly subjected soldiers to uncertain risks for legitimate governmental reasons and then failed to warn them so that they could protect themselves against those risks.

A second gambit was to distinguish several recent radiation exposure cases that had upheld postdischarge failure-to-warn claims by emphasizing the larger doses and more certain causation involved there, considerations relevant to the merits but quite irrelevant to those cases and to the issue before him—that is, the scope of the *Feres* immunity. (Since Weinstein's decision, at least two courts of appeals have upheld such claims despite *Feres*.)[86] Finally, he noted that the "discretionary function" exception to the Federal Tort Claims Act might bar the claims even apart from *Feres* because the use of Agent Orange involved valid military objectives—a fact that would immunize the government's decision to *use* the herbicide but was quite irrelevant to a claim of subsequent failure to *warn*. (As for Weinstein's "artful pleading" objection, it could be met by confining recovery to those claims that were truly the result of new, postdischarge acts or omissions (for example, failure to warn when new information came to light, resulting in new or additional damage).

On the family members' claims, Weinstein had to take a different tack, for he had earlier made the innovative ruling that *Feres* did not bar them. Instead, he rejected the wives' claims on causation grounds. Their expert medical testimony, he ruled, was "guarded and unpersuasive" and lacked any "factual foundation" necessary for admissibility. This last reason was extremely controversial and potentially far-reaching as a basis for summary judgment, as I showed in the previous section, and he had not relied on it in any previous written opinion. (His summary judgment decisions in the opt-out and civilian cases were not issued until May, three months later.) Surprisingly, therefore, he did not defend this approach, but merely cited two cases without elaboration or explanation, cases whose applicability to Agent Orange was not at all obvious. As to the children's birth defect claims, he granted Taylor's request to dismiss them without prejudice. Instead of responding directly to the government's contention that Weinstein's own rejection of the children's causation evidence required dismissal on the merits, he used the occasion to denounce the government's "harsh and unyielding view of its relationship to the veterans, their wives and children in this litigation," emphasizing the possibility that persuasive causation evidence might become available to the children in the future.[87]

Both of these suggestions reveal interesting complexities of Weinstein's self-conception in the Agent Orange case. Although the Justice Department's opposition to dismissal without prejudice does seem petty and mean-spirited, Weinstein's castigation of the "vindictive" government was unfair, perhaps even hypocritical on his part. It was Weinstein, after all, who had stressed *ad nauseam* that there was no evidence that Agent Orange had caused the plaintiffs' harm, a conclusion that made it plausible for the government to disclaim responsibility, even in the VA context. (Indeed, Weinstein's disdain for the PMC's causation evidence may have discouraged further VA research on Agent Orange.) Moreover, it was his action dragging the government back into the case only a few months before trial and without a real opportunity for adequate discovery or preparation, an action (as we have seen) of doubtful validity, that had caused the government to refuse to participate in the settlement negotiations. His own special masters had reported that the government was actually doing a great deal for the veterans, and his own fairness opinion had detailed these contributions, including pending legislation (subsequently enacted) designed "to provide full compensation if scientific studies support this result."[88]

If the government was guilty of anything, then, it was guilty of protecting all too effectively what it viewed (with strong support from Weinstein's own rulings and remarks) as the general public's interest in not submitting to ill-founded raids on the United States Treasury. (As I discussed in Chapter 10, however, the government's recalcitrance in connection with the design and implementation of the distribution plan is more difficult to justify.)

The Chemical Companies' Claims

Shortly after the settlement, the chemical companies asserted contribution and indemnity claims against the government for the lion's share of their $180 million liability.[89] They then quickly served the government with a discovery onslaught, including an enormous number of demands to admit the companies' factual allegations.[90] When the government sought more time to respond, Weinstein ordered it to answer all of them and to serve its own discovery requests on the companies—all without delay. In July, after the government lawyers had complied and just before the date for responding to the government's first discovery requests in the history of the Agent Orange case, the companies' lawyers rushed into court and obtained an order—*ex parte*, because (they argued) government counsel were unavailable and could not be notified in time—staying the government's discovery.[91]

On July 24, the companies moved for summary judgment against the opt-outs primarily on the basis of the government contract defense, contending that there was no issue of fact.[92] From the government's perspective, this contention was the height of disingenuousness; it was the companies' *ex parte* stay of discovery, after all, that had prevented the government from showing that issues of fact *did* exist. The companies' strategy seemed to have worked when, the next day, Weinstein rejected the government's request that the stay be lifted, although assuring Maskin that the case would not be tried until the government had its chance for discovery.[93] Still, as to the summary judgment motion, this obviously placed the government in an extremely awkward position, the legal equivalent of having to fight with one arm tied behind its back. As a nonparty to the case for more than three years, the government had conducted no discovery of its own. Now that it was a party, the court had barred discovery indefinitely. Thus the government must oppose the companies' summary motion judgment by essentially relying upon what a poorly funded, often chaotic plaintiffs' team had managed to uncover.

On August 31, Maskin filed his papers opposing the companies' motion.[94] They clearly signaled a high-level Justice Department policy decision to attack the companies' government contract defense not only in the Agent Orange case but in all cases in which such a defense might be raised. Because the government's own military and procurement interests had been the basis for the legal rule recognizing such a defense, its challenge was especially significant; the defense was bound to be less persuasive if its intended beneficiary, the government, strongly repudiated it.[95]

But the government did not simply challenge the defense on generalized policy grounds. In a brief burning with an indignation seldom found in the passionless papers customarily filed by government litigators, it denounced the chemical companies' invocation of the defense in the Agent Orange case. For five years, the brief began, the companies had provided the court with a "one-sided story . . . without meeting significant opposition." Now, by obtaining the discovery stay, they had made opposition all but impossible. The brief then cited numerous documentary exhibits in the case, some of which remained under seal, that undercut the companies' claims. Far from having been dragooned into producing Agent Orange for the government, as they had always argued, the companies had vigorously promoted and competed for the opportunity to do so. "Profit, and not compulsion or patriotism," the brief charged, had motivated them to produce Agent Orange. Nor had the companies merely responded to the specification established and controlled by the government, or invariably met those specifications. And as to the parity-of-knowledge requirement of the defense, the brief cited eleven documents, including the smoking gun memorandum, which demonstrated that the companies had withheld evidence of dioxin toxicity from the government.

The government's arguments, which received wide publicity, clearly precluded summary judgment on the government contract defense, and Weinstein denied it from the bench on September 5.[96] But despite the clear factual issues and damaging evidence the gov-

ernment had raised, Weinstein subsequently reversed field and upheld the defense—tentatively in his fairness opinion and then
unequivocally in his May 8, 1985, decision dismissing the opt-out
claims. "The government," he asserted then, "knew as much as, or
more than, the defendant chemical companies about the possible
adverse health effects of Agent Orange as it was used in Vietnam."[97]
If Weinstein's refusal to submit the causation issue to the jury is
questionable, as I have argued, his refusal to submit the government
contract defense, which involved neither expert testimony nor admissibility of evidence issues, seems clearly wrong.

But even if the companies could successfully interpose the government contract defense, their claims must founder on two other shoals.
First, the policy justifications for the defense implied (and Weinstein
had earlier suggested) that it could be only as broad as the governmental immunity conferred by *Feres/Stencel*.[98] This meant that if the
companies succeeded in establishing the defense, it must be at the
price of establishing that immunity. That would defeat the companies' claims against the government as surely as it would bar those of
the veterans and family members.

Even more formidable was their second obstacle—causation. When
Weinstein rejected the direct claims by the veterans and family members on causation grounds, it became inevitable that he must dismiss
the companies' third-party claims as well. The companies' contribution and indemnity theories required them to demonstrate that they
and the government shared a common liability, but Weinstein had
now rejected the government's liability. To get around this, the defendants contrived another imaginative theory. Even if the government had violated no duty to the plaintiffs, they argued, it nevertheless
owed a duty to the manufacturers to use Agent Orange in a manner
that would not result in liability for them. Judge Pratt, however, had
rejected this "reverse warranty" theory, and Weinstein also thought
it far-fetched.[99]

Still, one element of this theory—the claim that the government
could have participated in the settlement and influenced the companies' decision to settle—gave the judge one more chance to excoriate
the government. As Maskin argued against these claims on April 15,
1985, Weinstein broke in to insist that the government had been
aware of the settlement negotiations a year earlier. Maskin, who had
been as shocked as anyone when he learned of the settlement,[100]
replied that Feinberg's letter three days before the settlement, inviting

the government's participation, had been misaddressed and was never received; more important, this eleventh-hour invitation could not have been meaningful. Weinstein, finding this assertion "weird," suggested that if Maskin did not know, "it was because you deliberately wanted *not* to know." When Rivkin jumped in to offer "proof" that Maskin knew, Weinstein said emphatically, "Well, I don't need any proof . . . If you didn't know, it must have been because you didn't want to know, you deliberately decided not to know."[101]

Nevertheless, Weinstein still could not swallow the companies' indemnity arguments. The government "stonewalled," he told Rivkin, "and you took a chance. You were both right." Although the government had been "very unfair to its contractors," he added, the law was on its side, and it owed the companies nothing. In formally dismissing the claims on May 9, Weinstein would go even further, writing that the government's "benign detachment . . . may be cruel" as to the veterans and "shortsighted" as to its contractors. "Undoubtedly, the United States will pay a high price for its present position," he predicted, including indemnification demands by future contractors and "lingering resentment by veterans and their families."[102]

With this ominous, gratuitous warning, the Agent Orange litigation came to an end at the trial court level. (Weinstein would soon file his remaining written opinions, and numerous appeals would be taken.)[103] As Weinstein approached the door leading to his chambers, he paused and turned to the roomful of lawyers, veterans, and onlookers. "Goodbye, everybody," he said, beaming broadly. "If I don't see you again, I want you to know I have fond affection for all of you. Who knows, we may be together again later on." And with a genial wave of his hand, he left the courtroom.[104]

III

THE FUTURE

12

Versions of Legal Reality

THE story of the Agent Orange case in the trial court has now been told. The narrative must now be placed within a larger web of meaning so that we can begin to evaluate and learn from it. This is no simple task. For one thing, the litigation continues; first-level appeals have only recently been heard.[1] It may be years until the dispute is finally resolved, and many years more until the legal system can fully digest and assimilate it. We are still too close to the case and the war that spawned it to attain the detached, disinterested perspective from which scholarly analysis should proceed.

Another problem is that the case, like other complex social phenomena, can plausibly be understood in many different ways. Like the fabled elephant "seen" differently by each blind man, the Agent Orange case is a melange of stories, each true from some vantage point, each false from another, and all incomplete and thus inevitably misleading.

To many of the veterans, as I suggested earlier, the case was a morality play performed on a stage—the court. From that stage they hoped to express their deepest aspirations for justice, retribution, fraternity, and social (or perhaps even cosmic) coherence. Searching for some explanation for the devastating physical and psychological conditions that many veterans suffered upon their return, they fastened upon Agent Orange. That a synthetic chemical should seem a plausible scapegoat for their ills was understandable. They lived in a milieu, after all, in which reputable scientists and mass media sympathetic to their cause proclaimed a growing, chemically caused cancer epidemic and in which public cancerphobia had become widespread enough to receive some judicial recognition in tort cases. The fact that no such epidemic has yet been demonstrated was largely irrelevant to the rhetorical power of the claim, especially when made on behalf of those who already saw themselves, with considerable justification, as the forgotten victims of an unpopular war. Michael Ryan probably spoke for many veterans when he said, "What happened to Kerry was not an act of God, it was an act of Dow."[2]

The veterans' lawyers had a somewhat different view of the case. As professionals, of course, they valued the case as a means to help the veterans. But its meaning for some of the lawyers transcended their clients' immediate interests. To Yannacone and a few colleagues in the consortium, for example, the case was also a tactic in a larger "public interest" struggle to control the threat of toxic chemicals in contemporary life. Some of the lawyers who later entered the case saw it as a high-visibility, high-stakes contest in which they could seek fame and fortune. Through it they might enlarge their personal injury practices while smiting the chemical industry, their frequent, much-despised adversary.

The veterans and their lawyers were divided in another sense. The veterans expected the law to provide the essential elements of simple justice—their "day in court," with comprehensible narrative evidence, a clear determination of guilt or innocence, and a swift, straightforward remedy. Their lawyers knew, however, that this view of adjudication was chimerical, the legal equivalent of the elementary civics-textbook view of politics. They knew that many of the complex, technical aspects of the Agent Orange case contradicted their clients' intuitive notions of justice and even defied common sense. The intricacies of class action, choice-of-law, sovereign immunity, statistical causation, and the government contract defense (to name just a few) simply had no counterpart, no coherent meaning, in the veterans' experiences. Their lawyers might understand, at least at a technical level, how a case that was essentially identical to one that was settled for almost $200 million could be thrown out of court a year later for being without merit. But the veterans, lacking the highly stylized training and specialized conceptual apparatus that we call "professionalism," could not. For them, the law had become profoundly mystifying, alien, and unjust.

To the Agent Orange manufacturers—"repeat players" in the mass toxic tort game—the case was a crucial indication of their future economic viability. It presented a critical opportunity to demonstrate that "legal blackmail" (as Rivkin described the class action) would not succeed. It was a fundamental test of strength against the avaricious, implacable plaintiffs' bar—the chemical companies' version of Armageddon. To the federal government, another repeat player, Agent Orange was not merely an extremely important legal precedent and potential budgetary threat; the revelation of the government's treatment of millions of veterans and family members was dramatic, front-page news with deep political reverberations.

To the judges, the case was a legal Gordian knot, an unprecedented intellectual conundrum, an almost impossible administrative tangle that threatened to transmogrify tort litigation and deplete the court's capacity to render justice. Agent Orange fascinated them, but most of the time they wished it would go away. To the law professors, it was a dream case, the perfect hypothetical made flesh; it would quickly enter their classrooms and their textbooks.

To the larger American society, the case had several meanings. As the final inquest into our conduct of the Vietnam War, it reinforced a desire for national catharsis that was always close to the surface of public consciousness. This complicated quest for understanding and justification became especially salient as the tenth anniversary of the harrowing American evacuation of Saigon approached. But along with Love Canal and the asbestos cases, Agent Orange was also a visible symbol of society's effort, which began in earnest only during the 1970s, to come to terms with the more specific risks created by the chemical revolution.

A third, related problem in evaluating the Agent Orange case is that the relevant criteria are in principle or in application irreducibly subjective, political, and value-laden. One may begin with the chief instrumental goal of the tort system—deterrence of unduly dangerous activity. To this must be added other goals—compensation, risk-spreading, administrative efficiency, decisional accuracy, and process-oriented values such as procedural fairness, litigant autonomy, judicial self-restraint, and fidelity to legislative intent.[3] Such evaluative criteria are difficult or impossible to put into operation, and they almost always point in different directions. Trade-offs must be established between, for example, litigant autonomy and administrative efficiency, or between deterrence and risk-spreading, yet no social consensus concerning these trade-offs exists. Some of these criteria are intelligible only if applied to some baseline, empirical notion of what the tort system *is*. Yet any serious effort to evaluate the Agent Orange case cannot be satisfied by a merely descriptive account; it must also confront the normative question of what that system (at least as applied to mass toxic exposures) *ought to be.*

These problems converge when one considers the class action settlement. How should one evaluate it? The veterans, the beneficiaries of the settlement, do not speak clearly on this question. Most have been mute, and the others, as the fairness hearings revealed, speak with many different voices. To Michael Ryan, the settlement was a sellout; to Frank McCarthy, it offers a glimmer of hope for the future.[4] All entered the case with multiple objectives, some of which no mere legal decision or settlement fund could possibly fulfill. To the veterans, as to most people, the law's procedural complexities, doctrinal refinements, and evidentiary demands often seem to have no relationship to their intuitive, common-sense view of what justice requires, especially in their own case. Frank McCarthy surely echoed the frustration of many veterans when, a year and a half after the settlement, he rued having "wasted more than seven years of my life on a lawsuit that went nowhere, denied us our day in court, and produced a few hundred dollars a year for a relative handful of veterans."[5]

From the more professional perspective of the specialists—the lawyers for both sides and the court—the settlement reflected their best judgments about the strength of the contending legal and factual claims, discounted by the various contingencies of litigation. As Chapters 8 and 9 revealed, Judge Weinstein did dictate some of the principal terms of the settlement agreement. And by increasing the uncertainty on certain issues, such as choice of law, reducing it on others, such as punitive damages, and emphasizing different risks to each side, he cajoled the lawyers into subscribing to the agreement. Still, their assent was not in any conventional sense coerced; they remained free to reject settlement and proceed to trial. The most that can be said with certainty is that the nature of class action litigation in a mass tort case, especially the judge's commanding position, constrained their choices and influenced their judgments. To say more would be to cast serious doubt on their ability and determination to protect their clients' interests, at least as the lawyers defined those interests. The record does not justify such an indictment.

From another perspective, however, that is precisely the point: a legal structure that gives the judge so many levers with which to move lawyers—for example, control over their fees, their leadership position in the case, their access to the jury, and most of the legal rules to be applied—is in a sense *inherently* intimidating, if not coercive, at least in the hands of an adroit strategist like Weinstein. Viewed that way, Yannacone's assessment of the settlement—that it "only reflects the judge's masterful skill in extracting money from the defendants"—seems plausible but incomplete; the settlement also reflected Weinstein's ability to wring concessions from plaintiffs anxious to get before a jury.

From a third perspective, the settlement reflected neither the merits of the parties' claims nor the judge's awesome powers; instead, it was quite literally a tribute to the staggering litigation costs that a case of this kind entails. From that vantage point, the settlement amount was (as the defendants viewed it) the "nuisance value" of the Agent Orange case on the eve of trial. Given the incentives created by our tort system and the roughly $100 million already spent, the plaintiffs could extract $180 million from the other side. In a different system—one, say, like India's, in which plaintiffs must post a substantial bond with the court before they may file suit, or one like England's, in which losing plaintiffs must pay the defendants' litigation costs—the case's settlement value might have been negligible.[6] It was from this third vantage point that Weinstein's evaluation of the $180 million class action settlement as "fair" could be presented as logically consistent with his subsequent decision to dismiss the opt-out cases.

This multiplicity of perspectives also confounds the question of the court's role in the Agent Orange case. How should the performance of Judge Pratt and Judge Weinstein be evaluated? On one view, Weinstein flagrantly abused his exalted position. He pushed the parties here, pulled them there, reformulated legal doctrine, self-consciously used procedural rules to shape desired substantive outcomes, emphasized one thing to the PMC and another to the chemical companies, employed special masters to do as agents what he as principal knew he should not do directly (for example, communicating with each side *ex parte*), articulated his views of the merits publicly, and used evidentiary rulings to decide fundamental factual disputes. In a sense, he played a massive game of chicken in which he made highly questionable decisions while working for a settlement that would render them invulnerable to appeal. Through these stratagems, he transformed the court from the essentially reactive, umpirelike institution that Pratt embodied into that of an active, engaged policymaker.

On another view, however, Weinstein's extraordinary moves were no more than was demanded by an extraordinary case like Agent Orange. His legal innovations—his propensity to "make things up as he goes along"—can be seen as the quintessential work of the

common-law judge, "working the law pure" as it is applied to un-
foreseen cases in unprecedented circumstances, devising judicial solutions in an area of policy in which legislatures have been content to
permit the courts to take the lead. Indeed, from this vantage point, it
was Pratt, not Weinstein, who failed to discharge the ancient judging
function of recognizing when the received legal rules are no longer
adequate to the case before the court and then modifying them (within
limits) to meet new conditions.[7]

How can one rationally choose between such disparate versions of
legal reality? The answer, perhaps unsurprisingly, is that one cannot.
Just as no logical principle can tell us exactly when a precedent loses
its compelling analogical force and becomes an "unconvincing" basis
for deciding the new case before us, so no jurisprudential canon can
prescribe the precise point at which creative common-law reasoning
by analogy loses its legitimacy and becomes an arbitrary exercise in
judicial usurpation. Both of these versions of judicial performance in
Agent Orange capture important elements of the truth; each, taken
alone, also remains seriously incomplete.

I do not mean to suggest that no such normative canon exists, only
that it gets rather fuzzy as one moves away from the core of familiar
principles and fact situations to the jurisprudential margins where the
Agent Orange case lies. Nor do I believe that the case's novelty necessarily makes the judges' performance immune from criticism. First,
as in any litigation, some of the issues in Agent Orange—for example,
the applicability of federal common law and the temporal sequence of
the distribution—lie close to the conventional core, and their resolutions can be evaluated by more or less conventional analytical standards. Second, even when a judge's ruling seems correct or at least
reasonable, the process of argument used to reach it may be deficient.
Examples include Pratt's belated epiphany concerning the relationship between the causation and government contract defense issues
and Weinstein's choice-of-law decision. Finally, a judge's conduct
may be objectionable on the more general grounds that it distorts the
judicial role or disables the legal system from functioning appropri-
ately. Pratt's prolonged failure to move the litigation to trial and
Weinstein's insistence on forcing the government to stand trial without discovery and (a much closer question) his refusal to send the
opt-out cases to the jury are examples.

The earlier chapters are studded with criticisms of this kind. In a
sense, however, they are beside the point. The true significance of the
Agent Orange case transcends the question of whether a particular

judge decided this or that legal issue correctly. That is a valuable inquiry, to be sure, and one to which legal commentators are already beginning to turn.[8] But the case raises a far more profound and troubling set of questions that now must be confronted, not only by lawyers but by society in general. These questions revolve around one fundamental issue: how should the legal system handle the problem of potentially toxic chemicals to which large numbers of people are exposed but whose effects on individuals are difficult to discern? The remainder of this chapter and the next, which will necessarily be somewhat technical in nature, are devoted to exploring it.

I wish to emphasize at the outset how limited the domain of this issue may be. Because some of the problems raised by the Agent Orange case are distinctive and affect relatively few civil cases, it would be foolish to redesign the entire tort system solely to deal with them. (There are respectable arguments, of course, that the tort system fails to achieve its purposes and should therefore be scrapped entirely in favor of alternative systems of compensation and deterrence.[9] Although I indicate below some of the reasons why I do not endorse this view, at least in its most comprehensive, apocalyptic forms, that issue is well beyond the scope of this project, which is concerned with the special problems created by mass toxic exposure cases.) Even the mass torts—the airliner crash that leaves hundreds dead, the collapse of a building that kills thousands, the conflagration that destroys a school or neighborhood—are not implicated in this critique. Although difficult issues are often involved in these cases, the problems of litigation management (with the possible exception of choice of law in airline disasters) are fairly tractable to now-conventional legal techniques.

Indeed, the analysis that follows does not concern even all mass *toxic* torts. As noted in Chapter 1, certain difficulties arising in previous cases, such as indeterminate defendants (DES and asbestos) and governmental immunity (swine flu), were addressed through legislative or judicial changes within a general tort law framework, such as market share liability in DES cases and waiver of sovereign immunity and liability requirements for victims of Guillain-Barre syndrome (GBS) in swine flu cases. When proof of causation was difficult, it was seldom because of the indeterminate plaintiff problem that plagues the proof of Agent Orange causation. In those cases, victims typically manifested symptoms rarely caused by known chemical agents other than the one being challenged. In particular, asbestosis and, to a lesser extent, mesothelioma are considered asbestos-specific pathologies and are often precursors of asbestos-caused cancer; the vaginal adenocarcinoma caused by DES is also exotic and specific to that disease. GBS, although not caused *only* by the swine flu vaccine, is a rare condition, and the vaccine is known to be a cause.[10]

In at least one important respect, as Judge Weinstein has observed, the Agent Orange case was actually *easier* than many other mass toxic tort cases.[11] By the time of Weinstein's fairness opinion in September 1984, much high-quality epidemiological and other research evidence sponsored by the government had become available. But the case also presented many distinctive problems. Most important was the difficulty of proving that Agent Orange harmed the plaintiffs, in view of the fact that it apparently produces no unique symptoms (other than chloracne, which is not usually a precursor of others). It also involved large scale, because of the number of potential plaintiffs, defendants, and insurers; spatial dispersion, because of the large number of jurisdictions having plausible claims to provide the governing law; temporal dispersion, because of the duration of exposure and the fact that injuries might not fully manifest themselves for twenty or more years; and enormous cost, because of all the factors listed above.

Although the Agent Orange case was probably the first to combine indeterminate causation, large scale, spatial dispersion, temporal dispersion, and enormous cost, one would be foolish to assume it will be the last. Moreover, even cases that lack some of these features—say, cases arising from long-term mass exposure to toxic wastes associated with nonspecific, long-latency diseases but occurring within only one jurisdiction—may create similar problems. In those cases—perhaps few in number but disproportionately significant and costly—legal techniques that proved serviceable in the past may be inadequate. New ones must be devised.

Very broadly speaking, there are three possible ways in which the legal system might attempt to deal with cases of this kind. I shall, with no claim to originality, call them (1) the traditional tort approach, (2) the public law tort approach, and (3) the nontort approach. As I shall maintain, the law governing mass toxic exposures in the future should draw upon all three.

The Traditional Tort Approach

The traditional approach views a case like Agent Orange essentially as an ordinary tort dispute writ large. This view represents an individualistic orientation to litigation, grounded in three linked principles: the primacy of the individual claimant, the necessity for full compensation (including a residual "pain and suffering" award) based on fault (or a faultlike criterion such as defect), and the sanctity and indissolubility of the conventional attorney-client relationship.

In this view, each individual possesses an absolute right to the integrity of his or her personhood. If injured, he or she possesses the right to recover damages that compensate not simply for out-of-pocket expenses and other economic losses wrongfully caused by the defendants but for invasion of dignitary and other subjective interests, particularly pain and suffering. And these rights can be fully vindicated only if the claimant can control how the case is planned, presented, or settled through a lawyer of his or her choosing.

The traditional tort approach reflects the ideology and self-interest of plaintiffs' personal injury bar, especially those lawyers who are unlikely to be selected to manage class actions and to earn the fees and notoriety that go with that status. But the traditional view is also deeply embedded in American legal traditions and individualistic liberal values that sanctify certain doctrines and institutions—the fault standard, private control of litigation, trial by jury, the dominance of "reasonableness" criteria, the preponderance-of-the-evidence rule for proof of causation, and a relatively passive judicial role in tort cases.

In the Agent Orange case, the traditional view was articulated by a curious alliance of defendants' lawyers and counsel for the opt-out plaintiffs. Their positions converged on a critique of the class action as a vehicle for litigating such cases and of the settlement in which the action culminated and which reflected its defects. The class action, in this view, has no place in mass toxic tort litigations; it is, in Rob Taylor's words, an "engine of destruction."[12] A class action corrodes the individual attorney-client relationship. The intimate contact and consultation that force lawyers to educate their clients, respond to their wishes, and litigate faithfully and vigorously are supplanted by a condition of amorphous anonymity. Meaningful communication, trust, and accountability become impossible. In effect, individual litigants lose their personal attorneys. They must settle instead for representation by the court-designated lead counsel, whose loyalties are diffuse and whose incentives may be different.

A class action transforms the judge's role, greatly magnifying his power to mold the case. This power can be abused, and this fact relegates the lawyers and their clients to subsidiary roles. And mass tort class actions can mock the traditional ideal of due process. In particular, courts interpreting Rule 23, using notions of "constructive notice" and "adequate class representation," obscure the fact that many individuals do not know that their rights are being adjudicated and that their own lawyers are merely watching from the sidelines.

The mass tort class action, by centralizing the case geographically (usually in a large metropolitan area), deprives many plaintiffs of their customary right to choose the jurisdiction in which they will litigate. This right gives them access to local judges familiar with the local laws that are supposed to be applied to their disputes and to juries responsive to local values. If the class contains individuals from many diverse areas, the individual litigant cannot readily predict which jurisdiction's law will ultimately be applied by the court. Thus the individual plaintiff's choice of forum, so fundamental in our private law jurisprudence, loses much of its value.

The class in a mass tort case consists of individuals whose situations and interests may differ vastly from one another. This heterogeneity far exceeds that in, say, an antitrust or securities class action, in which individual claims tend to be small and purely financial in nature. In a mass tort case, individual claims may be quite large and highly personalized; the inequities of subjecting all individuals to uniform class treatment are correspondingly increased. In such a class, for example, any settlement fund, when distributed on a wholesale basis, is almost certain to result in a lower recovery than some individuals (especially the most seriously injured) would receive by litigating on their own. (This assumes, of course, that they could prove individual causation—a serious problem in individual indeterminate plaintiff situations, as we saw in the preceding chapter.) The class's benefit, in this sense, becomes less than the sum of its individual members' benefits.

Finally, the fuel that powers a class action—attorneys' fees—is measured and dispensed by judges. This dependency compromises the autonomy of the class lawyers, distorts their litigation and settlement strategies, and encourages many to coast along on the efforts of a few in the hopes of sharing in the recovery. Although the courts are supposed to counteract these unfortunate tendencies, they cannot always do so as a practical matter.

This critique of class actions lies at the core of the traditional tort approach to mass exposure litigation. The Agent Orange case suggests that at least some of these concerns are warranted. Although Agent Orange was not a lawyers' case when McCarthy and Yannacone first designed it, it eventually became one. As the case proceeded, the relationship between the veterans and their lawyers (first the consortium, then the PMC) became more and more attenuated; indeed, the settlement was bitterly attacked by many veterans in part because it was negotiated by lawyers whom they had not retained, did not know, and whose motives they did not trust.

Even continued control of the class action by Yannacone, who clearly enjoyed a special rapport with the veterans, might not have averted this problem. This is not a comment on Yannacone's idiosyncratic personality and style; rather, it testifies to the dynamics of mass tort litigation, in which power tends to flow from the lawyers with individual clients to the lawyers with the financial, legal, and administrative resources to underwrite and manage the protracted, expensive venture. Weinstein had no illusions on this score, as Chapter 10 revealed. In class actions, he reminded Yannacone, the nominal representative plaintiffs "are only names" and "the case is turned over to the lawyers," among whom "the people who put up the money will insist on a say as to how the litigation is conducted. They won't allow others to spend endlessly without control."[13] Thus we should not be surprised to learn, as Chapter 8 taught, that when it came to deciding whether and how to settle the Agent Orange case, the financiers— lawyers without clients—called the tune, creating troublesome conflict-of-interest issues.

Weinstein's realistic account of class action management, of course, modestly omits any special role for the court. But if the Agent Orange case teaches us anything about mass tort class actions, it is that the lawyers lose control of the litigation when the judge decides to control the lawyers. The levers of judicial control are far more numerous and powerful than in a conventional case. Pratt cautiously pressed some of them, as when his special master molded the PMC and threatened that Ashcraft & Gerel might receive no fees. Weinstein, however, was less restrained. He boldly pressed all the levers; thus he favored class members over opt-outs in his rulings on statutes of limitations, indeterminate plaintiffs, and alternative liability, and he designed the settlement and distribution plan.

The judge's awesome power in such a case, magnified by the distinctive features of a mass tort case, is an important reason why many commentators prefer the class action form. It facilitates what has come to be called "managerial judging," a variety of judicial techniques designed to resolve cases in an expeditious fashion rather than leave them to the vagaries and pace of a lawyer-centered adversary process.[14] Managerial judging promises much to many; I shall show why in the next section. But the judge's power is also troubling. It may be (as Lincoln once said of the presidency) "more power than a bad man should have or a good man should want." If it can be used to prevent lawyers from running the case to serve their selfish purposes, it also permits an appointed, life-tenured official to impose personal views of substantive justice and public policy on the parties—and through them, on society at large. Judge Weinstein's behavior illustrated both possibilities. With some important exceptions, he deployed his power with extraordinary skill, judgment, and self-restraint; he produced a result that on the whole struck most observers as efficient and fair. But this performance provides scant assurance concerning the judiciary generally. By all accounts, Weinstein is an extraordinary man and an extraordinary judge. Large social structures such as legal systems, however, are not designed by or for such people, nor is it wise to assume that they will often be in a position to run them.[15] Here, we do well to recall James Madison's warning that "enlightened statesmen will not always be at the helm."[16]

The Agent Orange case also confirms some of the other concerns that traditionalists voice about mass tort class actions. Class notice was arguably inadequate, especially as to the nature of the distribution plan and the time allowed for opting out of the class. Very different kinds of claims—cancers, birth defects, miscarriages, and chloracne, for example—were lumped together in the class, and many plaintiffs' choices of forum were overridden. Had the case gone to trial, numerous other shortcuts, compromises, and distortions would doubtless have been necessary simply to manage the massive aggregated case.

But if the traditional tort view spotlights the vices of mass tort class actions, it is obscure and unhelpful as an approach to managing Agent Orange–type cases. Indeed, it essentially denies that any extra-party management is either necessary or appropriate, insisting that any approach other than the traditional one would be a cure worse than the disease. Rob Taylor, whose opt-out cases were dismissed in May 1985, maintains that Agent Orange could have been litigated as a traditional tort case without overwhelming the court system. "Only" 7,600 veterans were named plaintiffs and intervenors in the Agent Orange proceeding, he argues, a smaller number than in the asbestos cases. Instead of a class action, the issues common to all plaintiffs could be tried in a consolidated, multidistrict action process, after which the cases would be remanded for individual trials of the remaining issues in the local courts in which they were originally filed. Although some trials could last a year, he urges, few would actually go that far; if plaintiffs won the early ones, defendants would quickly settle the rest. Contrary to the PMC's strategy in Agent Orange, he adds, plaintiffs could keep the cases simple, obtaining protective orders against defendants' perverse efforts to complicate them.

Taylor's optimism, however, seems Panglossian, perhaps even reckless in a case like Agent Orange. It is true that looking across the many individual cases, some issues may divide neatly along common/uncommon or generic/specific lines, permitting a single consolidated trial. But as Judge Pratt's experience suggests, the most important and complex issues, especially specific causation, knowledge, and damages, do not so divide. (Consolidated discovery, to be sure, is sometimes feasible even outside the class action framework.) Nor is it entirely clear what would happen if hundreds or thousands of cases were remanded to the local, originating courts. If, for example, it would be necessary to present most of the causation evidence each time in order to establish specific causation, the arrangement Taylor envisions could actually be more costly and protracted than the present system.

Finally, the asbestos experience, cited by Taylor, is hardly reassuring. According to a 1983 study of the costs of that litigation, the total compensation and litigation expenditures from the early 1970s through 1982 were approximately $1 billion. Of the total spent by defendants and insurers to close cases during that period, 63 percent went for the parties' legal fees and litigation expenses, while only 37 percent was paid to injured parties.[17] Although this percentage may have increased since 1982 as the size of plaintiffs' jury verdicts has grown and encouraged settlements, the traditional tort approach as applied to mass toxic exposures like asbestos is obviously an exceedingly expensive, lawyer-intensive way to compensate victims and deter manufacturers from marketing excessively risky products. Moreover, the asbestos litigation entailed few of the costly indeterminate plaintiff and proof difficulties that Agent Orange and some other toxic substances present.

The traditional tort approach, one must conclude, is not so much a serious response to the special problems posed by Agent Orange–type cases—the problems of proof of causation, scale, spatial dispersion, time span, and cost—as an ostrichlike avoidance of them. Even if this approach is considered adequate for most conventional cases and even for some mass tort cases—a proposition that some commentators vigorously deny[18]—its shortcomings in cases like Agent Orange are severe. That is reason enough to search for alternatives.

The Public Law Tort Approach

In a provocative article published in 1984, David Rosenberg of Harvard Law School advanced a quite different conception of mass toxic tort litigation.[19] Refining and elaborating arguments put forth by a number of commentators since the late 1970s,[20] Rosenberg emphasized two defects in the traditional tort approach when applied to many mass exposures. First, the preponderance-of-the-evidence rule, coupled with the difficulty of distinguishing among the many possible causes of the injury, prevents individual victims of such exposures from proving specific causation. At best, the individual can prove membership in a large population subjected by that exposure to a statistical "excess risk" of that injury. Second, the costs of individually litigating a claim in a mass exposure case typically exceed the individual's expected recovery. By discouraging even valid claims, these defects result in inadequate deterrence and compensation.

In place of the traditional approach, Rosenberg advocates what he calls a "public law vision of the tort system." This vision contains two central elements. First, the preponderance rule would be replaced by a "proportional liability" rule, under which the court would apportion liability according to the percentage of injuries attributable to a defendant's activity. This attribution could be determined wholly through statistical analysis, need not exceed the traditional 50 percent preponderance level, and could be based on increased risk, not just on actual harm. Second, the public law approach would employ class actions culminating in nonindividualized damage assessment devices, such as damage scheduling, in which compensation would be paid on the basis of general categories and scheduled amounts, and insurance fund judgments, in which defendants would be required to create a fund to pay victims over a long period of time.

Under Rosenberg's approach, the link between these two elements—proportional liability based on statistical evidence, and class actions and remedies—reveals the fundamental conceptual, ideological, and operational differences between the traditional tort and the public law view. The public law approach is not seen simply as a way to vindicate individual rights more effectively. Instead, it employs aggregative, mass tools (such as class actions, statistical evidence, and group-based remedies) to achieve certain *collective* purposes. These purposes include deterring socially injurious activity, encouraging an efficient allocation of social resources, expressing social solidarity, and augmenting the government's legislative, regulatory, and wealth-redistributing policies. This collective litigation mode is thought to harmonize the interests of the individual victim and those of society in mass exposure cases by reducing costs that would otherwise impede individual prosecution of valid claims.

Individual and collective interests sometimes conflict, however, and when they do, the public law approach sacrifices the former to the latter. For example, Rosenberg would make class litigation mandatory in mass tort actions, barring individuals with an especially strong case or a higher-than-average expected recovery from litigating on their own. This is necessary, he argues, to prevent individual litigants from free-riding on the efforts of others, from depleting a limited damages fund, and from creating binding precedents prematurely on certain issues.[21] Stripped to its essentials, however, this proposal amounts to making one's substantive rights turn on subordinating one's interests to those of the group.

In the public law vision, even causation is a social, aggregated phenomenon. Unlike the traditional approach, it emphasizes not the individual, discrete, or contingent quality of injuries, but rather their "centralized corporate sources, statistical predictability, massive scale, and relative uniformity of disease risks."[22] It also stresses an essentially identical relationship of all victims to injurers and to the toxic agent. Because harms from mass exposures are seen to be caused and suffered in common and reflect mass technological processes and economic concentrations, the legal rules for litigating them should, in this view, be similarly aggregative. In this sense, Rosenberg argues, the public law approach is the procedural counterpart of the liability-expanding changes in product law in recent years, changes that courts have increasingly attempted—without much success—to mold to the structure of a mass-production, mass-distribution, mass-consumption economy.

The public law vision necessarily magnifies the role and discretion of judges—an exaltation of abstract principle and unaccountable power that rests uneasily with our democratic traditions.[23] In many respects, Weinstein's performance in the Agent Orange case was the quintessential expression of this judge-centered vision, presenting a classic instance of the occasional influence of academic theories on judicial decisions. Weinstein, citing Rosenberg, actively implemented the public law vision. For example, he approved the class action, enthusiastically endorsed statistical evidence and the "weak" version of the preponderance rule, and designed a distribution plan based on categorical statuses and awards rather than individualized ones. He adopted a "classwide solution" to the indeterminate plaintiff problem, which incorporated the concepts of proportional liability and probabilistic causation. He decided to apply "national consensus" law, used alternative liability devices to keep all defendants in the case, and doggedly searched for a "comprehensive" solution to what he defined as a large social policy problem, a search that took him to great lengths to involve the government as the preeminent collective institution.

Rosenberg's theory, like many academic creations, was conceived at several removes from institutional reality. His arguments for the public law approach are, as he candidly observed, "relatively abstract: I have considered no specific toxic agent, disease risk, or epidemiological methodology."[24] The Agent Orange experience therefore provides perhaps the first actual test of his claims. It is a highly imperfect, incomplete test, of course, if only because the case never went to trial. Firm conclusions about the effects of his approach would have to await a careful, partly quantitative study, which would have to include assumptions about how the litigation would have proceeded in a more conventional fashion. Clearly, the new procedures—at least in Weinstein's adept hands—produced some real benefits, economizing on costs, avoiding inconsistent verdicts, and tending to equalize the parties' litigation resources. The class action permitted a relatively comprehensive litigation remedy (the distribution plan), which assured a controlled, equalized access to the settlement fund and focused public attention on legislative and other possible remedies.

There is, of course, another side to the ledger. The availability of a class action, for example, may have enabled plaintiffs' attorneys to litigate for many years at great cost a case that would not—and, if Weinstein's evaluation of the merits is correct, should not—have survived nearly so long under the traditional tort approach. Rosenberg contends that a public law system, even one that included a regime of proportional liability for mass exposure claims, would not encourage "nuisance" claims.[25] Again, however, the Agent Orange case, by revealing how contingent such litigation is and thus how hard it is for plaintiffs' lawyers—the system's gatekeepers—to predict its course, casts some doubt on this assurance. Again, supposing that Weinstein's view is correct, a worthless litigation managed to acquire, at least partly through the agency of the class action, a nuisance value of at least $180 million on the eve of the trial. And defendants were obliged to spend perhaps $100 million or more just to reach that point. If Weinstein is also correct that even his "low" attorneys' fee awards will not chill the litigious fervor of the plaintiffs' bar, then there seems a great risk that a public law tort system will encourage lawyers to bring even more such cases. Finally, a recent decision by the Supreme Court could possibly restrict the ability of state (and perhaps federal) courts in class action cases to apply the forum state's law to out-of-state class members.[26] If it does, the efficiency advantages of nation-wide class actions like Agent Orange will be correspondingly reduced.

Even when these and other possible problems with the class action are acknowledged, its potential advantages may well outweigh the disadvantages in Agent Orange–type cases. But the public law approach goes well beyond the use of class actions; indeed, some of its other elements raise additional difficulties that class actions may only magnify. Rosenberg, for example, advocates the widespread use of statistical evidence to prove causation in mass tort cases. All causation is statistical, he maintains, and the search for nonstatistical, "particularistic" evidence is thus misguided and futile. He further points out, as Weinstein did, that courts "regularly admit" such evidence in some other kinds of cases, such as civil rights and antitrust litigation.

These assertions seem somewhat beside the point. While it is true that causal statements are irreducibly probabilistic, this does not imply that in mass exposure cases the proof requirement should be satisfied with nothing more than an epidemiological study showing a statistical "excess risk" to a population of which plaintiff is a member. It is not clear whether Rosenberg would dispense with the additional requirement (which Weinstein insisted on in the opt-out cases) that a plaintiff adduce expert medical testimony supporting specific causation, evidence at least tending to exclude other possible causes of the injury based on family and medical history, exposure data, and so on. Rosenberg offers no justification for omitting this requirement, yet its confirmatory and probative value may be important. If, on the other hand, he would require it, there is much less to his argument against particularistic evidence than meets the eye.

Rosenberg's appeal to precedent in the judicial use of statistical evidence is also questionable, if only because the demands that mass exposure cases impose on statistical analysis seem far more difficult to satisfy. In employment discrimination cases, for example, statistical evidence is generally used to create certain presumptions that defendants can in principle, and often do in practice, readily rebut. If plaintiffs show that an employer has a lower-than-expected representation of a minority group or women in its labor force, the employer can conduct its own study and perhaps show that the relevant labor pool should be defined differently or that "business necessity" justified its hiring pattern.

In mass exposure cases, however, a defendant whose product is said to be associated with a statistical "excess risk" is in a decidedly poor position to rebut that showing even if the defendant is in fact causally innocent. Conducting an epidemiological study of cancer causation in the population is not at all like conducting a labor market study. In the latter, the relevant data are almost all objective (wage levels, demographic characteristics, job categories) and readily available from existing records. In the former, however, neither of these conditions is likely to obtain; moreover, numerous confounding variables (for example, alternative causes) are possible. Statistical evidence in a mass tort case, then, greatly compounds the risk of error.

It is important to note that Rosenberg's causation approach has never been tested in an actual case; in previous mass toxic tort disputes, the epidemiological evidence has demonstrated either a powerful causal connection (DES and asbestos) or a weak or nonexistent one (Agent Orange and Bendectin). A case involving an epidemiologically derived probability of causation that was significant but less than 50 percent would create far more serious evidentiary difficulties. Until such a case arises, then, the feasibility of Rosenberg's approach must remain highly conjectural.

An even more fundamental concern about the public law approach has recently been advanced by Peter Huber.[27] His point is a simple but compelling one: if we truly wish our society to be safer, our decision-making institutions must concern themselves with whether a particular substance increases the risk not of a particular harm, but of the *totality* of harm, taking into consideration any preexisting risks that the new substance may reduce.

Huber observes that new technologies, be they pharmaceuticals, nuclear power, or chemical products, tend to displace more health risks than they create. Moreover, because these new risks are relatively "public" and thus subject to centralized monitoring and regulation, they are usually more effectively controlled than the old, predominantly "private" risks that they supplant. Public risks, to which mass toxic tort litigation (including Agent Orange) is almost exclusively directed, are desirable whenever they displace more risk than they create. Unfortunately, he contends, several features of our legal system—especially its bias in favor of old, private risks and against new, mass-produced ones, and its related tendency to ignore *natural* risks in defining baseline entitlements against which the law must measure new risks—lead to regressive risk management policies.

Huber's critique seems generally correct and has considerable significance for public policy. For present purposes, however, his more interesting argument is this: "The judicial system is . . . incapable of engaging in the aggregative calculus of risk created and risk averted that progressive public-risk management requires . . . The judicial role sought (and achieved) by many commentators [of whom Rosenberg is the exemplar] is imprudently biased against many progressive, risk-reducing (though still risky) technologies. This bias significantly hinders our progress towards a healthier, safer environment."[28] The public law approach, in short, only exacerbates the disabilities and distortions of the tort system as a regulator of environmental, product, and other mass exposure risks.

The public law approach, Huber suggests, is generally biased against newer, mass-produced risks for several reasons. First, the plaintiffs' mass tort bar focuses on new, "exotic" risks, which not only "stand out against the otherwise grey background of ubiquitous hazard" but are better documented. In addition, the cases that these lawyers bring are not concerned with risk displacement potential; instead they target "deep-pocket" defendants. Judges and juries, moreover, are vulnerable to these same biases. Second, Huber contends, calculations of excess risk in mass tort litigation, especially under the public law approach, "are almost certain to adopt a simplistic, disease-specific focus on risk while entirely ignoring the collateral, risk-reducing benefits" that the challenged product generates. Specifically, courts do not analyze the risks created by actual or potential substitutes in the same "risk market." In the case of the Dalkon

Shield, for example, these risks would include the maternal deaths, abortions, and fetal abnormalities that the product would have prevented, as well as the risks associated with other contraceptives that might be resorted to instead.

Further, Huber argues, it is usually easier for plaintiffs to show that a defendant's product caused a statistical "excess risk" than it is for the defendant to show that it caused a compensating statistical "decreased risk." As a result, he asserts, *net* risk—the only appropriate policy-relevant measure—"simply cannot be evaluated from raw, disease-specific, epidemiological statistics." Courts also ignore the contribution to net risk reduction of the increased social wealth (jobs, income, and "consumer surplus") that a defendant's activities may create. More generally, courts are poorly equipped to trace out the interactions and indirect effects of risk decisions.

The force of Huber's provocative analysis of the likely effect of the public law approach ultimately turns on empirical questions, some of which are at this point impossible to answer. Do we really know more about new risks than we know (or could learn) about old ones? Perhaps, but that may be a result of research priorities, not an ineluctable consequence of our legal system. Are judges and juries in mass tort cases always duped by plaintiffs' lawyers' strategic choices? As mentioned in Chapter 11, there have been some notable exceptions (Bendectin). Do courts inevitably ignore risk substitutes? In fact, Weinstein *did* refer to the risks to American soldiers had Agent Orange not been used, and his formulation of the government contract defense makes relevant whether the government made an informed benefit/risk decision. (On the other hand, Weinstein's failure to analyze this question systematically may actually underscore the truth of Huber's general point.) Is Huber correct that "the risk assessment scales are now clearly biased in favor of the public-risk plaintiff"? Perhaps, but the outcome of the Agent Orange opt-out cases is evidence to the contrary. (On the other hand, if defendants are peculiarly disadvantaged by our relative ignorance about background or natural risks and about the risk-reducing effects of increased wealth, the scales may indeed be as biased as he suggests.)

In principle, at least, courts *could* ask the kinds of risk questions that Huber correctly regards as essential. Moreover, the public law approach—which does, after all, promise a more comprehensive, technocratic perspective on risk issues—*could* be implemented in ways that would encourage courts to undertake such an inquiry rather than obscure it and that would minimize the danger of error. Ultimately, the value of the public law approach in mass toxic tort litigation depends on how judges actually define and implement it through their reasoning and procedures.

One glimpse of how this might work has recently been offered by Judge Weinstein himself. His experience with the Agent Orange case and his study of other toxic tort disputes has led him to propose consideration of a number of procedural changes for litigating "mass disasters," especially those that spill across state borders. In addition to class actions, Weinstein mentions creation of a federal common law of choice-of-law in such cases, use of court-appointed technical expert witnesses, special court administration and personnel arrangements, establishment of administrative claims commissions, consolidation of related litigation in specialized courts, and other procedural techniques. In particular, he proposes creation of a Federal National Disaster Court, constituted on an *ad hoc* basis by temporary assignment of federal judges with expertise in handling litigation that meets the criteria—for example, large potential damages, numerous parties, multiple jurisdictions—of a "substantial national disaster." This court would decide on a single applicable substantive law, employ flexible procedures for aggregating and consolidating claims, make emergency payments to needy victims, and award limited damages (that is, neither punitive nor pain-and-suffering awards).[29]

Some of these reforms are probably desirable and might be grafted onto a traditional tort system. Many, however, bear the earmarks of the public law approach; they are aggregative, judge-controlled, and molded to collective concerns rather than those of individual litigants. Their attractiveness also depends in part on the magnitude of the "boundary problem"—the need for clear, defensible criteria for allocating litigation to a special court rather than an ordinary one. Only those relatively few disputes that are unsuitable for adjudication under conventional rules and procedures should be separated out for special treatment.

This boundary question is not merely or even chiefly a technical one; it goes to the very heart of our legal system. Although courts have innovated far more successfully during the last few decades than most legal commentators thought possible, neither the judicial process nor tort law itself is infinitely plastic. Neither may be able to absorb the kinds of changes that the public law approach entails without being transformed into something quite different—something alien, misshapen, and dysfunctional. As we begin to understand just how much courts must change if they are to play the larger, more ambitious role that the public law vision demands of them, we may conclude that alternative visions of reform, including some that subordinate the courts to other risk-regulating institutions, are preferable. That is the subject of the final chapter.

My account of the Agent Orange case provides one reason to search for alternatives—the hope of reducing massive, unproductive litigation costs, long delays, uncertainty, and unhealthy reliance on exceptional judicial performance. The likelihood that the public law approach will prove incompatible with sound risk regulation provides a second reason. But there is a third, more speculative reason to seek alternatives. Traditionally, the individualistic, corrective justice focus of tort law and its basis in widely shared community norms gave it a distinctive claim to moral legitimacy.[30] In recent years, that claim has been frequently contested on a number of grounds, including the movement from fault to functional criteria of liability, the attenuation of individual loss-bearing through widespread insurance, tort law's high litigation costs, and its dissimilar treatment of similarly situated people. By taking the giant step to a wholly aggregative, distributive justice approach—one in which individual A is compensated by company B even though A may not have been harmed by B or indeed by *any* responsible actor (other than Mother Nature)—the public law structure might well destroy whatever residual moral justification remains for shifting A's loss to B through tort adjudication. If so, we might be wise to acknowledge candidly the changed assumptions that exist and to pursue their implications for institutional and doctrinal change. We should not pretend that we are still operating in the moral universe of tort law when mass toxic exposure problems render it anomalous.

13

Alternatives

THIS book is not the place to present and defend a full-blown alternative legal structure for the control of mass toxic exposures. That task would require a level of empirical investigation, legal and political analysis, and institutional design well beyond the scope of the present project. Even at this point, however, it is possible to identify the main elements that such a structure might contain. These elements, which draw upon proposals previously advanced by others in diverse contexts, relate to the three broad policy goals most pertinent to the mass exposure problem: compensation of victims and deterrence of undue risk creation at reasonable administrative cost. The first two goals are discussed separately, and the third is treated as a constraint on each of them.

Compensation

From the perspective of economic efficiency, tort law should not be justified as a compensatory device; instead, it is simply a means of deterring dangerous activity. Compensation objectives can be better met through "first-party" insurance (purchased by or for victims) than through "third-party" insurance (which injurers purchase to cover liability claims by victims). (The appropriate mix as between private and social forms of first-party insurance is a topic I do not pursue here.) Potential victims can ordinarily spread their own losses through insurance more cheaply than manufacturers or other injurers can. To the third-party liability insurance system that tort law has spawned, victims are necessarily a broad, undifferentiated, and therefore relatively unpredictable and inefficient insurance category.

Private first-party insurance enables the insured to select optimal coverage, based on knowledge concerning potential losses and risks. It enables the insurer to appraise and monitor risks at relatively low cost and to administer more cheaply claims filed by its own clients. Under first-party insurance, compensation generally requires only proof that a loss has occurred, not proof that a particular injurer or agent has caused it. For individuals who cannot afford to insure themselves and for risks that they do not or cannot adequately anticipate and thus insure against, first-party losses can be socially insured—at some budgetary cost, of course. Social insurance can spread risks very broadly and achieve some redistributional goals at far lower administrative expense than tort liability can.

There is also a strong argument on grounds of distributive justice that compensation through first-party private and social insurance is fairer than compensation through the tort system. (This is especially true if injurers can be made—through an injury tax or through subrogation of insurers to victims' claims—to finance the compensation fund according to the accident costs that their activities impose.) The tort system, after all, favors certain kinds of victims—for example, those fortunate enough to have been injured by defendants who are identifiable, negligent, solvent, and without strong technical defenses; those who have access to a good, contingent-fee lawyer and can afford to wait for a recovery; and those whose claims are small relative to their defendants' litigation costs. (Tort law also compensates only victims of *accidents*, as distinguished from those who are disabled through illness, genetic predisposition, or in other ways, but that is another issue.) Yet it is difficult to see why, as an equitable matter, these factors ought to determine whether or not a claim is compensated. In contrast, compensation through first-party insurance does not turn on any of these fortuities. The tort system, as others have observed, resembles nothing so much as an expensive lottery, and while lotteries may be fair for selecting draftees or awarding door prizes, they are perverse mechanisms for compensating injuries.[1]

In addition, the systems of nontort compensation that are already in place, although not universal or wholly adequate, are quite extensive. According to a recent analysis by Stephen Sugarman, most tort victims would not suffer substantial income loss in the absence of tort damages. Private, employment-related sick leave benefits and workers' compensation, supplemented in some states by public temporary disability insurance schemes, cover most workers' income replacement needs, which for most are short-term only. For long-term partial and total disabilities and death, Social Security, workers' compensation, and private insurance provide workers with incomplete but substantial income replacement. The main gaps relate to victims who are under working age, long-term unemployed, nonwage earners who perform economically valued functions, and those in transient employment. As for medical expenses, private and public insurance leaves about 85 percent of the population "reasonably well-protected against the risk of incurring substantial medical expenses, including expenses resulting from torts." Here the main gap is for those who are unemployed.[2]

Nontort schemes, to be sure, do not compensate for pain and suffering (except perhaps for disfigurement awards in workers' compensation). But that is a category of damage that people are manifestly unwilling to insure against on their own. Again the important point is not that existing nontort compensation is complete; tort damages, especially in more serious cases, are not complete either, especially if litigation costs are taken into account. It is that nontort compensation is already substantial and could (again, at some cost) readily be expanded.

Despite these facts, an increasing number of courts and observers view compensation as a principal goal of the tort system. As a political matter, redistributive purposes have become more prominent. To a rationalistic, security-conscious society, random misfortune seems an unacceptable basis for making individuals bear concentrated losses. As noted above, first-party insurance is far from universal. The impoverishment of uninsured individuals who suffer injuries is seen not simply as a private tragedy but also as a social cost that legal policy can mitigate. Existing, widespread liability insurance has externalized liability costs, removing much of the sting from legal rules that make injurers pay. Finally, institutional defendants such as business firms or governments—blameworthy or not, insured or not—are increasingly viewed as efficient loss spreaders.[3]

How can compensation of mass exposure victims best be achieved at reasonable cost? The asbestos cases suggest that even when a chemical's causation of harm is rather clear, the existing tort system imposes enormous costs, long delays, and unpredictable outcomes. If causation is uncertain and other litigation obstacles exist, as with Agent Orange, these disadvantages are magnified. And as third-party insurance—the lifeblood of tort compensation today—becomes increasingly unavailable in response to court decisions expanding liability and damages, compensation becomes an even more dubious goal of tort law.[4]

If individuals purchased adequate first-party insurance or their losses were adequately covered by social insurance, these problems would be inconsequential. Tort law in mass exposure cases could be relegated to a secondary role. A first-party insurer would be subrogated to the compensated victim's claim; tort law would simply adjust losses between the victim's and the injurer's insurers, which would (as they do now) develop relatively low-cost ways to resolve allocation disputes and would also compensate injuries that somehow fell between the cracks of the expanded insurance system. In the long run, expanded first-party and social insurance, perhaps combined with a rule that reduced tort judgments by the amount of "collateral benefits" paid by such insurance, would provide an efficient, predictable compensation mechanism for mass exposure losses and would reduce tort law to an interstitial role.[5] (Such changes could have undesirable distributional and deterrence effects, discussed below.)

That day, however, is surely distant. Individuals often fail to pay heed to low-risk events like mass toxic exposures, and even if they do, they may be unable to afford to insure against them or may find such insurance unavailable in the market. Resistance to expanded social insurance has become a hallmark of the politics of the 1980s.

Still, even in the short run and without increasing federal expenditures, insurance might be used to displace tort law more than it does now. Collective bargaining, for example, could extend first-party insurance for economic losses (that is, wage loss plus medical and other out-of-pocket expenses, perhaps including legal fees) to more persons and perhaps, depending on their individual preferences for coverage and on "moral hazard" problems, to more of their losses. If private insurance markets are thought deficient in this area because individuals systematically undervalue such low-probability risks, first-party coverage for economic losses could even be mandated, as government often does for automobile accidents and as lenders often do for risks to property. It is true that defining the insurable event in the case of toxic harms and enforcing the insurance requirement are more difficult than for these other hazards. But if compensation were confined to net economic losses, those difficulties might be minimized. Even today, incentives to sue could be reduced without defeating compensation goals by deducting insurance benefits from tort awards.

To this point, the discussion has been concerned with mass exposures generally. Workplace-related mass exposures like Agent Orange and asbestos, however, involve special considerations. For them, analysis must begin with the existing workers' compensation scheme.[6] This scheme could be strengthened by reducing claimants' incentives to circumvent it. If, for example, wage replacement rates were increased beyond their present levels (usually two-thirds of preinjury wages) and existing biases against long-latency occupational diseases were lessened, the tort remedy against product manufacturers and employers, so attractive to individual victims but so costly to the system as a whole, could more justifiably be limited or eliminated.

There are arguments, of course, against increasing workers' compensation awards. Some of these arguments oppose the federal intervention that would almost certainly accompany such reforms, while others concern the possible effects of awards on work incentives. But so long as workers' compensation awards remain far below the level of tort recoveries, even after tax, a kind of market in victims' remedies will continue to attract claimants and their lawyers to the tort system lottery. Only closing that gap can lure them away.[7] Employee tort actions against manufacturers, of course, could simply be prohibited without altering the existing workers' compensation structure, but that approach seems politically unlikely; no state has yet pursued it, presumably because the trial lawyers have successfully convinced the public that such a one-sided change would be unfair, if not unconstitutional.

Even (or especially) if statutory awards were increased relative to tort recoveries, however, employers and insurance companies would resist coverage of long-latency diseases with alleged but uncertain causal links to widely used chemical substances. As the VA's response to the non-chloracne Agent Orange claims suggests (see Chapter 2), even the broad coverage formulas of administrative compensation programs may not clearly encompass such claims. Coverage will be especially doubtful if, in addition to the question of whether the illness was workplace-related, smoking or other possible confounding causes exist, as they did for many asbestos and Agent Orange claimants. In such cases, the obstacles to proving causation in the tort system would largely be replicated in the statutory scheme.

These problems could be addressed by adopting special presumptions and other burden-shifting techniques to facilitate claimants' proof in Agent Orange–type cases. Numerous proposals of this kind have been advanced in Congress, and others have been urged on the courts, most notably, in the Agent Orange case itself.[8] Two points, however, should be emphasized. First, the virtue of such an approach depends critically upon the strength of the underlying scientific data suggesting a causal relationship in general between employment and a disease; otherwise, burden-shifting would arbitrarily move the cost of scientific ignorance from plaintiffs to defendants, who may not be any better situated to reduce it. (This concern, it will be recalled, led Judge Weinstein to reject burden-shifting in favor of a public law remedy—his "classwide solution".) Where, as with asbestos, the causal relationship appears to be strong, burden-shifting is an appealing approach; where, as with Agent Orange, the data on causation are relatively weak, it is not. This in turn suggests that discrete, substance-specific schemes of burden-shifting, in which the formulation of the presumptions can be precisely tailored to the state of scientific knowledge and other substance-specific factors, should be preferred to broad, generic ones in which the formulations must necessarily be cruder.

A second caveat is that even substance-specific programs may function very differently than expected. Experience with the one established substance-specific scheme—the black lung benefits program—invites caution. Despite relatively reliable data about the risks and victims of black lung, the costs of the program quickly mushroomed, far exceeding anyone's predictions. The presumptions proved so elastic that coverage became almost universal, effectively transforming a disease compensation program into a pension program for miners and their families. Indeed, because of the logic of coverage expansion, many individuals receiving benefits have never worked in a mine! The administration of the program has been highly politicized, and it raises troubling questions of equal treatment as between coal miners and other workers vulnerable to occupational disease, and as between miners who smoke and those who do not. It is not surprising, then, that the black lung program is almost invariably cited by opponents of federalization and "reform" of workers' compensation for long-latency diseases.[9]

Although some of these difficulties might be remedied in newly created programs, another approach—what I shall call prelitigation settlement incentives—may be more promising. One version has been advanced by Jeffrey O'Connell, coauthor of the original no-fault automobile insurance plan. It would create powerful incentives for defendants in tort cases to pay the economic losses of personal injury claimants prior to litigation (the proposal is in this sense "nontort"), while allowing defendants to continue to litigate claims that they deem especially weak.[10]

In O'Connell's version, a defendant would be given the option to foreclose a claim by offering, within a specified period after the claim is filed, to pay the claimant's net economic losses (that is, economic losses less collateral benefits) for as long as those losses continue to accrue. Claimants would be obliged to accept such offers in total satisfaction of their claims, except in intentional harm cases and certain others (including cases of death and long-term total disability) in which such limited payments would be deemed "unconscionable."

Since defendants are already free to make such offers and claimants to accept them, what new incentives would O'Connell create to induce them to make such offers? And what compensating advantages to claimants would justify compelling them to accept the offers in lieu of pursuing their tort remedy? Under O'Connell's proposal—what one critic has called a "gross sort of swap" of rights[11]—a defendant that refused to make the offer would be barred from interposing at trial the defenses of contributory or comparative fault, assumption of risk, or product misuse; the burden of proof might be shifted to defendant; trial would be expedited; and successful claimants would be entitled not only to tort damages (including pain and suffering) but to costs and counsel fees as well. For claimants, the advantage would be the same as that mandated in workers' compensation and no-fault automobile insurance plans—the prospect of being made financially (albeit perhaps not emotionally) whole immediately and without the need for costly, uncertain litigation.

The terms of O'Connell's trade-off could be altered, of course, if it were thought desirable to strengthen the incentives for defendants to make the offers or to "sweeten" the compensation for claimants. As with any scheme to compensate nontraumatic injuries, causal defenses must be retained to distinguish those injuries for which defendants should be held responsible from the ubiquitous injuries attributable simply to adverse health outcomes or preexisting conditions.[12] But certain noncausal defenses, such as statutes of limitations (which often bar claims in toxic tort cases) could be precluded for defendants who insist on litigating. Alternatively (or in addition), presumptions favoring plaintiffs could be triggered; the compensation amount in the binding offer could be subject to certain ceilings, as in workers' compensation, and estoppel rules might be liberalized in plaintiffs' favor. One standard objection to such measures—that they preclude victims from, and penalize defendants for, asserting their common-law rights—seems no more compelling now than similar claims were three-quarters of a century ago when the courts (eventually) rejected challenges to workers' compensation statutes. And O'Connell's scheme, by excepting death and serious disability cases and by retaining *causal* defenses, is less vulnerable to these objections than workers' compensation, which usually contains no such exceptions and requires only a less-than-causal employment linkage.

How would this proposal affect tort litigation in general and mass toxic tort cases in particular? In general, one would expect defendants to be more willing than at present to settle with individuals having relatively strong claims (thereby avoiding higher, common-law damage awards and the scheme's litigation penalties). As to very weak claims, defendants would be less willing to make a binding offer under the scheme since the net economic losses would exceed the expected value of such claims. But they would presumably settle many of those claims outside the scheme for less than net economic losses; even with the litigation advantages that the scheme confers, the expected value of the claims might still be lower than the litigation costs. The effect on "middling" claims is difficult to predict, for it would depend on parties' litigation costs, the expected outcome at trial, claimants' net economic losses, and their willingness to settle for less than net economic losses.

In mass toxic tort cases, however, the costs of litigation are usually high, and plaintiffs often confront formidable causal defenses.[13] Defendants therefore would often have little incentive to make the binding offer even if their failure to do so would preclude them from asserting certain noncausal defenses; those defenses are ordinarily unimportant in such cases compared to the causal defenses that would remain. Since under O'Connell's plan, claimants could not compel defendants to make the offer, the plan would probably make little difference. Finally, as O'Connell acknowledges, his plan would tend to redistribute compensation from nonnegligent claimants, who would not benefit from barring most noncausal defenses, to negligent ones, who would benefit.[14] In short, his proposal might encourage more prelitigation settlements but only of the strongest (and perhaps some "middling" claims), while probably not reducing litigation of the highest-cost cases.[15]

Other variants of the prelitigation settlement incentives approach, however, are possible. Guido Calabresi has recently suggested the bare outlines of a system consisting of three remedies. The first would be a compensation plan limited to economic losses, on the workers' compensation model. The second would be a tort remedy for claimants who refuse the statutory compensation; it would condition recovery, however, on proof of negligence, not strict liability, and would allow some or all of the traditional common-law defenses. The third remedy would permit defendants to refuse to pay the statutory compensation and instead to interpose some, but not all, traditional defenses in tort. In the second and third (that is, tort) remedies, the defendant, if liable, would pay damages higher than would be paid in the first. Ideally, Calabresi would calibrate the damages in the tort remedies to create incentives for claimants to litigate only strong claims and for defendants to litigate only weak ones.[16]

Here, too, there are difficulties. At the most general level, we should recognize that settlements, while often desirable, are not an unmitigated social blessing. Litigation, by enabling courts to develop and apply legal rules, clarifies legal rights and obligations. Any scheme that encourages settlement, therefore, inhibits that clarifying function and thus nourishes legal uncertainty. This may tend to engender future disputes and other social costs.[17] Let us assume, however, that on balance society wishes to promote settlements. Then, in designing a scheme, the incentives to litigate rather than to accept or pay compensation should be geared not to the strongest and weakest claims, which are precisely those that the parties are most likely to settle anyway, but to the middling claims, as to which liability and damages are most uncertain and are therefore (except in cases like Agent Orange) least likely to settle. Moreover, a multitiered remedial structure like Calabresi's would be extremely complex, making a great deal turn on precisely how the trade-offs within and between each tier were designed. Finally, it is not clear how damage schedules can be calibrated categorically in advance to create desirable litigation/settlement incentives, as Calabresi envisions.

Despite these problems with particular prelitigation settlement incentive proposals, some such structure can probably be designed, perhaps after some trial and error, that will be superior to the status quo on balance. For mass toxic tort cases that fall outside the workers' compensation system, cases in which causation is likely to be an important, costly-to-litigate, and morally salient issue, a functionally and politically viable scheme probably requires three design principles. First, *either* party, not simply the defendant, should be able to litigate in tort if it wishes. This will not only make the plan more even-handed and thus politically acceptable; it will also have the virtue of encouraging fuller compensation for the strongest cases and no compensation (at least in tort) for the weakest. Second, a party that insists upon litigating must be placed at some significant risk or disadvantage in order to activate more robust incentives to settle, for claimants' economic losses, all but the very strong and the very weak claims. Third, the structure should not be too complex or create boundary problems (as the "add-on" no-fault automobile insurance plans have) that simply invite more litigation—now over whether the dispute is in or out of the new system. So long as resort to the new system is voluntary, of course, boundary problems should not be serious, and parties in high-cost, high-uncertainty, Agent Orange–type cases may find prelitigation settlement incentives relatively attractive.

Deterrence

If tort law can be said to have any distinctive functional purpose, it is to deter the creation of undue risks. In principle, deterrence can be accomplished in two ways—"market" deterrence (in which society assesses actors for the accident costs created by their activity, but leaves to the actors the decision of whether to proceed with it), and "collective" deterrence (in which society evaluates the activity and makes a collective decision about whether and how to prevent or reduce it through various forms of regulation).[18]

Deterrence ordinarily operates by shaping the behavior of one or more of three parties—government, potential injurers, and potential victims. At this point, the relationship between deterrence and compensation becomes crucial to the design of legal policy toward mass toxic exposures. In practice, market deterrence shapes the behavior of potential injurers and victims by facing injurers with the prospect of having to pay tort damages and by facing potential victims with the prospect of being denied full compensation (through the doctrines of contributory negligence or comparative fault). An essential feature of a court is that its judgment must perform double service; that is, the damage award must—at once and with the identical sum of money— both compensate the victim and deter the injurious activity. For a number of reasons, however—causation rules, the immunity or absence from the case of certain entities that contributed to the injury, failures of proof, technical defenses, broad jury discretion in awarding damages—the amount that a plaintiff should receive as a matter of sound compensation policy may be far different from the amount a defendant should be charged as a matter of sound deterrence policy. For reasons to be discussed in a moment, the disjunction between the levels of optimal compensation and optimal deterrence is likely to be especially great in mass exposure cases.

This extremely tight linkage in tort law between compensation and deterrence constitutes a serious institutional limitation of courts. In contrast, collective deterrence does not depend upon victims' suing for and recovering damages; it influences behavior in other ways. In principle, therefore, society could *decouple* its compensation and deterrence goals, pursuing them through wholly separate mechanisms— the former through nontort insurance schemes and the latter through administrative regulation. For accidental injuries, New Zealand has done just that.[19] This approach is particularly appealing where the limitations of market deterrence result largely from its preoccupation with a compensation objective that can, as we have just seen, be met tolerably well in other, nontort ways. In that situation, it is natural to suppose that a system of pure collective deterrence, one neither distracted nor weakened by the often-competing imperatives of tort-based compensation, would permit society to have it both ways. Not surprisingly, some commentators have ardently advocated that approach.

In the real world, however, no legal system that employs only collective deterrence is likely to manage these risks as well as a mixed system that employs both forms. Administrative regulation, as we shall see, exhibits significant shortcomings of its own that under the best of circumstances cannot be wholly remedied in the near future. Moreover, tort law can sometimes—albeit probably not in most mass toxic exposure cases (for reasons about to be discussed)—achieve significant deterrence at an acceptable cost. It would therefore be unwise, as well as politically naive, to abandon tort law altogether in the almost certainly vain hope that pure collective deterrence and pure nontort compensation would somehow solve the existing problem. Until we have greater reason to be confident of the efficacy of proposed regulatory reforms, we are well advised to retain tort law—although hopefully much diminished in scope and importance—as a safety valve.

The important question, then, is not whether a mixed system is either desirable and inevitable—it is both—but what the mix of its elements ought to be.[20] I argue that the system for mass toxic exposure risks should employ both market and collective deterrence but should subordinate the former to the latter. Furthermore, it should focus on the behavior of government and injurers, not that of victims.

For many types of risky activities, the deterrence effect on behavior of prospective tort liability, even at the margin, is doubtful. The vagueness of the negligence standard, the extralegal incentives for risk reduction and self-protection that already exist, widespread insurance, individuals' inattention to low-probability risks and their ignorance about the content of legal rules—these and other factors suggest that many liability rules have no significant deterrence effect, a suggestion supported by a growing body of empirical evidence.[21]

In certain areas of activity, to be sure, it is more plausible to believe that market deterrence may significantly shape behavior. Prominent examples are the generation, transportation, and disposal of identifiable toxic wastes and the manufacture of drugs, vaccines, and some other potentially toxic products (such as asbestos and Agent Orange) to which large numbers of consumers or workers are exposed. In each of these domains, the potential injurers are rationally calculating, profit-maximizing firms—what one commentator has called "high-attention" or "problem-solving" actors.[22] They see that the scope of tort liability and the magnitude of damages have steadily expanded, that the availability of liability insurance is rapidly dwindling, and that even the involvement of government—as purchaser or regulator—cannot render their liability risks predictable. Their activities are also ones in which victim self-protection is least feasible; here, potential victims tend to be poorly situated to avoid injuries that may take decades to manifest themselves or to bear large, uninsured losses. In these areas, market deterrence can be an important influence.

Even here, however, several countervailing factors weaken market deterrence. In mass exposure cases like Agent Orange, these factors include long latency periods, problems of proving causation, the possibility of potential defendants' insolvency, and impediments to bringing and sustaining litigation. In addition, clear, generally applicable liability rules are unlikely to emerge from common-law adjudication that involves particular substances, highly fact-specific circumstances, and growing opportunities—because of liberalized jurisdictional and choice-of-law rules—to litigate similar issues in multiple forums that may apply different rules and reach disparate results. This diffuseness mutes the signals upon which effective market deterrence depends.[23] (Even the published decisions in the Agent Orange case, which did not involve the problem of multiple forums, provide manufacturers with astonishingly little guidance concerning their future liability risks as to *other* potentially toxic chemicals.) And although tort law sometimes succeeds in revealing information damaging to injurers that might otherwise remain secret, such revelations can take decades to occur, as they did in the asbestos litigation.[24] For all these reasons, it may not be surprising that even product manufacturers appear not to be much deterred by the threat of tort liability.[25]

On the other hand, if some of these obstacles to liability are dismantled through a public law approach, the chief result may be to effectively *overdeter*, to discourage the taking of risks from which society might well benefit. Overdeterrence can also result from what some, seeking to make a virtue of necessity, celebrate as tort law's strength—the profound *uncertainty* it engenders in the minds of corporate executives, liability insurers, and defendants' lawyers.[26] What this view overlooks, however, is that uncertainty is costly to society, not just to manufacturers. As Huber suggests, individual juries acting in isolated tort cases with few constraints on the amount of damages seem especially prone to overdeter some risky activities and underdeter others. The effect of soaring insurance premiums on the availability of certain vaccines, some medical specialties, and other risky but valuable activities are dismal portents of this problem. In mass exposure situations, then, the deterrence value of tort law is either highly questionable or too crude and unpredictable.[27]

In comparison, collective deterrence through administrative regulation of risks has much to recommend it. Unlike market deterrence, it breaks the highly constraining and artificial linkage between compensation and deterrence; it focuses on direct deterrence through *ex ante* prevention of injuries rather than indirect deterrence through *ex post* compensation of them; it can be triggered by a much lower level of proof of causation than the tort system can; and it permits a social rather than an individual valuation of the cost of accidents. Collective deterrence can influence individuals and institutions, including the government itself, that are not parties to an adjudication but are nevertheless well positioned to reduce accident costs; it involves decision-making by a technically expert, policy-oriented, politically responsive, enduring body (the agency) rather than a generalist, accident-oriented, insular, and *ad hoc* body (the jury); it can send clearer, faster, and more consistent signals to people than a succession of jury verdicts can, concerning precisely what is expected of them; it can deploy a far richer but less costly array of inducements, positive and negative, for compliance; and it can accomplish these ends at relatively low social cost. In principle, at least, collective deterrence seems considerably more promising as a vehicle for achieving the goals of a public law vision than even a reformed, aggregated tort law.[28]

Administrative regulation is no panacea, of course, and its defects must be squarely faced and reckoned with. Collective deterrence suffers from all of the limitations of political decision-making generally, as well as those associated with predicting and penalizing individual behavior. It is not enough to enumerate the weaknesses of courts in assessing risk and then simply to add, as Huber does, that "even in the agencies, comparative risk regulation is not all that it should be." A fuller account of the institutional competence issue would take note of the recent, well-documented studies of one regulatory disaster after another, including the area of environmental policy. These studies portray a long litany of systematic deficiencies, including inadequate resources, poor data bases, sluggish proceedings, hostility to economic analysis, weak leadership, political vulnerability, lack of public support and participation, secrecy, sporadic enforcement, under- and overdeterrence, inability to set priorities, lawlessness, and many others. Indeed, the long tortuous history of efforts to regulate 2,4,5-T itself—it was not completely banned until 1985, fifteen years after being withdrawn from use in Vietnam—supports this indictment.[29]

The question of who should regulate toxicity risks, then, is a choice between institutions that each display characteristic defects. The shortcomings of courts in adjudicating mass toxic tort cases are highly relevant to that decision, of course, but they do not by themselves determine its outcome. In any event, the choice is not either-or. In any imaginable future—one in which social and first-party insurance for such injuries will remain incomplete, many serious risks will remain unregulated, and regulatory agency enforcement will remain inadequate—market deterrence through decentralized tort litigation must continue to play an important role in controlling mass exposure risks. Even if insurance provided adequate compensation in such cases, we would undoubtedly still need some interstitial, backup mechanism to augment administrative deterrence efforts; in that event, private enforcement of regulatory standards through the courts (perhaps motivated by bounties to successful plaintiffs) might well be the most efficient instrument.[30] But administrative regulation, not tort law, should be expected to provide the great bulk of deterrence in this area.

This primacy of regulation implies four corollaries for an effective nontort approach. Significantly, advocates of the public law approach should find each of these congenial. First, as Huber and some others have urged, regulatory standards concerning the appropriate, socially acceptable level of risk should ordinarily be binding on juries in subsequent tort cases, a conclusiveness that existing tort law doctrine rejects.[31] Without having some strong reason to doubt that an existing administrative standard manifests society's best judgment as to what that level ought to be (as where the standard is clearly out of date or was developed for some other purpose), twelve lay men and women convened on a single occasion to decide a single dispute with little more guidance than a "reasonableness" criterion should not be permitted to override or second-guess the considered risk-benefit judgment of an expert regulatory agency established to speak authoritatively on such matters for society as a whole. This principle is not an abject surrender to the tyranny of expertise; it is an insistence that expertise be controlled by accountable public institutions, not by *ad hoc* unaccountable ones. Until private and social insurance schemes that assure adequate compensation to victims are in place, however, the principle probably cannot be politically implemented.

Second, publicly funded research on the nature and effects of substances to which large numbers of people are exposed should be substantially increased, and private incentives to generate risk information should be strengthened. Although additional research seems an innocuous proposal, it actually raises controversial resource and political issues for hard-pressed agencies during a period of fiscal and regulatory retrenchment. Research on toxic substances is costly—a two-year animal study can cost more than $250,000—and may return significant benefits only in the long run;[32] meanwhile, research must compete for funding with many other important regulatory activities, such as rulemaking and enforcement. In 1984, the EPA was operating with no more inflation-adjusted dollars than in 1973, when its regulatory responsibilities were far more limited.[33] Indeed, federal funding of research on toxic substances actually declined in *absolute* terms by more than one-third between 1982 and 1984; in 1985 it rose slightly but still remained below the 1980 spending level.[34] As a result, our ignorance concerning environmental risks is appalling—we have no risk information on 90 percent of the substances already in the environment, and the number of new substances, especially with the advent of bioengineering, is increasing steadily.[35] Yet the social costs of this ignorance may prove to be very high, as the asbestos and vinyl chloride problems suggest.[36]

Knowledge of this kind is a "public good," however, and the tort system, by often basing liability on what manufacturers "knew or should have known," may discourage them from seeking more such knowledge. Thus we cannot rely on the market to stimulate "enough" knowledge, and government must finance or require much of the research to produce it.[37] Recent regulations that require industry to notify agencies, employees, and the public about toxic risks, although presenting certain problems, are an important advance.[38] Collective bargaining over workplace-related risk information can also be encouraged.[39] New ways can be sought to reduce the ability of political-bureaucratic considerations to distort government information, perhaps by strengthening the influence of external scientific advisory bodies.

Improved risk information would not only create better incentives for private decisions about acceptable levels of risk and strengthen social confidence in public regulation. It might also stimulate the kinds of "technological fixes" that have great promise for controlling certain kinds of risks. (Recently, for example, a patent was issued for microbes that can eat toxic material in the environment, probably including dioxin and PCBs.)[40] In addition to increased funding and private incentives for long-term toxicological and related research, flexible reserves should be created to support a limited number of shorter-term, policy-oriented research projects driven by unforeseeable public health emergencies, such as swine flu, AIDS, and other natural or chemical toxins.

Third, if collective deterrence is to be effective, far greater attention must be given to the actual *implementation* of regulatory policy on toxic substances. Reforms along these lines have been proposed by others.[41] One frequently neglected aspect of the implementation problem, which is exacerbated by the decentralized, highly privatized structure of the American political and economic systems, deserves special emphasis. Effective policy implementation must ultimately depend largely upon voluntary compliance by firms. This in turn requires that government either provide direct subsidies for compliance,[42] which is probably politically infeasible, or establish a strong, credible monitoring and enforcement program that makes compliance economically rational for firms. That credibility is weakened when the government appears to countenance suppression and distortion of important risk information in the hands of regulated firms, as occurred recently when Eli Lilly officials received minimal punishments for serious violations, or when the government abandons its enforcement activity in the face of rapidly expanding regulatory responsibilities, as the EPA did in connection with the hazardous waste program during the early 1980s.[43] (Indeed, in February 1986 the EPA, faced with a political stalemate over future funding for the program, began to plan for a phaseout of toxic dump cleanups.)[44]

For these reasons, it may be desirable to conscript private citizens and organizations into toxic monitoring and enforcement activities in order to augment governmental efforts and increase the costs of noncompliance. This might be done in several ways. Existing incentives for citizens or groups to bring "private attorney general" lawsuits to enforce established regulatory standards could be strengthened. Additional monitoring and disclosure duties could be imposed on firms. The accounting rules of the Securities and Exchange Commission might require corporations to disclose contingent tort or regulatory liabilities for potential toxic substances violations. William Drayton, a former EPA official, has proposed that firms dealing with toxic substances be required to retain "certified public toxics auditors" to investigate and report upon firms' compliance with regulatory obligations, much as certified public accountants are obliged to sign audited financial statements and disclosure documents on behalf of firms regulated under the securities laws. Drayton has also suggested requiring that liabilities under the hazardous waste laws "run with the land," encouraging an acquiring company to investigate such risks before completing the purchase lest it be held liable for its seller's violations. This might stimulate a kind of toxics substance–related title insurance and warranty system.[45]

Finally, any nontort approach to mass exposures must attend to the problem of boundaries. First, it must soften or eliminate certain boundaries by integrating any new nontort compensation remedies with the extensive, complex systems of private and social insurance and welfare benefits that already exist, in order to assure both fairness and administrative efficiency.[46] Second, if such an approach would preserve some role for tort actions (either traditional or public law), it must delineate a defensible boundary between the realms of tort and nontort remedies. Otherwise, the availability of one remedy may weaken the other, much as employees' tort actions against manufacturers have circumvented the workers' compensation scheme. A system of prelitigation settlement incentives attempts to avoid the boundary problem by creating an option for either party to invoke one remedy or the other. Without such a system, however, the boundary can be defined only by carefully enumerating the characteristics of a claim that will qualify it for a particular remedial alternative. The limitations of language and the ingenuity of litigating lawyers make this a difficult task. Even a clear definition of "mass tort" would not suffice; as noted earlier, not all mass tort claims demand a nontort approach. Still, the boundary problem is probably not insuperable.[47]

In the end, the response of the legal system to the problem of mass toxic exposures will be shaped largely by forces outside its control. Scientific progress will make it possible to detect ever smaller quantities of chemical substances in the environment. It is important in this regard to recall that in the twenty-year period bracketed by the use of Agent Orange in Vietnam and the Agent Orange litigation, the level at which dioxin can be scientifically detected has dropped from parts per million to parts per billion (or less)—a factor of 1,000![48] Indeed, a new kind of mass spectrometer said to be capable of detecting dioxin residues in food at concentrations as low as one part per *trillion* is now being sold to supermarket chains.[49] As this methodological advance continues, ever lower levels of contamination will become matters of public debate and concern. In addition, knowledge about the toxic effects of such chemicals is a relentlessly dynamic process, driven not only by human curiosity but by lawsuits, publicity, politics, and other factors. Again, the explosion of federally supported research on dioxin's effects during the 1970s and 1980s is an instructive example.

Although it is certainly possible that increased scientific knowledge about these risks will render them more acceptable to society, the history of public controversy over these issues suggests that the contrary is more likely. As the environmental burden of chemical substances increases, paced by economic growth, technical innovation, and the continuing integration of all aspects of social life, public demands for effective risk management will intensify. These demands are by now deeply structured, driven by our society's growing risk aversion and commitment to environmental values, both of which seem firmly embedded in our political culture.[50] By raising the stakes in addressing mass toxic risks, these scientific, economic, social, and political developments will make legal solutions more urgent and more controversial.

This chapter and the Agent Orange experience on which it draws suggest that the future law governing mass toxic exposures must amalgamate the traditional, public law, and nontort approaches into a complex remedial structure. The Agent Orange case, like all great lawsuits, was unique in some ways. But it can recall us to some more general, now-familiar truths. Our law, spurred by resourceful litigants and creative judges, constantly changes under the pressure of new social challenges. Tort cases, built upon flexible norms and decided by socially responsive juries, have become principal instruments of those changes.

In Agent Orange, Judge Weinstein's problem-solving decisions imaginatively reconceptualized and reconstructed tort law for mass exposures, combining its traditional features with an innovative public law design. That eclecticism, however, combined some of the most worrisome features of each approach. By preserving traditional tort concepts—for example, each litigant's right to an individualized adjudication of specific causation and damages—he hoped to draw upon tort law's distinctive moral integrity and coherence, an important source of legitimacy. But those concepts were prohibitively expensive and manifestly unworkable in the context of a case like Agent Orange, as Weinstein fully appreciated. He therefore tried to graft several elements of a new species, the public law remedy, onto the traditional tort law stock.

The resulting hybrid, however, engendered new difficulties even as it boldly grappled with old ones. It sacrificed individual litigants' interests to collective ones. It relied heavily upon inevitably flawed, limited epidemiological techniques. It exalted and personalized the judge's role in controlling, directing, and terminating the litigation. It created a dependency upon massive class actions and upon the motives of the financiers and lawyers who support and manage them. It further weakened the already atttenuated relationship between lawyers and clients. It resorted to procedural shortcuts and necessarily crude, categorical distributions. It encouraged "nuisance suits." More generally, it attempted to shoehorn an aggregative, probabilistic, policy-oriented methodology into legal forms designed to express individualistic, moralistic, corrective justice values. In Agent Orange, Weinstein's approach ended up compromising and distorting both the new methodology and the old forms—and did so at an extremely high cost.

A nontort approach was not really available to Judge Weinstein, for it necessarily requires legislative action and must then be implemented by an administrative agency. He nonetheless drew heavily on the nontort approach when he fashioned the settlement and designed the final, legislative-type distribution plan. These actions exemplified the principal virtues of nontort solutions, achieving a semblance of rough justice at a relatively low social cost. But these innovations, developed in a nontort spirit, also revealed some of the characteristic dangers of that approach, including procedural shortcuts, substantive compromises, and use of crude remedial categories.

The law of the future governing mass toxic exposures must receive extensive, probing public debate. For exposures that entail the kind of causal indeterminacy, scale, spatial and temporal dispersion, and cost exhibited by the Agent Orange case, the law should look primarily to nontort techniques of deterrence, compensation, and dispute resolution. It should stress regulatory standards supported by improved risk information, enhanced public and private enforcement of these standards, a reformed workers' compensation scheme for occupational exposures, and expanded private or social first-party insurance of economic losses from nonoccupational exposures. Private insurers should be subrogated to victims' claims; if the victims' compensation came from public funds, a tax should be imposed, assessed as directly on the risk-generating activity as the determinacy of causality and the potential for effective deterrence permit. In either case, alternative nontort techniques for dispute resolution should be encouraged for settling the issues that remain.[51]

Until such a system is in place, however, tort law must continue to govern mass exposure cases that cannot be satisfactorily resolved by traditional tort actions or by existing nontort approaches. The analysis presented in Chapter 12 suggests that some version of the public law model may well be necessary to deal with those cases. That analysis also indicates, however, that the model's scope should be carefully confined. I do not doubt that well-designed reforms can ameliorate some of its most objectionable aspects. But the Agent Orange experience suggests that other troubling ones will inevitably remain.

The most serious challenge to the future law of mass exposures is to avoid the kind of institutional mismatch against which Huber and others have warned.[52] The prospect of such a mismatch may actually be the greater danger posed by the public law approach in Agent Orange–type cases. By exacerbating the poor fit between problem solver and problem—between the radically decentralized, dispute-oriented institutions of tort law and the task of rational, comprehensive risk management—the new approach could discourage the very risk-taking that in the long run may make our society both wealthier and safer.[53] It would be a cruel but all-too-familiar irony if, by stifling technological change, this well-intentioned "procedural" law reform sacrificed the promise of substantive justice that social and scientific innovation holds out to us.

NOTES • INDEX

Notes

I conducted personal and telephone interviews with most of the key participants in the Agent Orange case; the names of those people and the dates of the interviews are listed below. Several of those interviewed insisted that some or all of their remarks be treated as confidential, and one person asked that the interview itself be so treated. Wherever possible, however, I have provided full attribution in the notes.

David Dean: Jan. 14, 1985; May 20, 1985 (telephone); Nov. 15, 1985 (telephone).
Kenneth Feinberg: Sept. 13, 1984 (telephone); Nov. 29, 1984; Mar. 5, Apr. 11, 1985.
Albert Fiorella: Apr. 23. 1985.
Allen Friedman: Feb. 5, 1985; July 17, 1985 (telephone).
Arthur J. Galligan: Jan. 9, 1985.
Dr. Arthur Galston: Oct. 11, 1985.
Robert Heinemann: Apr. 15, 1985; Feb. 4, 1986 (telephone).
Thomas Henderson: Jan. 9, Apr. 15, 1985; May 14, 1985 (telephone); July 15, 1985 (telephone); Jan. 23, 1986 (telephone); Feb. 4, 1986; Feb. 7, 1986 (telephone).
William Krohley and David R. Gross: Jan. 15, 1985.
Irving Like: Apr. 23, 1985.
Arvin Maskin: Mar. 14, 1985; June 14, 1985 (telephone); July 8, 1985 (telephone); July 19, 1985 (telephone).
Frank McCarthy: Mar. 6, 1985; May 10, 1985 (telephone); Jan. 24, 1986 (telephone).
Benton Musslewhite: Mar. 18, 1985.
John O'Quinn: Oct. 25, 1985 (telephone).
Hon. George C. Pratt: Jan. 27, 1986 (telephone).
Leonard L. Rivkin: Jan. 14, Mar. 19, Apr. 23, 1985; July 22, 1985 (telephone); Nov. 15, 1985 (telephone).
Michael and Maureen Ryan: Feb. 5, Feb. 6, 1986; Feb. 7, 1986 (telephone).
Shira Scheindlin: Apr. 15, 1985.
Steven Schlegel: Feb. 5, 1985; Feb. 7, 1986 (telephone).

David I. Shapiro: Jan. 9, Mar. 15, 1985; June 6, 1985 (telephone).
Morton Silberman: Mar. 6, 1985.
Barton Stichman: May 24, 1985.
Dr. Jan Stolwijk: Oct. 23, Oct. 28, 1985.
Robert A. Taylor, Jr.: May 24, 1985; May 30, 1985 (telephone).
Dr. Harvey Wachsman: Feb. 27, 1986 (telephone).
Victor John Yannacone, Jr.: Feb. 6, Mar. 19, 1985; Jan. 30, Feb. 6, Feb. 27, 1986
  (telephone).

The Agent Orange litigation, formally designated as *In re 'Agent Orange' Product Liability Litigation* (MDL No. 381), is cited as *AO*.

1. A New Kind of Case

1. On the new synthetic chemicals, see U.S. Council on Environmental
Quality, *Environmental Quality 1983* (Washington, D.C.: U.S. Government
Printing Office, 1983).
2. Yannacone interview.
3. Aristotle, *Nichomachean Ethics,* bk. 5, sec. 4, 1131b25–1132b20.
4. See Richard Epstein, *Modern Products Liability Law* (Westport, Conn.:
Quorum Books, 1980). For an intellectual history of the evolution of this
branch of law, see George Priest, "The Invention of Enterprise Liability: A
Critical History of the Intellectual Foundations of Modern Tort Law," 14
Journal of Legal Studies 461 (1985).
5. Statistics on magnitude of the Agent Orange case and administration
of the fund are from interviews with Robert Heinemann, clerk of the court,
United States District Court for the Eastern District of New York, and from an
examination of the docket sheet on Jan. 31, 1986. On the number of law firms:
written communication from Steven Schlegel, Feb. 10, 1986.
6. The legal literature on mass toxic torts is already large and growing.
See, e.g., "Special Project: An Analysis of the Legal, Social and Political
Issues Raised by Asbestos Litigation," 36 *Vanderbilt Law Review* 573 (1983);
David Rosenberg, "The Causal Connection in Mass Tort Cases: A 'Public
Law' Vision of the Tort System," 97 *Harvard Law Review* 849 (1984); Peter
Huber, "Safety and the Second Best: The Hazards of Public Risk Management
in the Courts," 85 *Columbia Law Review* 277 (1985); Richard Epstein, "The
Legal and Insurance Dynamics of Mass Tort Litigation," 13 *Journal of Legal
Studies* 475 (1984).
7. The most important DES cases are *Sindell* v. *Abbott Laboratories,* 26 Cal.
3d 588, 607 P.2d 924, 163 Cal. Rptr. 132, *cert. denied,* 449 U.S. 912 (1980);
Payton v. *Abbott Laboratories,* 386 Mass. 540, 437 N.E. 2d 171 (1982); *Collins* v.
Eli Lilley & Co., 116 Wis.2d 166, 342, N.W. 2d 37 (1984); and *Abel* v. *Eli Lilley
& Co.,* 418 Mich. 311, 343 N.W.2d 164 (1984). For an overview of the DES
litigation, see Harlan Abrahams and Bobbee Joan Musgrave, "The DES Lab-
yrinth," 33 *South Carolina Law Review* 663 (1982). The most important asbestos
cases are *Borel* v. *Fibreboard Paper Products Corp.,* 493 F.2d 1076 (5th Cir.
1973); *Beshada* v. *Johns-Manville Products Corp.,* 90 N.J. 191, 447 A.2d 539 (1982);

Keene Corp. v. *Insurance Co. of North America,* 667 F.2d 1034 (D.C. Cir. 1981), *cert. denied,* 452 U.S. 1007 (1982). For a tendentious overview of the asbestos litigation, see Paul Brodeur, *Outrageous Misconduct: The Asbestos Industry on Trial* (New York: Pantheon, 1985).

8. Classes were certified in several mass tort actions, notably the Hyatt Regency Skywalk and Bendectin cases, but these certifications were reversed on appeal. *In re Bendectin Products Liability Litigation,* 749 F.2d 300 (6th Cir. 1984); *In re Federal Skywalk Cases,* 680 F.2d 1175 (8th Cir. 1982). On remand in the Skywalk case, a class was certified by the trial court: 95 F.R.D. 485 (W.D. Mo. 1982). In addition, a class action was upheld by an appellate court pending full review: *Union Light, Heat & Power Co.* v. *U.S. District Court,* 588 F.2d. 543 (6th Cir. 1978), *cert. dismissed,* 443 U.S. 913 (1979).

9. *In re Johns-Manville Corp.,* Nos. 82B 11, 656 to 82B 11, 676 (Bankr. S.D.N.Y. filed Aug. 26, 1982).

10. Punitive damages were awarded in *Froud* v. *Celotex Corp.,* 107 Ill. App. 3d 654, 437 N.E.2d 910 (App. Ct. 1982); *Moran* v. *Johns-Manville Sales Corp.,* 691 F.2d 811 (6th Cir. 1982); *Thiry* v. *Armstrong World Industries,* 661 P.2d 515 (Okla. Sup. Ct 1983); *Neal* v. *Carey Canadian Mines, Ltd.,* 549 F. Supp. 357 (E.D.Pa. 1982).

11. See Chapter 9.

12. See discussion in the *AO* "fairness opinion," 597 F. Supp. 740, 819–43 (E.D.N.Y. 1984) (Weinstein, C.J.), hereinafter cited as *AO,* Fairness Opinion, analyzed in Chapter 9.

13. See, e.g., Ernest Weinrib, "The Natural Law of Tort" (unpublished).

14. On asbestos as the cause of asbestosis and mesothelioma, see, e.g., Margaret R. Becklake, "Asbestos-related Diseases of the Lung and Other Organs: Their Epidemiology and Implications for Clinical Practice," 114 *American Review of Respiratory Disease* 187 (1976). On DES as the cause of vaginal adenocarcinoma, see, e.g., Arthur L. Herbst, Hans Ulfendahl, and David C. Poskanzer, "Adenocarcinoma of the Vagina: Association of Maternal Stilbestrol Therapy with Tumor Appearance in Young Women," 284 *New England Journal of Medicine* 878 (1971).

15. For a comparison of the DES, asbestos, and Agent Orange cases, see Epstein, "Legal and Insurance Dynamics of Mass Tort Litigation."

16. Veterans' goals in *AO* case: interviews with McCarthy, Yannacone, and Barton Stichman, Vietnam Veterans of America Legal Services. See also Chapter 3.

17. See Philip Shabecoff, "Most Toxic Dumps Violate Deadline," *New York Times,* Dec. 7, 1985, at A1; Stuart Diamond, "U.S. Toxic Mishaps in Chemicals Put at 6,928 in 5 Years," *New York Times,* Oct. 3, 1985, at A1; Diamond, "U.S. Names 403 Toxic Chemicals That Pose Risk in Plant Accidents," *New York Times,* Nov. 18, 1985, at A1; William Greer, "Radon May Endanger 8 Million Homes," *New York Times,* Nov. 17, 1985, at E6.

18. The Superfund law is 42 U.S.C. secs. 9601–57 (1982). Amendments to it are currently pending in Congress.

19. See Congressional Budget Office, *Hazardous Waste Management: Recent*

Changes and Policy Alternatives (Washington, D.C.: U.S. Government Printing Office, May 1985), at 31; Philip Shabecoff, "E.P.A. Proposes Addition of 38 Toxic Waste Sites to Cleanup List," *New York Times,* Sept. 6, 1985, at B7. On the growing list of sites, see letter to editor from Lee M. Thomas, administrator, E.P.A., *New York Times,* Sept. 18, 1985, at A26. For a legal analysis of the Love Canal incident, see William Ginsburg and Lois Weiss, "Common Law Liability for Toxic Torts: A Phantom Remedy," 9 *Hofstra Law Review* 859 (1981).

20. For an analysis of the Three Mile Island incident, see Charles Perrow, *Normal Accidents: Living with High-Risk Technologies* (New York: Basic Books, 1984). Two consolidated cases on the Bhopal incident have been filed in the United States District Court for the Southern District of New York. See Tamar Lewin, "Carbide Is Sued in U.S. by India in Gas Disaster," *New York Times,* Apr. 9, 1985, at A1; Stuart Diamond, "Combined Bhopal Suit Is Filed," *New York Times,* June 29, 1985, at D1. On the Sequoya Fuels incident, see William Robbins, "Untested Process Was in Use at Time of Fatal Gas Leak," *New York Times,* Jan. 6, 1986, at A1.

21. See Jethro Lieberman, *The Litigious Society* (New York: Basic Books, 1981); compare Marc Galanter, "Reading the Landscapes of Disputes: What We Know and Don't Know (and Think We Know) about Our Allegedly Contentious and Litigious Society," 31 *U.C.L.A. Law Review* 4 (1983).

22. See, e.g., Guido Calabresi, *The Costs of Accidents* (New Haven: Yale University Press, 1970); Peter Schuck, *Suing Government: Citizen Remedies for Official Wrongs* (New Haven: Yale University Press, 1983).

2. The Chemical and the Courts

1. On the early development of 2,4-D and 2,4,5-T, see, e.g., John Dux and P. J. Young, *Agent Orange: The Bitter Harvest* (Sydney: Hodder and Stoughton, 1980), chap. 1; Thomas Whiteside, *The Pendulum and the Toxic Cloud* (New Haven: Yale University Press, 1979), chap. 1.

2. On the testing and use of Agent Orange in Vietnam, see *AO* Fairness Opinion at 775–77; Fred Wilcox, *Waiting for an Army to Die: The Tragedy of Agent Orange* (New York: Vintage Books, 1983); Whiteside, *Pendulum,* chap. 1.

3. See *AO,* Fairness Opinion at 797–99; *AO,* 565 F. Supp. 1263, 1266–74 (E.D.N.Y. 1983); Whiteside, *Pendulum,* chap. 1.

4. Interview with Arthur Galston, chairman, Department of Biology, Yale University.

5. Galston, "Herbicides: A Mixed Blessing," *Bioscience,* Feb. 1979, at 85–90.

6. See *AO,* Fairness Opinion at 778–80; *AO,* 565 F. Supp. 1263, 1277 (E.D.N.Y. 1983).

7. Dux and Young, *Agent Orange,* chap. 3; lecture by Arthur Galston, Yale Law School, Mar. 26, 1985.

8. On the Bionetics study, see *AO,* Fairness Opinion at 776; Dux and

Young, *Agent Orange*, chap. 3; Galston lecture. On the suspension of 2,4,5-T, see *AO*, Fairness Opinion at 776.

9. On the veterans' assimilation, see James Jacobs, *Social Foundations of Civil-Military Relations* (New Brunswick, N.J.: Transaction Books, 1986), chap. 7; Charles Figley and Seymour Levantman, eds., *Strangers at Home: Vietnam Veterans since the War* (New York: Praeger, 1980), chaps. 8, 9, and 14; Paul Starr, *The Discarded Army: Veterans after Vietnam* (New York: Charterhouse, 1973), chap. 8.

10. Robert Klein, *Wounded Men, Broken Promises* (New York: Macmillan, 1981), at 177–78.

11. See Jacobs, *Social Foundations*, chap. 7.

12. On what was known about dioxin generally, see Whiteside, *Pendulum*; Wendy Wagner, "Environmental Regulation under Scientific Uncertainty: A Case Study on the EPA's Cancellation of 2,4,5-T," *Journal of the National Association of Administrative Law Judges* (forthcoming 1986). For a current review, see Fred Tschirley, "Dioxin," 254 *Scientific American* 29 (1986).

13. On the veterans' health problems, see Dux and Young, *Agent Orange*, at chap. 4; Wilcox, *Waiting*, at 6; Whiteside, *Pendulum*, at 135–36; Robert Klein, *Wounded Men*, at chap. 6; Michael Uhl and Tod Ensign, *G.I. Guinea Pigs* (New York: Playboy Press, 1980), at chap. 10. Letter from Richard Severo, *New York Times* reporter, to author, July 21, 1985.

14. On the VA's response, see Jacobs, *Social Foundations*; Barbara McClure, "Medical Care Programs of the Veterans Administration," Congressional Research Service Report No. 83–99 (1983) at 1; Uhl and Ensign, *G.I. Guinea Pigs*, at chap. 10; Klein, *Wounded Men*, at chap. 6; Wilcox, *Waiting*, at chap. 6.

15. On the veterans' organizational activity, see Sar Levitan and Karen Cleary, *Old Wars Remain Unfinished* (Baltimore: Johns Hopkins University Press, 1973), at 19; Figley and Levantman, *Strangers at Home*, at xxx, 316–17; Klein, *Wounded Men*, at 53–54; Uhl and Ensign, *G.I. Guinea Pigs*, at 222; Jacobs, *Social Foundations*. Quote is from Figley and Levantman, *Strangers at Home*, at xxv.

16. Yannacone interview.

17. On changes in the legal system, see Owen Fiss, "The Forms of Justice," 93 *Harvard Law Review* 1 (1979). On the use of statistical or epidemiological evidence, see Richard Hoffman, "The Use of Epidemiology in the Courts," 120 *American Journal of Epidemiology* 190 (1984).

18. On relaxation of ethical restrictions, see, e.g., *Bates* v. *State Bar of Arizona*, 433 U.S. 350 (1977). This trend has been strengthened most recently in *Zauderer* v. *Office of Disciplinary Counsel*, 105 S.Ct. 2265 (1985).

19. On the transformation of product liability law, see George Priest, "The Invention of Enterprise Liability: A Critical History of the Intellectual Foundations of Modern Tort Law," 14 *Journal of Legal Studies* 461 (1985).

20. On the defendant's duty of care, see *MacPherson* v. *Buick Motor Co.*, 217 N.Y. 382, 111 N.E. 1050 (1916); *Henningsen* v. *Bloomfield Motors, Inc.*, 32

N.J. 358, 161 A.2d 69 (1960). On the further enlargement of the duty, see *Restatement (Second) of Torts,* sec. 402A(2) (b) (St. Paul, Minn.: American Law Institute Publishers, 1965).

21. See *Greenman* v. *Yuba Power Products, Inc.,* 59 Cal. 2d 57, 377 P.2d 897 (1963).

22. On design defects, see, e.g., *Barker* v. *Lull Engineering Co., Inc.,* 20 Cal. 3d 413, 573 P.2d 443 (1978). For scholarly debate, see, e.g., Richard Posner, "Strict Liability: A Comment," 2 *Journal of Legal Studies* 205 (1973); Steven Shavell, "Strict Liability versus Negligence," 9 *Journal of Legal Studies* 1 (1980).

23. On causation generally, see William Prosser and Page Keeton, *The Law of Torts,* secs. 41–42 (St. Paul, Minn.: West Publishing Co., 1984). On special burden-shifting rules, see, e.g., *AO,* Fairness Opinion, 597 F. Supp. 740, 819–28.

24. On the substantial factor rule, see Prosser and Keeton, *Law of Torts,* sec. 41; *Restatement (Second) of Torts,* sec. 431(a). Both requirements created extremely difficult problems in Agent Orange: see especially Chapters 7, 9, and 11. On the increasing use of statistical evidence, see *AO,* Fairness Opinion at 839–41.

25. The 1948 case was *Summers* v. *Tice,* 33 Cal. 2d 80, 199 P.2d 1 (1948). The DES case was *Sindell* v. *Abbott Laboratories,* 26 Cal. 3d 588, 607 P.2d 924, 163 Cal. Rptr. 132, *cert. denied,* 449 U.S. 912 (1980).

26. On damages, see *Dillon* v. *Legg,* 68 Cal. 2d 728, 441 P.2d 912 (1968); *Molien* v. *Kaiser Foundation Hospitals,* 27 Cal. 3d 916, 616 P.2d 813, 167 Cal. Rptr. 831 (1980). On tort awards of $1 million or more, see "Special Report of Defense Trial Lawyers' Task Force on Litigation Cost Containment," 27 *For the Defense* SR1, SR9 (Sept. 1985). But see "Much-Cited Numbers on Verdicts Are Misleading," *Legal Times,* Feb. 17, 1986, at 6.

27. On the increase in punitive damages, see Mark Peterson, *Punitive Damages: Preliminary Empirical Findings* (RAND Institute for Civil Justice, August 1985); *Grimshaw* v. *Ford Motor Co.,* No. 19–77–61 (Super. Ct., Orange Cty., Cal., Feb. 7, 1978), *aff'd as amended,* 119 Cal. App. 3d 757, 174 Cal. Rptr. 348 (1981); *Toole* v. *Richardson-Merrel Inc.,* 251 Cal. App. 2d 689, 60 Cal. Rptr. 398 (1967).

28. See Guido Calabresi, *The Costs of Accidents* (New Haven: Yale University Press, 1970). The place of Calabresi's work in the evolution of tort doctrine is analyzed in George Priest, "The Rise of Law and Economics," Working Paper No. 7, Civil Liability Program, Yale Law School (1982).

29. Critics of these developments include Richard Epstein, *Modern Products Liability Law* (Westport, Conn.: Quorum Books, 1980); Priest, "Invention of Enterprise Liability"; John Wade, "On the Effect in Product Liability of Knowledge Unavailable Prior to Marketing," 58 *New York University Law Review* 734 (1983). On the erosion of manufacturer defenses, see Epstein, *Modern Products Liability Law;* Priest, "Invention of Enterprise Liability."

30. On the expansion of tort liability, see, generally, Peter Schuck, *Suing*

Government: Citizen Remedies for Official Wrongs (New Haven: Yale University Press, 1983). On criticism of *Feres* immunity, see Note, "The Federal Tort Claims Act: A Cause of Action for Servicemen," 14 *Valparaiso University Law Review* 527 (1980); Note, "From *Feres* to *Stencel:* Should Military Personnel Have Access to FTCA Recovery," 77 *Michigan Law Review* 1900 (1979).

31. On asbestos personal injury litigation, see Note, "The Manville Bankruptcy: Treating Mass Tort Claims in Chapter 11 Proceedings," 96 *Harvard Law Review* 1121 (1983); Paul Brodeur, *Outrageous Misconduct: The Asbestos Industry on Trial* (New York: Pantheon, 1985). Borel decision: *Borel v. Fibreboard Paper Products Corp.,* 493 F.2d 1076 (5th Cir. 1973); On asbestos property damage litigation, see, e.g., Rich Arthurs, "Will Asbestos Property Cases Follow Injury Cases' Pattern?" *Legal Times of Washington,* Mar. 25, 1985, at 1; "Asbestos Suit Won by Greenville, S.C.," *New York Times,* Jan. 26, 1986, at A17.

3. The Agent Orange War

1. Reutershan's story: McCarthy interview; McCarthy letter to author, Oct. 30, 1985; John Dux and P. J. Young, *Agent Orange: The Bitter Harvest* (Sydney: Hodden and Stoughton, 1980), at 109–10; Fred Wilcox, *Waiting for an Army to Die: The Tragedy of Agent Orange* (New York: Pantheon, 1983), at 99–100; *Reutershan v. The Dow Chemical Company,* No. 78-CV-14365 (N.Y. Sup. Ct., N.Y. County), filed July 20, 1978.

2. McCarthy's story: McCarthy interview. See also Robert Klein, *Wounded Men, Broken Promises* (New York: Macmillan, 1981), at 175–81.

3. Interviews with Yannacone, McCarthy.

4. McCarthy's search for a new lawyer and discussions with Yannacone: McCarthy interview; McCarthy letter to author, Oct. 30, 1985; Yannacone interview. Yannacone's version: Yannacone interview. McCarthy's recollection: McCarthy letter, Oct. 30, 1985.

5. The class action: Yannacone interview; original complaint in *Reutershan et al. v. The Dow Chemical Co. et al. and the United States of America,* No. 78-CV-4253 (S.D.N.Y.) filed Jan. 8, 1979; Memorandum Supporting Plaintiffs' Amended Verified Complaint (July 15, 1979).

6. See "Advisory Committee's Notes to Proposed Rule of Civil Procedure," 39 F.R.D. 69, 103 (1966), discussed in *AO,* 100 F.R.D. 718 (E.D.N.Y. 1983) (Weinstein, C.J.). See also Chap. 1, n. 8, *supra.*

7. Interviews with McCarthy, Yannacone.

8. Interview with Michael and Maureen Ryan.

9. Michael Winerip, "The Law Firm That Toxic Waste Built," *New York Times,* Nov. 22, 1985, at B2.

10. Interviews with Rivkin, Yannacone.

11. See, e.g., *Ezaugui v. Dow Chem. Corp.,* 598 F.2d 727 (2d Cir. 1979).

12. Interviews with McCarthy, Ryan.

13. Interviews with Dean, Like, Fiorella.

14.   Yannacone interview; Susan Milstein, "Crusader Who Lost His Way," 6 *American Lawyer*, Apr. 1984; letter from McCarthy to author, Oct. 30, 1985.

15.   Musslewhite interview.

16.   The details of how Yannacone went about obtaining help and why his efforts ultimately failed have been chronicled in Milstein, "Crusader." That article is based upon interviews and on internal memoranda exchanged by the members of Yannacone & Associates, some of which I possess.

17.   Yannacone's deposition, Feb. 23, 1985, used to support Memorandum in Support of Plaintiffs' Motion Pursuant to Rules 52(b) and 59(e) to Reconsider the Order of January 7, 1985, Which Approved the Settlement (Mar. 7, 1985), at 22.

18.   On the early organization, activities, and budgeting of consortium: interviews with Like, Yannacone, Fiorella, Dean; Milstein, "Crusader."

19.   Interviews with Yannacone, Like, Fiorella; Milstein, "Crusader."

20.   Interviews with Like, Fiorella.

21.   Yannacone's deposition, Feb. 23, 1985, used to support Memorandum in Support of Plaintiffs' Motion, at 83–84.

22.   Yannacone's account of the study: Yannacone interview. Like's account: letter from Like to author, Aug. 14, 1985. "Swan song": testimony at hearing on Mar. 5, 1985; see transcript of hearing at 228–29.

23.   Interviews with Yannacone, Like, Dean, Fiorella; Milstein, "Crusader."

24.   Confidential portions of interviews with several lawyers.

25.   W. Stuart Dornette and Robert Cross, *Federal Judiciary Almanac* (New York: John Wiley & Sons, 1984), at 33.

26.   *AO*, 475 F. Supp. 928 (E.D.N.Y. 1979).

27.   Remarks at Symposium on Mass Torts after Agent Orange, Brooklyn Law School, Feb. 27, 1985.

28.   Transcript of hearing, June 21, 1979, at 74; Like interview.

29.   *AO*, 475 F. Supp. 928, 936 (E.D.N.Y. 1979).

30.   Yannacone's views on pleadings: written communication to author, Nov. 29, 1985. Pratt's criticism: transcript of hearing, Oct. 3, 1979, at 6–7.

31.   *AO*, 506 F. Supp. 737 (E.D.N.Y. 1979), *rev'd*, 635 F.2d 987 (2d Cir. 1980), *cert. denied*, 454 U.S. 1128 (1981).

4. Judge Pratt Rules

1.   Transcript of hearing, Dec. 12, 1983, at 14.

2.   On the evolution and scholarly criticism of sovereign immunity, see Peter Schuck, *Suing Government: Citizen Remedies for Official Wrongs* (New Haven: Yale University Press, 1983), chap. 2.

3.   Tort Claims Act: 28 U.S.C. secs. 1291, 1346, 1402, 1504, 2110, 2401, 2402, 2411, 2412, 2671–80.

4.   *Feres* v. *United States*, 340 U.S. 135 (1950). For the most recent, em-

phatic, and perhaps extreme reaffirmation of *Feres*, see *United States* v. *Shearer*, 105 S. Ct. 3039 (1985).

5. Interviews with Yannacone, Like, McCarthy, Musslewhite.

6. Rivkin interview.

7. *Stencel Aero Engineering Corp.* v. *United States*, 431 U.S. 666, *rehearing denied*, 434 U.S. 882 (1977).

8. Transcript of hearing, Feb. 1, 1980, at 67–68.

9. See, e.g., *Tillett* v. *J. I. Case Co.*, 756 F.2d 591, 596–600 (7th Cir. 1985).

10. Musslewhite interview.

11. Dean interview.

12. Yannacone's claim: written communication to author, Nov. 29, 1985. Like's version: letter from Like to author, Aug. 14, 1985. The Second Circuit granted leave to appeal on Jan. 16, 1980.

13. *Eisen* v. *Carlisle & Jacquelin*, 417 U.S. 156 (1974).

14. "Advisory Committee's Notes to Proposed Rule of Civil Procedure," 39 F.R.D. 69, 103 (1966).

15. See Dow's Memorandum of Law in Opposition to Certification of Plaintiffs' Action as a Class Action (Sept. 26, 1979), at 28–44. The case in which the court certified a class for limited purposes only and later rescinded it was *Payton* v. *Abbott Labs*, 100 F.R.D. 336 (D. Mass. 1983).

16. *AO*, 635 F.2d 987 (2d Cir. 1980), *cert. denied*, 454 U.S. 1128 (1981).

17. Decision on prisoners: *Owens* v. *Haas*, 601 F.2d 1242 (2d Cir.), *cert. denied*, 444 U.S. 980 (1979). Feinberg's dissent: *AO*, 635 F.2d at 995.

18. Twerski made this argument in remarks at the Symposium on Mass Torts after Agent Orange, Brooklyn Law School, Feb. 27, 1985. The Supreme Court on the special relationship: *Feres* v. *United States*, 340 U.S. 135, 143 (1950).

19. Dissatisfaction with plaintiffs' brief: Yannacone interview; written communication from Yannacone to author, Nov. 29, 1985. Supreme Court refusal: *AO*, 454 U.S. 1128 (1981). Weinstein's observation: *AO*, Fairness Opinion at 754.

20. Pratt's decision: *AO*, 506 F. Supp. 762 (E.D.N.Y. 1980). Weinstein later modified important aspects of that decision, as discussed in Chapter 7.

21. *AO*, Fairness Opinion at 810–16.

22. Id. at 800.

23. Serial trials approach: interviews with Like, Fiorella; written communication from Yannacone to author, Nov. 29, 1985.

24. Plaintiffs' Memorandum in Support of an Application for Serial Trials, June 23, 1980, at 25–26.

25. Interviews with Yannacone, Dean, Like.

26. Interviews with Rivkin, Silberman.

27. Pratt's original order barring discovery was issued on May 18, 1979. It was modified on Feb. 5, 1980, to permit only voluntary discovery. See discussion in *AO*, 506 F. Supp. 762 at 797. Pratt's fears: transcript of hearing, Nov. 22, 1979, at 17.

5. Discovery Begins

1. Yannacone interview.
2. Dean interview.
3. Susan Milstein, "Crusader Who Lost His Way," *American Lawyer*, April 1984.
4. Interviews with Yannacone, McCarthy, Like, Fiorella; Milstein, "Crusader."
5. Dean interview.
6. Interviews with McCarthy, Fiorella, Like; Milstein, "Crusader."
7. See Ashcraft & Gerel et al.'s Motion to Establish Steering Committee to Coordinate Discovery, filed Jan. 16, 1981; interview with Robert Taylor, Jr.; Milstein, "Crusader"; Motion and Brief in Support of Motion to Establish a Steering Committee and Appoint Liaison Counsel, filed Jan. 16, 1981.
8. Robert Klein, *Wounded Men, Broken Promises* (1981) at 55–65; Bernard Weintraub, "Vietnam Invites 4 U.S. Veterans to Visit Hanoi," *New York Times*, Dec. 13, 1981, at A1; Tony Bliss, "Bobby Muller's Vietnam Veterans of America: Troubled Past, Uncertain Future," *Soldier of Fortune*, May 1984, at 30.
9. Transcript of hearing, Jan. 30, 1981, at 8, 18–19, 204–6.
10. Transcript of hearing, Jan. 30, 1981, at 207–10, 211–12, 214. See also Plaintiffs' Memorandum Opposing Motion by Certain Non–Class Action Attorneys for Order Establishing Steering Committee (Jan. 26, 1981).
11. On the differences among AOVI, VVA, and Citizen Soldier, see Klein, *Wounded Men*, at 176–77; Michael Uhl and Tod Ensign, *G.I. Guinea Pigs* (New York: Playboy Press, 1980), at 55–65, 175–81; Bliss, "Bobby Muller's Vietnam Veterans," at 30.
12. Interviews with Dean, Musslewhite, Yannacone.
13. Federal Rules of Civil Procedure, Rule 23 (d).
14. Transcript of hearing, Jan. 30, 1981, at 97.
15. GAO report: Uhl and Ensign, *G.I. Guinea Pigs*, at 212–16; "G.A.O. Report Says Agent Orange Tests Are Inadequate," *New York Times*, Oct. 26, 1982, at A19. Citizen Soldier survey: Uhl and Ensign, *G.I. Guinea Pigs*, at 213–14.
16. McCarthy interview; "2 Vietnam Heroes Disrupt Carter Talk," *Arizona Republic*, May 31, 1979, at C1; Klein, *Wounded Men*, at 162–63.
17. David Binder, "Administration Widening Investigation of Herbicide Effects on Veterans," *New York Times*, May 29, 1979, at A18; Uhl and Ensign, *G.I. Guinea Pigs*, at 207; Fred Wilcox, *Waiting for an Army to Die: The Tragedy of Agent Orange* (New York: Vintage Books, 1983), at chap. 8; "Traces of a Toxic Chemical Found in Vietnam Veterans," *New York Times*, Dec. 13, 1979, at A18; "U.C.L.A. Researchers Given Pact for V.A. Study of Agent Orange," *New York Times*, May 6, 1981, at A26; "Prejudice and Agent Orange," *New York Times*, Sept. 1, 1981, at A18; "Furor Looms at Herbicide Hearing," *New York Times*, Nov. 18, 1981, at A25; "Agency to Yield on Herbicide Issue," *New York Times*, Oct. 16, 1982, at A6; lecture by Arthur Galston at Yale Law School, Mar. 26, 1985.

18. Veterans' Health Care, Training, and Small Business Loan Act of 1981, Pub. L. No. 97-72, 95 Stat. 1047–64.

19. Uhl and Ensign, *G.I. Guinea Pigs,* at 210; Comment, "Agent Orange as a Problem of Law and Policy," 77 *Northwestern University Law Review* 48, 55 (1982); Barbara McClure, "Veterans' Benefits and Services: Major Legislation in the 98th Congress," Congressional Research Service Issues Brief No. IB83110 (1984) at 4; "G.A.O. Report," *New York Times,* Oct. 26, 1982, at A19.

20. Yannacone's suit against the VA was *Ryan v. Cleland.* The 1974 Supreme Court decision was *Johnson v. Robison,* 415 U.S. 361 (1974). Pratt denied the claim in *Ryan v. Cleland,* 531 F. Supp. 724 (E.D.N.Y. 1982).

21. The request was filed on Jan. 8, 1981, and was never acted upon. See Defendants' Petition for a Writ of Mandamus (Apr. 29, 1983).

22. *AO,* 534 F. Supp. 1046, 1058 (E.D.N.Y. 1982).

23. Confidential portions of interviews with certain lawyers for plaintiffs and defendants.

24. Pratt's decision of Feb. 24, 1982: *AO,* 534 F. Supp. 1046 (E.D.N.Y. 1982).

25. Schreiber's appointment: Pretrial Order No. 35, published at 94 F.R.D. 173 (E.D.N.Y. 1982). Defendants' desire for special discovery master: Rivkin interview.

26. Pratt interview.

27. See, generally, Wayne Brazil, "Referring Discovery Tasks to Special Masters: Is Rule 53 a Source of Authority and Restrictions?" 1983 *American Bar Foundation Research Journal* 143.

28. Schreiber interview.

29. Shapiro interview.

30. Interviews with Musslewhite, Dean, Fiorella.

31. Milstein, "Crusader"; interviews with Like, Fiorella, Yannacone. The negotiations between the consortium and Ashcraft & Gerel and the Musslewhite group are further detailed in Musslewhite's deposition of Feb. 23, 1985, used to support Memorandum in Support of Plaintiffs' Motion Pursuant to Rules 52(b) and Rule 59(e) to Reconsider the Order of January 7, 1985, Which Approved the Settlement (Mar. 7, 1985), at 13–15.

32. Milstein, "Crusader."

33. Dean interview.

34. Id.

35. Memo to File (Mar. 25, 1965), by E. L. Chandler (of Diamond Alkali) concerning meeting of Mar. 24, 1965, Exhibit BB to Plaintiffs' Memorandum in Opposition to Defendant The Dow Chemical Company's Motion for Summary Judgment on the Government Contract Defense (Apr. 25, 1983). On how the consortium learned of it: Letter from Like to author, Aug. 14, 1985.

36. Dean interview.

37. *AO,* Fairness Opinion at 777.

38. Memo by Hercules official, Exhibit FF to Plaintiff's Memorandum in Opposition to Dow's Motion for Summary Judgment.

39. Reply Memorandum of Defendant Dow in Support of Its Motion for Summary Judgment on the Government Contract Defense (May 2, 1983), at 19–29.

40. Such verdicts are not unknown. See, e.g., Thomas Hayes, "Texaco Must Pay $11 Billion Award, Texas Court Rules," *New York Times*, Dec. 11, 1985, at A1. (The judgment against Texaco included $3 billion in punitive damages.)

41. Interviews with Yannacone, Dean, Like, Fiorella.

42. Interviews with Rivkin, Silberman.

43. Settlement discussions: interviews with Fiorella, Like, Dean; letter from Rivkin to author, Nov. 21, 1985; confidential portions of interviews with certain defendants' lawyers. Yannacone denies this account, according to his written communication to author, Nov. 29, 1985.

44. Richard Severo, "Jury Awards $58 Million to 47 Railroad Workers Exposed to Dioxin," *New York Times*, Aug. 27, 1982, at A9. Almost two years later, an appellate court reversed on the basis of procedural errors and ordered a new trial: *Lowe* v. *Norfolk & Western Rwy. Co.*, 124 Ill. App. 3d 80, 463 N.E.2d 796 (1984). The defendants' reaction: Rivkin interview.

45. Dean interview.

46. Confidential portion of interview with a defendant's lawyer.

6. Three-Cornered Struggle

1. Transcript of hearing, Mar. 21, 1983, at 3616.

2. Yannacone interview.

3. Transcript of hearing, Dec. 13, 1982, at 2566–67.

4. *AO*, 98 F.R.D. 557 (E.D.N.Y. 1983); Schreiber interview.

5. Maskin interview.

6. Schreiber interview.

7. For Judge Weinstein's analysis of this issue, see *AO*, Fairness Opinion at 796–97.

8. Trade secrets problem: *AO*, 96 F.R.D. 578 (E.D.N.Y. 1983) and *AO*, 97 F.R.D. 424 (E.D.N.Y. 1983). Media access: *AO*, 96 F.R.D. 582 (E.D.N.Y. 1983). *In extremis* depositions: *AO*, 96 F.R.D. 587 (E.D.N.Y. 1983).

9. Memorandum, Feb. 27, 1983, from Keith Kavenagh to Yannacone & Associates.

10. Interview with Steven Schlegel.

11. See Defendants' Motion for Adjournment of the Date for Trial of the Government Contract Defense (Mar. 16, 1983).

12. Transcripts of hearings: Mar. 21, 1983, at 3619–20, 3631; Mar. 28, 1983, at 3695–3704.

13. Yannacone interview.

14. *AO*, 565 F. Supp. 1263 (E.D.N.Y. 1983).

15. See Chapter 10.

16. *AO*, Fairness Opinion at 832.

17. Memorandum of The Dow Chemical Company in Support of Its Mo-

tion for Summary Judgment on the Government Contract Defense (Apr. 20, 1983); Plaintiffs' Memorandum in Opposition to Defendant The Dow Chemical Company's Motion for Summary Judgment on the Government Contract Defense (Apr. 25, 1983).

18. *AO*, 565 F. Supp. at 1276, 1277.

19. Transcript of hearing, Nov. 12, 1982, at 2314.

20. Rivkin interview; see also Chapter 7.

21. Interviews with Like, Dean.

22. Interviews with Like, Schlegel, Fiorella; Susan Milstein, "Crusader Who Lost His Way," *American Lawyer*, Apr. 1984; Yannacone's written communication to author, Nov. 29, 1985; Yannacone interview.

23. Interviews with Henderson, Schlegel.

24. Yannacone interview.

25. Milstein, "Crusader."

26. Interviews with Like, Yannacone, Schlegel, Henderson.

27. Yannacone interview.

28. Interviews with Like, Yannacone.

29. Yannacone interview.

30. Interviews with Like, Dean.

31. Memorandum from Yannacone to Yannacone & Associates Management Committee, June 3, 1983.

32. Like interview; letter from Like to author, Aug. 14, 1985.

33. Interviews with Fiorella, Dean.

34. Interviews with Henderson, Yannacone.

35. Henderson interview.

36. Curriculum Vitae of Samuel Epstein, appended to Epstein's Causation Affidavits, submitted with Plaintiffs' Second Supplemental Opposition to Defendants' Motion to Dismiss or, in the Alternative, for Summary Judgment (Mar. 11, 1985).

37. Interviews with Like, Fiorella, Dean.

38. Like interview.

39. Plaintiff's Notice of Motion for Order Relieving Yannacone & Associates as Lead Counsel, filed Sept. 21, 1983.

40. Interviews with Henderson, Schlegel, Fiorella. Yannacone denies this claim: Yannacone interview.

41. Henderson interview; Milstein, "Crusader."

42. Interviews with Schlegel, Henderson.

43. Milstein, "Crusader"; transcript of hearing, Sept. 20, 1983, at 6575–76.

44. Henderson interview; Milstein, "Crusader."

45. Interviews with Like, Fiorella.

46. Yannacone interview.

47. See, e.g., remarks of Stanley Chesley in transcript of hearing, Sept. 26, 1984, at 26.

48. Letter from Pratt to Judge Andrew Caffrey, chairman, Multidistrict Litigation Panel, requesting reassignment, Oct. 13, 1983.

7. Enter Judge Weinstein

1. Confidential portions of interviews with plaintiffs' and defendants' lawyers.

2. Weinstein's treatises: *Cases and Materials on Evidence* (Mineola, N.Y.: Foundation Press, 1983); *Weinstein's Evidence* (Albany, N.Y.: M. Bender, 1975); *CPLR Manual* (with Harold Korn and Arthur Miller), (New York: Bender, 1980); *Elements of Civil Procedure, Cases and Materials* (with Maurice Rosenberg and Hans Smith) (Mineola, N.Y.: Foundation Press, 1970). Landmark cases: *Hall* v. *E. I. DuPont de Nemours & Co., Inc.*, 345 F. Supp. 353 (E.D.N.Y. 1972); *Hart* v. *Community Sch. Bd. of Brooklyn, N.Y., Sch. D. #21*, 383 F. Supp. 699 (1974); *In re Franklin National Bank Securities Litigation*, 92 F.R.D. 468 (E.D.N.Y. 1981), *aff'd sub nom. Federal Deposit Insurance Corp.* v. *Ernst & Ernst*, 677 F.2d 230 (2d Cir. 1982). His political background: Friedman interview.

3. Interviews with Dean, Rivkin, Maskin.

4. Interviews with Dean, Krohley and Gross, Friedman.

5. The following account is based on the transcript of hearing, Oct. 21, 1983, at 6807–21; and on Friedman interview.

6. Milstein, "Crusader Who Lost His Way," *American Lawyer*, Apr. 1984.

7. Interviews with Dean, Henderson.

8. Milstein, "Crusader"; written communication from Yannacone to author, Nov. 29, 1985.

9. McCarthy interview.

10. Transcript of hearing, Oct. 21, 1983, at 6822; interviews with Friedman, Yannacone.

11. McCarthy interview.

12. Interviews with Dean, Krohley and Gross.

13. Friedman interview.

14. Interviews with Rivkin, Dean, Scheindlin.

15. Scheindlin interview.

16. Friedman interview.

17. Like interview.

18. See George Priest and Benjamin Klein, "The Selection of Disputes for Litigation," 13 *Journal of Legal Studies* 1, 14–17 (1984).

19. Interviews with Friedman, Feinberg, Shapiro.

20. Interviews with Henderson, Dean, Schlegel, Like.

21. Interviews with Henderson, Like, Musslewhite.

22. Musslewhite interview; Musslewhite's deposition, Feb. 23, 1985, submitted in support of Rule 59 Motion.

23. Schwartz affidavit, docketed June 4, 1985, at 11–12.

24. Musslewhite interview.

25. Musslewhite interview.

26. Dean interview.

27. The PMC agreement and the individual contributions are discussed in *AO*, 611 F. Supp. 1452, 1454–55 (E.D.N.Y. 1985). "The golden spike": Musslewhite interview. Tom Henderson states that he contributed as much money as the others: letter from Henderson to author, Feb. 4, 1986.

28. Schlegel interview.

29. *Waga & Spinelli, Inc.* v. *Agent Orange Plaintiffs' Management Committee et al.*, No. 84-CV-4246 (D. N.J.).

30. Dean interview.

31. Fiorella interview.

32. Interviews with Friedman, Scheindlin.

33. Dean interview.

34. Wayne Brazil, "Special Masters in Complex Cases: Extending the Judiciary or Reshaping Adjudication?" 53 *University of Chicago Law Review* 394 (1986).

35. Scheindlin interview.

36. Interviews with Scheindlin, Musslewhite.

37. Scheindlin interview.

38. Friedman interview.

39. Friedman interview.

40. *AO*, 100 F.R.D. 718 (E.D.N.Y. 1983), *mandamus denied*, 725 F.2d 858 (2d Cir. 1984), *cert. denied*, 104 S. Ct. 1417 (1984).

41. Id. at 725–28.

42. Id. at 728–35. *Eisen* decision: *Eisen* v. *Carlisle & Jacquelin*, 417 U.S. 156 (1974).

43. *AO*, 725 F.2d 858 (2d Cir. 1984), *cert. denied*, 104 S. Ct. 1017 (1984). Stay of class notification: Order of U.S. Court of Appeals, Second Circuit, Staying Pre-Trial Order Number 72 Pending Determination of Petition for Mandamus (Dec. 23, 1983). It was vacated on Jan. 9, 1984: Order of U.S. Court of Appeals, Second Circuit (Jan. 9, 1984).

44. *AO*, 100 F.R.D. at 724.

45. *AO*, 580 F. Supp. 690 (E.D.N.Y. 1984).

46. Kearse's opinion: *AO*, 635 F.2d 987 (2d Cir. 1980), *cert. denied*, 454 U.S. 1128 (1981). See also discussion in Chapter 4.

47. Dean interview.

48. *AO*, Fairness Opinion at 845–47.

49. *AO*, 506 F. Supp. 762 (E.D.N.Y. 1980).

50. Weinstein's governmental immunity opinion: *AO*, 580 F. Supp. 1242, *mandamus* denied, 733 F.2d 10 (2d Cir. 1984), *appeal dismissed*, 745 F.2d 161 (2d Cir. 1984).

51. *AO*, 611 F. Supp. 1223 (E.D.N.Y. 1985).

52. *Orken* v. *United States*, 239 F.2d 850 (6th Cir. 1956).

53. *Stencel Aero Engineering Co.* v. *United States*, 431 U.S. 666, 676–77 (1977) (Marshall, J., dissenting).

54. *AO*, 580 F. Supp. at 1248.

55. *Chappel* v. *Wallace*, 462 U.S. 296 (1983).

56. Transcript of hearing, Dec. 19, 1983, at 41–55; Scheindlin interview.

57. *Hinkie* v. *United States*, 715 F.2d 96 (3d Cir. 1983), *cert. denied*, 104 S. Ct. 1276 (1984); *Mondelli* v. *United States*, 711 F.2d 567 (5th Cir. 1983), *cert. denied*, 465 U.S. 1021 (1984); *Monaco* v. *United States*, 661 F.2d 129 (9th Cir. 1981), *cert.*

denied, 456 U.S. 989 (1982); *Lombard* v. *United States*, 690 F.2d 215 (D.C. Cir. 1982), *cert. denied*, 462 U.S. 1118 (1983); *Scales* v. *United States*, 685 F.2d 970 (5th Cir. 1982), *cert. denied*, 460 U.S. 1082 (1983); *Gaspard* v. *United States*, 713 F.2d 1097 (5th Cir. 1983), *cert. denied*, 104 S. Ct. 2354 (1984); *AO*, 506 F. Supp. 762 (E.D.N.Y. 1980) (Pratt, J.).

58. Respondents' Answer to Petition for Writ of Mandamus (Mar. 30, 1984), at 13.

59. *Kohn* v. *United States*, 680 F.2d 922, 926 (2d Cir. 1982).

60. Maskin interview.

61. See Motion to Amend the Order of February 16, 1984, for Certification Pursuant to 28 U.S.C. Section 1292(b) (Feb. 27, 1984), which Weinstein denied by endorsement on the motion; letter from Maskin to Weinstein, Mar. 7, 1984, on which Weinstein denied relief by endorsement on Mar. 11, 1984; United States' Motion for Reconsideration of Preliminary Pretrial Order No. 91, (Mar. 12, 1984), which Weinstein denied from the bench on Mar. 19, 1984. See transcript of hearing, Mar. 19, at 57.

62. Transcript of hearing, Mar. 5, 1984, at 38–39.

63. *AO*, 565 F. Supp. at 1274; transcript of hearing, Feb. 15, 1984, at 43–44.

64. *AO*, 733 F.2d 10 (2d Cir. 1984).

65. *AO*, 745 F.2d 161 (2d Cir. 1984).

66. Spencer Williams, "Mass Tort Class Actions: Going, Going, Gone?" 98 F.R.D. 323 (1983); quote is from Henderson interview.

67. Henderson interview.

68. Henderson interview; written communication from Yannacone to author, Nov. 29, 1985.

69. Henderson interview.

70. Transcript of hearing, Jan. 18, 1984, at 7–20; interviews with Henderson, Dean.

71. Written communication from Henderson to author, Feb. 4, 1986.

72. Henderson interview.

73. Interviews with Henderson, Scheindlin.

74. See the discussion in *AO*, Fairness Opinion, analyzed in Chapter 9.

75. Interviews with Rivkin, Silberman.

76. Dow's Memorandum in Opposition to Utilization of Enterprise Liability, Market Share Liability or Other Theories of Alternate Liability Or, in the Alternative, for Allocation of Liability in Proportion to Levels of Dioxin in Each Manufacturer's Product (Nov. 30, 1983); Monsanto's Memorandum of Law Concerning Plaintiffs' Burden of Proving Responsibility of a Particular Defendant for the Injury of a Particular Plaintiff (Dec. 1, 1983).

77. Transcript of hearing, Feb. 15, 1984, at 37–44.

78. Rivkin interview.

79. Transcripts of hearings: Sept. 26, 1984, at 20; Oct. 1, 1984, at 55.

80. McCarthy interview.

81. Interviews with Scheindlin, Friedman.

82. Written communication from Yannacone to author, Nov. 29, 1985.

8. Fashioning a Settlement

1. Interviews with Friedman, Scheindlin, Feinberg, Shapiro.

2. Feinberg interview.

3. Jack Weinstein, "The Role of the Court in Toxic Tort Litigation," 73 *Georgetown Law Journal* 1389, 1392 (1985).

4. Feinberg interview.

5. On special masters, see Wayne Brazil, "Special Masters in the Pretrial Development of Big Cases: Potential and Problems," 1984 *American Bar Foundation Research Journal* 287. Weinstein had used special masters in *Hart v. Community Sch. Bd. of Brooklyn, N.Y. Sch. D. #21*, 383 F. Supp. 699 (1974).

6. Galligan interview.

7. Federal Rules of Civil Procedure, Rule 53(b). *La Buy* v. *Howes Leather Co.*, 352 U.S. 249 (1957), but see *Mathews* v. *Weber*, 423 U.S. 261 (1976).

8. Feinberg interview.

9. Yannacone interview.

10. Transcript of hearing, Mar. 12, 1984, at 58.

11. Feinberg interview.

12. Interviews with Shapiro, Feinberg.

13. Shapiro interview.

14. Garment interview.

15. Shapiro interview.

16. Interviews with Shapiro, Feinberg, Musslewhite.

17. Interviews with Garment, Shapiro.

18. Weinstein's demand was transmitted by telephone about Apr. 24, 1985: personal communication from Maskin to author, December 1985.

19. Maskin interview.

20. Letter from Maskin to Weinstein, Apr. 24, 1984, Appendix D to *AO*, Fairness Opinion.

21. Memorandum from Garment, Apr. 24, 1984 (Re: Political Justification for Federal Government Involvement in Settling Agent Orange Cases).

22. Maskin interview.

23. Motion of the United States to Strike the Submission of Federal Tort Claims to the Advisory Jury (Apr. 25, 1984). Weinstein's ruling: order dated May 2, 1984; Maskin interview. Weinstein's earlier use of advisory jury: *Birnbaum* v. *United States*, 436 F. Supp. 967, 988 (E.D.N.Y. 1977); see also Federal Rules of Civil Procedure, Rule 39(c).

24. Shapiro interview.

25. Rivkin interview.

26. Shapiro interview.

27. Dean interview.

28. Interviews with Dean, Scheindlin; transcript of hearing, May 4, 1984, at 70–73; Heineman interview.

29. The following account of the settlement negotiations is a composite from interviews with a number of people who were present, including Dean, Feinberg, Shapiro, Musslewhite, Rivkin, Silberman, and Krohley and Gross.

30. The insurance disputes that resulted in litigation included *Hercules v. Aetna,* Docket No. CV-82-854 (D. D.C.), which concerned defense costs and was settled quickly, and *Travelers* v. *Monsanto, Liberty Mut., and Insurance Company of North America,* Docket No. CV-81-3485 (S.D.N.Y.). This case, which continued for more than three years and was settled in June 1984, involved a dispute over which of several different policies covered the Agent Orange risks; one insurer alleged that Monsanto had failed to disclose to it information regarding known dangers and risks. See Answer filed by Liberty Mutual, Mar. 25, 1982. For the role of insurance disputes in the asbestos litigation, see "Special Project: An Analysis of the Legal, Social, and Political Issues Raised by Asbestos Litigation," 36 *Vanderbilt Law Review* 573, 709–30; James Peeples, "Asbestos Litigation and Theories of Insurance Coverage," *Federation of Insurance Counsel Quarterly* 323 (1982).

31. Musslewhite's sworn statement, referred to in Chapter 5, is in his deposition, Feb. 23, 1985.

32. Id.

33. Communication with Steven Brower, special deputy clerk for Agent Orange, U.S. District Court for the Eastern District of New York, Feb. 14, 1986.

34. Musslewhite's deposition, Feb. 23, 1985, at 82–83.

35. Interviews with O'Quinn, Musslewhite.

36. See, e.g., *Kothe v. Smith,* 771 F.2d 667 (2d. Cir. 1985). On Weinstein, see *Almanac of the Federal Judiciary* (Chicago: LawLetters, Winter 1984), at 57.

37. See, e.g., Wayne Brazil, "What Lawyers Want from Judges in the Settlement Arena," 106 F.R.D. 85, 90 (1985); see also Peter Schuck, "The Role of the Judge in Settlement: The Agent Orange Example," 53 *University of Chicago Law Review* 337 (1986).

38. Remarks by Richard Duesenberg at Conference on Litigation Management, Yale Law School, Oct. 4, 1985.

39. Shapiro's fees: letter from Robert C. Heinemann, clerk of court, to author, Oct. 2, 1985. Feinberg's fees: Monthly Status Report on Agent Orange Settlement Fund, dated February 4, 1986. The $750,000 total includes $230,000 to Lawrence Novey, Feinberg's associate.

40. Quoted in Michael Winerip, "The Law Firm That Toxic Waste Built," *New York Times,* Nov. 22, 1985, at B2.

41. Confidential portion of an interview with a defendant's lawyer.

42. Confidential portion of an interview.

43. Ari Press, "A Fast Deal on Agent Orange," *Newsweek,* May 21, 1984, at 56.

44. "Companies Comment on Pact," *New York Times,* May 8, 1984, at B4.

45. Dean interview; Press, "A Fast Deal."

9. A Question of Fairness

1. McCarthy interview.
2. Interviews with McCarthy, Dean.

3. Ralph Blumenthal, "Veterans Accept $180 Million Pact on Agent Orange," *New York Times*, May 8, 1984, at A1; transcript of hearing, May 24, 1984, at 267. McCarthy's assertion: McCarthy interview.

4. Ryan interview.

5. *AO, Fairness Opinion* at 756.

6. Yannacone interview.

7. Taylor interview.

8. See Appendix A, *AO,* Fairness Opinion at 862 and paragraph 10 at 865.

9. Interviews with Ryan, Yannacone. See Chapter 10.

10. See paragraph 13 of settlement agreement, *AO,* Fairness Opinion at 865.

11. James Jacobs, *Social Foundations of Civil-Military Relations* (New Brunswick, N.J.: Transaction Books, 1986), chap. 7.

12. Musslewhite interview; Musslewhite deposition, Feb. 23, 1985, at 117; Taylor interview.

13. See paragraph 7 of settlement agreement, *AO,* Fairness Opinion at 865.

14. Deboer testified at the fairness hearing, Brooklyn, Aug. 9, 1984; see transcript of hearing at 402.

15. Shapiro's letter to Weinstein is dated May 10, 1984.

16. See, e.g., transcripts of hearings: Sept. 26, 1984, at 20; Oct. 1, 1984, at 55.

17. Interviews with McCarthy, Ryan, Yannacone, Dean, Henderson.

18. Written communication from Henderson to author, Feb. 4, 1986.

19. *City of Detroit* v. *Grinnell Corp.*, 495 F.2d 448 (2d Cir. 1974), discussed in *AO,* Fairness Opinion at 761–62.

20. My distillation of the principal themes emerging from the testimony is a composite drawn from the transcripts of the hearings. See summary in *AO,* Fairness Opinion at 764–65.

21. Id. at 764.

22. Transcript of hearing, San Francisco, Aug. 24, 1984, at 256–58.

23. Transcript of Aug. 24 hearing, at 417–75. On paranoid rhetoric in American history, see Richard Hofstadter, *The Age of Reform* (New York: Alfred A. Knopf, 1955) at 60–94.

24. See testimony of Rena Kopystenski, transcript of hearing, Brooklyn, Aug. 8, 1984, at 178.

25. See testimony of Carol Delaney, transcript of hearing, Brooklyn, Aug. 10, 1984, at 675.

26. *AO,* Fairness Opinion at 857.

27. Transcript of hearing, Aug. 24, 1984, at 378.

28. Friedman interview.

29. Letter from Heinemann, clerk of court, to author, Oct. 2, 1985.

30. See, e.g., Blumenthal, "Veterans Accept"; Ari Press, "A Fast Deal on Agent Orange," *Newsweek*, May 21, 1984, at 56.

31. See transcripts of fairness hearings.

32. *AO,* Fairness Opinion at 763, 775.

33. Id. at 857–58.

34. My discussion and analysis of the fairness opinion in the following pages generally tracks the sequence and structure of Weinstein's own analysis.

35. See Memorandum in Support of Plaintiffs' Motion Pursuant to Rules 52(b) and 59(e) to Reconsider the Order of January 7, 1985 Which Approved the Settlement (Mar. 7, 1985), at 186–201, and supporting exhibits. Allegations controverted on appeal: letter from Like to author, Oct. 2, 1985.

36. Transcript of hearing, Feb. 6, 1985, at 44–45.

37. Confidential portion of an interview with a defendant's lawyer.

38. The intention of the Federal Rules of Civil Procedure not to affect substantive rights: 28 U.S.C. §2072 (1976).

39. *AO*, Fairness Opinion at 833–34.

40. Samuel Estep, "Radiation Injuries and Statistics: The Need for a New Approach to Injury Litigation," 59 *Michigan Law Review* 259 (1960); Glen Robinson, "Probabilistic Causation and Compensation for Tortious Risk," 14 *Journal of Legal Studies* 779 (1985); Richard Delgado, "Beyond *Sindell:* Relaxation of Cause-in-Fact Rules for Indeterminate Plaintiffs," 70 *California Law Review* 881 (1982); David Rosenberg, "The Causal Connection in Mass Exposure Cases: A 'Public Law' Vision of the Tort System," 97 *Harvard Law Review* 849 (1984).

41. *Allen* v. *United States,* 588 F. Supp. 247 (D. Utah 1984).

42. *State of West Virginia* v. *Charles Pfizer & Co.,* 440 F.2d. 1079, 1086 (2d Cir.), *cert. denied,* 404 U.S., 871 (1971).

10. Compensations

1. Author's notes of hearing, Feb. 6, 1985; transcript of hearing at 195–96; Ryan interview.

2. On the lawyers' financing of the litigation, see *AO,* 611 F. Supp. 1296 (E.D.N.Y. 1985) (Weinstein, C.J.), referred to hereinafter as Initial Attorneys' Fee Opinion.

3. Pre-Trial Order No. 32, July 23, 1984.

4. My account of the fee hearings is extracted from the transcripts of hearings held on Sept. 26 and Oct. 1, 1984.

5. Rivkin interview; editorial, *New York Times,* Mar. 8, 1985, at A34.

6. Plaintiffs' Memorandum on Causation (no date); written communication from Henderson to author, Feb. 4, 1986.

7. See Memorandum Concerning Plaintiffs' Lawyers' Application for Attorneys' Fees and for Reimbursement of Expenses, filed Dec. 13, 1984.

8. Rivkin interview.

9. My discussion and analysis of Weinstein's Initial Attorneys' Fee Opinion is based on the opinion itself, except where otherwise noted here.

10. *AO,* Fairness Opinion at 786.

11. Interviews with Krohley and Gross; Feinberg; Scheindlin; confidential portion of interview with another special master.

12. Author's notes of hearing, Feb. 6, 1985; transcript of hearing at 33–35. Some lawyers report that Weinstein "tends to award low attorneys' fees": *Almanac of the Federal Judiciary* (Chicago: LawLetters, Winter 1984), at 57.

13. Author's notes of hearing, Feb. 6, 1985; transcript of hearing at 187; Silberman interview.

14. Author's notes of hearing, Feb. 6, 1985; transcript of hearing at 16–19.

15. Interviews with Rivkin, Feinberg.

16. Author's notes of hearing, Feb. 6, 1985; transcript of hearing at 73–74.

17. Yannacone's Petition for Award of Attorneys' Fees and Reimbursement of Expenses and Disbursements Advanced (Aug. 31, 1984).

18. Rivkin interview.

19. Dean interview.

20. Interview with Dr. Harvey Wachsman of Pegalis and Wachsman.

21. Yannacone interview.

22. Feinberg interview.

23. "Orangemail: Why It Got Paid," *New York Times*, Mar. 8, 1985, at A34.

24. Author's notes of hearing, Feb. 6, 1985; transcript of hearing at 186.

25. Dean interview.

26. *AO*, 611 F. Supp. 1296 (E.D.N.Y. 1985). Scheindlin's report appears at 611 F. Supp at 1347.

27. *AO*, Memorandum and Order on Attorneys' Fees and Final Judgment, issued on Jan. 7, 1985. This opinion was not published in the official federal reports.

28. Schreiber's remarks were made at Symposium on Mass Torts after Agent Orange, Brooklyn Law School, Feb. 27, 1985.

29. Musslewhite interview. See John Moore, " 'Master of Disaster' Builds Reputation for Mega-Settling," *Legal Times*, April 1, 1985, at 1. Musslewhite's First Supplement, and Brief in Support of, Motion Filed under Rule 59 and 60 of F.R.C.P. Concerning the Court's Final Judgment (Jan. 7, 1985), at 5.

30. *AO*, 611 F. Supp. 1452, 1454 (E.D.N.Y. 1985); Musslewhite interview.

31. Memorandum and Order on Attorneys' Fees.

32. Memorandum of Law in Support of Motion by Dean, Falanga & Rose to Invalidate Fee Sharing Agreement (May 16, 1985).

33. See Chapters 6 and 7.

34. *AO*, 611 F. Supp. 1452 (E.D.N.Y. 1985).

35. Memorandum and Order on Attorneys' Fees at 7.

36. Musslewhite's Motion Filed under Rule 59 and 60 of F.R.C.P. Concerning the Court's "Final Judgment" with Respect to the Settlement of the Class Claims against the Defendant Chemical Companies (Jan. 16, 1985), and two supplements thereto; and Taylor's Motion Pursuant to Rules 52(b) and 59(e) to Reconsider the Order of January 7, 1985, Which Approved the Settlement, Mar. 7, 1985. See transcript of hearing, Feb. 6, 1985, at 186, where Weinstein granted Musslewhite's petition to resign. Yannacone's and Musslewhite's depositions, Feb. 23, 1985, were used to support Taylor's motion.

37. Author's notes of hearing, Mar. 18, 1985; transcript of hearing at 59, 82.

38. See *AO*, 611 F. Supp. 1396 (E.D.N.Y. 1985) (Weinstein, C.J.), referred to hereinafter as Distribution Plan Opinion, at 1401; communication with Steven Brower, special deputy clerk for Agent Orange, U.S. District Court for the Eastern District of New York, Feb. 14, 1986; Feinberg interview.

39. See Petition for Writ of Mandamus and for Other Relief to Honorable Jack B. Weinstein, United States District Judge, Eastern District of New York (Apr. 3, 1985), at 18–19.

40. *AO*, Fairness Opinion at 782–95.

41. Letter from Feinberg to Garment, May 16, 1984.

42. Garment interview.

43. Letter from Garment to Maskin, May 24, 1984; letter from Maskin to Garment, June 19, 1984.

44. Letter from Feinberg to Maskin, July 23, 1984; letter from Maskin to Feinberg, July 31, 1984.

45. Garment interview.

46. The Garment–Horowitz conversation is memorialized in Garment's file memorandum of Oct. 17, 1984.

47. Horowitz's note to Garment was dated Jan. 11, 1985. The article was from the November 1984 issue of the *Journal of the National Cancer Institute*.

48. Letter from Garment to Maskin, Nov. 16, 1984; letter from Maskin to Garment, Dec. 10, 1984. Maskin's claim about the earlier meeting: Maskin interview.

49. Garment interview; letter from Maskin to Garment, Mar. 5, 1985; Feinberg interview.

50. *AO*, Fairness Opinion at 858–61.

51. Feinberg interview.

52. Plaintiffs' Preliminary Plan for Allocation and Distribution of Settlement Fund, filed Nov. 15, 1984. PMC's request for $100,000: letter from Henderson to Weinstein, June 28, 1984. Weinstein's approval order was dated Aug. 2, 1984.

53. Henderson interview; written communication from Henderson to author, Feb. 4, 1986.

54. Vietnam Veterans Agent Orange Committee of Texas, Proposal for the National Foundation for Vietnam Veteran Assistance (Feb. 28, 1985).

55. Report of the Special Master Pertaining to the Disposition of the Settlement Fund (Feb. 27, 1985). The exposure test is discussed in Appendix J.

56. Feinberg interview.

57. James Feron, "A Postal Worker in Yonkers Slays His Wife and a Son, Then Himself," *New York Times*, Mar. 5, 1985, at B2; Larry Cole and Don Singleton, "Boy, 3, Survives Carnage," *New York Daily News*, Mar. 6, 1985.

58. Author's notes and transcript of hearing, Mar. 5, 1985; see also Ralph Blumenthal, "Vietnam Veterans Argue over Agent Orange Fund," *New York Times*, Mar. 6, 1985, at A18.

59. McCarthy interview.

60. Overheard by the author.

61. Yannacone interview.

62. The account of Yannacone's speech is from author's notes and transcript of hearing, Mar. 5, 1985, at 217–28; see also letter from Yannacone to Weinstein, Feb. 26, 1985.

63. Feinberg interview.

64. Testimony of Diana Hackett in transcript of hearing, Mar. 5, 1985, at 56–78.

65. Ryan interview.

66. Feinberg interview.

67. Changes in *AO*, Distribution Plan Opinion from Feinberg plan: in form and amount of death benefit, 611 F. Supp. at 1420–21; in the exposure requirement, id. at 1414–16; in the structure of endowments, id. at 1432. See also letter from Feinberg to Weinstein, Apr. 1, 1985.

68. For an argument that tort principles should not govern the distribution in an Agent Orange–type settlement, see Charles Silver, "Just Utilization of Class Action Settlement Funds" (1986, unpublished). On appellate courts precluding fact-finding in passing on settlements, see, e.g., *West Virginia* v. *Pfizer*, 440 F.2d 1079, 1086 (2d Cir. 1971), cert. denied, 404 U.S. 871 (1971).

69. See, e.g., *Greenfield* v. *Villager Industries, Inc.*, 483 F.2d 824 (3d Cir. 1973).

70. *In re Chicken Antitrust Litigation*, 669 F.2d 228, 235 (5th Cir. 1982). *Manual for Complex Litigation* (St. Paul, Minn.: West Publishing Co., 1985), at sec. 30.212.

71. Weinstein discussed the temporal sequence in *AO*, Fairness Opinion at 763–64. *Chicken Antitrust* actually refutes Weinstein: see 669 F.2d at 235. Even the special master who prepared the distribution plan expressed concern about the due process problems created by Weinstein's temporal sequence. Feinberg's remarks were made at Conference on Litigation Management, Yale Law School, Oct. 4, 1985.

72. On Weinstein's use of *cy pres*, see Distribution Plan Opinion at 1402–03. The precedents referred to are *West Virginia* v. *Chas. Pfizer & Co.*, 440 F.2d 1079 (2d Cir.); *In re Folding Carton Antitrust Litigation*, 557 F. Supp. 1091 (N.D. Ill. 1983).

73. *AO*, Distribution Plan Opinion at 1410–12.

11. The Final Act

1. The facts, documents, and legal arguments surrounding the original protective orders and the subsequent developments relating to public disclosure are recited at *AO*, 104 F.R.D. 559 (E.D.N.Y. 1985) (Weinstein, C.J.).

2. *AO*, Fairness Opinion at 769–70.

3. *AO*, 104 F.R.D. at 562–77.

4. Author's notes and transcript of hearing, Feb. 6, 1985. Weinstein's formal opinion, *AO*, 104 F.R.D. 559, was issued one week later on Feb. 13.

5. *In re Franklin National Bank Securities Litigation*, 92 F.R.D. 468 (E.D.N.Y.

1981), *aff'd sub nom. Federal Deposit Insurance Corp.* v. *Ernst & Ernst,* 677 F.2d 230 (2d Cir. 1982).

6. Notice of Appeal of Magistrate's Pretrial Order No. 33, Mar. 14, 1985.

7. Motion for Recusal from Further Involvement in the Cases of Certain Plaintiffs Who Have Opted-Out in Certain Line Cases from the Class Action (Jan. 11, 1985), referred to hereinafter as Recusal Motion, at 4; Taylor interview.

8. *AO,* Fairness Opinion at 756–57; letter from Friedman to author, Sept. 19, 1985.

9. See Defendants' Memorandum in Support of Their Motion for Summary Judgment against Plaintiffs Who Opted Out of the Class (July 24, 1984).

10. Taylor interview; author's notes of hearing, Mar. 18, 1985; transcript of hearing at 7–8.

11. See Federal Rules of Civil Procedure, Rule 56.

12. See, e.g., *Heyman* v. *Commerce and Industry Ins. Co.,* 524 F.2d 1317 (2d Cir. 1975), citing *U.S.* v. *Diebold, Inc.,* 369 U.S. 654 (1962).

13. *Donnelly* v. *Guion,* 467 F.2d 290 (2d Cir. 1972); *SEC* v. *Research Automation Corp.,* 585 F.2d 31, 33 (2d Cir. 1978).

14. *Aetna Cas. & Surety Co.* v. *Giesow,* 412 F.2d 468, 471 (2d Cir. 1969); *Amer. Mfrs. Mut. Ins. Co.* v. *Amer. Broadcasting-Paramount Theatres,* 388 F.2d 272 (2d Cir. 1967) at 278.

15. *Wells* v. *Oppenheimer & Co.,* 101 F.R.D. 358 (S.D.N.Y. 1984). For a critical view of this acknowledged trend, see Robert Sayler, "Rule 56: Some Notes on a Decent Rule with a Shady Past," *An ADR Manual for Judges,* draft (Center for Public Resources, October 1985) at 135.

16. *Ferebee* v. *Chevron Chemical Co.,* 736 F.2d 1529 (D.C. Cir.), *cert. denied,* 105 S.Ct. 548 (1984), quote at 1534–35.

17. Opt-Out Plaintiffs' Opposition to Defendants' Motion to Dismiss or, in the Alternative, for Summary Judgment, filed Sept. 18, 1984.

18. Transcript of hearing, Sept. 18, 1984, at 17–54.

19. Plaintiffs' Supplemental Memorandum in Support of Plaintiffs' Opposition to Defendants' Motion for Summary Judgment, Exhibit 1 (Oct. 16, 1984).

20. See depositions of Dr. Ronald Codario, id. at 234; Dr. Alan Levin at 471–72; Dr. Ellen Silbergeld at 320–21; Dr. Alistair Hay at 212–13; Dr. Marvin Schneiderman at 144–50; and Dr. Lennart Hardell at 77.

21. Transcript of hearing, Dec. 10, 1984, at 114–20.

22. Taylor interview; transcript of Dec. 10 hearing at 103–06, 109–10.

23. Id. at 106–08, 114–20.

24. Id. at 122–23.

25. Weinstein's stay of certification was dated Dec. 29, 1984. His order to require Carnow to testify was dated Jan. 24, 1985.

26. Recusal Motion.

27. Transcript of hearing, Jan. 18, 1985. Taylor's appeal: Petition for Writ

of Mandamus, Apr. 3, 1985. Second Circuit's summary affirmance: order dated May 8, 1985, docket number 85-3023.

28. First Singer affidavit, Jan. 21, 1985; second Singer affidavit, Feb. 28, 1985.

29. See affidavits of, e.g., Alfred R. Johnson, Jan. 16, 1985; Bernard W. Fong, Oct. 5, 1984; Donald E. Sprague, Jan. 17, 1985; Samuel S. Epstein, Mar. 13, 1985.

30. Affidavit of Samuel S. Epstein, Attesting to Causation in the Case of William J. Fraticelli (Mar. 13, 1985), at 4.

31. Epstein affidavit (Mar. 10, 1985), submitted in support of Plaintiffs' Second Supplemental Opposition to Defendants' Motion to Dismiss or, in the Alternative, for Summary Judgment (Mar. 11, 1985).

32. Defendants' Supplemental Memorandum in Opposition to Plaintiffs' Motion for Partial Summary Judgment and Reply Memorandum in Further Support of Defendants' Motion to Dismiss and/or for Summary Judgment (Apr. 29, 1985).

33. Author's notes of hearing, Apr. 15, 1985.

34. Summary judgment decision in opt-out cases: *AO*, 611 F. Supp. 1223 (E.D.N.Y. 1985), referred to hereinafter as Opt-Out Opinion. *Lilley* decision: *AO*, 611 F. Supp. 1267 (E.D.N.Y. 1985).

35. David Kleinbaum, Lawrence Kupper, and Hal Morganstern, *Epidemiologic Research: Principles and Quantitative Methods* (Belmont, Calif: Lifetime Learning Publications, 1982); Malcolm Pike, "Epidemiology and Risk Assessment: Estimation of GI Cancer Risk from Asbestos in Drinking Water and Lung Cancer Risk from PAHs in Air," in David Hoel, Richard Merrill, and Fredericka Perera, eds., *Risk Quantitation and Regulatory Policy* (Cold Spring Harbor Laboratory, 1985), at 55–64; Bert Black and David Lilienfeld, "Epidemiologic Proof in Toxic Tort Litigation," 52 *Fordham Law Review* 732, 751–64 (1984).

36. Interview with Dr. Jan Stolwijk, chairman, Department of Epidemiology and Public Health, Yale University Medical School.

37. James Gillette, "Biological Variation: The Unsolvable Problem in Quantitative Extrapolations from Laboratory Animals and Other Surrogate Systems to Human Populations," in Hoel, Merrill, and Perera, *Risk Quantitation*, at 199–209; Stolwijk interview.

38. Note, "Tort Actions for Cancer: Deterrence, Compensation, and Environmental Carcinogenesis," 90 *Yale Law Journal* 840–50 (1981); Stolwijk interview.

39. Remarks by Weinstein at Section on Evidence, American Association of Law Schools meeting, New Orleans, Jan. 5, 1986.

40. Stolwijk interview.

41. Remarks by Dr. Leon Gordis, chairman, Department of Epidemiology, School of Hygiene and Public Health, Johns Hopkins University, at faculty workshop, Yale Law School, Nov. 18, 1985.

42. Gordis remarks; Stolwijk interview.

43. Alastair Hay, *Chemical Scythe: Lessons of 2,4,5-T and Dioxin* (New York: Plenum Press, 1982), at 47; *International Agency for Research on Cancer, Monographs on the Evaluation of the Carcinogenic Risk of Chemicals to Humans*, suppl. no. 4 (1982) at 238.

44. Black and Lilienfeld, "Epidemiological Proof" at 746.

45. Even Khristine Hall and Ellen Silbergeld, "Reappraising Epidemiology: A Response to Mr. Dore," 7 *Harvard Environmental Law Review* 441, 445–46 (1983), which advocates greater use of epidemiological evidence by courts, makes clear that additional evidence is required as well, such as proof of exposure and of injury.

46. *Johnston v. United States*, 597 F. Supp. 374, 412–13 (D. Kans. 1984).

47. Michael Dore, "A Commentary on the Use of Epidemiological Evidence in Demonstrating Cause-in-Fact," 7 *Harvard Environmental Law Review* 429 (1983); Richard Hoffman, "The Use of Epidemiology in the Courts," 120 *American Journal of Epidemiology* 190–91 (1984); Stolwijk interview.

48. Stolwijk interview.

49. Opt-Out Opinion, at 1241.

50. See, e.g., *Bieghler v. Kleppe*, 633 F.2d 531 (9th Cir. 1980).

51. Defendants' Supplemental Memorandum (Apr. 29, 1985).

52. Friedman interview.

53. See, e.g., *Shatkin v. McDonnell Douglas Corp.*, 727 F.2d 202 (2d Cir. 1984); *United States v. Esle*, 743 F.2d 1465 (11th Cir. 1984); *Soden v. Freightliner Corp.*, 714 F.2d 498 (5th Cir. 1983); *Tabatchnick v. G. D. Searle & Co.*, 67 F.R.D. 49 (D. N.J. 1975); *Cunningham v. Rendezvous, Inc.*, 699 F.2d 676 (4th Cir. 1983).

54. See, e.g., *Barrel of Fun, Inc. v. State Farm Fire & Casualty Co.*, 739 F.2d 1028 (5th Cir. 1984); *Toys "R" Us, Inc. v. Canarsie Kiddie Shop, Inc.*, 559 F. Supp. 1189 (E.D.N.Y. 1983); *In re Swine Flu Immunization Products Liability Litigation*, 508 F. Supp. 897 (D. Colo. 1981), *aff'd sub. nom. Lima v. U.S.*, 708 F.2d 502 (10th Cir. 1983).

55. See, e.g., *State v. Tyler*, 77 Wash. 2d 726, 466 P.2d 120 (1970), *vacated on other grounds*, 408 U.S. 937 (1972); *Brugh v. Peterson*, 183 Neb. 190, 159 N.W.2d 321 (1968); *Jackson v. Johns-Manville Sales Corp.*, 750 F.2d 1314 (5th Cir. 1983); *Moe v. Avions Marcel Dassault-Breguet Aviation*, 727 F.2d 917 (10th Cir.), *cert. denied*, 105 S.Ct. 176 (1984); *Wilk v. American Medical Association*, 719 F.2d 207 (7th Cir. 1983), *cert. denied*, 104 S.Ct. 2398 (1984); *Securities and Exchange Commission v. Carriba Air, Inc.*, 681 F.2d 1318 (11th Cir. 1982); *Litton Systems, Inc. v. A.T.&T. Co.*, 700 F.2d 785 (2d Cir. 1983), *cert. denied*, 104 S.Ct. 984 (1984).

56. See, e.g., *Ellis v. International Playtex, Inc.*, 745 F.2d 292 (4th Cir. 1984); *Kehm v. Procter & Gamble Mfg. Co.*, 724 F.2d 613 (8th Cir. 1983).

57. See, e.g., *Mannino v. International Mfg. Co.*, 650 F.2d 846 (6th Cir. 1981); *U.S. v. Aluminum Co. of America*, 35 F. Supp. 820 (S.D.N.Y. 1940).

58. See Chapter 7.

59. Feinberg interview; confidential portions of other interviews.

60. On the social costs of litigation, see James Kakalik and Abby Robyn, *Costs of the Civil Justice System: Court Expenditures for Processing Tort Cases*

(RAND Institute for Civil Justice, 1982). On making litigants bear more of the costs, see Richard Posner, *The Federal Courts: Crisis and Reform* (Cambridge, Mass.: Harvard University Press, 1985), pts. 2 and 3; Posner, "The Summary Jury Trial: Some Cautionary Observations," 53 *University of Chicago Law Review* 366 (1986).

61. *AO*, Fairness Opinion at 838, 842.

62. Id. at 842.

63. Id. at 837.

64. See, e.g., David Rosenberg, "The Causal Connection in Mass Exposure Cases: A 'Public Law' Vision of the Tort System," 97 *Harvard Law Review* 851, 866–68 (1984).

65. See, e.g., transcript of hearing, May 4, 1984 at 71–72; Friedman interview.

66. *Almanac of the Federal Judiciary* (Chicago: LawLetters, Winter 1984), at 58.

67. Remarks at Section on Evidence, American Association of Law Schools meeting, New Orleans, Jan. 5, 1986.

68. Fleming James & Geoffrey Hazard, *Civil Procedure* (Boston: Little, Brown, 1985), sec. 8.11; Richard Lempert, "Civil Juries in Complex Cases: Let's Not Rush to Judgment," 80 *Michigan Law Review* 68 (1981); Thomas Jorde, "The Seventh Amendment Right to Jury Trial of Antitrust Issues," 69 *California Law Review* 1 (1981).

69. See, e.g., Peter Huber, "Safety and the Second Best: The Hazards of Public Risk Management in the Courts," 85 *Columbia Law Review* 277, 319–20 (1985).

70. West Virginia case: "7 at Monsanto Lose a Lawsuit over Dioxin Ills," *New York Times*, May 1, 1985, at A20. *Bendectin* case: *In re Bendectin Products Liability Litigation*, 749 F.2d 300 (6th Cir. 1984).

71. Recusal Motion.

72. PMC class action: Eighth Amended Complaint by Plaintiffs (July 23, 1984).

73. Defendants' Motion for Partial Summary Judgment on Their Third-Party Claims against the United States and in Opposition to The United States' Motion to Dismiss or for Summary Judgment, filed Mar. 21, 1985. Pratt had dismissed the defendants' third-party complaints in his opinion at 506 F. Supp. 762 but had never entered an order of dismissal. Weinstein tentatively addressed the government liability issue in a preliminary memorandum of Feb. 16, 1984. In May, Diamond Shamrock moved that he reconsider the conclusions of his preliminary memorandum.

74. See, e.g., *AO, Fraticelli v. Dow Chemical Co. et al.*, 611 F. Supp. 1285 (E.D.N.Y. 1985).

75. *Sharkey et al. v. U.S.*, No. 697-84-C, filed Dec. 27, 1984. The government filed its motion to dismiss on Mar. 27, 1985.

76. *Ryan v. Public Health Service et al.*, Civ. No. CV-84-2237, dismissed June 4, 1985.

77. Maskin interview.

78. *AO*, 506 F. Supp. 762, 779 (E.D.N.Y. 1980).

79. Transcript of hearing, June 22, 1984, at 35–36.

80. Transcripts of hearings: Oct. 30, 1984, at 4, and Dec. 10, 1984, at 60–70; *AO*, 603 F. Supp. 239, 242 (E.D.N.Y. 1985).

81. McCarthy declaration, Sept. 12, 1984, is Exhibit C to United States of America's Memorandum of Law in Support of Its Motion to Dismiss All Actions against the United States Regarding the Court's Orders to Show Cause Why Cases against the United States Should Not Be Dismissed (Sept. 20, 1984).

82. Transcript of hearing, Dec. 10, 1984, at 60–70; Maskin interview.

83. Plaintiffs' Motion to Dismiss the Minor Children Pursuant to Rule 41(a)(2) (Jan. 24, 1985). Maskin's opposition: transcript of hearing, Feb. 6, 1985, at 200–02.

84. *AO*, 603 F. Supp. 239 (E.D.N.Y. 1985).

85. Transcript of hearing, Oct. 11, 1984, at 90.

86. *Cole* v. *United States*, 755 F.2d 873 (11th Cir. 1985); *Molsbergen* v. *United States*, 757 F.2d 1016 (1985). For a nonradiation case reaching the same result, see *West* v. *United States*, 729 F.2d 1120 (7th Cir. 1984). See, generally, Note, "Postdischarge Failure to Warn: Judicial Response to Veterans' Attempts to Circumvent the *Feres* Doctrine," 30 *Villanova Law Review* 263 (1985); Comment, "An Interpretation of the *Feres* Doctrine after *West* v. *United States* and *In re 'Agent Orange' Product Liability Litigation*," 70 *Iowa Law Review* 737 (1985).

87. *AO*, 603 F. Supp. at 247–48.

88. *AO*, Fairness Opinion at 750, 851–57. The then-pending legislation, the Veterans' Dioxin and Radiation Exposure Compensation Standards Act, Pub. L. 98-542, was adopted Oct. 24, 1984.

89. Defendants' Motion for Partial Summary Judgment on Their Third-Party Claims against the United States.

90. See, e.g., Defendants' First, Second, Third, Fourth, and Fifth Requests for Admission Directed to the Third-Party Defendant the United States of America (Mar. 9, 1984).

91. Weinstein's *ex parte* stay order was dated July 11, 1984; Maskin interview.

92. Defendants' Motion for Summary Judgment against Plaintiffs Who Opted Out of the Class (July 24, 1984).

93. Transcript of hearing, July 25, 1984, at 16–20.

94. United States' Memorandum in Opposition to Defendants' Motion for Summary Judgment Based on the Government Contract Defense (Aug. 31, 1984).

95. See John Riley, "Defoliant Makers Lashed," *National Law Journal*, Sept. 17, 1984, at 1, 24; Maskin interview.

96. Riley, "Defoliant Makers"; Ralph Blumenthal, "U.S. Challenges Agent Orange Suppliers' Defense," *New York Times*, Sept. 8, 1984, at 5; transcript of hearing, Sept. 5, 1984, at 40.

97. *AO*, Fairness Opinion at 799; *AO*, Opt-Out Opinion at 1263.

98. *AO*, 580 F. Supp. 1242, 1247 (E.D.N.Y. 1984).

99. *AO*, 506 F. Supp. 762, 781–82 (E.D.N.Y. 1980); *AO*, 611 F. Supp. 1221, 1223 (E.D.N.Y. 1985). For a case upholding an analogous theory in the context of a claim by an asbestos manufacturer against the United States for indemnity and breach of warranty in connection with its liability for injuries to a civilian worker at a Navy shipyard not subject to *Feres*, see *Johns-Manville Sales Corp.* v. *United States*, 622 F. Supp. 443 (N. D.Cal 1985).

100. Maskin interview.

101. Transcript of hearing, Apr. 15, 1985, at 116–17.

102. *AO*, 611 F. Supp. 1221, 1222 (E.D.N.Y. 1985).

103. Letter from Robert C. Heinemann, clerk of court, to author, Oct. 2, 1985.

104. Author's notes of hearing, Apr. 15, 1985.

12. Versions of Legal Reality

1. As of Jan. 31, 1986, more than fifty appeals had been assigned docket numbers by the United States Court of Appeals for the Second Circuit: communication with Steven Brower, special deputy clerk for Agent Orange, U.S. District Court for the Eastern District of New York, Feb. 14, 1986.

2. On Agent Orange as scapegoat: *Report of the Royal Commission on the Use of and Effects of Chemical Agents on Australian Personnel in Vietnam* (Canberra: Australian Government Publishing Service, 1985), epilogue. On "cancer epidemic": id. See, generally, National Cancer Institute, *1985 Annual Career Statistics Review*. On cancerphobia in tort cases, see, e.g., *Arnett* v. *Dow Chem. Co.*, Case No. 729586 (California Superior Court Mar. 21, 1983); *Devlin* v. *Johns-Manville Co.*, 292 N.J. Super. 556, 495 A.2d 495 (1985). Michael Ryan quote: Ryan interview.

3. On the instrumental goals of tort law, see, e.g., Guido Calabresi, *The Costs of Accidents: A Legal and Economic Analysis* (New Haven: Yale University Press, 1970), chap. 3; Peter Schuck, *Suing Government: Citizen Remedies for Official Wrongs* (New Haven: Yale University Press, 1983), chap. 1. On process-oriented values, see, e.g., Jerry Mashaw, *Due Process and the Administrative State* (New Haven: Yale University Press, 1985).

4. Ryan interview; McCarthy interview.

5. McCarthy interview.

6. England's fee-shifting rules: J. Robert S. Prichard, "A Systemic Approach to Comparative Law: The Effect of Cost, Fee and Financing Rules on the Development of the Substantive Law" (1984, unpublished).

7. For a more theoretical analysis of Weinstein's role in the settlement, see Peter Schuck, "The Role of Judges in Settling Cases: The Agent Orange Example," 53 *University of Chicago Law Review* 337 (1986). On common-law judging, see, e.g., Benjamin Cardozo, *The Nature of the Judicial Process* (New Haven: Yale University Press, 1921).

8. See, e.g., Note, "An Interpretation of the Feres Doctrine after *West* v. *United States* and *In re 'Agent Orange' Product Liability Litigation*," 70 *Iowa Law*

Review 737 (1985); William Blechman, "Agent Orange and the Government Contract Defense: Are Military Manufacturers Immune from Products Liability?" 36 *University of Miami Law Review* 489 (1982); Frank Lalle, "Agent Orange as a Problem of Law and Policy," 77 *Northwestern University Law Review* 48 (1982); Robert Sand, "How Much Is Enough? Observations in Light of the Agent Orange Settlement," 9 *Harvard Environmental Law Review* 283 (1985).

9. See Stephen Sugarman, "Doing Away with Tort Law," 73 *California Law Review* 555 (1985), and sources cited there.

10. Waiver in swine flu cases: see *Lima v. United States,* 708 F.2d 502, 503 (10th Cir. 1983). On causal relation between swine flu vaccine and GBS, see *In re Swine Flu Immunization Products Liability Litigation,* 508 F. Supp. 897 (D. Colo. 1981), *aff'd,* 708 F.2d 502 (10th Cir. 1983).

11. Remarks at Section on Evidence, American Association of Law Schools meeting, New Orleans, Jan. 5, 1986.

12. Taylor interview.

13. Transcript of hearing, Feb. 6, 1985, at 195–96.

14. See Judith Resnik, "Managerial Judges," 96 *Harvard Law Review* 374 (1982); E. Donald Elliott, "Managerial Judging and the Evolution of Procedure," 53 *University of Chicago Law Review* 306 (1986).

15. James Landis, *The Administrative Process* (New Haven: Yale University Press, 1938), at 41: "Most government affairs are run by men of average capabilities, and it is necessary to supply such men with a routine and ready-made technique."

16. Federalist No. 10, in *The Federalist Papers,* ed. Benjamin Wright (Cambridge: Harvard University Press, 1961).

17. James Kakalik, Patricia Ebener, William Felstiner, and Michael Shanley, *Costs of Asbestos Litigation* (Santa Monica: RAND Corporation, 1983), at vi–vii.

18. See Sugarman, "Doing Away with Tort Law."

19. David Rosenberg, "The Causal Connection in Mass Exposure Cases: A 'Public Law' Vision of the Tort System," 97 *Harvard Law Review* 849 (1984).

20. See, e.g., Jeffrey Tauberman, "Statutory Reform of 'Toxic Torts': Relieving Legal, Scientific, and Economic Burdens on the Chemical Victim," 7 *Harvard Environmental Law Review* 177 (1983) and sources cited at n. 48. The earliest advocate of proportional or probabilistic liability was Samuel Estep, "Radiation Injuries and Statistics: The Need for a New Approach to Injury Litigation," 59 *Michigan Law Review* 259 (1960). See also Glen Robinson, "Probabilistic Causation and Compensation for Tortious Risk," 14 *Journal of Legal Studies* 779 (1985).

21. Rosenberg, "Causal Connection" at 913.

22. Id. at 855.

23. See, e.g., Alexander Bickel, *The Least Dangerous Branch: The Supreme Court at the Bar of Public Opinion* (Indianapolis: Bobbs-Merrill, 1962); Schuck, *Suing Government,* at chap. 7.

24. Rosenberg, "Causal Connection" at 928.
25. Id. at 896.
26. *Phillips Petroleum Corp.* v. *Shutts,* 105 S.Ct. 2965 (1985). For a discussion of interaction of choice-of-law rules and former decisions in mass toxic exposure cases, see Peter Huber, "Have Lawsuit, Will Travel," *Regulation* 25 (Sept./Oct. 1985).
27. Peter Huber, "Safety and the Second Best: The Hazards of Public Risk Management in the Courts," 85 *Columbia Law Review* 277 (1985).
28. Id. at 278. See also Chris Whipple, "Redistributing Risk," *Regulation* 37 (May/June 1985).
29. Jack Weinstein, "Preliminary Reflections on Managing Disasters," 11 *Columbia Journal of Environmental Law* 1 (1985).
30. See O. W. Holmes, Jr., *The Common Law* (Boston: Little, Brown, 1881); Weinrib, "The Natural Law of Tort" (1985, unpublished).

13. Alternatives

1. For an argument that the focus on accidents is arbitrary and unsound, see Stephen Sugarman, "Doing Away with Tort Law," 73 *California Law Review* 555 (1985). On the tort system as a lottery, see Jeffrey O'Connell, *The Lawsuit Lottery: Only the Lawyers Win* (New York: Free Press, 1979); TRB, "The Tort Explosion," *New Republic,* Nov. 18, 1985, at 4; Jack Weinstein, "The Role of the Court in Toxic Tort Litigation," 73 *Georgetown Law Journal* 1389 (1985).
2. Sugarman, "Doing Away with Tort Law" at 645–48.
3. Id. at 591.
4. On the unavailability of liability insurance, see, e.g., Stuart Diamond, "Insurance against Pollution Is Cut," *New York Times,* Mar. 11, 1985, at A1; Elizabeth Kolbert, "Midwives Face Threat of High Insurance Cost," *New York Times,* Sept. 29, 1985, at 56; Richard Madden, "Liability Insurance Cost Is Soaring for Localities," *New York Times,* Sept. 30, 1985, at B1; David Hilder, "Liability Insurance Is Difficult to Find Now for Directors, Officers," *Wall Street Journal,* July 10, 1985, at 1; Kim Masters, "Malpractice Insurance Crunch: Some Big L.A. Firms Have to 'Go Bare,' While Others Scramble for Coverage," *Legal Times,* Nov. 18, 1985, at 1.
5. On arguments for and against "collateral benefits" rule, see Richard Epstein, James Gregory, and Harry Kalven, *Cases and Materials on Torts* (Boston: Little, Brown, 4th ed. 1984), at 784–91.
6. See W. Kip Viscusi, "Structuring an Effective Occupational Disease Policy: Victim Compensation and Risk Regulation," 2 *Yale Journal on Regulation* 53 (1985); Leslie Boden and Carol Jones, "Occupational Disease Remedies: The Asbestos Experience" (1985, unpublished).
7. See Jeffrey O'Connell, "Workers' Compensation as a Sole Remedy for Employees But Not Employers," 28 *Labor Law Journal* 287 (1977); O'Connell, "Bargaining for Waivers of Third-Party Tort Claims," 1976 *University of Illinois Law Forum* 435.

8. Proposals in Congress: American Enterprises Institute Legislative Analyses, *Toxic Torts: Proposals for Compensatory Victims of Hazardous Substances* (Washington, D.C.: American Enterprise Institute, 1984). Burden-shifting urged in Agent Orange: *AO, Fairness Opinion* at 837.

9. On the black lung program, see W. Kip Viscusi, "Structuring an Effective Occupational Disease Policy." Many beneficiaries have never worked in a mine: Feinberg interview. Program cited by opponents to reform: see, e.g., remarks of numerous opponents of Rep. George Miller's H.R. 5735 and H.R. 3175 in *Occupational Health Hazards Compensation Act of 1982: Hearings on H.R. 5735 Before the Subcommittee on Labor Standards of the House Committee on Education and Labor*, 97th Cong. 2d Sess. (1983); and *Occupational Disease Compensation Act of 1983: Hearings on H.R. 3175 Before the Subcommittee on Labor Standards of the House Committee on Education and Labor*, 98th Cong., 1st Sess. (1983).

10. Jeffrey O'Connell, "Foreclosing Claims for Personal Injury from Toxic Substances by Defendants' Tender of Claimants' Net Economic Losses," 2 *Virginia Journal of Natural Resources* 203 (1982). O'Connell elaborated on and generalized this idea in "Offers That Can't Be Refused: Foreclosure of Personal Injury Claims by Defendants' Prompt Tender of Claimants' Net Economic Losses," 77 *Northwestern Law Review* 589 (1983).

11. Sugarman, "Doing Away with Tort Law" at 619.

12. See Patricia Danzon, "The Medical Malpractice System: Facts and Reforms," in Martin Baily and Warren Cikins, eds., *The Effects of Litigation on Health Care Costs* (Washington, D.C.: The Brookings Institution, 1985), at 34–35.

13. For an argument that judges and juries are dismantling the causal defense barriers *sub rosa*, see E. Donald Elliott, "Why Courts?: A Comment on Robinson's Probabilistic Causation," 14 *Journal of Legal Studies* 799 (1985).

14. O'Connell, "Offers" at 612–13.

15. For another, more fundamental critique of O'Connell's approach, see Sugarman, "Doing Away with Tort Law" at 624–28.

16. Guido Calabresi, "Commentary on the Dodd and Gorton Amendments to S.100 (the Kasten Bill)," Working Paper no. 34, Yale Law School Program in Civil Liability, June 1985.

17. On the social costs of settlement, see Richard Posner, "The Summary Jury Trial: Some Cautionary Observations," 53 *University of Chicago Law Review* 366 (1986); Owen Fiss, "Against Settlement," 93 *Yale Law Journal* 1073 (1984).

18. On deterrence, see Guido Calabresi, *The Costs of Accidents: A Legal and Economic Analysis* (1970) at chaps. 5, 6.

19. Craig Brown, "Deterrence in Tort and No-Fault: The New Zealand Experience," 73 *California Law Review* 976 (1985).

20. See Calabresi, *Costs of Accidents* at 312; Calabresi, "Torts—The Law of the Mixed Society," 56 *Texas Law Review* 519 (1978); Howard Latin, "Problem-Solving Behavior and Theories of Tort Liability," 73 *California Law Review* 677, 738–42 (1985).

21. See, e.g., sources cited in Sugarman, "Doing Away with Tort Law" at 561–91, esp. n.12; Patrick Atiyah, *Accidents, Compensation and the Law* (London: Weidenfeld and Nicolson, 3d ed. 1975), at 606–07; Robert Ellickson, "Of Coase and Cattle: Dispute Resolution among Neighbors in Shasta County," 38 *Stanford Law Review* (forthcoming, 1986). But see Robert Lindsey, "Businesses Change Ways in Fear of Lawsuits," *New York Times*, Nov. 18, 1985, at A1.

22. See Latin, "Problem-Solving Behavior" at 680.

23. See Peter Huber, "Have Lawsuit, Will Travel," *Regulation* 18 (Sept./Oct. 1985). See Sugarman, "Doing Away with Tort Law" at 611–13; Peter Schuck, *Suing Government: Citizen Remedies for Official Wrongs* (New Haven: Yale University Press, 1983) at chap. 6.

24. See E. Donald Elliott, "Goal Analysis Versus Institutional Analysis of Toxic Compensation Systems," 73 *Georgetown Law Journal* 1357, 1358n.6 (1985).

25. George Eads and Peter Reuter, *Designing Safer Products: Corporate Responses to Product Liability Law and Regulation* (Santa Monica: RAND Corporation, 1983), discussed in Sugarman, "Doing Away with Tort Law" at 588.

26. Written communication from Henderson to author, Feb. 4, 1986.

27. Huber, "Have Lawsuit" at 285–90; Jane Stein, "The High Cost of Suing," *National Journal*, Feb. 25, 1984 (study of obstetricians and gynecologists); "Insurers Tell Why Costs Are Up for Daycare," *New York Times*, July 19, 1985, at A15. But see Julie Kosterlitz, "FTC Probes Possible Insurance Boycott," *National Journal*, Nov. 30, 1985, at 2719.

28. See, e.g., Richard Pierce, "Institutional Aspects of Torts," 73 *California Law Review* 917, 931–40 (1985); Elliott, "Goal Analysis" at 1372–75.

29. On the limitations of political decision-making, see Charles Wolf, "A Theory of Non-Market Failures," 55 *Public Interest* 114 (Spring 1979). On the problems of predicting and penalizing behavior, see Calabresi, *Costs of Accidents* at 107–13; Rosenberg, "The Causal Connection in Mass Exposure Cases: A 'Public Law' Vision of the Tort System," 97 *Harvard Law Review* (1984) at 926–28. Huber on risk regulation: "Safety and the Second Best: The Hazards of Public Risk Management in the Courts," 85 *Columbia Law Review* (1985) at 332. For studies of regulatory performance, see, e.g., Senate Committee on Government Operations, *Study on Federal Regulation* (1977). On regulating 2,4,5-T, see Wendy Wagner, "Environmental Regulation under Scientific Uncertainty: A Case Study on the EPA's Cancellation of 2,4,5-T," *Journal of the National Association of Administrative Law Judges* (forthcoming, 1986).

30. See Richard Stewart and Cass Sunstein, "Public Programs and Private Rights," 95 *Harvard Law Review* 1195 (1982).

31. See Huber, "Safety and the Second Best" at 332–35; Elliott, "Goal Analysis" at 1375. *Restatement (Second) of Torts*, 288c (1965) rejects this approach.

32. Stolwijk interview, Galston interview.

33. William Drayton, *America's Toxic Protection Gap: The Collapse of Compli-*

ance with the Nation's Toxic Laws (Washington, D.C.: Environmental Safety, 1984), at 2.

34. Data supplied by Neal Armstrong, Comptroller's Office, U.S. Environmental Protection Agency, Oct. 18, 1985.

35. See National Academy of Sciences, Steering Committee on Identification of Toxic and Potentially Toxic Chemicals for Consideration by the National Toxicology Program, *Toxicity Testing: Strategies to Determine Needs and Priorities* (Washington, D.C.: National Academy Press, 1984), at 125–26; Clarence Davies, "Coping with Toxic Substances," 1 *Issues in Science and Technology* 72–73 (1985).

36. See Paul Brodeur, *Outrageous Misconduct: The Asbestos Industry on Trial* (New York: Pantheon, 1985). See David Doniger, "Federal Regulation of Vinyl Chloride: A Short Course in the Law and Policy of Toxic Substances Control," 7 *Ecology Law Quarterly* 497 (1978).

37. On information markets generally, see Ejan Mackaay, *Economics of Information and Law* (Boston: Kluwer-Nijhoff, 1980). On the tort system's discouragement of information-seeking, see Guido Calabresi and Alvin Klevorick, "Four Tests for Liability in Torts," 14 *Journal of Legal Studies* 585 (1985); Marion Blankopf, "Incentives for Producing and Disseminating Information on Toxic Risks" (1985, unpublished).

38. See Tim Atkeson, "Toxics Regulation and Product Liability: Decreasing Exposure in the Workplace, Increasing Exposure in the Courts," 13 *Environmental Law Report* 10418 (December 1983); Blankopf, "Incentives for Producing."

39. See *Oil, Chemical and Atomic Workers Local Union No. 6-418, AFL-CIO* v. *N.L.R.B.,* 711 F.2d 348 (D.C. Cir. 1983); Blankopf, "Incentives for Producing."

40. "Bacteria Eat Toxic Materials," *New York Times,* Aug. 17, 1985, at 36.

41. On proposed reforms, see, e.g., Sugarman, "Doing Away with Tort Law" at 651–59.

42. See William Baumol and Edwin Mills, "A New Strategy for Toxic Waste: Paying Companies to Obey the Law," *New York Times,* Oct. 27, 1985, at F3.

43. Philip Shenon, "Lilly Pleads Guilty to Oraflex Charges," *New York Times,* Aug. 22, 1985, at A16; Mosher, "Who's Afraid of Hazardous Waste Dumps? Not Us, Says the Reagan Administration," 14 *National Journal* 952–57 (1982); Mosher, "EPA Still Doesn't Know the Dimensions of Nation's Hazardous Waste Problems," 15 *National Journal* 769–99 (1983).

44. Philip Shabecoff, "Lack of Money Might Halt Toxic Cleanup Soon, U.S. Officials Say," *New York Times,* Jan. 26, 1986, at 17.

45. Drayton, *America's Toxic Protection Gap* at 15.

46. For one ambitious effort to eliminate boundaries by creating a comprehensive scheme of compensation and deterrence, see Sugarman, "Doing Away with Tort Law" at 642–64.

47. For an effort to define those claims requiring special causation rules

within a tort framework, see Richard Delgado, "Beyond *Sindell:* Relaxation of Cause-in-Fact Rules for Indeterminate Plaintiffs," 70 *California Law Review* 881 (1982).

48. Stolwijk interview.

49. Keith Schneider, "Detecting Food Contaminants," *New York Times,* Feb. 6, 1986, at D2.

50. Aaron Wildavsky and Mark Douglas, *Risk and Culture* (Berkeley: University of California Press, 1982). Kathy Bloomgarden, "Managing the Environment: The Public's View," 6 *Public Opinion* 47 (1983).

51. See, e.g., Harry Wellington, "Asbestos: The Private Management of a Public Problem," 33 *Cleveland State Law Review* 375 (1984–85); Center for Public Resources, *Manual for Judges,* draft (October 1985).

52. See Stephen Breyer, *Regulation and Its Reform* (Cambridge, Mass.: Harvard University Press, 1982); Bruce Ackerman et al., *The Uncertain Search for Environmental Quality* (New York: Free Press, 1974); Elliott, "Goal Analysis" at 1372–75.

53. See Aaron Wildavsky, "Richer Is Safer," 60 *Public Interest* 23 (Summer 1980).

Index

DATE DUE

GAYLORD			PRINTED IN U.S.A.